THE LOVE OF KRISHNA

The Fourteenth Publication in the Haney Foundation Series

University of Pennsylvania

THE LOVE OF KRISHNA

The Kṛṣṇakarṇāmṛta of Līlāśuka Bilvamaṅgala

Edited with an Introduction by

FRANCES WILSON

UNIVERSITY OF PENNSYLVANIA PRESS

PHILADELPHIA

Library of Congress catalog card number: 74–153426

ISBN: 0–8122–7655–8

Publication of this book has been made possible by a grant from the Haney Foundation of the University of Pennsylvania

Printed in the United States of America

PREFACE

> The mediaeval religious movements of India, with their devotional Sanskrit texts and highly scholastic sectarian commentaries, do not appear to have received as much recognition in Europe as they deserve. In India they still constitute the basis of the living faiths of the people; but the texts themselves, always reverentially acknowledged, are yet hardly accessible and seldom critically studied.[1]

Since Professor De wrote this in 1938, there has been serious and productive attention in the West to devotional Sanskrit texts and to the mediaeval religious movements of India. Much remains to be critically studied. The work presented on the following pages is an effort in such critical study: The *Kṛṣṇakarṇāmṛta*, a devotional anthology of mediaeval Vaishnava hymns, has been critically edited.

I have been able to accomplish this critical edition because of the guidance of many teachers of the University of California at Berkeley; the support of the United States Fulbright Foundation in India and the American Institute of Indian Studies; and aid from the personnel and facilities of some fifty libraries in India, Europe, and the United States.

It is a pleasure to express my gratitude to the numerous people of the above scholarly institutions who have been important to accomplishing various phases of this critical edition. Especially, it is a pleasure to express my gratitude to Professor M. B. Emeneau who has ever guided my Sanskrit studies and to Śrīramaṇa Ācārya who was my first and most constant Sanskrit teacher in India.

1. The *Kṛṣṇa-karṇāmṛta*, ed. Sushil Kumar De, University of Dacca. Oriental Publication Series No. 5 (Dacca, 1938), p. lxx.

TABLE OF CONTENTS

General Abbreviations ix

Introduction 3
Text-Critical Problem. 6
Identity of the Author. 16

Manuscripts Used. 29
Meanings of the Letters by Which the Bilvamañgala Manuscripts Are Identified 29
System of Numbering by Which the Verse Sequence of Kṛṣṇakarṇāmṛta Manuscripts Is Described. 30
Description of the Manuscripts. 32
Interrelationships of the Manuscripts 86
Diagram of the Manuscript Relationships. 90
Methodological Principles for the Text Criticism of the Kṛṣṇakarṇāmṛta 91

The Kṛṣṇakarṇāmrta Text and Translation 94
Century I 94
Century II 140
Century III 184
Additional Verses. 226

Appendix 235
Critical Apparatus 235
Abbreviations Used in the "Critical Apparatus". 235
Śataka I 236
Śataka II 261
Śataka III. 285
Additional Verses. 314
Synoptic Charts of Verse Sequences 319
Guide to Reading "Chart of Standard Verse Sequences" . . 319
Chart of Standard Verse Sequences. 324

Notes to Chart of Standard Verse Sequences 416
Guide to Reading "Chart of Additional Verse Sequences" . 418
Chart of Additional Verse Sequences 422
Notes on the Additional Verses. 433
Abbreviations Used in "First Line Index of 66 Additional Verses with Notes". 433
First Line Index of 66 Additional Verses with Notes. 434

List of Works Cited. 447

Index of Meters. 453

Index of Standard Verses 459

GENERAL ABBREVIATIONS

KK Kṛṣṇakarṇāmṛta

° The degree sign is used to indicate that only a part of a word—the first, last, or middle part—is noted.

st. standard. When prefixed to a century number (e.g. KK st. 1) or a verse number (e.g. KK st. 1.1), st. indicates that this is the usual position of the century or verse in the mainstream (2=) tradition. See p. 90 for a description of the mainstream tradition.

* If the aberrant tradition (3≠) does not include a st. verse, or includes the st. verse in an unusual position, thus indicating some doubt as to the validity of the verse or its position for a critical text, the verse in question is marked with an asterisk. (e.g. st. 1.1*) In two sections in the Appendix the asterisk is used otherwise. The other uses are described in the appropriate places: "Guide to Reading 'Chart of Standard Verse Sequences'" and "Notes on Additional Verses."

add. additional. In addition to the 330 st. vss. found in the KK, some 66 other verses are found in one or more of the mss. used for the text in this dissertation. These verses are designated by add. plus their *pratīka* (e.g. add. āttaṃ padavyāṃ). See "Notes on Additional Verses" for further information.

≠ This sign indicates that the ms. versions, to which it is appended, is a hypothetical, reconstructed version.

INTRODUCTION

The Kṛṣṇakarṇāmṛta (KK) is a collection of four line verses which have as their theme the loving adoration (*bhakti*) of the Lord Kṛṣṇa. Every verse expresses this *bhakti*, and whatever the manner of expression—narrative, lyric, dramatic—it is rarely accomplished without a vivid pictorial reminder of Kṛṣṇa. Over and over again the following characteristics and others like them are described: His body is cloud dark and clothed with shimmering yellow garments like streaks of lightning; his cherry lips are anointed with the nectar of smiles and flute music; his breath is honey; his face and eyes are lotuses; his feet are sunbeams; circlets of bells sound on his hands and feet; a golden thread is hung around his hips; a peacock plume is on his head; he is the Ocean of Mercy, the Lake of the Oversoul, and the Splendour which is the home of Lakṣmī.

Along with this descriptive material, then, we have dramatic and narrative fragments from the Kṛṣṇa story or lyric expression of the soul's love and longing for Kṛṣṇa. Whatever the material the whole of the composition must be accomplished within a four line verse, for every verse is a unit and unrelated to the next except as each relates to Kṛṣṇa *bhakti.*

The KK collection of verses gives expression to almost every sort of Kṛṣṇa *bhakti*. All the sentiments (*rasas*) associated with *bhakti* are evoked: There is the loving adoration of the mother, friend, lover, and slave. These are the metaphors used by the poet to tell of the soul's longing for the Lord Kṛṣṇa. Perhaps the dominant *rasa* is that of erotic love. The Bengali Vaishnava commentators on the KK, especially Kṛṣṇadāsa Kavirāja, have construed all the verses of the short Bengali version (see A and B mss. in the "Description of Manuscripts" section) as expressions of a woman in love, but, on the face of it, it seems easier to construe those verses which have reference to the child Kṛṣṇa, e.g. KK st. 1.24, as expressions of a mother. Actually, the poet does not seem overly concerned that the metaphors, which he uses to express the soul's inexpressible love and longing, be consistent. There are verses in which words appropriate to the adoration of the child Kṛṣṇa and words appropriate for the adoration of the lover Kṛṣṇa are surrealistically combined, e.g. KK st. 1.31.

In other ways the KK is a comprehensive collection of Kṛṣṇa hymns (*stotras*). The *stotras* refer to the whole range of Kṛṣṇa stories, and all of Kṛṣṇa's principal wives and paramours are mentioned one by one in the verses throughout the collection. The fact that Śrī, Lakṣmī, the milkmaids (gopīs), Rādhā, and Rukmiṇī are all present has been used by those who are interested in the identity of the author, Līlāśuka Bilvamaṅgala to define his date and doctrine.

Aside from the above description of the content of the KK there are some features of meter, prosody, and arrangement of verses which are described below because they are basic to a description of the KK sufficient for a discussion of the text-critical problem.

Like many other collections of Sanskrit *stotras* and eloquent verses (*subhāṣitas*) the verses are written in a great variety of meters. Some thirty-four are used. The Vasantatilaka is the most frequent in the first century of the standard version (st. 1). The Śārdūlavikrīḍita is overall the most frequent meter. Its greater length provides space for elaborate descriptions or for dramatic episodes with lively dialogues.

Although the various versions of the KK collection of verses are markedly different in the number and sequence of verses which they include, all the versions arrange the verses in one or more centuries (*śatakas*) which, in fact, usually included 101 to 112 verses.

The Bengali version (see A and B mss. in the "Manuscripts Used" section) contains a single century of verses. This century, which is the first century of the standard version (st. 1), was brought back to Bengal by Caitanya. He obtained it while on a pilgrimage in South India.[1] The KK is a South Indian text (see p. 6). There has been much discussion (see "The Text-Critical Problem" section) as to whether Caitanya, c. 1510, made a partial or a complete copy of the South Indian version of the KK (see C through V mss. in the "Description of the Mss." section). If he made a complete copy, then two centuries (st. 2. and 3) of the present South Indian version, which has three centuries, are later additions to the century (st. 1) current in South India c. 1510.

Whatever the form of the KK c. 1510 A.D., today the first century of the standard version of the KK (KK st. 1) is an authoritative work for the followers of Caitanya in Bengal.[2] In South India the work includes three centuries and is not an authoritative work for any sect.

Although the work includes three centuries in South India, it is only the verses of the second century (st. 2) which are quoted. Many KK st. 2 verses can be quoted even by those with just the usual store of

1. *The Kṛṣṇa-karṇāmṛta*, ed. Sushil Kumar De, University of Dacca Oriental Publication Series No. 5 (Dacca, 1938), p. ix.

2. *Ibid.*, p. x.

Sanskrit verses remembered from childhood. On the other hand, even those South Indians whose professional life is connected with Sanskrit quote only from KK st. 2.

My pandit from Tuluva, A. S. Acharya, told me that fond fathers repeat KK st. 2.57 over the cribs of their baby sons. This verse and the name Mukunda are thought to be connected with the increased possibility of further sons.

Professor V. Raghavan told me that KK st. 2.2, 2.65, 2.71, 2.82, and 2.106 used to be part of a Bhāratanāṭyam dancer's repertoire. He mentioned add. govālamūle also which he considers part of the KK.

In other parts of India—in Maharashtra, West India, Madhyadeśa—one gets the inpression that the KK collection is not a popular, often quoted text. Some of the verses, e.g. st. 2.57 and st. 2.108, might be very well known but not their occurrence in the KK. Northern pandits may know and write about the KK, but they do not remember it as part of their childhood home life. It is not part of their domestic or religious life. For example, Svāmī Śrīāmadāsa Jī Śāstrī, head of Cār Saṃpradāya Āśrama in Vṛndāvana, has written an extensive Hindī commentary on the Bengal version of the KK.[3] The Svāmī told me that he worked on this commentary as a scholarly endeavour while in Benares. At his Āśrama in Vṛndāvana KK verses were never used for *saṃkīrtanas*.

The Y version (Northern mss.) shows that the KK collection reached West India and Madhyadeśa and was popular there from c. 1400–1700 A.D. From a descriptive point of view the Y version is not a version of the KK: Except for Y50 mss. the mss. of the Y version do not arrange the verses into centuries; no Y version is named *Kṛṣṇakarṇāmṛta*; finally, about one half the verses in any Y ms. are not found in the mss. named KK. and about one half the verses in the mss. named KK are not found in any Y ms. The KK mss. and the Y mss. share about 150 verses. It is only a close study of the Y sub-versions and the various KK sub-versions which show that the Y version, its verses and varying sequences, developed organically from the KK tradition and is an aberrant version of the KK. For further description of the "evolution" of the Y version, see the "Interrelationships of Manuscripts" section.

3. *Kṛṣṇakarṇāmṛta*, Hindi commentator Śrīrāmadāsa Śāstrī (Vṛndāvana: Cār Saṃprādaya Āśrama, n.d.), 336 pp.

Although the Y version of the KK about 1700 A.D. ceased to be a popular source for expression of Kṛṣṇa *bhakti* in North India, the author is well-known there today. Around Ujjain, according to Vyākaraṇācārya Gopīnāthaśāstrī[4] of that city, Bilvamaṅgala is identified with the Braj poet, Sūrdās, a devotee of Kṛṣṇa who lived about 1550 A.D. in Agra.[5] Almost every part of India has some tradition which presents Bilvamaṅgala as a native of that part. These traditions are more prevalent in South India. It is almost certain that the author of the KK was a South Indian, because about 25 per cent of the verses in all versions of the KK demonstrate the initial assonance of Dravidian poetry[6] (See Y mss. in the "Description of Manuscripts" section).

The Text-Critical Problem

In 1938 S. K. De's critical edition of the Bengal version (see B mss). was published from Dacca.[7] In this edition he sought to establish the precedence of this version, which he designates by the term 'recension', over the South Indian version (or recension). C through V mss., described in the "Manuscripts Used" section, are the mss. which give the evidence for this version.

In 1935 Professor De had written an article in the ABORI[8] of which the introduction to his critical edition was a restatement. His argument for the precedence of the Bengal version included the following points. (1) The testimony for the Bengal version is uniform; the testimony for the Southern version is not.

> It is clear that most of the Bengal Mss, as well as the printed Bengal edition, agree in giving definitely one section, viz, the first, with 112 verses; but there is no agreement in the respective number of

4. Professor S. L. Katre relayed this information from Gopīnāthaśāstrī in a conversation at Nagpur University in December of 1964.

5. J. N. Farquhar, *An Outline of the Religious Literature of India* (Oxford: Oxford University Press, 1920), p. 316.

6. Amar Nath Raya, "Reviews: The Kṛṣṇakarṇāmṛtam," *The Indian Historical Quarterly*, Vol. XV, No. 1 (March, 1939), p. 150.

7. De, op. cit., 451 pp.

8. S. K. De, "A Note on the Text of Kṛṣṇa-karṇāmṛta," *Annals of the Bhandarkar Oriental Research Institute*, Vol. XVI, Parts 3–4 (April–July, 1935), pp. 173–188.

> verses in the so-called three Śatakas or Āśvāsas of the South Indian Mss and printed edition.[9]

To establish the above De has cited Bengali mss. (B), South Indian mss. (C21 D1 P71 V1), and a very anomalous Maharasthrian ms. (Y38).[10] De also considers difficult the designation, *śataka* (century), which occurs in the colophons found in P71, the printed edition with the commentary of Pāpayallaya Sūri. P71, like all other KK mss., does not have exactly 100 vss. in a century, but many more. Some mss. have several less. (2) The second and third centuries of the Southern version, which are not found in the Bengal version, were added to the first century sometime after Caitanya procured his copy of the Bengal version in South India c. 1510.

To establish the above De gives the information about Caitanya presented above on page 4. He concludes:

> It would thus appear that the tradition regarding the KK obtaining in Bengal from the beginning of the 16th century is not altogether negligible. [He goes on to say:] The date of Pāpayallaya Sūri, on the other hand, is not known, but he could not have been a very early writer. As he refers to the well known commentator Mallinātha (Peddibhaṭṭa), who flourished in the 14th century, he must have lived considerably after that date. But if he flourished in the 15th century and if at that time the text of the KK was known in three Āśvāsas as he presents it, it is not likely that Caitanya would have brought back to Bengal the tradition of only one Śataka of the work, on which his immediate disciples and followers wrote commentaries. It would, therefore, be reasonable to assume that the two other Śatakas apparently unknown to him but known to Pāpayallaya Sūri and to comparatively recent South Indian and Western Mss, arose at a somewhat later date.[11]

(3) Rūpa Gosvāmin, a contemporary and disciple of Caitanya, lived towards the end of the 15th and the first half of the 16th century. He knew only the first century of the KK and did not accept the other two centuries as part of the poem.

---

9. De, KK, p. vii.
10. *Ibid.*, pp. i–ix.
11. *Ibid.*, pp. xi–xii.

To establish the above De examines the works of Rūpa Gosvāmin.

Rūpa Gosvāmin... compiled a Sanskrit anthology, entitled *Padyāvalī* [Z11], of Kṛṣṇaite devotional verses. In the concluding verse of this work he tells us (no. 387) that in compiling his anthology he has deliberately refrained from including the verses of Jayadeva and Bilvamaṅgala.... That Rūpa Gosvāmin has strictly fulfilled his undertaking is obvious from the fact that in his anthology not a single verse occurs which can be traced to the first Śataka of the KK (in either recension), which alone was apparently known to him as genuine. On the other hand, some of the verses occurring in Pāpayallaya Sūri's second and third Āśvāsas are given in Rūpa Gosvāmin's anthology, not with Bilvamaṅgala's name but ascribed to different authors or cited anonymously.[12]

That Rūpa Gosvāmin knew only the first Śataka of the KK and did not accept the other two Śatakas as parts of the poem is also confirmed by the way in which he cites Bilvamaṅgala and his works in his *Bhakti-rasāmṛta-sindhu* [Z12] and its supplement *Ujjvala-nīla-maṇi* [Z14]. In the *Bhakti-rasāmṛta*° (ed. Murshidabad 1924) there are six quotations with the direct superscription *yathā karṇāmṛte*. These are: *ānamrām asita*° (p. 202), *mādhuryād api madhuram* (p. 203), *akhaṇḍa-nirvāṇa-rasa*° (p. 379), *amūnyadhanyāni* (p. 670), *nibaddha-mūrdhāñjali*° (p. 671), *tvacchaiśavam* (p. 674). All these verses occur in the first Śataka of the KK respectively as: i, 54; i, 64 (=Bengal Text i, 65); i, 96 (=Bengal Text i, 99); i, 41; i, 30 and i, 32. But in the *Bhakti-rasāmṛta*°, again, Rūpa Gosvāmin cites some other verses with *yathā bilvamaṅgale* or with *yathā bilvamaṅgala-stave*. These are: Bilvamaṅgala:

P. 296 *cintāmaṇiś caraṇa*° [Y2 vs. 189, Y11 vs. 87, Y21 vs. 83, Y31 vs. 255]

P. 386 *ayi paṅkaja-netra* [Y2 vs. 239, Y11 vs. 241, Y21 vss. 189 and 318, Y31 vs. 305]

P. 456 *hastam utkṣipya yāto'si*=KK iii, 94 [KK st. 3. 97]

P. 472 *rādhā punātu*=KK ii, 25 Bilvamaṅgala-stava:

P. 626 *advaita vīthī-pathikaiḥ.* [Y21 vs. 489, Y31 vs. 245]

12. *Ibid.*, p. xiii. De lists the verses which occur in KK centuries 2 and 3 and Z11. For these verses see Z11 in the "Description of the Mss." section.

None of these verses occur in the first Śataka of the KK; but two of them, as noted above, are found respectively in the second and third Śatakas. Eggeling notes (*op. cit.* p. 1475) that four of these verses occur in the *Sumaṅgala-Stotra* [Y33]... ascribed to Bilvamaṅgala. In the *Ujjvala-nīla-maṇi* (ed. Kāvyamālā 95, Bombay 1913), again, Rūpa Gosvāmin cites only one verse (p. 493, *stoka-stoka-nirudhyamāna°*) with *yathā karṇāmṛte*, and this verse occurs in the first Śataka as verse no. 21. There are three other quotations with *yathā bilvamaṅgale:*

P. 277 *rādhe'parādhena vinaiva* [Y21 vs. 484]

P. 285 *ayi murali mukunda°* = KK ii, 11.

P. 435 *rādhā-mohana-mandirāt* [add. rādhāmohana°]

None of these verses can be traced in the first Śataka of KK; and only one, as noted above, is found in the second.[13]

(4) The anthologies indicate that the second and third centuries, but not the first century, have many verses which are probably original to other sources.

To establish the above De examines some of the major anthologies.

The SKM [Z5], which was compiled in Bengal in 1205 A.D., does not cite Bilvamaṅgala at all, an omission which probably confirms the story of Caitanya's discovery of the work in the South and its introduction into Bengal. Nor does the Sbhv [Z2] or SML [Z7] quote Bilvamaṅgala. On the other hand, some verses occurring in the second and third Āśvāsas of the Southern recension are ascribed to other authors or cited anonymously.[14]

(5) Gopāla Bhaṭṭa was a Vaiṣṇava who is said to have come from Southern India; yet the authorship of the third Śataka... seems to have been unknown to him or not recognised by him. [To establish the above De points out]..... that KK iii, 82 [st. 3.84]....., which is assigned to Śāradākāra in the *Padyāval*, is cited anonymously by Gopāla Bhaṭṭa in his *Hari-bhakti-vilāsa* [Z13].[15]

From these five considerations or arguments, De concludes that it is very doubtful whether the second and third Āśvāsas given in the

13. *Ibid.*, pp. xvi–xvii.

14. *Ibid.*, p. xviii.

15. *Ibid.*

> South Indian recension originally belonged to the poem itself. These two Śatakas are unknown as a part of the poem to the Bengal tradition. One cannot be absolutely sure about the question of genuineness or interpolation in a mediaeval Sanskrit text; but it seems probable that in Bengal, where the work was studied at a distance from its reputed place of origin and where it acquired a certain sanctity, the tradition of the text was better preserved and less modified. It is undoubted that verses of other authors, some known and some unknown, went into the making of the last two Śatakas and swelled their bulk. But it is also possible that these two Śatakas prevailing in Southern India were not mere imitative supplements deliberately composed in their entirety by some later suthors and tacked on to the original first Śataka. Their nucleus might have been drawn from verses occurring in other Stotra-like works composed by or ascribed to Bilvamaṅgala; and around this might have been woven verses of less known writers which, with their authorship forgotten, came to be confused with the genuine verses of Bilvamaṅgala.
>
> On this point, however, it is difficult to arrive at a definite conclusion without examining in detail other works attributed to Bilvamaṅgala. With regard to such other works the items of information are too vague or meagre in the different catalogues of Mss in which they are noticed, and few of them are accessible or available in print.[16]

At this point De examines the only Bilvamaṅgala mss., which are not obviously KK mss., available to him. These mss. were Y51, Y52, and part of Y33. None of these mss. contains verses from the KK st. 1, except that in Y33

> the first Maṅgala-śloka, is found to be identical with the first Maṅgala-śloka of the first Śataka of the KK.[17]

From the examination of this evidence De makes his final conclusion:

> It would appear from the above discussion of available materials that we can trace a considerable number of verses of the second and third Śatakas of Pāpayallaya's text in other works at-

---

16. *Ibid.*, pp. xviii–xix.
17. *Ibid.*, p. xxi

tributed to Bilvamaṅgala, while the citations in the anthologies (including the *Padyāvalī*) assign some of the verses of these Śatakas to other authors. We can thus account for more than 30 out of 110 verses in the second Śataka and more than 40 out of 102 verses in the third Śataka, which are for the most part derived from the *Bilvamaṅgala Kośa-kāvya* [Y51], the *Kṛṣṇa-Stotra* [Y52], the *Sumaṇgala-Stotra*, or from other unknown works of Bilvamaṅgala, from which the *Bhakti-rasāmṛta*° and *Ujjvala-nīla-maṇi* cite some verses. We should be able to trace also other verses if we could examine in detail all the works assigned by tradition to Bilvamaṅgala. But these instances are enough to raise the presumption that the nucleus of the second and third Śatakas, which probably arose in later times, was made up by verses culled from other poems ascribed to Bilvamaṅgala, but into its sewlling bulk verses of a similar character by other poets also found their way.[18]

In a footnote De cites Y15 (for description see "Description of Manuscripts" section) as evidence to further substantiate the statement of the last sentence quoted above:

> That independent collections of Kṛṣṇaite Stotras were made in later times and ascribed to Bilvamaṅgala is clear from a curious Devanagari Ms which exists in the Bhandarkar Institute collection (no. 429 of 1887–91 [Y15]). It consists of 29 folios comprising 379 verses, being a collection of miscellaneous devotional poems similar to those described above (some of the verses being common). The work is called simply Bilvamaṅgala in the colophon; but the authorship is ascribed to Śrī-paramahaṃsa-parivrājakācārya-paṇḍita Vopadeva, who was apparently its compiler. The date of the Ms is given as Saṃvat 1681 (=A.D. 1625).[19]"

In the Addenda to his critical edition De adds further material to this footnote. He cites Y11 and describes it at length from Brown's presentation of Y11 (see "Description of Mss." section) in *Eastern Art*.[20] De finds four verses in Y11 which occur also in the Bengal version of the KK.[21]

18. *Ibid.*, p. xxiv–xxv.
19. *Ibid.*, p. xxv, n. 1.
20. *Ibid.*, pp. 371–378.
21. *Ibid.*, p. 373.

He also cites here[22] the poem *Kālavadha* of Kṛṣṇalīlāśuka, which is the ninth entry in the YY10 codes (see "Description of the Mss." section), but does not note the half verse (KK st. 1.31 ab) in the *Kālavadha* which is also found in the Bengal version of the KK.

Before evaluating De's consideration of the text-critical problem of the KK according to the findings of this present research, a résumé of some articles, which deal with this problem, is presented.

In a February, 1944, issue of the *Adyar Library Bulletin*, H. G. Narahari summarises De's consideration of the text critical problem and goes on to say:

> All this reasoning could have been accepted had it not been for the discovery of the Adyar Library MS. described above. [This ms. is Y1.[23] For its description see Y1 in "Description of Mss." section.] It was copied in A.D. 1418, and includes in its text verses grouped as Cantos II and III in all editions of the KK. which do not claim to represent what has been called the Bengal recension. This silences once and for all the assumption that the KK. originally contained only Canto I. It also proves beyond doubt that at least 68 years before *Caitanya*, tradition accepted the genuineness of Cantos II and III of the KK. Pāpayallayasūri and others who came after him originated no new school, but only followed this old tradition regarding the text of the *Kṛṣṇakarṇāmṛta*. If Caitanya took back with him to Bengal only Canto I of the KK., it should be because only so much was available to him.[24]

De in the *Indian Historical Quarterly* of June, 1944, replies:

> It should be understood at the outset that although ascribed to Bilvamaṅgala, the work described by Mr. Narahari is called *Viṣṇu-stuti*, and not *Kṛṣṇa-karṇāmṛta*. The two works, on his showing, are not co-extensive in content and arrangement; nor can the one, as we

22. *Ibid.*, p. 378

23. My description of Y1 varies in insignificant details from the description by H. G. Narahari. Because I was able to compare my copy of Y1 with H. G. Narahari's description and the original ms., I believe my description is the more accurate.

24. H. G. Narahari, "Manuscript Notes: An Early Manuscript of the Kṛṣṇa-karṇāmṛta of Bilvamaṅgala," *The Adyar Library Bulletin*, Vol. VIII, Pt. 1 (February, 1944), p. 44.

> shall see presently, be regarded as a version of the other. His claim, therefore, that his manuscript is one of *Kṛṣṇa-karṇāmṛta* is as unwarranted as the heading, "An Early Manuscript of the *Kṛṣṇa-karṇāmṛta* of Bilvamaṅgala," of his article is surprising and misleading. In reality his article gives an account of another interesting but independent work ascribed to Bilvamaṅgala, which is of the same type as the similarly ascribed *Sumaṅgala-stotra*, *Bilvamaṇgala-stotra*, *Kṛṣṇa-stotra*, and *Bilvamaṇgala-kośa-kāvya*, discussed in the Introduction to my edition of the *Kṛṣṇa-karṇāmṛta* (Dacca University, 1938) pp. xxi–xxiv, and the *Bāla-gopāla-stuti* [Y11] considered in the Addenda at pp. 371–78. Eggeling and Bendall noticed the manuscripts of the first two works respectively, while O. C. Gangoly and W. Norman Brown gave an account of the last work; but none of them claimed, as they could not indeed claim, that these works are identical with the *Kṛṣṇa-karṇāmṛta* or even represent a version of it. I have already discussed the question at some length and have tried to show that these apocryphal works are *independent* collections of miscellaneous Kṛṣṇaite verses ascribed to Bilvamaṅgala, which supply the nucleus of the Second and Third Āśvāsas of the South Indian recension. We can, therefore, trace a good number of the verses of these two Āśvāsas in all of them, but no verse of the First Āśvāsa occurs in any of them. This conclusion is not assailed in the least by material revealed by Mr. Narahari's discovery. On the contrary, it only confirms what I anticipated when I said that "we should be able to trace also other verses if we could examine in detail all the works assigned by tradition to Bilvamaṅgala."
>
> Much has been made of the date 1418 A.D. of the manuscript, *Viṣṇu-stuti.* But this date does not prove that the Second and the Third Āśvāsas of the KK existed before it, but only confirms that such independent collections existed at that date and supplied material for the making of these later Āśvāsas.[25]

In rebuttal of De's reply to Narahari, K. Kunjunni Raja wrote in the March, 1946, issue of *The Indian Historical Quarterly.*[26] He repeated this

25. S. K. De, "Miscellany: The Viṣṇu-stuti and Kṛṣṇa-karṇāmṛta," *The Indian Historical Quarterly*, Vol. XX, No. 2 (June, 1944), pp. 179–180.

26. K. Kunjunni Raja, "The Text-Problem of the Kṛṣṇakarṇāmṛta," *The Indian Historical Quarterly*, Vol. XXII, No. 1 (March, 1946), pp. 66–71.

rebuttal in his book, *The Contribution of Kerala to Sanskrit Literature.*[27]

Kunjunni Raja directs his argument against De's statement given above. He quotes, "I have already discussed... [through]... but no verse of the First Āśvāsa occurs in any of them." Against this statement Kunjunni Raja cites the 12 KK st. 1 verses found in Y2, Y11, and Y14.[28] These 12 KK st. 1 vss. are given in the appropriate columns in the "Synoptic Chart of Standard Verse Sequences".

Kunjunni Raja goes on:

> If the presence of some verses from the second and third cantos of the KK. in other works attributed to Bilvamaṅgala is accepted as sufficient evidence to indicate that the nucleus of these cantos "was supplied by verses taken from the genuine or spurious works of Bilvamaṅgala", we will have to accept that same is the case with the first canto also, since verses from that are found in some of the works attributed to Bilvamaṅgala.
>
> Dr. De's suggestion about the *Stotra* works attributed to Bilvamaṅgala being the nucleus of the last two cantos of the KK. presupposes the assumption that those collectanea of verses are earlier than the two cantos of the KK. Now since verses from such works are found even in the first canto, we will have to assume, if we accept Dr. De's argument, that all the three cantos of the KK. are later than these apocryphal works. But this does not seem to be the case. A close study of some of these Stotra works attributed to Bilvamaṅgala shows that they are later compilations from various sources and cannot claim to be the nucleus of the KK.[29]

The various sources[30], which Raja goes on to cite, are much the same cited under Y mss. in the "Description of the Manuscripts" section.

Raja concludes:

---

27. K. Kunjunni Raja, *The Contribution of Kerala to Sanskrit Literature* (Madras: University of Madras, 1958), 310 pp.

28 The numbers, which K. Kunjunni Raja assigns to the KK st. 1 verses found in Y14, are different than those given in the "Synoptic Chart of Standard Verse Sequences." Since those given in the "Synoptic Chart" are from a copy of the Y14 ms. and those in Raja's book are taken from the original ms., it is to be assumed that Raja's numbers are the correct ones.

29. Raja, *The Contribution of Kerala*, p. 38.

30. *Ibid.*, pp. 38–39.

"It is quite possible that the text of the KK. was not entirely free from interpolations. It was also subject to the fate of all the popular works like the *Bhartṛhariśatakas* and the *Amarukaśataka*. The presence of some interpolated verses is no evidence to the spurious nature of a poem."[31]

The above statements by De, Narahari, and Raja give the most careful and cogent expressions to the text critical problem and the resultant controversy about its proper resolution.

The analysis given in the "Interrelationships of the Mss." section in this work supports Narahari's position that the South Indian KK and the *Viṣṇu-stuti* are versions of the same work. De, however, is quite right when he maintains that Narahari has in no way demonstrated their identity. A description of the present day South Indian KK and the *Viṣṇua-stuti* gives no basis for asserting their identity. It is the Vijayanagara version (represented by the DG, G1, G2, N1, and N21 mss.) with some evidence that it dates from before 1535 A. D. which is the "missing link" which reveals their relationship. For the full argument that all the Y versions are versions of the KK, see the "Interrelationships of the Mss." section and the "Diagram of the Manuscript Relationships".

Since my findings and interpretations of them conflict with those of Professor De, I must examine his arguments which are presented above on pp. 6–10. Arguments one, two, and three give good evidence that Caitanya obtained the KK as a text with but one century (KK st. 1) in South India c. 1510. These three arguments establish the strongest point in favor of the authority of the Bengal version. The only real objections to these arguments is that De seems to believe that he has established more than the great probability that Caitanya obtained the KK as a text with but one century (KK st. 1) in South India c. 1510. For example, the fact that Rūpa Gosvāmin did not know of the South Indian version of the KK (see argument 3) means only that this version of the KK was probably not known in Bengali Vaishnava circles during the last part of the 16th century. It does not mean that this version of the KK was probably unknown throughout the whole of India.

The evidence which De gives for the fourth argument is faulty.

31. *Ibid.*, p. 39.

The SKM [Z5] includes a verse, KK st. 1.106, from the Bengal version. It is cited anonymously. Therefore, the second and third *āśvāsas* of the Southern recension are not the only ones to include an anonymous verse from an anthology. Of course the second and third centuries (or *āśvāsas*) contain several such anthology verses; the first century contains but one.

The fifth argument and the evidence for it are valid. The point established is not a major one.

De concludes from these arguments or considerations that the second and third centuries of the KK are later additions adapted from other works ascribed to Bilvamaṅgala. Accordingly, he predicts and finds many works (Y51, Y52, Y53), ascribed to Bilvamaṅgala, which include vss. from the second and third centuries. Unfortunately, he also finds such a work (Y11) with four verses from the first century. Mention of this work is made in the Addenda. Evidently it came to this notice after publication was under way. Also he must have forgotten these four verses when some years later he asserts that no verse from the first century occurs in any of the

> collections of miscellaneous Kṛṣṇaite verses ascribed to Bilvamaṅgaṅa, which supply the nucleus of the Second and Third Āśvāsas of the South Indian recension.

Aside from the four verses from the first century noted in the Addenda, Raja finds 8 verses. In favor of the authority of the Bengal version and De's prediction is the fact that compared with the second and third centuries few verses from century one are found in the collections of miscellaneous Kṛṣṇaite verses ascribed to Bilvamañgala.

The Identity of the Author

There are many legends about Līlāśuka Bilvamañgala and many elaborate scholarly conjectures about his identity. The following will not be a comprehensive presentation of these although the great number and variety of legends about Bilvamañgala are interesting and delightful. A selection of the most telling information and theories will be given below.

Date. First of all the date of the author and of the KK text, which is ascribed to him, will be considered. The earliest firm date for the KK is provided by its mention by Gaṅgādevī in her *Madhurāvijaya*.[32] The author was a wife of Kampana who ruled at Conjeevaram about 1367 A.D. Kampana was a prince of the Vijayanagara empire who defeated the sultan at Madurai (Madhurā). *Madhurāvijaya* celebrates this event.[33] In the introduction to her work Gaṅgādevī salutes, among others, the poet who wrote the *Karṇāmṛta*:

mandāramañjarīsyandi-
makarandarasābdhayaḥ /
kasya nā 'hlādanāyā 'laṃ
karṇāmṛtakaver giraḥ // (Sarga I, verse 12)
For whom are the words of the *Karṇāmṛta* poet
not adequate for refreshing?—
the words which are like an ocean of elixir
of the honey which oozes from the
blossoming clusters of a tree of
paradise.

The earliest possible mention of the author, Bilvamaṅgala, is at the end of the *Sarvamūla* of Madhvācārya.[34] The text ends:

iti śrīmadānandatīrthabhagavatpādācāryaviracitā
kṛṣṇastutiḥ saṃpūrṇā. bilvamaṅgalaḥ sādhuḥ.
śrīkṛṣñārpaṇam astu. sarvamūlaṃ saṃpūrṇam.[35]

There has been some discussion as to what "bilvamaṅgalaḥ sādhuḥ" might mean here. It is possible that it is an auspicious saying. My Madhvaite pandit, A.S. Acharya, who pointed out the above text to me, explained that, in appending "bilvamaṅgalaḥ sādhuḥ", Madhva might have been calling attention to a good and saintly if simple person, named Bilvamaṅgala, who was a member of Madhva's circle of students and devotees. B. N. K. Sharma, the Madhvaite scholar, told me that, according to tradition, "bilvamaṅgalaḥ sādhuḥ" is supposed to have been spoken by Madhva. Professor Sharma felt that to understand it as a

32. *Madhura Vijaya or Virakamparaya Charita*: *An Historical Kavya by Ganga Devi*, ed. G. Harihara Sastri and V. Srinivasa Sastri (Trivandrum, 1924).

33. *Ibid.*, p. i.

34. *Śrīmat Sarvamūlam; The Collected Works of Madhvācārya*, Vol. III, ed. R. Kṛṣṇācārya and Rāmācārya (Bombay: Nirnaya Sagar Press, 1892), folio 1149.

35. *Ibid.*

mantra would be questionable. He offered no opinion about interpretting "bilvamaṅgalaḥ sādhuḥ" as a reference to the poet. There is no traditional meaning assigned to these words. A modern Madhvaite pandit, P. Hayagrīvācārya Guttal of Deccan College, has written an article on the possible meanings of these words as a *mantra* or as a reference to the poet.[36]

Whether "bilvamaṅgalaḥ sādhuḥ" is found in the manuscript of the *Sarvamūla*, which dates from the time of Madhva, is not known. The date of Madhva has been estimated to be 1199–1294 or 1238–1317 A.D. Professor Sharma prefers the later.[37] Neither date conflicts with the evidence of the *Madhurāvijaya.*

Many Malayalī Sanskritists have concerned themselves with the date of Bilvamaṅgala, whom they consider to be a Malayalī.

A. Govinda Wariyar[38] and K. Rama Pisharoti[39] believe that there are three Bilvamaṅgalas, whom they call the Villamaṅgalam Svāmiyārs, Villaṅgalam Svāmiyārs, or the Vilvamaṅgalam Svāmiyārs. Pisharoti[40] says that Villamaṅgala is correct, for the second Villamaṅgala Svāmiyār refers to his family as Kodaṇḍamaṅgalam or Cāpamaṅgalam which corresponds to Villumaṅgalam. *kodaṇḍa* and *cāpa* mean "bow" in Sanskrit; *villu* means "bow" in Malayalam. These references are from the *Siricindhakavva* [see YY10 (14)], a Prākrit *kāvya* which illustrates the *Prākṛta Prakāśa* of Vararuci. I quote them from Raja's chapter on Bilvamaṅgala in his book, *The Contribution of Kerala to Sanskrit Literature.*

kodaṅḍamaṅgalavacogadite hi dhāmni
śrīkṛṣṇadarśanaparaḥ kiḷa karṇabhṛtyaḥ (?)/(Canto I)
cāva (Skt. cāpa-) maṃgaladharo jaīsaro
villamaṃgaladharo vahoi jo / (Canto XII)[41]

---

36. P. Hayagrīvācārya Guttal, "śrīmadānandatīrthabhagavatpādācāryāṇāṃ sarvamūlagranthāntyavākyam idam. bilvamaṅgalaḥ sādhuḥ iti", *Saṃskṛti* (Poona, 1960?).

(The text was available to me from an offprint which provided little bibliographical information.)

37. B. N. K. Sharma, *A History of the Dvaita School of Vedānta and its Literature*, Vol. I (Bombay: Booksellers' Publishing Co., 1960), pp. 101–103.

38. A. Govinda Wariyar, "Vilvamaṅgalam Svāmiyārs," *The Indian Historical Quarterly*, Vol. VII, No. 2 (June, 1931), pp. 334–358.

39. K. Rama Pisharoti, "Kṛṣṇas of Kerala," *Bulletin of the Rama Varma Research Institute*, Vol. VI, Part 2 (July, 1938), pp. 69–86.

40. *Ibid.*, pp. 70–71, n. 3.

41. Raja, *The Contribution of Kerala*, p. 45.

Pisharoti[42] believes this confusion of names existed at the time of the first Villamaṅgala Svāmiyār.

According to Wariyar and to Pisharoti the first Bilvamaṅgala was the author of the KK and lived in the ninth century A.D. The second was the grammarian, Kṛṣṇalīlāśuka, who lived about 1200 A.D. He wrote the *Puruṣaknra* commentary on *Daiva.*[43] The third was the court poet of Mānavada, prince of Calicut in the 17th century.

The third Bilvamaṅgala need not be dicussed. About the first Bilvamaṅgala, Pisharoti[44] and Wariyar[45] point out that there is a tradition in Kerala that Villamaṅgalam Svāmiyār founded the Padmanābha temple in Trivandrum. The date for founding the temple is 827 A.D. according to Pisharoti.[46] In refutation of the above Ullur S. Paramesvara Aiyar[47] cites the *Anantaśayanakṣetramāhātmya* which gives Divākara, a Tulu brahmin, as the founder of the temple. Raja[48] says that Pisharoti's method of arriving at the date of 827 A.D. is incorrect.

Both Raja and K. Raghavan Pillai, present day Sanskritists from Kerala, seem to believe that the first and second Bilvamaṅgalas of Pisharoti and Wariyar are one and the same. His date is about 1300 A.D. Raja writes:

> It may be safely assumed that Kṛṣṇalīlāśuka, author of the *Puruṣakāra*, is identical with the author of the *Śrīcihnakāvya* [Pkt. Siricindhakavva YY10 (14)] and that he flourished towards the beginning of the fourteenth century.... Since even the KK shows the deliberate art of a scholar devotee, there is nothing against identifying its author Līlāśuka with the grammarian Līlāśuka. If this identification is accepted, his date can be fixed by about 1300 A.D., since he quotes Vopadeva [in the *Puruṣakāra*[49]] who lived in the second half of the thirteenth century, and since Gaṅgadevī refers to him in the second half of the fourteenth century A.D.[50]

42. Pisharoti, *op. cit.*, p. 71, n. 3.

43. *The Daiva of Deva with the Puruṣakāra commentary of Kṛṣṇalīlāśuka*, ed. T. Ganapato Sastri, Trivandrum Sanskrit Series No. 1 (Trivandrum, 1904?).

44. Pisharoti, *op. cit.*, pp. 77–78.

45. Wariyar, *op. cit.*, p. 335.

46. Pisharoti, *op. cit.*, p. 71–72.

47. Ullur S. Paramesvara Aiyar, "Saint Vilvamaṅgala", *Proceedings and Transactions of the All-India Oriental Conference, Trivandrum*, 1937 (Poona, 1938), p. 473.

48. Raja, *The Contribution of Kerala*, p. 41

49. *Ibid.*, p. 44.

50. *Ibid.*, p. 47

Phillai has very kindly given me an English translation of an article of his written in Malayalam.[51] He presents the grammarian and poet, Līlāśuka, as the probable author of the anonymous *Līlātilaka*, a 14th century work on Malayalam grammar. Thus, Līlāśuka would have written grammars on Sanskrit, Prakrit, and Malayalam.

If Līlāśuka Bilvamaṅgala does belong to the 14th century, then we must account for verses from the KK which are quoted by earlier poets. Since all Southern versions of the KK include KK st. 2.65 quoted by Kṣemendra (see Z22) and KK st. 2.70 quoted by Hemacandra and Vidyākara (see Z23 and Z25) and since all these authors were considerably prior to 1300 A.D., it is necessary to account for the appearance of verses quoted by them.

There are several other verses (see those found in Z5) like st. 2.65 and st. 2.70, but these two verses are the earliest and evidence of their early occurrence is best.

One way to account for verses which are original to collections such as the KK but which are not original to the author to whom the verses of the collection are attributed is to assume that the author of the verses did not put the collection together. Those that did assemble and arrange the verses inadvertently included verses not written by the author. It seems to me that this is a fair assumption although my impression of the authorship of the KK is not that of Raja and Pillai.

My imagination, instructed first hand by the myriad Kerala and all-India traditions about Bilvamaṅgala—and by the Madhvaite evidence as well as by textual studies, conjures a very popular poet-saint, a *parivrājaka* who wandered over the whole of India composing Kṛṣṇaite verses about the time of Madhva. These verses were much admired by the 14th century grammarian Kṛṣṇalīlāśuka who incorporated fragments in some *stotras* and a *kāvya* he wrote (see YY10, especially on p. 72 of the "Mss. Used" section). Of course it has to be assumed that the writer of the *stotras* in YY10 is the 14th century grammarian who wrote the *Puruṣakāra* commentary on *Daiva*. This assumption is made on two other assumptions; 1) The grammarian who wrote the *Puruṣakāra* and the grammarian who wrote the *Śrīcihnakāvya* are identical because they are both grammarians with the same name Kṛṣṇalīlāśuka. 2) The writer of the

51. K. Raghavan Pillai, "On the Līlātilaka" [an English translation by Pillai of the original in Malayalam published in the *Matṛbhūmi* (June 10 and 17, 1962)].

Kālavadhakāvya etc. and the *Śrīcihnakāvya* are the same, because the colophon of YY10, wherein they are both found, indicates this.

If the 14th century grammarian was the admirer—or writer—of Bilvamañgala verses, it is pertinent to the history of the KK that in his poetic composition, the *Kālavadha*, he juxtaposed lines found only in KK st. 1 and lines found only in the Y version. If the 14th century grammarian did juxtapose the lines, it would agree with the history, given on p. 87 ff. of the "Mss. Used" section, which is derived from the textual evidence of the KK versions.

Before going on to the legends associated with Bilvamañgala, it should be noted here that since Rādhā is frequently mentioned in the KK, she has to be reckoned with when calculating the dates possible for the KK. This calculation is doubly difficult for there is much dispute as to the date of her arrival on the literary scene in North India, on the one hand, and in South India, on the other.[52]

Legends. In the first verse of the KK is the line

cintāmaṇir jayati somagirir gurur me

which has been interpreted by the commentators in many ways.

Pāpayallaya Sūri, as do many of the other commentators, gives two possible readings. 1) Somagiri is the guru of Līlāśuka and *cintāmaṇi* (jewel of wishes) is an epithet of Somagiri. Kṛṣṇadāsa Kavirāja identifies Somagiri mentioned in KK st. 1.1 with Īśānadeva mentioned in KK st. 1.110.[53] 2) Cintāmaṇi is the name of a courtesan who was the first guru

---

52. S. L. Katre, "Kṛṣṇa, Gopas, Gopīs, and Rādhā" (offprint of an article from the *P. K. Gode Commemoration Volume*) 10 pp.

53. V. Raghavan of Madras states and most of the past and present day Sanskritists from Kerala believe that KK st. 1.110 gives further biographical information about Līlāśuka. They believe the correct reading for nīvī- in line a to be nīlī-. This is a popular name for girls in Kerala. I have found no textual evidence for reading nīlī- in any KK ms. which I have seen. Nīlī would be the name of Līlāśuka's mother and Dāmodara, the name of his father.

The textual evidence for Nīlī is found in the "Vṛttiratna," a biographical group of verses found in YY10 and YY11 mss. YY10 ms. is the ms. with the *Śrīcihnakāvya.* It includes many *stotras* besides the grammatical commentary. Everything in the ms., according to the colophon, is attributed to Kṛṣṇalīlāśuka. The "Vṛttiratna." which is called "Gopālastotra" in YY10, is quoted in its entirety in the "Description of Mss." section under YY10 (4). (It is probably called "Gopālastotra" in YY10 because of the

of Līlāśuka. There is a long story connected with this reading. The story, I hear, has been dramatised and produced on the Bengali and the Andhra stage. I have seen the play done in Tamil by the Ramakrishna Kripa Amateurs on October 10, 1964, in Mylapore. Dr. (Miss) S. S. Janaki kindly interpreted for me. The Tamil play I saw had very much the same story told by Swami Vivekananda when he was in America.[54] This story is told briefly in Nābhādāsajī's *Bhaktamālā*[55] which was written about 1600 A.D.[56] The story often includes a passage wherein Bilvamañgala blinds himself with needles or thorns. His motives and actions are the same as those told of Sūrdās.

The story of Bilvamañgala and Cintāmañi is set on the banks of the Kṛṣṇaveṇa River, the Ganges, at Kākkatturuttu near Tṛkkaṇāmatilakam in Kerla, or at Puttancira in North Parur also in Kerala[57], etc., according, very often, to the nativity of the teller.

The earliest datable telling of the Cintāmañi story is by Kṛṣṇadāsa Kavirāja[58] towards the end of the 16th century. There are two other early stories about Bilvamañgala. In the Vallabhaite *Saṃpradāyakuladīpikā*, written by Gada in 1554, it is told that Bilvamañgala, when reborn become Jayadeva. Seshagiri Sastri says that this might suggest that Bilvamañgala was earlier than Jayadeva.[59]

The following is the report given by Dasgupta of a tradition reported in the *Vallabhadigvijaya* by Jadunāthajī Mahārāja.

> According to the *Vallabha-dig-vijaya* there was a king called, Vijaya of the Pāṇḍya kingdom in the south. He had a priest Devasvāmin, whose son was Viṣṇusvāmin. Śukasvāmin, a great religious reformer of North India, was his fellow-student in the Vedānta; it is difficult to identify him in any way. Viṣṇusvāmin went to Dvārakā, to Bṛndāvana, then to Purī, and then returned home. At an

first of the three initial verses which are not closely connected with the main body of the "*stotra*."). Vss. 11 and 12 give the information that Nīlī was the mother of Līlāśuka and Dāmodara, his father.

54. *The Complete Works of Swami Vivekananda*, Vol. I (Calcutta, 1957), pp. 485–488.

55. *Śrīnābhādāsajīviracitā Śrībhaktamālā* (Bombay: Vaibhav Press, 1924), p. 46.

56. Farquhar, *op. cit.*, p. 317.

57. Raja, *The Contribution of Kerala*, pp. 32–33.

58. De, KK, p. 8.

59. Raja, *The Contribution of Kerala*, p. 43.

advanced age he left his household deities to his son, and having renounced the world in the Vaiṣṇava fashion, came to Kāñcī. He had many pupils there, e.g., Śrīdevadarśaṇa, Śrīkaṇṭha, Sahasrāci, Śatadhṛti, Kumārapada, Parabhūti, and others. Before his death he left the charge of teaching his views to Śrīdevadarśaña. He had seven hundred principal followers teaching his views; one of them, Rājaviṣṇusvāmin, became a teacher in the Andhra country. Viṣñusvāmin's temples and books were said to have been burnt at this time by the Buddhists. Vilva-maṅgala, a Tamil saint, succeeded to the pontifical chair at Śrīraṅgam, Vilva-maṅgala left the pontifical chair at Kāñcī to Deva-maṅgala and went to Bṛndāvana. Prabhā-viṣṇusvāmin succeeded to the pontifical chair; he had many disciples, e.g., Śrīkaṇṭhagarbha, Satyavatī Paṇḍita, Somagiri, Narahari, Śrāntanidhi and others. He installed Śrāntanidhi in his pontifical chair before his death. Among the Viṣṇusvāmin teachers was one Govindācārya, whose disciple Vallabhācārya is said to have been. It is difficult to guess the date of Viṣṇusvāmin; it is not unlikely, however, that he lived in the twelfth or the thirteenth century.[60]

Another literary source of Bilvamañgala legends is, according to Kavi, the 13th Skandha of the Uriya *Bhāgavata Purāṇa*. This Skandha is devoted to

> the glorification of Bilvamaṅgala, whose name is accounted for by the presence of a *bilva* tree [woodapple tree] in the front of the house of his nativity.[61]

Works. Works attributed to Līlāśuka Bilvamañgala and discussed elsewhere will not be mentioned here. Unlike the works discussed elsewhere—for the most part in the "Mss. Used" section—the following works have no verses in common with the KK.

Most of the *stotras* attributed to Kṛṣṇalīlāśuka and written in the Malayalī script are included in the YY10 and the YY11 codices. See YY10 and YY11 in the "Description of the Mss." section. Two other such *stotras* are deposited in the University of Kerala Mss. Library.

60. Surendranath Dasgupta, *A History of Indian Philosophy*, Vol. IV (Cambridge: University Press, 1949), p. 383.

Durgāstava. This has been published as the Durgāstutiḥ by Ullur S. Paramesvara Aiyar.[62] The ms., which contains this *stotra* was formerly deposited in the Trivandrum Palace Library. The ms. is Trivandrum Palace Library No. 1172 G. Malayalam script, palm leaf, folios 2, 12 inches by 1½ inches, 20 lines to a side. The Palace Library Catalogue[63] remarks that the work is about the deity in the temple at Harikanyāpura. The concluding portion indicates that it is also known by the titles, *Mālinīstuti* (from the meter in which it is composed) and *Mūlakanyāstuti* and that the author had written another work, *Stotraratna* by name.

Dakṣiṇāmūrtistava. This has been published by T. Ganapati Sastri.[64] It is from the same codex as the above Durgāstava. The ms. no. is 1172 Q.

Sarasvatīnakṣatramālā. All information on this *stotra* is from the *Stotrasamāhāra*:

> This stotra in praise of goddess Sarasvatī probably derives the name nakṣatramālā from the fact that the stotra alone consists only of 27 stanzas. The colophon mentions the work as consisting of 32 stanzas but the manuscript contains only 31. The edition is based on a manuscript (No. L. 722) kindly lent to us [University of Kerala Manuscripts Library] by Sri Raman Vasudevan Nambuthiry, Patiñjattiyeṭattu Mana, Kanayannoor.[65]

Sūryastotram. Baroda Oriental Institute No. 13091 (a).

Malayalam script, palm leaf, folios 1, size and lines to a side not known. Begins: svasti.

---

61. M. Ramakrishna Kavi, "Literary Gleanings: No. 9 Bilvamañgalasvāmin," *The Quarterly Journal of the Andhra Historical Research Society*, Vol. III, Part 1 (July, 1928), p. 67.

62. Aiyar, *op. cit.*, pp. 481–482.

63. *A Descriptive Catalogue of the Sanskrit Manuscripts in H.H. The Maharajah's Palace Library Trivandrum*, Vol. V, ed. K. Sāmbaśiva Śāstrī (Trivandrum, 1938), p. 1795.

64. *Abhinavakaustubhamala and Dakshinamurtistava of Krishnalilasukamuni*, ed. T. Ganapati Sastri, Trivandrum Sanskrit Series No. 2 (Trivandrum, 1905).

65. *Stotrasamāhāra*, Part 1, ed. K. Raghavan Pillai, University of Kerala Sanskrit Series No. 211 (Trivandrum, 1964), p. iii.

kāmaṃ dhāmāni tattatsuravaraparișadgātranityādhivāsā-
nnāsīranaitihāsānyapahasanapadaṃ vīramīmāṃsakānām /
kiṃ taccintābhirābhistribhuvana... bhogasākṣīyadīyaṃ
tejassāmrājyametattapanavijayate sarvato nirvivādam //1//

Ends:

iti bhagavati bhāvanānatābhīṣṭavarṣa
vyasanikarasahasre ko vibhakteḥ pravāhaḥ /
jayatu jayatu jaitrastotramūrtyāvatīrṇaḥ
katihṛdayavilaṅghyaḥ kṛṣṇalīlāśukīyaḥ //14//
iti kṛṣṇalīlāśukakavimuninā viracitaṃ trayodaśaśloka-
saṃkhyaṃ sūryastotraṃ samāptam.

Collated from hand copy by Adyar Library copyist. Adyar Library had the ms. on loan from Baroda Oriental Institute.

Kṛṣṇāhnikakaumudī. Universitäts Bibliothek Tübingen No. Ma I 230. Bengali script, paper, folios 28 (incomplete), size not known, 12 lines to a side.
Begins: śrīrādhākṛṣṇau jayatāṃ.

rajanicaramayāme stokatārābhirāme
kimapi kimapi vṛndādeśajātābhinandā /
vitatirakṛta rādhākṛṣṇayoḥ svāpabādhā-
matimṛduvacanānāṃ śārikāṇāṃ śukānāṃ //1//

Final folios are missing.
Collated from photographic copy.

Mitra[66] describes a ms. of the same text. He describes the text as "Poetical descriptions of Kṛṣṇa's amatory career in Vṛndāvana."[67] He gives the end:

tantrāśliṣṭe sati madhumade kiñcidarddhāviśiṣṭe /
pratyāsannaḥ samadanamado yaḥ saṃstaḥ parīṣṭe //

To Kṛṣṇalīlāśuka, the grammarian, is ascribed a commentary *Kṛṣṇalīlāvinoda* on Bhoja's *Sarasvatīkaṇṭhābharaṇa.*[68] M. Ramakrishna

---

66. Rājendralāla Mitra, *Notices of Sanskrit Mss.*, Series I, Volume IX (Calcutta, 1888), pp. 60–61.

67. *Ibid.*

68. Kavi, *loc. cit.*

Kavi was evidently the first to note this commentary. I have been unable to trace its whereabouts. Kavi[69] mentions two other grammars by Līlāśuka: the *Subantasāmrājya* and the *Tiṅantasāmrājya.* These could not be traced, but there is a helpful note in the preface to the Trivandrum *Curator's Library Catalogue:*

> Puruṣakāra (Vide page 1189.) From the verse "etat subantasāmrājyamedhitaṃ nayasaṃpadā / kṛṣṇacandrājñayā guptaṃ kṛtārthayatu sajjanān //" we gather that the title of the work is Subantasāmrājya. The subsequent portion dealing with Tiṅantaprakriya may be Tiṅantasāmrājya. The passage: "yad uktaṃ puruṣakāre bahayatītyudāhṛtya—iṣṭhani yat phiṣaḥ, kāryaṃ, taṇṇāvapyatidiśyate. na ceṣṭhani yiṭ phiṣo bhū bhāvaśca' bhuvo yiṭ sanniyogaśiṣṭatvāt. tena nyāse/bhāvayatīti cintyā prāptiḥ.' occurring in Mādhavīya Dhātuvṛtti is a quotation taken from the commentary on the Sūtra *iṣṭhe yuk ca* in Tiṅantasāmrājya. So on the authority of Mādhava, we may believe that Tiṅantasāmrājya was also known as Puruṣakāra.[70]

Kṛṣṇalīlāśuka has written a commentary on the *Kenopaniṣad* called *Śaṅkarahṛdayaṅgamā.* Raja accepts it as a work of the grammarian and the poet.[71] He describes it.

> There are two *Bhāṣyas* on the Upaniṣad both ascribed to Śaṅkara; Līlāśuka tries to effect a reconciliation between the two, and show what was really intended by the Bhāṣyakāra; at times he gives original interpretations also.[72]

There are three mss. of this commentary: Madras Government Oriental Library No. 2962 and University of Kerala Manuscripts Library Nos. L. 1246B and T. 1255. The last mentioned ms. is a copy of the first. It has been published in the *Annals of Oriental Research.*[73]

69. Kavi, *loc. cit.*

70. *A Descriptive Catalogue of Sanskrit Manuscripts in the Curator's Office Library, Trivandrum,* Vol III, ed. K. Sāmbaśiva Śāstrī (Trivandrum, 1938), pp. i–ii.

71. Raja, *The Contribution of Kerala,* p, 47

72. *Ibid.,* p. 48.

73. This information is from Raja, *The Contribution of Kerla,* p. 48, n. 101. (Edited by S. Subrahmanya Sastri, *Annals of Oriental Research,* Madras University, 1952.)

MANUSCRIPTS USED

This section includes both manuscripts and printed editions used to prepare the Kṛṣṇakarṇāmṛta text in this edition.

Colophons and verses quoted from these manuscripts are markedly corrupt. They appear in the following pages as they are in the manuscript. They are without correction or emendation.

Meanings of the Letters by Which the Bilvamaṅgala Manuscripts are Identified

Bengal version of the KK written in both the Devanāgarī and Bengali scripts

- A ms. not reported by S. K. De and without a commentary (c)
- B Bengal version as reported by S. K. De, KK

Southern version of the KK written in the Devanāgarī script

- C mss. with the Pāpayallaya Sūri c (P. Sūri c)
- D mss. without a c
- E mss. with the Kṛṣṇa Paṇḍita c (*śataka* 2 only)
- F printed edition with old Marāthī c (*śataka* 1 only)

Southern version of the KK written in the Grantha script

- G mss. without a commentary
- H mss. with the P. Sūri c

Southern version of the KK in the Kannada script

- K mss. without a c

Southern version of the KK written in the Malayalam script

- M mss. without a c

Southern version of the KK written in the Nandināgarī script

- N mss. without a c

Southern version of the KK written in the Telugu script

- P mss. with the P. Sūri c
- Q ms. with the Bālagopāla *ślokavārtika*
- R mss. with the Rāmacandra c
- S mss. with the Brahmābhaṭṭa c
- T mss. without a c
- U mss. with an old Telugu verse translation
- V printed editions with a modern Telugu gloss and the above verse translation

Bengal recension associated with the Northern anthologies of Bilvamañgala verses

W mss. with the Vanamālin c

X mss. with a Vallabhaite c

Northern anthologies of Bilvamañgala verses

Y

Stotras, anthologies, kāvyas of Kṛṣṇalīlāśuka written in Dravidian scripts.

YYO

Collections of refrain vss. which have the same line d or a (or part of same) as a vs. (or vss.) which appears in the KK

YY50

Anthologies and other works in which KK vss. are found

Z

System of Numbering by Which the Verse Sequence of the KK Mss. Is Described

(This system does not apply to Y and Z mss.)

Numbers are assigned to mss.	according to verse sequence[1] in both *śataka* 1				and *śataka* 3.	
	a	b	c	d	a	d
0–9	a				a	
10–19	a					d
20–29		b			a	
30–39		b				d
40–49			c		a	
50–59			c			d
60–69				d	a	
70–79				d		d

[1] Verse sequences a b c d in *śataka* 1:

a Sequence is as in standard (or critical) version.

b Sequence of vss. 66 and 67 of the standard version is reversed.

c Vs. 57 of the standard version is omitted.

d Both b and c sequence of a are present.

Verse sequences a d in *śataka* 3:

a Sequence is as in standard (or critical) version.

d Sequence of vss. 79 and 80 of the standard version is reversed.

Sequence aa (Numbers 1–9 are assigned to mss. with this sequence. Number 0 designates the group or part of the group of mss. with this sequence.) is found in the standard (or critical) version and, most characteristically, in mss. which provide the oldest testimony. These mss. are A, B, and W of the Bengal or Caitanyaite tradition and DG, G1, G2 and N1 of the Vijayanagara (see DG) tradition. These latter mss. have otherwise a very atypical organization of verses.

Sequence ba (Numbers 21–29 are assigned to mss. with this sequence. Number 20 designates the group or part of the group of mss. with this sequence.) is found, most characteristically, with the Brahmabhaṭṭa commentary (S mss.), the Rāmacandra commentary (R mss.), and the short version of the P. Sūri commentary (C21, C22, H21, and H31). It should be noted here that N21 has an atypical verse sequence which places it with the Vijayanagara tradition. N21 is exceptional.

Sequence ca (Numbers 41–49 are assigned to mss. with this sequence. Number 40 designates the group or part of the group of mss. with this sequence.) is found only in Maharashtrian mss. The reverse is not true: Some Maharashtrian mss. have other verse sequences.

Sequence dd (Numbers 71–79 are assigned to mss. with this sequence. Number 70 designates the group or part of the group of mss. with this sequence.) is found, most characteristically, with the long version of the P. Sūri commentary (P71, P72).

Sequences ad (Numbers 11–19 are assigned to mss. with this sequence. Number 10 designates the group or part of the group of mss. with this sequence.); bd (Numbers 31–39 are assigned to mss. with this sequence. Number 30 designates the group or part of the group of mss. with this sequence.); cd (Numbers 51–59 are assigned to mss. with this sequence. Number 50 designates the group or part of the group of mss. with this sequence.); da (Numbers 61–69 are assigned to mss. with this sequence. Number 60 designates the group or part of the group of mss. with this sequence.) are considered to result from mixing of the centuries of the different versions.

About the variant readings which are reported in the mss. with the various sequences aa, ba, ca, and dd:

The readings of aa and dd vary most markedly from each other.

The number of non aa mss. recording an aa variant is usually very small.

ba mss. are more frequently found among this small number than are the ca mss.

As one would expect, however, both ba and ca mss. read much more frequently with the aa mss. in *śataka* 3.

Description of the Manuscripts

Two signs are used in the following section.

x placed before a manuscript indicates that it was only partially collated.

o placed before a verse or a manuscript indicates that the vs. or the ms. was not collated.

A and B mss. represent the Bengal and Caitanya version of the KK. Caitanya (1486–1533 A.D.) brought back a copy of the KK st. 1 only from his pilgrimage in Southern and Western India.[1] In Bengal it is only this century (KK st. 1) which is considered to be the KK.

A1 Staatsbibliothek (Marburg) No. or. oct. 466. Devanāgarī script, paper, folios 17 (1–5, 6^{r}, 7^{r} are missing), 18–23 cm by 7–10 cm. Ms. includes first century only. Begins: First folios are missing. Ends: iti śrīlīlāśukabilvamañgalaviracitaṃ śrīkarṇāmṛtastotraṃ saṃpūrṇaṃ. śrīkṛṣṇāya namaḥ. śrī. śrī. śrī. śrī. saṃvat 1629 varṣe āṣāḍhasudī 9 guruvāsare leṣitaṃ vrā° jagannāthadāsavaiṣṇavakāsīdāsapaṭhanārthaṃ. vṛndāvanamadhye. A medical prescription, which is written in the same hand, follows. (1573 A.D., Vṛndāvana)

B1 refers to a group of Devanāgarī manuscripts with the commentary of Gopālabhaṭṭa which have been edited by S.K. De for his critical edition of the KK. De discusses this commentary and commentator in the introduction.[2]

---

1. The Kṛṣṇa-karṇāmṛta, ed. Sushil Kumar De, University of Dacca Oriental Publications Series No. 5 (Dacca, 1938), p. ix.

2. *Ibid.*, pp. xxx–li.

Of the Bengal commentaries the earliest appears to have been the *Kṛṣṇa-vallabhā* of Gopāla Bhaṭṭa, son of Harivaṃśa Bhaṭṭa and grandson of Nṛsiṃha of the Drāviḍa country.[3]

De considers at length the identity of the commentator and Caitanya's disciple of the same name. The evidence is equivocal. In his consideration he has noted the following about the commentary.

As the commentary quotes directly from the *Bhaktirasāmṛta-sindhu* and *Ujjvala-nīla-maṇi* of Rūpa Gosvāmin, the former of which work is dated expressly in Śaka 1463 (= 1541 A.D.), it could not have been composed before this date.[4]

B1-GA ms. (description from the KK edited by De) Benares Sanskrit College Library (Sanskrit University Sarasvati Bhavana) No. 42 described in the *Sūcī-patram*. Paper, folios (42, 8–14 are missing), 141 in., 11–17 lines to a side. (1605 A.D.)
Collated from the critical text of De who collated from a hand copy of the ms.

B1-GB ms. (description from the KK edited by De) Asiatic Society of Bengal No. III.C.107. Paper, folios 45, 11 in. by 43 in., 15 lines to a side.
Collated from the text of De who collated from the ms.

B1–GC ms. (description from the KK edited by De) Vaṅgīya Sāhitya Pariṣad No. 280. Modern paper, folios 30 (incomplete, ends with st. 1.59), 12¼ in. by 6 in., 14–15 lines to a side.
Collated from the text of De who collated from the ms.

B2 refers to a group of manuscripts with the commentary, *Subodhanī*, of Caitanyadāsa which have been edited by S. K. De for his critical edition of the KK. De discusses this commentary and commentator in the introduction. Nothing definite can be determined about the commentator. De notes the following about the commentary.

This commentary... often suggests interpretations which were appropriated and developed further by Kṛṣṇadāsa.[5]

3. *Ibid.*, p. xxx.
4. *Ibid.*, p. xli.
5. *Ibid.*, pp. lii–iii.

> If... Caitanyadāsa directed Kṛṣṇadāsa's literary activity, then he must have been a contemporary of Rūpa Gosvāmin, whose works were accepted by all Bengal Vaiṣṇava writers as authoritative. As such, the work would be almost contemporaneous with Gopāla Bhaṭṭa's *Kṛṣṇa-vallabhā*, which also quotes from the *Ujjvala-nīla-maṇi*.[6]

B2-CA (description from the KK edition by De) Dacca University Manuscript Library No. 2464. Bengali script, paper, folios 13, 16¾ in. by 5¾ in., 12–18 lines to a side.
Collated from the text of De who collated from the ms.

B2-CB (description from the KK edition by De) Vaṅgīya Sāhitya Pariṣad No. 21. Bengali script, paper, folios 26, 9½ in. by 4¼ in., 8–12 lines to a side. (1668 A.D.)
Collated from text of De who collated from the ms.

B2-CC (description from the KK edition by De) Bhandarkar Oriental Research Institute No. 326. Devanāgarī script, paper, folios 18, 11½ in. by 4¾ in., 14–15 lines to a side. (1757 A.D.)
Collated from text of De who collated from the ms.

B2-CD (description from the KK edition by De) Bodleian Library No. 230. Bengali script, paper, folios 16, 13½ in., by 5 in., 12 lines to a side.
Collated from text of De who collated from rotograph copy.

B3 refers to a group of manuscripts and a printed edition with the commentary *Sāraṅga-raṅgadā* by Kṛṣṇadāsa Kavirāja.
This commentary, according to De,

> is more well known... From the theological point of view this commentary possesses some importance, for Kṛṣṇadāsa was one of the most important theologians of the Bengal sect, who was trained in the authoritative school of the Vṛndāvana Gosvāmins... Although Kṛṣṇadāsa refers to Gopāla Bhaṭṭa as one of his Śikṣā-gurus..., it is remarkable that in his commentary he prefers to follow and develop the indications of Caitanyadāsa.[7]

B3-KA (description from the KK edition by De) Dacca University

6. *Ibid.*, pp. liv–v.
7. *Ibid.*, pp. lv–vi.

Manuscript Library No. 2358. Bengali script, paper, folios 30 (1–6 are missing), 15¾ in. by 3½ in., 6–14 lines to a side. (1743 A.D.) Collated from text of De who collated from the ms.

B3-KB (description from KK edition by De) Dacca University Manuscript Library No. 2454. Bengali script, paper, 12 in. by 5½ in., folios 30, 10–16 lines to a side.
Collated from text of De who collated from the ms.

B3-KC (description from KK edition of De) Dacca University Manuscript Library No. 3525. Bengali script, paper, folios 29 (1 missing at the end), 13½ in. by 6¼ in., 15–17 lines to a side.
Collated from text of De who collated from the ms.

B3-KD (description from the KK edition of De) Dacca University Manuscript Library No. 2415. Bengali script, paper, folios 56 (one folio missing at end), 11¼ in. by 5 in., 6–14 lines to a side.
Collated from text of De who collated from the ms.

B3-KP (description of this printed edition is from the KK edition of De) *Sāraṅga-raṅgadā* of Kṛṣṇadāsa Kavirāja, Murshidabad: Radharaman Press, Berhampore, 1916 A.D., 242 pp.
Collated from text of De who collated from printed edition.

C mss. with the Pāpayallaya Sūri commentary (P. Sūri c).
H and P mss. also have the P. Sūri c. Colophon to the commentary to each of the three *śatakas*: iti śrīpadavākyapramāṇapārāvārapārīṇavasumatitirumalabhaṭṭopādhyāyaputreṇa kodaṇḍamāmbāgarbhaśuktimuktāmaṇinā pāpayallayasūriṇā viracitāyāṃ śrīkṛṣṇakarṇāmṛtavyākhyāyāṃ suvarṇacaṣakaṃ samākhyāyāṃ prathamo 'dhyāyaḥ (dvitīyo 'dhyāyaḥ, tṛtīyo 'dhyāyaḥ).
From the introductory verses to P. Sūri's commentary Seshagiri Sastri concludes that P. Sūri

> ...refers to a hermit, named Yajñeśa, who performed the sacrifice called Vājapeya, and also to an ascetic, named Mukunda, who seemed to have been his preceptor... He does not aspire, he says, to such fame as was acquired by Peḍḍibhaṭṭa, that is Mallinātha...[8]

Mallinātha lived c. 1400 A.D.[9] Other authors quoted by P. Sūri

8. M. Seshagiri Sastri, *Report on a Search for Sanskrit and Tamil Manuscripts for the Year 1893–94*, No. 2, Madras, 1899, p. 51.

in his commentary are all earlier than Mallinātha. De gives an adequate summary of his references to other authors. (As everywhere De used P71 for his source when quoting the Southern recension of the KK or when quoting P. Sūri.)

In his commentary on KK i, 3 he quotes anonymously *muktā-phaleṣu cchāyāyāḥ* which occurs as a kārikā–verse in the *Rasārṇava-sudhākara* of Śiṅga-bhūpāla (ed. Trivandrum Sanskrit Series 50, Trivandrum 1916; i, 181, p. 41), belonging to the middle of the 14th century (see S. K. De, *Sanskrit Poetics*, i, p. 242–43). The verse is anonymously appropriated, apparently from the same source, in Rūpa Gosvāmin's *Ujjvala-nīla-maṇi* (Uddīpanaprakaraṇa, śl. 26, p. 223).—Besides the well known lexicon of Amara, Pāpayallaya Sūri quotes Viśva, Śabdārṇava (on i, 86; ii 64, 68; iii 59 etc.—lexicon), Halāyudha (on i 79—lexicon), Mukuṭa (on i 105; apparently Rāyamukuṭa on Amara), Sanatkumāra-saṃhitā (on iii 82, 96; a work on Vaiṣṇava mantras), Krama-dīpikā (on iii 97, 98, 99, 100; a work on Vaiṣṇava ritual), Bāhaḍa (on i 2), Lakṣmaṇa Bhaṭṭa Upādhyāya (on iii 83; whose comment on the verse *dhanuḥ pauṣpaṃ maurvī* is referred to).[10]

C21 Asiatic Society of Bengal No. 1230. Country paper, folios 37+44+40=121 (each *śataka* is separately numbered), $10\frac{3}{4}$ in. by $4\frac{1}{2}$ in., 10–12 lines to a side, 2500 *ślokas*. Appearance fresh. Commentary begins: śrīcintāmaṇigaṇapataye namaḥ. 2) and 3) śrīgaṇapataye namaḥ. Text ends: 1) iti śrīkṛṣṇakarṇāmṛtadvādaśottaraśatakaṃ samāptaṃ. 2) omitted. 3) iti śrīlīlāśukaviracite śrīkṛṣṇakarṇāmṛtastotraratne triśatakaṃ saṃpūrñaṃ.
Collated from a photographic copy.

C22 Bhandarkar Oriental Research Institute No. 492/1887–91. Country paper, 34 folios (ms. contains *śataka* 2 only), 10 in. by $6\frac{1}{5}$ in., 14–15 lines to a side. The usual colophon to the P. Sūri commentary is not appended to the *śataka* contained in this ms. The

9. A. Berriedale Keith, *A History of Sanskrit Literature* (Oxford: Oxford University Press, 1956), p. 87, n. 2.

10. De, *op. cit.*, p. xi, n. 1.

authorship of the commentary was determined by comparing it with the other commentaries. The colophon to the text reads: iti śrīlīlāśukaviracite karṇāmṛte dvitīyaṃ śatakaṃ. Commentary begins: śrīkṛṣṇāya namaḥ. Commentary ends: iti karṇāmṛtadvitīyaśatakaṭīkā samāptā. śake 1721 siddhārthināmavarṣe āṣāḍhāsita caturdaśyāṃ lekhanaṃ samāptam iti jñeyaṃ. śrīkṛṣṇajayakṛṣṇajayajayakṛṣṇa. kṛṣṇārpaṇam astu. (1799 A.D.). Collected during a search for Sanskrit mss. in Mahārāṣṭra.[11]

Collated from a photographic copy.

C51 Bhandarkar Oriental Research Institute 241/1880–81. Country paper (also modern paper with water marks used for folios 13–50 of the first *śataka*), folios 50+64+48=162 (each century is separately numbered), $10\frac{1}{4}$ in. by $4\frac{1}{2}$ in., 10–11 lines to a side. Appearance not very old. Text ends: 1) iti karṇāmṛtaśataka samāptam. 2) and 3) omitted. Commentary begins: śrīgaṇeśāya namaḥ (all centuries thus)

Collated from a photographic copy.

C52 Baroda Oriental Institute No. 308. Paper, folios 161. Commentary begins: 1) and 3) śrīgaṇeśāya namaḥ. 2) avighnam astu.

Collated from hand copy by Adyar Library copyist. Name of copyist is not noted on the copy of C52 nor on the copies of G1, G11, H21, and H31 which are by the same copyist.

DG The six DG manuscripts are deposited in the Tanjore Maharaja Serfoji's Saraswathi Mahal Library, Tanjore. In spring of 1965 these manuscripts were the subject of a final examination and discussion with Śrī P. V. Varadarajasarma, the curator of the library. It was concluded at this time that these six manuscripts are most likely 18th century Devanāgarī copies, made by library copyists, of old Grantha mss. deposited in the Tanjore library before the Nāyak kings took over about 1535 A.D. after the death of the great ruler, Kṛṣṇadevarāya (1509–1529 A.D.), at Vijayanagara. Tanjore was a dependency of the Vijayanagara empire.[12]

---

11. R. G. Bhandarkar, *Report on the Search for Sanskrit Manuscripts in the Bombay Presidency during the years 1887–8, 1888–9, 1889–90 and 1890–91* (Bombay: Government Central Press, 1897), p. 35.

12. P. P. S. Sastri, *A Descriptive Catalogue of the Sanskrit Manuscripts in the Tanjore Mahārāja Serfoji's Sarasvatī Mahāl Library Tanjore*, Vol. XIX (Srirangam: Sri Vani Vilas Press, 1934), p. x.

The DG mss. represent the same tradition as do G1 and G2 which see. The DG mss. probably represent a better copy of the tradition than do the G1 and G2 mss. One proof of this would be that G1 and G2 have vss. which appear twice in the ms. For example, G1 and G2 have KK st. 1.9 once in its standard position (KK st. 1.9) and a second time after KK st. 2.34 where this verse is often found in the Vijayanagara mss. (DG, G1, G2, N1, and N21). The DG mss. have no double occurrences of verses indicating that they were less conflated with the mainstream tradition of KK mss. The double occurrence of a verse in a manuscript can be quickly noted in the "Chart of Additional Verse Sequences." There we note that of the Vijayanagara mss. G1, G2, and N21 have at least one double occurrence of a verse. DG and N1 have no double occurrences.

According to Śrī Varadarajasarma, Grantha manuscripts were the first deposited in the library. The Telugu manuscripts were added when the Nāyak kings were in Tanjore (1535–1673 A.D.). Many of these Telugu manuscripts, however, are copies of the Grantha manuscripts. In the same way, Devanāgarī copies were made by Maharshtrian copyists when the Maratha kings were in Tanjore after 1676 A.D.,[13] but most of the Devanāgarī mss. were acquired when Mahārāja Serfoji, the Maratha king, ruled (1800–1832 A.D.[14]).

DG1 Tanjore Maharaja Serfoji's Saraswathi Mahal Library No. B. 4943/D. 20791. Country paper, 58 folios, 22.8 cm. by 9.7 cm., 8 lines to a side. DG1 has the standard sequence of centuries arranged thus: 2+3+1. The numbering of st. 2, st. 3, and st. 1 is in DG1, respectively, 1, 2, 3. Begins: st. 2) śrīgaṇeśāya namaḥ. śrīsarasvatyai namaḥ. śrīgurubhyo namaḥ. st. 3) śrīgaṇapatiye namaḥ śrīmudgalo jayati. st. 1) śrī. Ends: st. 2) iti śrīkarṇāmṛte prathamaśatakaṃ saṃpūrṇaṃ. st. 3) iti dvitīyaśatakaṃ samāptam. śrīkṛṣṇārpaṇam astu. śrīgaṇādhipataye namaḥ. śrīmudgalo jayati. śrījābālyai namaḥ. st. 1) iti śrīlīlāśukena viracite karṇāmṛtastotre tṛtīyaśatakaṃ samāptam. śrīmudgaleśo jayati. śrī.

Collated from two hand copies, the first by N. K. Rāmānujatātā-

13. *Ibid.*

14. *Ibid.*, p. xi.

cārya and the second by N. Ranganathasastri. The first hand copy was compared to the original manuscript by Davanathachariar and myself, the second, by N. K. Rāmānujatātācārya.

DG2 Tanjore Maharaja Serfoji's Saraswathi Mahal Library N. B.4957/ D.20804 (st. 2), No. B. 4946/D. 20815 (st. 3), No. B. 4952/D. 20823 (st. 1). Examination of these three mss. with Mr. P. V. Varadarajasarma determined them to be parts of the same manuscript. Country paper, folios 12+10+10=32 (each century is separately numbered), 25.5 cm. by 10.5 cm., 9–10 lines to a side. No date. DG2 has the standard sequence of centuries arranged thus: 2+3+1. The numbering of st. 2, st. 3, and st. 1 is in DG2, respectively, 1, 2, 3. Begins: st. 2) and st. 1) śrīgaṇeśāya namaḥ. st. 3) śrīgaṇeśāya namaḥ śrīgaṇeśaśāśviyo jayati. Ends: st. 2) iti karṇāmṛte prathamaśatakaṃ saṃpūrṇam.... idaṃ pustakaṃ raṅganāthapaṇḍitagāṇḍekareṇa likhitaṃ gaṇeśaśāstriṇāṃ dattam. śrī. st. 3) iti śrīlīlāśukena viracite karṇāmṛte dvitīyaśatakaṃ. st. 1) iti śrīlīlāśukena viracite karṇāmṛtastotre tṛtīyaṃ śatakaṃ samāptaṃ.

Collated from hand copy of manuscript by Tanjore copyist, N. Ranganatha Sastri, which was compared with manuscript by N. K. Rāmānujatātācārya.

DG3 Tanjore Maharaja Serfoji's Saraswathi Mahal Library No. B. 4954/ D. 20821 (st. 2 and st. 1) and No. B. 4949/D. 20801 (st. 3). Examination of these three mss. with Mr. P. V. Varadarajasarma determined them to be parts of the same manuscript. Country paper, folios 14+6+12=32 (Each century is separately numbered and each century is incomplete; see "Synoptic Charts of Verse Sequences." The final folios of st. 2, st. 1, and st. 3 are wanting; the initial folios [1–13] of st. 1 is wanting.), 23.5 cm. by 11.5 cm., 9–10 lines to a side. DG3 has the standard sequence of centuries arranged thus: 2+1+3. The numbering of st. 2, st. 1, and st. 3 is in DG3, respectively, 1, 2, 3. Begins st. 2) śrīgaṇeśāya namaḥ. śrīsarasvatyai namaḥ. śrīgurave namaḥ. mudgalo jayati. śubham astu. st. 1) folio missing. st. 3) śrīgaṇeśāya namaḥ. Ends: Final folios of all centuries are missing.

Collated from hand copy of manuscript by Tanjore copyist, N. Ranganatha Sastri, compared with manuscript by N. K. Rāmānujatātācārya.

DG4 Tanjore Maharaja Serfoji's Saraswathi Mahal Library No. B.4942/ D. 20795 (st. 2 and 3) and No. B. 4958 (a)/D. 24238 (st. 1). Examination of these three mss. with Mr. P. V. Varadarajasarma determined them to be parts of the same manuscript. Country paper, folios 62 (first 10 folios are missing), 25.5 cm. by 12 cm., 6–7 linės to a side. DG4 has a sequence of centuries as in DG1 and DG2. Begins: st. 2) folio is missing. st. 3) dvitīyaprārambhaḥ. st. 1) śrī. Ends: st. 2) iti śrīkarṇāmṛte prathamaṃ śatakaṃ. st. 3) iti līlāśukena viracite karṇāmṛte dvitīyaśatakaṃ samāptam. śrīr astu. st. 1) iti śrīlīlāśukena viracite karṇāmṛtastotre tṛtīyaṃ śatakaṃ samāptam. śrī śrīkṛṣṇo jayati. śrīrāmāya namah.

Collated from hand copy of manuscript by Tanjore copyist, N. Ranganatha Sastri, compared with manuscript by N. K. Rāmānujatātācārya.

DG5 Tanjore Maharaja Serfoji's Saraswathi Mahal Library No. B. 4945/D. 20814 (st. 2) and No. B. 4951/D. 20816 (st. 3). Examination of these mss. with Mr. P. V. Varadarajasarma determined them to be parts of the same manuscript. Country paper, folios 18 (Second century [st. 3] is incomplete and third century [st. 1] is missing; see "Synoptic Charts of Verse Sequences" section.), 19.5 cm. by 11 cm., 9–10 lines to a side. DG5 has the standard sequence of centuries arranged thus: 2+3. The numbering of st. 2 and st. 3 is in DG5, respectively, 1 and 2. Begins: st. 2) śrīgaṇeśāya namaḥ. śrīsarasvatyai namaḥ. śrīreṇukādevyai namaḥ. st. 3) śrīkṛṣṇakarṇāmṛte dvitīyaśatakam. Ends: st. 2) iti kṛṣṇakarṇāmṛte prathamaṃ śatakaṃ samāptam.

Collated from hand copy of manuscript by Tanjore copyist, N. Ranganatha Sastri, compared with manuscript by N. K. Rāmānujatātācārya.

DG6 Tanjore Maharaja Serfoji's Saraswathi Mahal Library No. B. 4958 (st. 2). Country paper, folios 9 (st. 1 and st. 3 are missing), 35.5 cm., 10 lines to a side. Begins: karṇāmṛślokadvitīyaśatakaprārambhaḥ. śrīgaṇeśāya namaḥ. Ends: rukmiṇīsatyabhāmāsametaśrīgopālakṛṣṇasvāmine namaḥ.

Collated from hand copy of manuscript by Tanjore copyist, N. Ranganatha Sastri, which was compared with manuscript by N. K. Rāmānujatātācārya.

D1 Asiatic Society of Bombay No. 1177. Paper, 11 folios, 14 in.

by 8½ in., 7 lines to a side. Begins: 1) śrīgaṇeśāya namaḥ. śrīnityānandāya namaḥ. 2) śrīkṛṣṇāya namaḥ. 3) śrīgopijanavallabhāya namaḥ. Ends: 1) iti śrīlīlāśukamunīviracitaṃ dvādaśastotraṃ ślokottaraśatasaṃkhyātaṃ śrīkṛṣṇāmṛtastotraratnaṃ prathamaśatakasaṃpūrṇaṃ śrīkṛṣṇārpaṇam astu. 2) iti śrīlīlāśukamuniviracitaṃ dvādaśaślokottaraśatasaṃkhyātaṃ karṇāmṛastotraratnadvitīyaśatakaṃ saṃpūrṇaṃ śrīrādhākṛṣṇārpaṇam astu. śrī. 3) iti śrīkṛṣṇalīlāśukamuniviracitaṃ śrīkṛṣṇāmṛtastotraratnākaraṃ tritiyaśatakaṃ saṃpūrṇaḥ.

Collated from a photographic copy. Mistakes in this mss. were so numerous that not all of them could be reported in the critical apparatus.

D11 Scindia Oriental Institute (Ujjain) No. 10010. Paper, number of folios and their size not known. Begins: 1) śrīkṛṣṇāya namaḥ. 2) śrīkṛṣṇāya namaḥ. 3) śrīgopālakṛṣṇāya namaḥ. Ends: 1) iti śrīkṛṣṇalīlāśukabilvamaṅgalaviracitakṛṣṇalīlāmṛtastotrasya prathamaśatakakarṇāmṛtaṃ samāptam. śrīkṛṣṇo jayati. idaṃ pustakaṃ gaṇapatirāvabhāuśarmaṇaḥ. 2) iti śrīlīlāśukaviracite śrīkṛṣṇakarṇāmṛte dvitīyaśatakaṃ samāptam astu. śrīkṛṣṇārpaṇam astu. 3) iti śrīkṛṣṇalīlāśukamuniviracite śrīkṛṣṇakarṇāmṛte tṛtīyaśatakaṃ saṃpūrṇaṃ. śrīkṛṣṇārpaṇam astu. śrīvikramanṛpatisaṃmata 1891 māghaśukla 10 ravivāsare liṣitaṃ bhāgavatopanāma karaghunāthasūnunā gaṇeśena svārthaṃ parārthaṃ ca. sainye gālhavaraṣisthānadurgasaṃnidhaṃ likhitam (1835 A.D.—Gwalior) Collated from hand copy of ms. by Vyākaraṇācārya Gopīkṛṣṇāśāstrī.

D12 Asiatic Society of Bengal No. 10416. Country paper, folios 47 (folios 1 and 2 missing), 8 in. by 5 in., 10 lines to a side. Begins: 1) missing. 2) begins with text: abhinava°. 3) begins with text: asti svastyayanaṃ. Ends: 1) iti śrīkarṇāmṛtastotrasaṃpūrṇam. śubhaṃ śrīgaṇeśāya namaḥ. śrīkṛṣṇabālacaritrāya namaḥ. 2) iti śrīlīlāśukaviracite kṛṣṇakarṇāmṛte tṛtīyaśatakaṃ saṃpūrṇam.... saṃvat 1826 varṣe śake 1681 āṣāḍaśudi (?) 3 ravivāsare. (1748 A.D.) Collated from photographic copy.

D14 Sanskrit University Sarasvati Bhavana (Varanasi) No. 18521. Folios 16 (folios 1 and 6 are wanting). No information on size and lines to a side. Contains century 2 only. Begins: 2) śrīgaṇeśāya namaḥ Ends: iti śrīkṛṣṇalīlāśukaviracite kṛṣṇakarṇāmṛtasto-

traratne dvitīyaśatakaṃ saṃpūrṇam. sarvātmā śrīrāmalikhitā tadbhaktanānā ātrī.
Collated from hand copy by unidentified copyist of the Sarasvati Bhavana.

D21 Deccan College (Poona) No. 6008. Stone printed on country paper with hand corrections in yellow pigment, folios 16+19+ +16=51 (Each century is numbered separately.), 8 in. by 3¾ in., 7–9 lines to a side. Begins: 1), 2), and 3) śrīgaṇeśāya namaḥ. Ends: 1) iti śrīlīlāśukaviracite dvādaśottaraśataśloke kṛṣṇakarṇāmṛtastotraratne prathamodhyāyaḥ samāptaḥ. śake 1707. 2) iti śrīkṛṣṇalīlāśukabilvamaṅgalaśrīcaraṇāryaviracitaṃ aṣṭottara ślokaṃ karṇāmṛtastotraratnaṃ nāma dvitīyodhyāyaḥ. 3) evaṃ śrīkṛṣṇadevasya karṇāmṛtaśatatrayam uccārayet sakṛd vipro vaiṣṇavaṃ padam āpnuyāt. iti śrīkṛṣṇalīlāśukabilvamaṅgalaśrīcaraṇāryaviracite kṛṣṇakarṇāmṛte tṛtīyodhyāyaḥ 3 śrīkṛṣṇārpaṇum astu. śake 1707 āṣāḍhaśuddha 9 idaṃ pustakaṃ hastākṣarajanārdanamāhādeva abhyaṃkareṇa likhitaṃ nārāyaṇadīkṣitakarvena saṃpāditam. (1764 A.D.)
Collated from manuscript.

D41 Bhārata Itihāsa Samshodhaka Maṇḍala (Poona) No. 65/1337. Country paper, folios 12, 22.5 cm. by 9.5 cm., 9 lines to a side. Contains the second century only. Begins: śrīgaṇeśāya namaḥ. Ends: iti śrīlīlāśukapaṇḍitaviracite karṇāmṛtaśatakaṃ saṃpūrṇam. śrīkṛṣṇārpaṇam astu. (Mr. G. Khare of the Bh. I. S. M. informs me that mss. D41, D43, and D44 were brought from Azre, a village in the mountains near Kohlapur.)
Collated from the manuscript.

D43 Bhārata Itihāsa Samshodhaka Maṇḍala (Poona) No. 65/568. Modern paper with water marks, 20 cm. by 10 cm., 10 lines to a side. Contains st. 2 only. Begins: śrīgaṇeśāya namaḥ. śrīgurucaraṇābhyāṃ namaḥ. Ends: iti śrīlīlāśukaviracite karṇāmṛte prathamaśatakaṃ saṃpūrṇam astu. See note in parenthesis at the end of D41. On the inside of the first folio, which is often left empty, 5 devotional verses have been inserted by a very different hand.
Collated from manuscript.

D44 Bhārata Itihāsa Samshodhaka Maṇḍala (Poona) No. 65/90. Modern paper with watermarks, 30 cm. by 13 cm., 10 lines to a side. Contains only st. 1 and st. 3. Begins: 1) and 3) begin with the texts (cintāmaṇir jayati and asti svastyayanaṃ, respectively). Ends: 1) iti śrīlīlāśukamuniviracitaṃ daśaślokottaraśatasaṃkhyākaṃ kṛṣṇakarṇāmṛtannāmastotraratnaṃ prathamo 'dhyāyaḥ. 3) iti śrīlīāśukaviracitāyāṃ śrīkṛṣṇakarṇāmṛte tṛtīyaḥ sargaḥ. See note in parenthesis at the end of D41.

Collated from manuscript.

D45 (Printed edition. Format and numbering as in mss. Bound with the *Adbhutarāmāyaṇa* which precedes the KK. Publishing information given on folio after KK.) Modern paper, folios 23 (numbered separately from the *Adbhutarñmāyaṇa*), 25.5 cm. by 15.5 cm., 12 lines to a side. Begins: 1) śrīgaṇeśāya namaḥ. 2) śrīmadrādhāvallabho jayaty atitarām. 3) begins with the text: asti svastyayanaṃ. Ends 1) iti śrīlīlāśukaviracite śrīkṛṣṇakarṇāmṛte prathamaśatakaṃ samāptam. 2) iti śrīlīlāśukaviracite śrīkṛṣṇakarṇāmṛte dvitīyaśatakaṃ samāptam. 3) iti śrīlīlāśukaviracite śrīkṛṣṇakarṇāmṛte tṛtīyaśatakaṃ samāptam. śrīmadrādhākṛṣṇacaraṇāravindārpaṇam astu. Publishing information: mumbaīmadhyeṃ. gaṇapata kṛṣṇājī yāṃce chāpakhānyāṃta kānhobā gaṇapatarāva yāṃce executor. rā. vi. nā. maṇḍalika va go. phaḍake yāṇīṃ chāpilem. āni. aṃtājī vāsudeva bāpaṭa., va nāro lakṣmaṇa dighe. yāṃṇīṃ prasiddha kelem. śake 1790 vibhavanāma saṃvatsare āṣāḍha śuddha 11 śī maṃgalavāra. (1868 A.D.)

Collated from printed edition.

D64 Bhandarkar Oriental Research Institute No. 147/1902–07. Country paper, folios 6+39=45 (st. 1 is separately paged; centuries 3 and 2, in this order, are numbered 1–23; folios 24–39 contain *subhāṣitas* from the *Śārṅgadharapaddhati*), 5⅕ in. by 8 in., 18–26 lines to a side. D64 has the standard sequence of centuries arranged thus: 1+3+2. The numbering, however, is as in the standard sequence. Begins: 1) śrīgajānano jayati. 3) and 2) as in 1). Ends: 1) iti śrīlīlāśukakṛte līlāmṛte prathamaśatakaṃ samāptam. 3) iti śrīlīlāśukaviracite karṇāmṛte tṛtīyaśatakaṃ samāptam. 2) iti śrīlīlāśukaviracite karṇāmṛte dvitīyaśatakaṃ samāptaṃ. kecit śārṅgadharīyāḥ ślokāḥ likhyate atha namaskṛtiḥ. calatkarṇanilodbhūta°.

Collated from hand copy by unidentified copyist.

D71 Tanjore Maharaja Serfoji's Saraswathi Mahal Library No. TS. 599/D. 20825. Country paper, folios 26, 9.4 cm. by 26.7 cm., 27 lines to a side. Begins: 1) śrīgaṇādhipatir jayati. 2) śrīgaṇeśāya namaḥ. 3) no introduction (Vs. 1 of the text is the verse which usually introduces the P. Sūri commentary to century 3. See add. vs. vyākhyāmudrā°.) Ends: 1) iti śrīlīlāśukakṛte śrīkṛṣṇakarṇāmṛtaprathamasargaḥ. 2) iti śrīlīlāśukaviracite kṛṣṇakarṇāmṛte dvitīyas sargaḥ. 3) iti śrīlīlāśukaviracite karṇāmṛte tṛtīyas sargaḥ. Collated from two hand copies, the first by N. K. Rāmānujatātācārya and the second by N. Ranganathasastri. The first hand copy was compared to the original ms. by N. S. Devanathachariar, the second by N. K. Rāmānujatātācārya.

E mss. with the commentary of Kṛṣṇa Paṇḍita (century 2 only). The identity of a Kṛṣṇa Paṇḍita of Benaras, who wrote *Kaṃsavadhanāṭaka* and *Pārijātāpaharaṇacampū*[15] in addition to many works on grammar and whose son was the guru of Bhaṭṭojīdīkṣita and Jagannāthapaṇḍita,[16] is discussed by Ranganathasvami. He does not mention this commentary. Aufrecht lists the E41[17] commentary as written by Śaṅkara and the E42[18] commentary by Kṛṣṇa Paṇḍita. Both E41 and E43 are without the colophon, which appears at the end of E42, stating that the commentary was written by Kṛṣṇa Paṇḍita at the request of Śaṅkara. The introductory verse no. 2 gives the impression that the commentary was written by Śaṅkara. See below for the colophon and the introductory verse.

Aufrecht[19] notes that the commentary by Śaṅkara has been published in the *Kāvyamālā* series. The *sūcīpatra* of the Nirnaya Sagara Press[20] was checked and this commentary was not listed in either of their *Kāvyamālā* series. A letter from the Nirnaya Sagara Press, in answer to an inquiry about this commentary, gave no further information.

E41 Bhandarkar Oriental Research Institute No. 465/1891–95.

15. S. P. V. Ranganathasvami, "On the Seshas of Benares," *The Indian Antiquary*, Vol. XLI (November, 1912), p. 249.

16. *Ibid.*, p. 251.

17. Theodor Aufrecht, *Catalogus Catalogorum*, Part III (Wiesbaden: Franz Steiner Verlag GMBH, 1962 reprint of 1896 edition), p. 26b.

18. Theodor Aufrecht, *Catalogus Catalogorum*, Part I (Wiesbaden: Franz Steiner Verlag GMBH, 1962 reprint of 1891 edition), p. 82a.

19. *Ibid.*, p. 119b.

20. *Nirṇayasāgarapres—prakāśita Saṃskṛta, Hindī, Gujarati Pustakoṃkā Sūcīpatra* (Bombay: Nirnaya Sagara Press, 1964), pp. 27–31, 40–44.

Country paper, folios 34 (last folios are missing), $8\frac{2}{5}$ in., 11–12 lines to a side. Commentary begins: śrīgaṇeśāya namaḥ.

jayati jagatinīlo viṭṭhalaḥ śliṣṭagātra
salilanidhiduhitrā vidyudullāsakāntyā /
kanakaharimaṇibhyāṃ saṃnidhitaṃ cāruniṣkaṃ
iti sakalamunīndrair dhyāyate yo hṛdābje //1//
śrīśaṅkareṇa nirupādhitayā vitīrṇāṃ
ṭīkāṃ prapāṃ sulalitāṃ saraloktidhīrām /
samyak praviśya vibudhāḥ haribhaktipānthāḥ
karṇāmṛtāni sarasāni muhur āpibantu //2//

Ends: last folios are missing.
Collected during a search for manuscripts in the Bombay Presidency, an area which in the period 1891–95 was designated both Gujerat and Maharashtra.
Collated from hand copy by unidentified copyist.

xE42 Bhandarkar Oriental Research Institute No. 257/Viśrāma (i). Modern paper with water marks, 64 folios, $12\frac{1}{4}$ in. by $4\frac{1}{5}$ in., 7 lines to a side. Commentary begins: śrīgaṇeśāya namaḥ. śrīkṛṣṇāya namaḥ. śubham astu. Two introductory verses, as in E41, follow. Commentary ends: iti śaṅkarapreritakṛṣṇapaṇḍitakṛtāyāṃ karṇāmṛtavyākhyāyāṃ daśottaraṃ dvitīyaṃ śatakaṃ saṃpūrṇam astu. śrīkṛṣṇārpaṇam astu.
Manuscript was part of the Visram Bagh Palace collection.
Partial collation from the manuscript.

xE43 Bhārata Itihāsa Samshodhaka Maṇḍala (Poona) No. 29/1799. Country paper, folios (First folio is much damaged. Folios 29, 30, 33, 34, 35, 36, 39, 43, and 44 are missing. Total number of folios not noted.), 21.2 cm. by 10 cm., lines to a side not noted. Begins: First folio is too damaged to decipher. Ends: Colophon to the text: iti śrīkarṇāmṛte dvitīyaśatam. No colophon after commentary. On outer side of final folio the following is noted in the same hand as the rest of the ms.: karṇāmṛta samāptaḥ idaṃ pustakaṃ. śamārādhyasya pustakam. Mr. G. Khare informs me that this ms. was obtained in Sholapur.
Partial collation from the manuscript.

F Only one incomplete copy (F41) of this commentary, written in Marāṭhī, was found. S. G. Tulpule, Professor of Marāṭhī at the

University of Poona, informed me that Vāmana, the writer of this commentary on the KK, is not the famous Vāmanapaṇḍita, who wrote the *Yathārthadīpikā* on the *Bhñgavata Purāṇa*. The guru of Vāmanapaṇḍita is Saccidānanda; the guru of Vāmana is Yogānandanātha. Also in the introduction (*adhyāya* 1) Vāmana apologizes for his ignorance of grammatical and rhetorical rules. Professor Tulpule said that Vāmana Paṇḍita would never have been so humble. Ashok Kelkar of Deccan College and G. Khare of Bh.I.S.M. express the same general opinion as above. All three Marāṭhī scholars say that the Marāṭhī of this commentary is not genuinely archaic.

F41 Deccan College Library (Poona) No. 18599 (Printed edition, format as in mss. Unbound. Incomplete, no information about publication date, etc.) Modern paper, folios 35 (first century only which is divided into five parts which are called *adhyāyas*—see "Synoptic Charts of Verse Sequences" section), 8 in. by 5 in., 12 lines to a side. No date. Begins: *Adhyāya* 1) śrīgajānano vijayate. śrīkṛṣṇakarṇāmṛtapānapātrīṭīke saha. Ends: *Adhyāya* 1) iti śrīkṛṣṇakarṇāmṛta. mahārāṣṭrabhāṣāvatārite. śrīpānapātrapadāñkite. saṃpūryate prathamādhyāya. iti śrīmad yogānandanāthapadānucaravāmanakṛtau bilvamañgalaviracita°. *śataka* 1) (after the end of the fifth *adhyāya*) iti śrīlīlāśukaviracite śrīkṛṣṇakarṇāmṛte prathamaśatakaṃ samāptam. (after end of commentary) iti bilvamañgalāparanāmalīlāśukaviracitaśrīkṛṣṇakarṇāmṛtavyākhyāyāṃ vāmanaviracitāyāṃ pānapātrasamākhyāyāṃ prathamaśatakaṃ saṃpūrṇam.

Collated from printed edition.

G For further information about G1 and G2 mss., see DG.

G1 Adyar Library (Madras) No. VB 524. Palm leaf, 34.5 cm. by 3.7 cm., 8–9 lines to a side. The Adyar Library pandits say this manuscript is possibly 400 years old. G1 has the standard sequence of centuries arranged thus: 2+3+1. It is bound with one other text, the KK with the P. Sūri commentary. Begins: 2) śrīkṛṣṇāya namaḥ. 3) and 1) no introductory phrases. Ends: 2) iti śrīkarṇāmṛte prathamaśatakaṃ saṃpūrṇam. hariḥ oṃ. iti līlāśukaviracite karṇāmṛte prathamaśatakaṃ saṃpūrṇam. śrīrāmāya namaḥ. 3) iti śrīkarṇāmṛte dvitīyaśatakaṃ saṃpūrṇam. 1) iti karṇāmṛte tṛtīyaśatakaṃ saṃpūrṇam. śrīkṛṣṇāya namaḥ.

Collated from a hand copy by an Adyar Library copyist. See end of C52 description.

G2 Tanjore Maharaja Serfoji's Saraswati Mahal Library No. B. 10174/D. 20794. Palm leaf, folios 15, 45.5 cm. by 3.8 cm., 8 lines to a side. Varadarajasarma informs me that this ms. predates the Nāyak kings. See notes on DG mss. G2 has the standard sequence of centuries arranged thus: 2+3+1. Begins: 2) beginning is damaged. 3) and 1) no introductory phrases. Ends: 2) hariḥ oṃ. karṇāmṛtaṃ prathamaṃ śatakaṃ samāptaṃ. hariḥ oṃ. śubham astu. om. 3) dviśataṃ samāptam. hariḥ oṃ. śubham astu. 1) ms. badly damaged.

Collated from hand copy by Ranganathasastri. Partial comparison of the hand copy with the original ms. was done by myself.

G11 Adyar Library No. 69276 (Old No. XXII. K. 45). Palm leaf (Śrītāla), folios 19, 10½ in. by 2½ in., 16 lines to a side. Begins: 1) hariḥ oṃ. śubham astu. 2) and 3) no introductory phrases. Ends: 1) iti śrīmat līlāśukamuniviracite śrīkṛṣṇakarṇāmṛtastotraratne prathamaśatakaṃ saṃpūrṇam. 2) omitted. 3) iti tṛtīyaśatakaṃ samāptam. rukmiṇīsatyabhāmāsametaśrīgopālakṛṣṇāya namaḥ. yintagranthaṃ nāgarukovigrāmattil gargagotrattil āpastamba-sūtrattil yajuḥ śākhādhyāyiyāna veṅkaṭarāmāvadhāniyal putran veṅkaṭeśvaran grantham. svahastalikhitam. śrīgurubhyo namaḥ. (Nagercoil)

Collated from hand copy by an Adyar Library copyist. See end of C52 description.

H See C mss.

H21 Adyar Library No. 70093 (Old No. XXIII. 0.2). Palm leaf, folios 109, 17 in. by 2 in., 8 lines to a side.

Collated from a hand copy by Adyar Library copyist. See the end of C52.

H31 Adyar Library No. 75730 (Old No. XXXIV. I. 27). Palm leaf, folios 93, 17 in. by 1½ in., 8 lines to a side. Entire colophon to to commentary on century 1: iti śrīvallabhasūriviracitāyāṃ karṇāmṛtavyākhyāyāṃ prathamo 'dhyāyaḥ. Last folio of hand copy is missing but the Adyar Library catalogue gives the information which occurs at the end of century 3:

The MS. was copied by Ramasavāmi on the 3rd day of the

Tamil month Āñi (Jyeṣṭha) of the encyclical year Kālayukti.[21]

Collated from a hand copy by an Adyar Library copyist. See end of C52.

K1 Mysore Oriental Research Institute No. C541. Palm leaf, folios 28, size (?), lines to a side (?). Begins: 1) śrīkṛṣṇāyau ramātmane parabrahmaṇe namaḥ. śrīrāmacandrāya namaḥ. śrīgaṇādhipataye namaḥ. 2) śrīrāmacandrāya paramātmane parabrahmañe namaḥ. śrīkṛṣṇāya namaḥ. dvitīyaśatakārambham. 3) tṛtīyaśatakaprārambham. śrīkṛṣṇāya namo namaḥ. śrīrāmacandrāya paramātmane parabrahmaṇe namaḥ. śrīrāma rāma. Ends: 1) iti śrīlīlāśukakaviviracite kṛṣṇakarṇāmṛtastotre prathamaśatakaṃ saṃpūrṇam. śrīkṛṣṇārpaṇam astu. śrī. śrī 2) iti śrīlīlāśukācāryaviracite kṛṣṇakarṇāmṛte dvitīyas sargaḥ, śrīrāmacandrārpaṇam astu. śrī. śrī. śrī. śrīrāmacandrāya namaḥ. 3) iti śrīlīlāśukakaviviracite kṛṣṇakarṇāmṛtastotre tṛtīyaśatakaṃ saṃpūrṇam. śrīkṛṣṇāya namo namaḥ.... śrīrāmacandrārpaṇam astu. st. 1.108 follows and concludes K1.

Collated from handcopy by unidentified copyist.

M1 Government Sanskrit College (Tripunithura) No. 1029/429. Palm leaf, folios 65, 7 in. by 2 in., 9 lines to a side. Begins: 1) hariḥ śrīgaṇapataye namaḥ avighnam astu. 2) and 3) no introductory phrases. Ends: 1) iti līlāśukaviracite karṇāmṛte prathamo 'dhyāyaḥ. prathamaśatakaṃ samāptaṃ. śrīkṛṣṇāya namaḥ. 2) iti līlāśuka viracite karṇāmṛte dvitīyo 'dhyāyaḥ. iti dvitīyaśatakaṃ samāptam. 3) śrīgurubhyo namaḥ. śubham astu. iti śrīkṛṣṇakarṇāmṛte tṛtīyaśatakaṃ samāptam.

Collated from hand copy of unidentified Sanskrit College copyist.

M6 University of Kerala Manuscripts Library No. 10729B. Palm leaf, folios 44, 12.8 cm. by 3.3 cm., 6 lines to a side. Manuscript contains century 2 only. Begins: 2) hariḥ gaṇapataye namaḥ. avighnam astu. Ends: 2) iti śrīlīlāśukena viracitaṃ śrīkṛṣṇakarṇāmṛtaṃ dvitīyaśatakaṃ saṃpūrṇam. śrīkṛṣṇāya namaḥ. śubham astu.

Collated from hand copy by K. Parameswaran Pillai. The hand

21. H. G. Narahari (under supervision of C. Kunhan Raja), *Descriptive Catalogue of Sanskrit Manuscripts in the Adyar Library*, Vol. V (Madras: The Adyar Library, 1951), p. 153.

copy was compared to the original manuscript by N. P. Nampiathiry.

M21 University of Kerala Manuscripts Library No. 6196A. Palm leaf, folios 96, 13 cm. by 3.4 cm., 8 lines to a side. Begins: 1) hariḥ śrīgaṇapataye namaḥ. avighnam astu. 2) and 3) no introductory phrases. Ends: 1) iti śrīkarṇāmṛte prathamo 'dhyāyaḥ. 2) iti dvitīyo 'dhyāyaḥ. 3) iti śrīkarṇāmṛte tṛtīyo 'dhyāyaḥ.

Collated from hand copy by K. Parameswaran Pillai. The hand copy was compared to the original manuscript by N. P. Nampiathiry.

xM24 (Printed edition.) *Kṛṣṇakarṇāmṛtam* (title from cover), Cochin: St Thomas Press, 1877 A.D., pp. 54, 10 cm. by 15 cm. (Publication information from edition deposited in the India Office: IO Book San. No. 1032. First pages of edition deposited in Government Sanskrit College, Tripunithura (Book No. 999), are missing. Begins: 1) hariḥ. gaṇapataye namaḥ. avighnam astu. 2) and 3) no introductory phrases. Ends: 1) iti prathamo 'dhyāyaḥ. 2) iti karṇāmṛtastotre dvitīyaśatakaṃ samāptam. 3) iti śrīmat karṇāmṛtaṃ tṛtīyaśatakaṃ samāptam.

Collated from hand copy by unidentified copyist of Government Sanskrit College Book 999.

Pages missing in Sanskrit College Book 999 were partially collated from IO Book San. No. 1032 by myself.

N1 Madras Government Oriental Library No. D. 9890. Palm leaf, folios 62, 10$\frac{3}{4}$ in. by 1$\frac{1}{8}$ in., 6 lines to a side. N1 has the standard sequence of centuries arranged thus: 2+3+1. The numbering of st. 2, st. 3, and st. 1 is in N1, respectively, 1, 2, 3. Begins: st. 2) śrīmatcaraṇāravindātmāṃ namaḥ. st. 3) śrīdakṣiṇāmūrtisabāya namaḥ. st. 1) śrībālakṛṣṇārpaṇam astu. śubham astu. Ends: st. 2) iti śrīlīlāśukena viracite śrīkṛṣṇakarṇāmṛtastotre prathamaṃ śatakam. st. 3) iti śrīlīlāśukena viracite śrīkṛṣṇakarṇāmṛtastotre dvitīyam śatakam. st. 1) (ms. damaged)... (cai) tramāsapañcabhyāṃ kṛṣṇapakṣake. vāre sthire 'likhatkarṇāmṛtaṃ śaṅkaranāmabhāk.

Collated from manuscript.

N21 Madras Government Oriental Library No. R. 4816. Palm leaf, (srītāla), folios 58, 8$\frac{1}{4}$ in. by 2 in., 12 lines to a side. N21 has the standard sequence of centuries arranged thus: 2+3+1. The numbering of st. 2, st. 3, and st. 1 is in N21, respectively, 1, 2, 3. Begins: st. 2) beginning is damaged. st. 3) no introductory phrase. st. 1) hariḥ oṃ. Ends: st. 2) and st. 3) no colophons or phrases. st. 1) iti śrīlīlāśukaviracitaṃ kṛṣṇakarṇāmṛtaṃ saṃpūrṇam. śubham astu. hariḥ oṃ. śrīgopālakṛṣṇāya namaḥ. śrīgopījanāhladakāya namaḥ śrīkṛṣṇāya mañgalaṃ. oṃ. śrī. śrī. śrī. śrī. śrī. Medical prescription in Kannarese follows.

Collated from manuscript.

xN22 Madras Government Oriental Manuscripts Library No. R. 12735. Palm leaf, folios 51, 22 cm. by 3.5 cm., 5–7 lines to a side. 1) śubham astu. 2) śubham astu. oṃ.\ 3) śubham astu. Ends: 1) no colophon or phrases. 2) śrīkṛṣṇāya. śrī. iti śrīlīāśukakaviviracite kṛṣṇakarṇāmṛtastotre dvitīyasatakaṃ saṃpūrṇam. 3) śrī. iti śrīlīlāśukakaviviracite kṛṣṇakarṇāmṛtastotre tṛtīyaśatakaṃ saṃpūrṇam. śrī. śrīkṛṣṇārpaṇam astu.

Presented to M.G.O.L. by manager of Ramaṇāśrama at Tiruvanamalai.

Partially collated from manuscript.

P see C mss.

P71 [Printed edition. Printed in Devanāgarī. Although this edition was printed in Devanāgarī script. it has been listed with the mss. in Telugu script. This has been done for the following reasons: 1) The foreword states:

> We are greatly indebted to Pandit S. Subrahmanya Sastrigal of Tanjore who... not only sent us the copy of both the text and this hitherto unpublished commentary... (p. iv)

Pandit Sastrigal's daughter, S. Sharada, now resident at the Adyar quarters of the Theosophical Society, informed me that her late father was associated with both the Tanjore Maharaja Serfoji's Saraswathi Mahal Library and the Adyar Library (1941–43). 2) P71 shares no similar tradition with any of the P. Sūri KK mss. deposited in the Saraswathi Mahal Library or the Adyar Library. P71 does share an almost identical tradition with the Saraswathi Mahal ms., collated in this edition under the sign, T71, which see.] *Sri Krishna Karnāmritam of Lila Suka with the commentary Suvarna Chasaka of Papayallaya Suri.* Sri Vani Vilas Sanskrit Series, No. 19, Srirangam: Sri Vani Vilas Press, 1926

A.D., pp. 207. Variants to colophon to commentary (See C mss.): All three colophons read °paśupati° for °vasumati°. Colophon 3 reads tṛtīya āśvāsaḥ (for tṛtīyo 'dhyāyaḥ). Text begins: 1) st. 3. 85 is given here as an introductory verse. 2) and 3) no introductory phrases. Text ends: 1) iti śrīlīlāśukaviracite śrīkṛṣṇakarṇāmṛte prathama āśvāsaḥ. 2) and 3) are the same with dvitīya and tṛtīya, respectively, for prathama.

Collated from xerocopy of IO Book San. B. 873 (i).

P72 Osmania University Library No. 414/233. Palm leaf. Ms. contains only centuries 1 and 2.

Collated from hand copy of manuscript.

Q exists in one single manuscript deposited in the Āndhra Sāhitya Pariṣad Granthālaya. C. Pāpayya Śāstrī very kindly supplied galley proofs in Devanāgarī of the edition which he was preparing from this single manuscript. The book has now been published. I have a copy of the title page and the foreword by V. Raghavan, who kindly supplied me with the same. The information given in Q71 derives from the galley proofs, the copy of the title page, V. Raghavan's foreword, the rough draft of Pāpayya Śāstrī's introduction, and conversation with both of these obliging persons.

xQ71 *Sri Krishnakarnamritam, Balagopala Keraliya Yatiswarakrita Bodhamrita Vartika*, ed. Ch. Papayya Sastri, Kakinada: Andhra Sahitya Parishat, 1965. Commentary ends: 1) iti śrībālagopālendrakeralīyayatīśvarakṛte karṇāmṛtavārtike bodhāmṛte prathamaṃ saṃpūrṇam. 2) iti śrīkṛṣṇakarṇāmṛtādhyātmavārtike dvitīyaśatakaṃ saṃpūrṇam. 3) iti śrīmatparamahaṃsaparivrājakācāryaśrīśaṅkarabhagavatpādakṛtaśārīrakamīmāṃsābhāṣyaparyāvartananiratena cidābhāsacitsvarūpanaranārāyaṇabhaktena śrīrāghavendrasarasvatīśiṣyena keralīyena bālagopālayatīndreṇa kṛtam idaṃ śrīkṛṣṇakarṇāmṛtādhyātmavārtikaṃ bodhāmṛtaṃ saṃpūrṇam. It is to be noted that Papayya Sastri informed me that 1) the manuscript is written on palm leaf in the Telugu script, 2) the ms. is without the text, 3) for publication he has taken an Āndhra edition with the commentary of Velagapūḍi Veṅganāmātya as a source for the text, 4) the number of the ms. is 3501–3502 of the Pariṣat collection. V. Raghavan has pointed out to me that the commentary, a metrical gloss takes the KK to be an allegory expressing Śaṅkara's *advaita* philosophy. The equivalents are given in the second and third verses which introduce the commentary to century 1: Kṛṣṇa is *ātman* and *īśa*, the *gopīs* are *cidvṛttis*, the *gopas* are *ahaṃkāras* etc., Kṛṣṇa's flute is the Vedānta, Kṛṣṇa's peacock feather crest is *jñāna*, Kṛṣṇa's beloved is *brahmavidyā*, and the cows are the *indriyas*. For collation the metrical and allegorical gloss was very difficult to interpret. Collation was partial and, it is to be hoped, accurate. Any accuracy is do to the guidance of my pandit, A.S. Acharya; any inaccuracy is, of course, mine.

R mss. have a commentary by Āvañca Rāmacandra Budhendra. This commentator has also written a commentary on Bhartṛhari's *Śatakatraya*. Kosambi[22] in his edition of this work discusses his place and date. When I visited Kakinada in connection with the Q71 publication, Papayya Sastri very kindly went with me to the village of Kāñjalūru, the home of Āvañca Rāmacandra Budhendra. Kāñjalūru is a few miles from Kakinada on the Ātreya River. A fifth generation descendant of A. Rāmacandra, A. Surya Narayana, related that the family had in times far past come from Southern Maharashtra, to Masulipatam, and finally to Kāñjalūru. The women in the family wear their saris in the Maharashtrian style, which is said not to be usual of the district.

It would seem that A. Rāmacandra based his commentary on that of Pāpayallaya Sūri.

R21 Madras Government Oriental Library No. R. 3040. Paper, folios 56, $10\frac{7}{8}$ in. by $9\frac{5}{8}$ in., 20 lines to a side. Ms includes *śataka* 1 only. Colophon to commentary: iti śrīmadraghunandanacaraṇāravindamakarandāsvādanakandalitasārasārasvatena. nityanirmalācāraparipūtena akhaṇḍatapaḥpracaṇḍamuniprakāṇḍamaṇḍaleśvaraśāṇḍilyamunigotrāvataṃsakoṇḍopaṇḍitatanūjena-sakalakavirājasamājakalpabhūjena vividhavidyāpravīṇāntarvāṇiśiromaṇinā gaṅgāmbikāśuktimuktāmaṇinā śrīmadāvañcakulābdhiparipūrṇacandreṇa śrīrāmacandrabudhendreṇa viracitāyāṃ śrīkṛṣṇakarṇāmṛtavyākhyāyāṃ bhagavadbhaktirasāyanasamākhyāyāṃ prathamo 'dhyāyaḥ. śrīrāmāya namaḥ.

Transcribed in 1919–1929 from a ms. of the Raja's Library, Bobbili.

---

22. *The Epigrams attributed to Bhartrhari*, ed. D. D. Kosambi, Singhi Jain Series No. 23 (Bombay: Bharatiya Vidya Bhavan, 1948 A.D.) pp. 36–37 of the Introduction.

Collated from a hand copy by V. Rangaswami. This hand copy compared with original ms. by E. S. Srinivasaraghavan.

R22 Madras Government Oriental Library No. R. 2615. Palm leaf, folios 92, 17⅛ in. by 1⅜ in., 5 lines to a side. Ms. includes century 2 only. Presented to the M.G.O.L. by M. R. Ry. Sātulūru Kṛṣṇamācāryulugāru, Tanuku, Kistna district.
Collated from hand copy by E. S. Srinivasaraghavan. This hand copy compared to the original by P. G. Sitharaman.

R23 Madras Government Oriental Library No. R. 2183. (This ms. is written in the Grantha script. Since it was the only available ms. of the *Bhagavadbhaktirasāyana* commentary, century 3, it was used and grouped here with the *Bhagavadbhaktirasāyana* mss. written in the Telugu script.) Palm leaf, folios 96, (Manuscript includes the second and third centuries only. For this edition only the third century was collated. It is written on the folios numbered from 122 to 218. No text is given with the commentary.)
Collated from a hand copy of century 3 by V. Subbiah Sastri. This hand copy compared with the original by R. Subbaratnam. Since R23 did not include a text, the critical apparatus does not distinguish citations as being from the commentary.

S mss. have commentary by Brahmābhaṭṭa. K. Rama Pisharoti informed S.K. De[23] that this commentary was a Malayalam commentary, evidently meaning a Sanskrit commentary written by a Malayalī. M. Krishnamachariar[24] considers the commentator to be an Āndhra, because he belonged to the Lohitagotra. The commentary on the last verse of the second century and the entire commentary on the third century were not found. It would seem that Brahmabhaṭṭa, like A. Rāmacandra, based his commentary on that of Pāpayallaya Sūri.

S21 Madras Government Oriental Manuscripts Library No. R. 1039. Palm leaf, folios 70, 14½ in. by ½ (?) in., 8 lines to a side. Manuscript includes all of century 1 and most of century 2 (see "Synoptic Charts of Verse Sequences"). Colophon to commentary on century 1:

23. De, *op. cit.*, p. xii, n. 1.

24. Krishnamachariar, *History of Classical Sanskrit Literature* (Madras: Tirumalai-Tirupati Devasthanams Press, 1937), p. 337, n. 6.

śrīmallohitagotradivyamaṇinā vyākhyātam ādyaṃ muhuḥ
nyagrodhāṃghripamūlavāsicaraṇadvaṃdvānatiṃ kurvatā /
brahmābhaṭṭabudhottamena śatakaṃ karṇāmṛtānāṃ mahat
ślokair dvādaśabhiḥ tadupari yutaśrīkṛṣṇasaṃprītaye //
iti śrīmatpālaṅkabrahmābhaṭṭakṛte karṇāmṛtavyākhyāne suvarṇāpātrīsamākhyāne dvādaśottaramādyaṃ śatakaṃ saṃpūrṇam. śrīgopālārpaṇam astu.

Collated from hand copy by V. Rangaswami. The hand copy was compared with the original manuscript by E. S. Srinivasaraghavan.

xT5 Tanjore Maharaja Serfoji's Saraswathi Mahal Library. No. B. 10176/D. 20796. Palm leaf, 15 folios, 34.7 cm. by 3.6 cm., 6–7 lines to a side. There are some indications (auspicious signs and a saying after st. 2.82) that the copyist considered st. 2.82 to be the final verse. T5 has the variant lines c and d in st. 2.82 which are found in D41, D43, N1, N21, R22 (as a variant reading), Y31, Y32. Begins: 1) śubham astu. avighnam astu. oṃ karṇāmṛtāni. 2) no introductory phrases. Ends: 1) iti śrīkṛṣṇalīlāśukamuniviracitaṃ dvādaśottaraśatasaṃkhyaśrīkṛṣṇakarṇāmṛtaṃ prathamaśatastotraṃ saṃpūrñam. śrīgopālakṛṣṇāya namaḥ. 2) śrīr astu. Collated from hand copy by N. Ranganathasastri. This hand copy compared with original manuscript by N. S. Devanathachariar. Original manuscript examined by myself together with P. Varadarajasarma.

T21 Madras Government Oriental Library No. 9891. Palm leaf, folios 80, $16\frac{1}{2}$ by $1\frac{1}{4}$ in., 6 lines to a side. Ends: 1) śrīkṛṣṇārpaṇam astu. prathamaśatakaṃ saṃpūrṇam. 2) iti līlāśukakṛte kṛṣṇakarṇāmṛte. dvitīyaśatakaṃ saṃpūrṇam. 3) breaks off before the end.

Collated from hand copy by C. N. Subramania Sastry. Hand copy compared with original manuscript by G. Subramanyam.

T71 Tanjore Maharaja Serfoji's Saraswathi Mahal Library No. B. 10170/D. 20792. Palm leaf, folios 35, 30.5 cm. by 3.1 cm., 6 lines to a side. T71 has the standard sequence of centuries arranged thus: 3+1+2. The numbering of st. 3, st. 1, and st. 2 is in T71, respectively, 1, 2, 3. Begins: st. 3) beginning is missing. st. 1) and st. 2) no introductory phrases. Ends: st. 3) śrīkṛṣṇārpaṇam astu. st. 1) śrīkṛṣṇārpaṇam astu. śrīrāmārpaṇam astu. śrī. st. 2) ends (or breaks off?) after st. 2.109. No signs or phrases.

Collated from hand copies by 1) N. K. Rāmānujatātācārya and 2) Ranganatha Sastri. Both of these hand copies compared to the original manuscript by N. S. Devanathachariar.

It is to be noted of this manuscript that it shares a tradition very close to that of P71. It has many evidences that it was copied from a ms. with the P. Sūri commentary, for example: 1) Introductory to st. 1.23 in the P71 ms. is the phrase: evaṃ manasi kṛṣṇe pratīyamāne cākṣuṣatāṃ prārthayate. T71 has before st. 1. 23: evaṃ manasi kṛṣṇe pratīyamāne ca. There are three other like instances. 2) After st. 3. 102 in P71 the commentary includes 7 verses from the *Kramadīpikā* V. 14–19.[25] T71 has the same several verses. There are two other like instances.

U mss. have a Telugu metrical gloss by Velagapūḍi Veṅganāmātya. No U manuscript ascribes this gloss to V. Veṅganāmātya, but it is the same metrical gloss which appears in the V printed editions and which is there attributed to Velagapūḍi Veṅganāmātya. No information is to be had about this commentator except that which is supplied by his name which means, Veṅgana, the government minister, from the village of Velaga. Velaga means *kapittha* in Sanskrit, wood-apple (*Feronia elephantum*) in English. Also of interest is the fact that *Aegle* (Skt. *bilva* [*Aegle marmelos*]) and *Feronia* are closely related genera of one species each.[26]

U1 Adyar Library No. 747147 (Old Shelf No. XXX. J. 37). Palm leaf, folios 43, 13½ in. by 1½ in., 9 lines to a side. Begins: 1) no introductory phrases. 2) śubham astu. avighnam astu. 3) avighnam astu. śubham astu. Ends: 1) ānandanāma saṃ. mārgaśirasu. 10 ādigavillirāmayyagāripratinivunna kramānancivaṭapu veṅkaṭāyaḍu karṇāmṛtālu trikāṇḍalu vrāśenū. śrīrāmārpaṇam astu. 2) ms. evidently ends with st. 2. 86. The Telugu metrical gloss to st. 2. 86 ends the folio. 3) again, ms. ends with st. 3. 101 and metrical gloss and no colophon or phrases.

Collated from hand copy of text by V. Narayanaswami Sastri.

UV The Telugu metrical gloss by V. Veṅganāmātya was impossible for me to collate. Rāmakṛṣṇa Śāstrī and Dr. (Mrs.) P. Saraswathi Mohan accomplished a partial collation for me. As was the

25. See "Description of Manuscripts" section Z41(S), pp. 40–41.

26. T. Burrow and M. B. Emeneau, *A Dravidian Etymological Dictionary* (Oxford: Clarendon Press, 1961), p. 381, (4535).

case with Q71, it was possible to determine very few variant readings. V2, which see, was the edition used to accomplish this collation.

V editions are Telugu printed editions of the KK with a word for word equivalence between words in the Sanskrit text and Telugu plus the Telugu metrical gloss by V. Veṅganāmātya.

V1 is printed in the Devanāgarī script with an English translation. It is placed with the V printed editions because V1 is a Devanāgarī transliteration of preceding V editions. Omitted in V1 is the word for word equivalence between words in the Sanskrit text and Telugu plus the Telugu metrical gloss by V. Veṅganāmātya. *Sri Krishna Karnamrita of Lilasuka*, ed. and trans. M. K. Acharya, Madras: V. Ramaswamy Sastrulu and Sons, 1958. pp. 176. Colophons: 1) śrīkṛṣṇakarṇāmṛtam. prathamāśvāsaḥ samāptaḥ. 2) śrīkṛṣṇakarṇāmṛtam. dvitīyāśvāsaḥ samāptaḥ. 3) tṛtīyāśvāsaḥ. śrīkṛṣṇakarṇāmṛtam samāptam.
Collated from printed edition.

xV2 *śrīlīlāśukayogendraviracitaśrīkṛṣṇakarṇāmṛtamu velagapūḍiveṅganāmātyaviracitāndhrapadyasahitamu*, Madras: V. Veṅkaṭakṛṣṇamu Seṭṭi and Sons, 1910. pp. 300. (Rāmakṛṣṇaśāstrī informs me that the title page indicates that T. Tēvapperumāḷḷayya did the word for word equivalence.) Colophons: 1) śrīkṛṣṇakarṇāmṛtamu prathamāśvāsamu. (After the colophon st. 1.111 and 112 are given with word for word equivalence but without the metrical gloss.) 2) śrīkṛṣṇakarṇāmṛtamu dvitīyāśvāsamu. 3) no colophon noted.
Collated from xerocopy of IO Book San. 21 D 16.

xV22 *śrīlīlāśukayogīndraviracitaṃbagu śrīkṛṣṇakarṇāmṛtamu.... velagapūḍiveṅganāmātyaracitāndhrapadyamūlatodaṃjerci ṭīkātātparyasahitaṃbagu*..., Madras: Vibudhamanohāriṇī Press, 1877. pp. 217. Colophons: 1) kṛṣṇakarṇāmṛtamu prathamāśvāsasaṃpūrṇamu. 2) kṛṣṇakarṇāmṛtamu dvitīyāśvāsasaṃpūrṇamu. 3) kṛṣṇakarṇāmṛtamu sarvambunu tṛtīyāśvāsasamāptamu.
Collated from IO Book San. 605.

V25 title as in V22, Madras: Vaṅkāyala Kṛṣṇasvāmi Seṭṭi, 1895. pp.
x 212. Colophons: 1) śrīkṛṣṇakarṇāmṛtamu prathamāśvāsamu. 2) śrīkṛṣṇakarṇāmṛtamu dvitīyāśvāsamu. 3) śrīkṛṣṇakarṇāmṛtamu sarvambunu tṛtīyāśvāsamu.
Collated from own copy.

W mss. with the *Bhaktavallabhā* commentary by Vanamālibhaṭṭa. Vanamālibhaṭṭa is the same commentator who wrote the *Bhaktavallabhā* commentary in the Y33 ms., which see.
The introduction found in W1 and Y33 mss. indicate that the commentator considered the two texts quite the same.

xW1 Sanskrit University Sarasvati Bhavana, Varanasi, No. 18265. Devanāgarī script, paper, number of folios and their size not known. No date. Begins: śrīrādhākṛṣṇau jayataḥ.
śrīmadgirivarādhīśaṃ
vṛndāraṇyapurandaraṃ /
kṛṣṇacandraprapadyehaṃ
bhaktānugrahakātaraṃ //1
nandavraje pāmaratā-
nānyatrāmaratāsamā /
yatra prātardivāsāyaṃ
bhaktaṃ vyaktaṃ paraṃ maha //2
kṛṣṇakarṇāmṛtasyaiṣā
ṭīkā śrībhaktavallabhā /
mūnir jareṇa bhaṭṭena
kriyate vanamālinā //3
Ends: iti śrīkarṇāmṛtastotraṃ saṃpūrṇam.
Collated from hand copy by unidentified copyist.

X[27] mss. According to Dasgupta,[28] Jayagopāla Bhaṭṭa, the son of Cintāmaṇi Dīkṣita, and the disciple of Kalyāṇarāja (grandson of Vallabha born in 1571 A.D.), wrote a commentary on the KK of Bilvamañgala. Besides this commentary he wrote a commentary on the *Sevāphala* and *Bhaktivardhinī* of Vallabha and on the *Taittirīya Upaniṣad.* The mss. listed below are not necessarily

27. So far there is little information on the Vallabhaite version. Of some side interest is the *Madhurāṣṭaka* of Vallabha. All eight vss. closely resemble KK st. 1.92 which is also found in the Y mss. Below is the first verse of the *aṣṭaka.*
adharaṃ madhuraṃ vadanaṃ madhuraṃ
nayanaṃ madhuraṃ hasitaṃ madhuraṃ /
hṛdayaṃ madhuraṃ gamanaṃ madhuraṃ
madhurādhipaterakhilaṃ madhuram //
Quoted from: *Stotraratnāvalī*, ed. anon. (Gorakhpur: Gītā Press, 1934), pp. 233.

28. Surendranath Dasgupta, *A History of Indian Philosophy*, Vol. IV (Cambridge: Cambridge University Press, 1949), 375.

attributed to Jayagopāle Bhaṭṭa. The anonymous X1, which is very fragmentary, seems to be a Vallabhaite commentary. X2 written by a Gopāla Bhaṭṭa, as is B1, seems to be a Bengali Vaishnava commentary according to De.[29]

X1 Madras Government Oriental Library No. D. 9899. Grantha script, paper, folios 22, 7½ in. by 4 in., 14 lines to a side. No date. Ms. contains only the first nine verses of st. 1 with an unidentified commentary. Begins: 1)
praṇamya viṭṭalādhīśaṃ puruṣottamamīśvaram /
līlāśukoktitātparyaṃ vivṛṇomi yathāmati //
The commentary to st. 1.1 contains reference to the following: 1) *Gopālatāpinyupaniṣad* 2) *Viṣṇupurāṇa* 3) puṣṭimārga 4) puṣṭipuruṣottama 5) *Brahmasaṃhitā* 6) *Gītagovinda*. Items 3) and 4), especially, suggest a Vallabhaite commentator.

xX2 Bhandarkar Oriental Research Institute No. 178/1879–80. Devanāgarī script, paper, folios 145, 5⅝ in. by 10 in., 24 lines to a side. Ends:
iti śrīlīlāśukabilvamaṅgalaviracitaṃ śrīkṛṣṇakarṇāmṛtaṃ stotraṃ
śrīgovindapadāravindabhajanatpaṃktākhilārthātryahaḥ
śrīmadbhāgavatārthaviśramabhavadbhadanyuṇā viśrutaḥ /
śrīrādhāramaṇāṃhrisaktamanasā gopālabhaṭṭena tat
putreṇa śravaṇāmṛtasya racitā ṭīkāstu satprītaye //1
vss. 2, 3, and 4 are omitted.
iti śrībhagavajjanacaraṇarājīvarajakvaṇikaśaraṇagopālabhaṭṭaviracitā śravanāhlādinī karṇāmṛtaṭīkā samāptāḥ.
Collated from ms.
According to vs. 1 of the ending the father of the Gopālabhaṭṭa, who wrote X2, was Śravaṇāmṛta. The father of Jayagopālabhaṭṭa was Cintāmaṇi Dīkṣita.

---

29. De, *op. cit.*, p. lxxxvii

30. Recently received was a copy of a Bīr Library ms. which represents a 7th sub-version of the Y versions. It includes the usual verses from KK st. 1 and so can be grouped with Y subversions 0–20. Following is a description of this ms. Vīrapustakālaya (Kathmandu) No. 79. Devanāgarī script, Madhyadeśīya paper, folios 65, 7½ in . by 3⅛ in., 6 lines to a side. Begins: oṃ śrīgaṇeśāya namaḥ. Ends: iti śrībilvamaṅgalaparamahaṃsasanyāsinā viractaṃ gopālasvarūpāṅkakāvyaṃ samāptaṃ śubhamastu. śrīrastu. śrīśāke 1661 vaiśākha śudi 2 śanivāsare likhitam idaṃ pustakaṃ śrīvīrabhadraśarmmaṇā. (1739 A.D.)

Collated from the hand copy of the manuscript.

Y mss. are North Indian anthologies of devotional verses attributed to Bilvamaṅgala. These anthologies include a varying number of verses (100–537 vss.) in varying arrangements. There are six[30] versions of this anthology if one considers it a single anthology with very varying versions. No manuscript includes less than 57 verses from the 328 standard verses of the KK; no manuscript includes more than 157 such verses. For distribution of the KK verses in Y mss., see "Synoptic Charts of Verse Sequences." All Y mss. are written in North Indian scripts: Devanāgarī, Bengali, Assamese, Śāradā, Newārī. If a Y ms. or a Y version is written in Devanāgarī, no note will be made in the description of the ms. or version; if a Y ms. or a Y version is written in another of the above 5 scripts, note of this script will be made in the description of the ms. or version.

Perhaps three things can be said of the non-KK verses:

1) Scattered throughout the verses, a little less frequently than is the case in the KK, are those verses which demonstrate the initial assonance characteristic of Dravidian poetry, for example, Y31 vs. 252 (Y2 vs. 183, Y13 vs. 84, Y21 vs. 180):

durvārapraṇayāvabodharasikair dhīrātmanāṃ mānasair
arvācīnarasaprasaṅgavimukhair ā kaṇṭham āsvāditam /
kurvāṇaṃ kim api priyaṃ nayanayoḥ kaumārakodgranthi me
sarvākāramanoharaṃ tata itas tejaḥ samujjṛmbhate //

2) There are many verses which echo the verses in the KK, for example, Y31 vs. 178 (Y2 vs. 86, Y13 vs. 228, Y21 vs. 144, Y51 vs. 74, Y61 vs. 105):

bhramadbhramarakuntalaṃ racitalolalīlālakaṃ
kalakvaṇitakiṅkiṇīlalitamekhalābandhanam /
kapolaphalakasphuratkanakakuṇḍalaṃ tanmaho
mama sphuratu mānase madanakeliśayyotthitam //

This verse has the same last line as st. 1.20. For other examples see, in the "Additional Verses" section in the Appendix, add. he kṛṣṇa viṣṇo, add. ālokya mātur.

3) As with the KK verses there are many which occur elsewhere. Two examples are the following: Y31 vs. 55 (Y2 vs. 68, Y13 vs. 209, Y21 vs. 128, Y51 vs. 76, Y61 vs. 107):

vande mukundam aravindadalāyatākṣaṃ
kundenduśaṅkhadaśanaṃ śiśugopaveṣam /

indrādidevagaṇavanditapādapadmaṃ
vṛndāvanālayam amuṃ vasudevabālam //

The above verse occurs as number 1 in the Nirnaya Sagara Press edition of the *Mukundamālā*.[31] It occurs not at all in the edition by K. Rama Pisharoti.[32] Y11 vs. 270 (Y21 vs. 326):

maheśvare vā jagatāṃ maheśvare
janārdane vā jagadantarātmani /
na bhedahetupratipattir asti me
tathāpi bhaktis taruṇenduśekhare //

The above verse occurs as number 300 in Kosambi's edition of Bhartṛhari's *Śatakatrayam*.[33]

Y(1–9), also known as YO, version of the Y anthology is represented by only three known mss. These mss. contain 11–12 verses from KK st. 1, 25–44 verses from KK st. 2, and 78–84 verses from KK st. 3. Like the other versions, the manuscripts contain many verses from st. 3, fewer from st. 2, and very few, if any, from st. 1. Version Y(1–9) arranges the KK verses, which it includes, closer to the arrangement of KK than does any other version, i.e., for the most part, it keeps the verses of st. 3 grouped together. See the "Synoptic Charts of Verse Sequences." Perhaps this closer resemblance to the KK sequence reflects a closer connection of YO with the KK tradition. YO is the version with the oldest dated ms. (Y1). If YO is the oldest version of the Y mss., it would be reasonable to expect the closer connection and resemblance.

Y1 Adyar Library No. PM 949 (Old No. XL. A. 116). Country paper, folios 10 (12–19+25–26), 9.8 in. by 3.8 in., 7 lines to a side. Begins: first 11 folios missing. Ends: st. 3.91 (Y1 vs. 212). iti śrībilvamaṅgalaviracitā mokṣadāyinī śrīviṣṇoḥ stutiḥ saṃpūrṇā. śrī. śrī. śubhaṃ bhavatu. viṣṇor bālakrīḍāsamāptaḥ. saṃvat 1475 varṣe caitra śudi 10 daśamyāṃ tithau mahaṃgovindasunasāraṃgasya vācanarthaṃ paṇḍitadevarājena stotramidaṃ vilikhad. śrīrastu. śubhaṃ bhavatu. lekhakapāṭhakayoḥ. śrī. kalyāṇonnatirastu. (1418 A.D.)

Collated from hand copy by unidentified copyist. Hand copy compared with the original by myself.

31. See "Description of the Manuscripts" section Z42(N).
32. See "Description of the Manuscripts" section Z42(A).
33. Kosambi, *op. cit.*, p. 118 of the text.

Y2 Bhandarkar Oriental Research Institute No. 292/1884–86. Modern paper with water marks for folios 1–9, 23–24 and country paper for folios 11–22 and 25, folios 25, $9\frac{7}{8}$ in. by $3\frac{7}{8}$ in., 9 lines to a side. Begins: śrīkṛṣṇāya namaḥ. Ends after 285 vss.: iti śrībilvamaṅgalaviracitaṃ śrīkṛṣṇabālacaritraṃ samāptam. saṃ. 1874 vaiśākhavadi 1 budhe likhitam idaṃ yodhapure purohita gopālalālena nijavicāragocarāyeti śrībālakṛṣṇaḥ prasanno bobhūtāt. śrī. (1818 A.D. at Jodhpur)
Collated from photographs.

xY3 British Museum No. Or. 2131a. Country paper, folios 3, size (?), 22 lines to a side. Begins: oṃ namaḥ śrīnārāyaṇāya. Ends after 207 vss.: iti paramahaṃsaparivrājakaśrībilvamaṅgalaviracita. śrīviṣṇoḥ stutiḥ samāptā. likhitapṛthvīdhareṇa.
Collated from a xerocopy.

Y(11–19), also known as Y10, version is represented by five known manuscripts. Four of these were used for this edition. These mss. contain 11–12 verses from KK st. 1, 35–46 verses from KK st. 2, and 83–84 verses from KK st. 3. In version Y10 verses of KK st. 3 were, for the most part, grouped together from st. 3.88 (Y2 vs. 89) to st. 3.69 (Y2 vs. 181). In version Y10 this group of st. 3 verses have been, as it were, made into a deck of verses which has been cut and shuffled and cut again with 31 verses inserted so that two groups of st. 3 verses are made: st. 3.88 (Y14 vs. 51) to st. 3.39 (Y14 vs. 101) and st. 3.8 (Y14 vs. 132) to st. 3.69 (Y14 vs. 189). This shuffling and formation of two groups can be partially seen in the "Synoptic Charts of Verse Sequences." This tradition is, most probably, almost as old as the YO version (see Y11). It is larger than the YO version and includes more verses from the KK and more verses which are not found in the KK.

xY11 Boston Museum of Fine Arts. An illustrated ms. reported upon by W. Norman Brown in *Eastern Art*.[34] Country paper, folios 6–9, 12, 14–19, 21, 23–24, 27–28, 30–33, 35, 38–42, 44–48, 50–54, 56, 59, size (?), 7 lines to a side where unillustrated, 10 lines to a side where illustrated. No date, but see end of this description. Ms. divided into two sections. Begins: 1) initial folios are missing.

34. W. Norman Brown, "Early Vaishnava Minature Paintings from Western India," *Eastern Art*, Vol. II (1930), pp. 167–206.

2) The second section, which begins immediately after the colophon to the first section, is but a continuation of the first part. Both the first verse in the second section and the colophon to the first section are numbered 109. There are no auspicious signs or salutations. Ends: 1) iti śrīparamahaṃsapravrājakaśrīpādabilvamañgalaviracitā śrībālagopālastutiḥ. iti māghapurāṇe bhagavadvākyam. 109. 2) final folios are missing.

W. Norman Brown concludes his estimate of the date of the manuscript:

> Some time about 1450 seems a fair guess, while a date as much as fifty years later, or even one fifty years earlier, although possible, would be open to question unless confirmed by unimpeachable evidence.[35]

The date 1450 or fifty years later would fit in with the evidence given in these descriptions. A date 50 years earlier, 1400 A.D., would indicate that the Y10 version was earlier than the Y0 version.

Collated from the plates (no. CI–CXX) which appeared with the article in *Eastern Art*.[36] The 40 ms. sides which these plates presented were completely collated. Photographs of 20 more ms. sides were obtained from the Boston Museum of Fine Arts. These have been partially collated.

Y12 Vishveshvaranand Vedic Research Institute (Hoshiarpur) No. 5080. Country paper, folios 23. The ms. is old, very fragmentary, and in complete disorder. Begins 1) oṃ namaḥ. śrigaṇeśasāradābhyāṃ namaḥ. 2) exactly as in Y11. Ends: 1) exactly as in Y11. 2) final folios missing. Readings etc. almost identical with Y11.

Collated from hand copy by unidentified copyist. The folios of the ms. were in complete disorder. They were copied in this disorder and their numbers not indicated. The numbers of the verses were, however, indicated.

Y13 Bodleian Library (Oxford) No. Chandra Shum Shere d 843. Country paper treated with sulfur, folios 39 (folios 1, 4–8, 38

35. *Ibid.*, p. 173.
36. *Ibid.*, pp. 168–203.

missing), 23.7 cm. by 6.6 cm., 5–6 lines to a side. Begins: 1) folio missing. 2) auspicious sign separates sections one and two. atha mahāpurāṇe bhagavadvākyaṃ. Y11 vs. 109 numbered 109. Ends: 1) iti śrīpāramahaṃsaparivrājakācāryaśrīpādavilvamaṅgalaviracitāṃ śrīgopālabālastutiḥ. Auspicious sign noted in description of the beginning of part two. 2) After 259 vss.: iti (destroyed) ...mahaṃsaparivrājakācāryaśrīpādaśrīvilvamaṅgalasamāpta. śubhaṃ bhava. (destroyed)... pāvakayoḥ. śubhaṃ (destroyed)... śrīviśveśvarabhavā (destroyed)... etam (destroyed)... śrīnārāy (destroyed)...

Collated from photographs. Photographs compared to original manuscript by myself.

Y14 Anup Sanskrit Library (Bikaner) No. 3107. Country paper, folios 10. Y14 has no colophon with in the ms. as in Y11, Y12, Y13. Begins: śrīgaṇeśāya namaḥ. Ends after 360 vss.: iti śrībilvamaṅgalaviracitaṃ śrīkṛṣṇastotraṃ.

Collated from hand copy by S. N. Savadi of Bh.O.R.I.

oY15 Bhandarkar Oriental Research Institute No. 429/1887–91. Country paper, folios 29. Ends: 1) iti paramahaṃsaparivrājakavilvamaṅgalaracitā vālagopālastutiḥ. 2) iti śrīparamahaṃsaparivrājakācāryapaṇḍitavopadevakṛte vilvamaṅgale kṛṣṇāvatāravaṇanaṃ samāptam. saṃvat saptāṣṭabhūpair mitaśaradimudā kāttike māsipakṣe kṛṣṇetyithyāṃ vyaliṣad adhikaṃ pārvatī (?) enaṃ. vārebhaumesvaparapaṭhanāyāniśaṃ śrīmukundārp (?) dhyānyāgāraṃ paramamamalavilvato maṅgalākhyaṃ likhitaṃ govardhanena. 1. (1625 A.D.)

Above information taken from ms.

Y(21–29), also known as Y20, version is represented by one ms. It is arranged somewhat in the manner of the two early versions, Y0 and Y10. It contains 537 verses as compared with the 360 verses of Y14 and the 383 vss. of Y33. Accordingly, it contains more verses from such sources as the *Bhāgavatapurāṇa*. It contains more echo verses, see, e.g., add. ālokya mātur. From the KK it contains 12 verses from st. 1, 51 verses from st. 2, and 86 verses from st. 3.

Y21 Baroda Oriental Institute No. 4221. Country paper, folios 35, 24 cm. by 10.5 cm., 11 lines/side. Begins: śrīgaṇeśāya namaḥ. atha bilvamaṅgalastotraṃ likhyate. Ends: vs. 537 (KK st. 3.41) iti śrībilvamaṅgalakṛtaśrikṛṣṇabālakrīḍāsaṃpūrṇo 'yaṃ granthaḥ.

śrīr astu. śubham astu. kalyāṇam astu. saṃvat 1682 varṣe kārtika-vadi 12 budhe likhitaṃ.... (1625 A.D.)
Collated from hand copy of unidentified copyist. Hand copy compared with original ms. by myself. Hand copy is not at all a true copy.

Y(31–39), also known as Y30, version is the Y version with the widest distribution. It is represented in 8 manuscripts. Six of these are written in the Devanāgarī script, one in the Śāradā script, and one in Nevārī script. Three of the Devanāgarī mss. have been used for this edition. The other five are also briefly described below since they all have some feature which contributes to defining this version of the Y mss. or to defining the whole Y tradition. This version contains no verses from KK st. 1, 53–56 vss. from KK st. 2, and 83–85 vss. from KK st. 3. It should be noted here that Y mss. 1–29 (Y0, Y10, Y20) include vss. from KK st. 1 and Y mss. 31–69 (Y30, Y50, Y60) do not. Perhaps the reason Y mss. 31–39 do not include vss. from the KK st. 1 is that these mss. represent a version which was put together after Caitanya's version (see A and B mss.) of the KK had become popular in North India sometime in the middle of the 16th century. The only Y30 ms. which. has a date is Y34. The date is 1630 A.D. The Devanāgarī script in the Y30 Devanāgarī mss.' which I have examined (Y32, Y33, Y34, Y37, Y38), do not approach the old styles used in Y1 and Y11. What has further encouraged this notion that the Y30 version was set up by some editor acquainted with Caitanya's version of the KK are two facts. 1) Vanamālibhaṭṭa, who has written a commentary to this version (see Y33), has written a commentary to Caitanya's version (see W1). Both commentaries have exactly the same introduction and the same first verse (KK st. 1.1). Also, they have the same name, *Bhaktavallabhā*, and they assign the same name, *Kṛṣṇakarṇāmṛta*, to both texts. One difficulty in assessing this material is the fact that the commentary to Y33 breaks off after Y33 vs. 200 and the colophon at the end of the ms. after Y33 vs. 383 names the text as the *Sumañgalastotra*. This contradicts the information in the introduction. 2) Unlike Y0 Y10 and Y20 mss., Y30 mss. group verses into sections which are given descriptive titles. An editor, who would rearrange such a ms. as a Y0 Y10 or Y20 ms. into

such a ms. as a Y30 ms., would delete the vss. which belonged to the Caitanyaite KK, the version of the KK which a Norths Indian editor would know in the 16 or 17th century. The section into which the Y30 version is divided are as follows: (If in the individual mss. there are significant variants to the following, they will be noted in descriptions of these mss. [Y31, Y32, Y33].)
iti kaumāram. occurs after vss. 1–69.
iti paugaṇḍam. occurs after vss. 70–115.
iti vayaḥsandhi. occurs after vss. 116–148.
iti kaiśorakeliḥ. occurs after vss. 149–233.
iti tāryuṇyam. occurs after 234–240.
iti kaviḥ prasādaḥ. samāptaṃ gokulacaritāmṛtam. occurs after vss. 241–271.
iti mathurācaritam. occurs after vss. 272–286.
iti dvārakācaritam. occurs after vss. 287–306.
iti nārāyaṇastutiḥ. occurs after vss. 307–331.
iti śivastutiḥ. occurs after vss. 332–337.
iti hariharastutiḥ. occurs after vs. 338.
iti kūrmaḥ. occurs after vs. 339.
iti nṛsiṃhastutiḥ, occurs after vss. 340–342.
iti vāmanaḥ. occurs after vs. 343.
iti rāmastutiḥ. occurs after vss. 344–355.
No further colophons occur (from 356–383), but vss. 356–371 are st. 2.56 refrain verses (see add. he kṛṣṇa viṣṇo) and vss. 372–380 are refrain verses (line d in vss. 372–380 is ko na mucyeta bandhanāt). Vss. 372–380 are *subhāṣitas*, not devotional Kṛṣṇa verses.

Y31 Scindia Oriental Institute (Ujjain) No. 6523. Paper, folios 23. Begins: śrīgaṇeśāya namaḥ. vs. 1 is st. 3.54. Ends: iti śrīmatparamahaṃsaparivrājakācāryaśrībilvamaṅgalaviracitaṃ vāsudevastotraṃ bilvamaṅgalaṃ nāma saṃpūrṇam. śubham astu. Y2 vs. 1 is appropriate as an introductory vs., but it appears here as the final verse (no. 381). This is the most obvious example of this sort of front to back shuffling of verses in the Y anthologies. Collated from hand copy by Gopīkṛṣṇaśāstrī.

Y32 Bhandarkar Oriental Research Institute No. 532/1891–95. Paper, folios 27 (final folio missing). Begins: śrīgokulanāyakāya namaḥ. The first verse which is numbered 1 is Y2 vs. 1; the second verse which is also numbered 1 is st. 3.54. Ends: breaks off at vs. 368:

yaṃ brahmā varuṇendra rudra maruta stunvanti divyai stavair
vedaiḥ sāṅgapadakramopaniṣadair gāyanti yaṃ sāmagāḥ /
dhyānāvasthitatadgatena manasā paśyanti yaṃ yogino
yasyāntaṃ na viduḥ surāsuragaṇāḥ devāya tasmai namaḥ //
This verse occurs in no other KK or Y ms. It does, as vs. 1, occur in Baroda Oriental Institute ms. No. 10342 (Bengali script, folios 4, 18 *ślokas*, 4 lines to a side). This Bengali ms. is otherwise indecipherable. Dr. Sen of Deccan College was unable to make out the verses because I was unable to provide him with verses to match the highly illegible writing. In Y32 before this verse occurs is the notation, anyatrāpi. Collated from hand copy by unidentified copyist.

xY33 India Office No. 564. Paper, folios 64, size is not known, 8–12 lines to a side in the part of the ms. with a commentary, 14 lines to a side in the part of the ms. without a commentary. Begins: śrīgāṇeśāya namaḥ.
śrīmadgirivarādhīśaṃ
vṛndāraṇyapurandaraṃ /
kṛṣṇacandraprapadehaṃ
bhaktānugrahakātaraṃ //1
nandavrajepāmaratā
nānyatrāmaratāsamā /
yatraprātardivāsāyaṃ
naktaṃ vyaktaṃ paraṃ mahaḥ //2
kṛṣṇakarṇāmṛtasyaiṣā
ṭīkāśrībhaktavatsallabhā /
bhūnirjjareṇa bhaṭṭena
kriyate vanamālinā // 3
vs. 1 of the text is KK st. 1.1 which seems to be in place of st. 3.54 which is not found in Y33. Ends: The commentary breaks off after Y33 vs. 200 (KK st. 3.79). The verses without commentary are entered from vs. 201 (st. 2.35) to v.s 383 after which is the colophon: iti śrīvilvamaṅgalakṛtaṃ sumaṅgalākhyaṃ stotraṃ samāptaṃ.
Collated from photographs.

oY34 University of Kerala Manuscripts Library No. 1655. Country paper, folios 21, size 32.5 cm. by 14.8 cm., 11 lines to a side. Begins: śrīgaṇeśāya namaḥ. vs. 1 is st. 3.54. Ends: vs 376 is Y33

vs. 380, vs. 377 is Y2 vs. 1. iti śrīmatparahaṃsaparivrājakācaryāśrīvilvamañgalaviracitaṃ śrīvāsudevastotravilvamañgalanāmadheyaṃ saṃpūrṇam. saṃ. 1687 māghe 13 jagannāthenālekhi. (1630 A.D.)
Collated from manuscript.

oY35 Bodleian Library No. Sansk. d. 72. Śāradā script, birch bark, folios 5 (23–28), 19 cm. by 26 cm., 15 lines to a side. Begins: first folios are missing. Ends: ms. is unumbered but final verse is Y33 vs. 33. The colophon occurs after this verse and the colophon lists the number of verses which are included within the various sections: kaumāra (69 vss.), paugaṇḍa (45 vss.), vayaḥsandhi (25vss.), kaiśorakeli (23 vss.), tāruṇya (20 vss.), kaviprasāda (does not occur), gokulacarita (91 vss.), mathurācarita (15 vss.—or 5?), dvārakācarita (20 vss.), nārāyaṇa (23 vss.), total 331 vss.—or 321?
Collated from photographs.

oY36 Vīrapustakālaya (Kathmandu) No. 1427. Nevārī script, country paper, folios 26 (incomplete), $9\frac{5}{8}$ in. by $2\frac{7}{8}$ in., 7 lines to a side. Begins: śrīkṛṣṇāya namaḥ. KK st. 3.54 is vs. 1. Ends: breaks off after vs. 281 (Y33 vs. 280, KK st. 2. 34).
Collated from hand copy.

oY37 Bhandarkar Oriental Research Institute No. 642/1883–84. Paper, folios 2, size not known, 19 lines to a side. Begins: beginning is damaged but vs 1 is Y33 vs. 311. After this beginning Y37 continues as the other Y30 mss.: iti nārāyaṇastutiḥ occurs after vss. 1–21 (Y33 vss. 311–331). Ends: final vs. 68 is Y33 vs. 383. śrīkeśavakleśanāśāya. madhureśāya vai namaḥ. iti śrīparamahaṃsaparivrājakācāryaśrībilvamañgalaviracitaṃ bilvamañgalanāmastotraśrīkṛṣṇaparasaṃpūrṇam agamat. śrikṛṣṇārpaṇam astu. lekhakapāṭhakayoḥ śamastu. dīnanāthena likhitam idaṃ svārthaṃ parāthaṃ ca. Obtained during search for mss. in Maharashtra.[37]
Collated from hand copy by unidentified copyist.

oY38 Bhandarkar Oriental Research Institute No. 628/1883–84. Modern paper with water marks, folios 12, 12 in. by $4\frac{1}{6}$ in., 18–19 lines to a side. Begins: śrīgaṇeśāya namaḥ. KK st. 1.1 fol-

37. R. G. Bhandarkar, *Report on the Search for Sanskrit Manuscripts in the Bombay Presidency during the year 1883–84* (Bombay: Government Central Press, 1887), p. 23.

lows. The first 79 vss. of this ms. are from st. 1 of the KK. Y38 vs. 79 is KK st. 1.81. Y38 includes no verses numbered 80–93. Y38 vs. 94 is Y33 vs. 94. After this verse the Y30 version continues through Y38 vs. 301 which is Y33 vs. 311 and Y37 vs. 1 which see. At this point the KK recommences with KK st. 3.23 which is numbered Y38 vs. 23. The rest of st. 3 is entered except for st. 3.28 and 106. Ends: The final two verses of Y38 are st. 1.111 and 112. They are numbered in the Y38 ms. as 107 and 108. Thus, in this ms. the Y30 version has been sandwiched within the KK. Obtained during a search for mss. in Maratha country.[38]
Collated from the manuscript.

Y(51–59), also known as Y50, version is the Bengalī version. It is found in 2 printed editions and 3 mss. All 5 are in the Bengali script. The 2 printed editions have been used for this edition. This version is the shortest version with only some 100 verses. It contains no verses from KK st. 1, 17–18 verses from KK st. 2, and 24–25 vss. from KK st. 3.

Y51 Reprinted in the Devanāgarī script in S. K. De's edition of the KK.[39] He gives the following information about the edition from which he took Y51.[40] *Bilvamaṅgalakośakāvya*, Bengalī prose trans. Yogīndranātha Bāgci, Berhampur-Murshidabad: Rāmadeva Miśra, śaka 1829 (1907 A.D.). Begins: Y51 vs. 1 is Y3 vs. 1. Ends: Y51 vs. 101 is KK st. 2.4.
Collated from reprint.

Y52 Variants to Y51 edition printed along with Y51 edition by S. K. De.[41] He gives the following information about the edition from which he took Y52.[42] *Bilvamaṅgalagosvāmikṛtaṃ Śrīkṛṣṇastotram*, Bengali verse trans. Jayagopāla Tarkālaṃkāra, Calcutta, B.E. 1224 (1817 A.D.). Begins: Y52 vs. 1 is Y3 vs. 1. Ends: Y52 vs. 109 is KK st. 2.4.
Collated from reprint.

oY53 Bangiya Sahitya Parisad No. 119/546. Substance not known, folios and size not known. Begins: oṃ namaḥ śrīkṛṣṇāya. Y53

38. *Ibid.*
39. De, *op. cit.*, pp. 330–342.
40. *Ibid.*, p. 330.
41. *Ibid.*, pp. 330–342.
42. *Ibid.*, p. 330

vs. 1 is Y3 vs. 1. Ends after 106 vss.: iti śrīvilvamañgalaviracitaṃ samāptam. After this colophon are three verses: 1) add. prabhātasaṃcāra° 2) is Y31 vs. 365. 3) is
yugmavānekālasomaśakavarṣasaṃpra-
namyanandasūnupādapadaladvaṃdvaham /
śrīlapūrvarāmaśarmatasya vilvamañgala-
prāṇakṛṣṇadattadāsapustikeyaṃ lekhakaḥ //
The copyist has translated the first line as yugma = two, vāne = five, kāla = 3, soma = 1 or śaka 1352 (or 1430 A.D.).
Collated from hand copy by unidentified copyist. After verse 60 the copy is almost illegible. A. S. Acharya of Deccan College helped decipher the final portion of the ms. This portion is evidently corrupt.

oY54 British Museum No. Add. 147696 b. Folios 43–56 of 78 folios bound in European book form, 17 lines to a side. Begins: śrikṛṣṇāya namaḥ. Y54 vs. 1 is Y3 vs. 1. Ends: Y54 vs. 119 is KK st. 2.7. iti villamañgalākhyaṃ kāvyaṃ samāptaṃ. Among the many extra verses included at the end of this ms. is KK st. 1.73 as Y54 vs. 109. KK st. 1.73 occurs in no other Y ms. No other KK st. 1 vs. occurs in a Y30 Y50 or Y60 ms. Ms. formerly in possession of Sir Wm. Jones.
Collated from xerocopy of ms.

oY55 India Office No. Tagore 176. Country paper, folios 9, 16⅜ in. by 2¾ in., 4 lines to a side. Begins: śrīgurave namaḥ. Y55 vs. 1 is Y3 vs. 1 Ends: Y55 vs. 104 is KK st. 3.96. iti śrībilvamañgalakṛtaṃ śrīkṛṣṇastotraṃ samāptam. ...
Collated from ms.

Y(61–69), also known as Y60, version is the Assamese version critically edited by Maheswar Neog.[43] Descriptions of the four mss. used by M. Neog are given below. Two other mss. of this version are not described here. M. Neog[44] has found the following verses used in the plays of the Assamese dramatist, Mādhavadeva (1492–1596 A.D.):[45]

43. *Bilvamañgala's Kṛṣṇa-Stotra*, ed. Maheswar Neog (Gauhati: Lawyer's Book Stall, 1962), 51 pp.

44. *Ibid.*, pp. 3–4.

45. Birinchi Kumar Barua, *History of Assamese Literature* (New Delhi: Sahitya Akademi, 1964), pp. 45, 52.

Y61 vs. 31 = KK st. 2.74
3
27 = KK st. 2.23
23
43 = KK st. 2.28
28
26 = KK st. 2.82
20 = KK st. 2.15

The Assamese version seems to be a combination of the first verses of the Y30 version plus 100 or so verses of the Bengali version: The first 32 verses of Y61 are equated with the Y31 vss.

Y61	Y31
1–4	1–4
5–9	6–10
10–12	13–15
13–20	17–24
21–23	31–33
24	35
25	226
26	39
27	34
28	42
29	38
30	37
31	41
32	11

Y50, the Bengali version, begins with Y61 vs. 32. The last 100 verses of the Assamese version Y60, have more or less the same sequence as the 100 verses of the Bengali version, Y50. The Assamese version contains no verses from KK st. 1, 22 verses from KK st. 2, and 44-45 verses from KK st. 3.

Y61 Department of Historical and Antiquarian Studies No. 445. Designated as (A) by Neog.[46] Paper, Assamese script, folios 12, 34 cm. by 10 cm., 7 lines to a side.[47] Begins: KK st. 3.54. Ends after 135 vss.

46. Neog, *op. cit.*, p. 1.

47. P. C. Choudhury, *A Catalogue of Sanskrit Manuscripts at the D.H.A.S.* (Gauhati: Dept. of Historical and Antiquarian Studies in Assam, 1961), p. 88.

Y62 Barpeṭā ms. No number. Designated as (B) by Neog[48] and noted to be undated. Begins and ends as in Y61.
Collated from critical edition by Neog.

Y63 Gauhati ms. No number. Designated as (C) by Neog[49] and noted to be dated 1725 śaka (1803 A.D.). Begins as in Y61. Ends after 134 vss.
Collated from critical edition by Neog.

Y64 Gauhati University ms. No number. Designated as (D) by Neog[50] and noted to be dated 1759 śaka (1837 A.D.). Begins and ends as in Y63.
Collated from critical edition by Neog.

YY(1–49), also YYo, designates the Dravidian manuscripts, very often quite singular, which include verses from the KK. These mss. may be *stotras*, anthologies, or *kāvyas*. They may or may not be attributed to Līlāsuka Bilvamañgala or to Līlāśuka or to Bilvamañgala. The few mss. used for collation are described below. Many other YYo mss. are mentioned, without the designation YYo, in the "Introduction" and in the "Notes on the Additional Verses" section.

YY1 University of Kerala Manuscripts Library No. C. 2501 B. Malayalam script, palm leaf, folios 40, 14 in. by 1½ in., 6 lines to a side. Dr. K. Raghavan Pillai, Curator of the library estimates the ms. to be 200 to 250 years old. Part 1 begins: gaṇapataye namaḥ. Part 1 ends after 177 vss.: śrīkṛṣṇāya namaḥ. hariḥ. Part 2 ends after 132 vss.:... śukamuniviracitāyāṃ bhāvanāmukuraḥ samāptaḥ. hariḥ. kṛṣṇa. Former owner was Nārāyaṇan Citran Nampūtiri, Cempaśśeri, Kuṭamālūr, Mānnānam, Koṭṭayam.
Collated from hand copy of Miss. P. Subhadradevi. Hand copy compared with original by N. P. Nampiathiri. YY1 seems to be the ms. from which Ullur Paramesvara S. Aiyar took the verses for the *Bālakṛṣṇastutih* (27 vss.)[51] and *Bhavanāmukuram* (27 vss.)[52]

48. Neog, *op. cit.*, p. 1.
49. *Ibid.*
50. *Ibid.*
51. Ullur S. Paramesvara Aiyar, "Saint Vilvamañgala," *Proceedings and Transactions of the Ninth All-India Oriental Conference, Trivandrum, 1937* (Poona, 1938), pp. 484–487.
52. *Ibid.* pp. 488–91.

which are published in the *Proceedings and Transactions of the All India Oriental Conference, 1937* after his article on "Saint Vilvamañgala."[53] He gives no source for these 54 vss. The blank spaces Aiyar leaves in the published verses match very well the damaged portions in the ms. As is always the case, however, the damaged portions have become more extensive.

About the verses which are found in the YY1 anthology: There are no KK vss. from st. 1, 21 from st. 2, and 3 from st. 3. The occurrence of these vss. can be noted in the "Synoptic Chart of Standard Verse Sequences." Otherwise YY1 includes many miscellaneous *subhāṣitas*, *Bhāgavata Purāṇa* vss., plus about 10 vss. which are found in one or more of the Y mss. It includes add. barhāpīḍaṃ (YY1 2.42) and add. udayagiri° (YY1 1.172). Like the Y collections it includes many extraneous elements.

YY2 University of Kerala Mss. Library (Trivandrum Palace Library Collection No. 1360). Malayalam script, palm leaf, folios 4, 4 in. by 1¾ in., 9 lines to a side. Begins: st. 3.105 is vs. 1. Ends: st. 2.35 is vs. 16. No colophon. 5 of the vss. in this *stotra* are from the KK. The others are unidentified.

YY2 vs.	1 is KK	st. 3.105
°	6 is	st. 2.102
o	14 is	st. 2.109
	15 is	st. 2. 35
	16 is	st. 3. 99

Collated from reading of manuscript by Miss. P. Subhadradevi.

xYY10 University of Kerala Manuscripts Library No. 17598. Malayalam, palm leaf, folios (see below), 53.5 cm. by 5.0 cm., 5-6 lines to a side. Appearance very old. Begins: beginning is damaged; begins with...., lakṣmaṇena ca. Ends: kṛṣṇalīlāśukasya yāṃ kīrtiṃ manoharaḥ puṣṇāti kṛṣṇānāṃ prītiṃ bhūyo bhūyo vijṛmbhatām. hariḥ oṃ. Before acquired by library, ms. belonged to Kāṭṭumāṭam Mana. Partial collation from printed edition based on this ms., from hand copy of a hand copy of this ms., and from the reading of the ms. by Miss P. Subhadradevi. For further information see below. The following *stotras* are included in this ms. The first eight *stotras* in the ms. are published in the *Stotrārṇavaḥ*, pub-

53. *Ibid.*, pp. 471–83.

lished in the Madras Government Oriental Manuscripts Series[54] from M.G.O.L. ms. R. 4320 of which I have a hand copy. R. 4320 is a hand copy, made for the M.G.O.L., from a ms. belonging to M. R. Ry. Śrīkumāra Nambūdirippāḍ, Kottamadam-mana, Andathode post, Malabar district. Comparison of R. 4320 and YY10 shows that R. 4320 is a copy of YY10. They share the same damaged portions. R. 4320 is a fairly correct copy of the first eight *stotras* in YY10 except for the extent designated for the "Mahākālāṣṭakam." In R. 4320 this *aṣṭaka* includes 25 vss.[55] In YY10 the "Mahākālāṣṭaka" includes only vss. 16–25. The first portion, vss. 1–15, gives biographical information about Līlāśuka. This is quoted in its entirety below; see fourth *stotra* below.
1) "Rāmacandrāṣṭaka," folio 1, 8 vss.
2) "Anubhavāṣṭaka," folio 1, 9 vss.
3) "Gaṇapatistotra," 40 vss.
4) "Gopālastotra," folios 1. Below is given M. Krishnamachariar's copy[56] of M. Ramakrishna Kavi's copy of the "Gopālastotra" from YY10. This copy is different somewhat than that which appears in the *Stotrārṇavaḥ*,[57] but both are copies from the same manuscript.

vacasi mama sannidhattāṃ
madhurasmitabharitamantharāpaṅgī /
karakalitalalitavaṃśā
kāpi kiśorī kṛpālaharī // 1
garvodriktadiśāgajendrapariṣatsevāpraṇāmādṛtaṃ
yātāyātasurendrasainyalaharīmauḷiprabhāvanditam /
valgatpārthivasārthamaṇḍalamahāyātrāravārādhitaṃ
kārsnyaṃ kāmabhuvāṃ buvāṃ gajamukhajyotiḥ kimapyāśraye //2
bhūmne bhuvanamādhuryasīmne saraḷasaṃpadāṃ /
sīmne sarasagopāśe dhāmne tatidamonnamaḥ //3
ajñānamadanajyotiḥprajñeśānapadāspadam /
ālambitanarākāramālambanamabhūtsatām //4

---

54. *Stotrārṇavaḥ*, ed. T. Chandrasekharan, Madras Government Oriental Manuscripts Series No. 70 (Madras, 1961), pp. 462–476.
55. *Ibid.*, pp. 468–469.
56. M. Krishnamachariar, *op. cit.*, p. 334.
57. T. Chandrasekharan, *op. cit.*, pp. 468–69.

amuṣya karuṇāpātramasti maskariṇāmmaṇiḥ /
ādityaprajñasamjñaṃ yadādityādadhikaṃ mahaḥ //5
nirjitassamadṛṣṭyai......... manmathaḥ /
ārjitairastrakusumairārādārādhyanyayau //6
ādityaprajñapādānāmādikāruṇyabhājanaṃ /
īśānadeva ityāsīt īśāno munitejasām //7
āspadasya hi yasyāsīdaśeṣaguṇasampadāṃ /
advitīya iti khyātirātmabuddhyā na kevalam //8
tayoranugrahāpāṅgasaṅkāntajñānasāgarāḥ /
sāgarā iva gaṃbhīrāssanti dhanyāḥ sahasraśaḥ //9
tayoreva kṛpāpātraṃ kṛṣṇalīlāśuko muniḥ /
yadāśramāṅgaṇe nityaṃ ramante tantravistarāḥ //10
tilakaṃ kulapālīnāṃ nīlīti nilayaṃ śriyāṃ /
yamaḷaṃ janayāṃcakre yaṃ ca kīrtiṃ ca śāśvatīṃ //11
yasya dāmodara nāma savitā savitṛ... bhaḥ /
anṛṇasya hi yasyāsannadhamarṇā marudgaṇāḥ //12
yasya tatpriyasarvasvaṃ rāghaveśānasaṃjñakaṃ /
vineyasavidhe yasya suhṛnnukrāya...... //13
yasya dakṣiṇakailāsalīlāpariṇataṃ mahaḥ /
carcācandanagandhena sugandhayati mānasam //14
kṛṣṇalīlāśukasyāsya kiśoramadhidaivatam /
(stu)tiratnamidaṃ brūte veṇuvādimukhendunā //15

5) "Mahākālāṣṭaka," folio 1, 10 vss.

6) "Kārkoṭakanavaratna," folio 1, 11 vss., vs. 1 evidently belongs in the *Mahākālāṣṭaka*:

tribhuvanajayavihārī viharatu hṛdi vo mahākālaḥ /
girivara... kucataṭaviluṭhitanayanatrayīsubhagaḥ //1

7) "Kṛṣṇavaradāṣṭaka," folio 1, 9 vss.

8) "Vṛndāvanastotra," folios 5 (also published by K. Raghavan Pillai[58] and M. Ramakrishna Kavi[59]), 60 vss.

9) "Kālavadhakāvya," (published by K. Raghavan Pillai[60] and

58. *Stotrasamāhāra*, Part I, ed. K. Raghavan Pillai, University of Kerala Sanskrit Series No. 211 (Trivandrum, 1964), p. i.

59. "Bṛndāvanastutiḥ," ed. M. Ramakrishna Kavi, *Tirumalai Sri Venkatesvara*, Vol. I, No. 3 (1932), pp. 225–30.

60. *Kālavadhakāvyam of Śrī Kṛṣṇalīlāśukamuni*, ed. K. Raghavan Pillai, University of Kerala Sanskrit Series No. 199, 22 pp.

M. Ramakrishna Kavi[61]). This *kāvya* contains 3 *sargas* of 53, 34, and 31 vss. Final colophon: iti śrīkṛṣṇalīlāśukasya kṛtau kālavadhe tṛtīyaḥ sargaḥ. samāptaṃ ca kāvyam.

10) "Kaustubhamālā," folios 3 (published by T. Ganapati Sastri[62] and K. Raghavan Pillai[63]), 47 vss.

11) "Tribhuvanasubhaga." folios 2 (published by K. Raghavan Pillai[64]), 13 vss.

12) "Viśvādhikastuti," folios 5, about 12 vss.

13) "Adbhutastuti," folios 2 (published by K. Raghavan Pillai[65]), 15 vss.

14) "Govindābhiṣeka," folios 20. This is a Prakrit *kāvya*, which illustrates the *Prākṛta Prakāśa* of Vararuci. The "Govindābhiṣeka" is also known as the *Siricimdhakavvaṃ*. The first canto is published in the *Bhāratīya Vidyā*.[66] The entire work is being published in successive issues of the *Journal of the Kerala University Oriental Manuscripts Library*.[67]

15. "Kṛṣṇāvatara," folios 24. Begins: govindāya namaḥ.... so 'vyāt... śānto vande. mūrdhnā modāt.....

The 24 folios seem to contain only such *maṅgalas* and *namaskriyas.* YY10 ends after this section.

YY10 vss. found in the KK and Y mss.

4) *Gopālastotra* vs. 1 is KK st. 3.74.

9) *Kālavadhakāvya*

vs. 1.4(ab) = Y2 vs. 54(ab) (Y2 vs. 54 is Y11 vs. 221, Y21 vs. 116, Y31 vs. 51, Y61 vs. 75):

mandasmitasnapitamugdhamukhāravindaṃ

---

61. Kālavadham," ed. M. Ramakrishna Kavi, *Tirumalai Sri Venkatesvara*, Serial publication of *sargas* 1–3 in Vol. I, Nos. 4 and 5 (1932), pp. 307–312 and 393–398.

62. *Abhinavakaustubhamala and Dakshinamurthstava* of *Krishnalilasukamuni*, ed. T. Ganapati Sastri, Trivandrum Sanskrit Series No. 2 (Trivandrum, 1905).

63. K. Raghavan Pillai, *Strotrasamāhāra*, p. ii.

64. *Ibid.*

65. *Ibid.*

66. A. N. Upadhye, "Siricimdhakavvaṃ," *Bhāratīya Vidyā*, Vol. III (1941–2), pp. 60–76.

67. "Śrīcihnakāvyam," ed. K. Raghavan Pillai, *Journal of the Kerala University Oriental Manuscripts Library*, Serial publication of *sargas* 1–7 in Vol. XII, No. 4 through Vol. XV, No. 4 (1963–1966).

mandānilākulitakomalakākapakṣam /
aṅgaṃ tadetadakhilavrajalocanānāṃ
maṅgalyamastu kimataḥ paramasti kṛtyam // Kāla° 1.4
mandasmitasnapanamugdhamukhāravinde
mandānilākulitakomalakākapakṣe /
gogopagopavanitājanapuṇyapūre
gopālabālatilake ramatāṃ mano me // Y31 vs. 51

o as. 1.5(ab)=KK st. 1.31 (ab)
piñchāvataṃsaracanocitakeśapāśaṃ
pīnastanīnayanapaṅkajalobhanīyam /
mandāravarṣabharitaṃ surasundarībhir
mandaṃ mṛdukvaṇitavenurasābhirāmam // Kāla° 1.5

2) *Anubhavāṣṭaka* vs. 5=Y2 vs. 185 (Y2 vs. 185 is Y11 vs. 86 [numbered 46], Y31 vs. 254):
na vacāṃsi na cittavṛtayaḥ
padamekaṃ paripātum īkṣate /
paramaṃ kimapīdamadbhutaṃ
paramapyadbhutam adbhutādbhutam // Y31 vs. 254

Variant readings to above verse from *Anubhavāṣṭaka* vs. 5: padametat parimātumīśate; punarapy (for paramapy); ms. damaged after punar apy.

YY11 University of Kerala Manuscripts Library No. 18229. Malayalam, palm leaf, 40.5 cm. by 4.5 cm., 6–7 lines to a side. K. Raghavan Pillai estimates this ms. to be 4–5 centuries old. It contains 48 *stotras*, seven which are, in the ms. or elsewhere, attributed to Līlāśuka.

16) "Bālagopālāṣṭakam" (published by K. Raghavan Pillai[68]). 10 vss. Vs. 3 is YY1 vs. 3.

19) "Anubhavāṣṭaka" (published by K. Raghavan Pillai[69]). This is the same *stotra* as YY10 *stotra* 2.

20) "Vṛttiratnam." This is the same *stotra* as YY10 *stotra* 4, named "Gopālastotra." vs. 1, variants to KK st. 3.74: b) madhurasmitaharitamandarāpāṅgī d) kiśorī. The following are variants to M. Ramakrishna Kavi's copy (see YY10 *stotra* 4): vs. 5) ādityaprajñapādaṃ vs. 7) īśānaveda (R. 4320 also reads

68. K. Raghavan Pillai, *Stotrasamāhāra*, p. iii.
69. *Ibid.*, pp. iii–iv.

thus) vs. 11) reads with the M. Ramakrishna Kavi copy and R. 4320 (nīlīti) vs. 15) vṛttiratnamidaṃ

21) "Mahākālāṣṭakam." This is the same *stotra* as YY10 *stotra* 5.

25) "Kārkoṭakanavaratnam." This is the same *stotra* as YY10 *stotra* 6.

30) and 34) "Nṛsiṃhanavaratnam." 30) and 34) are slightly different versions of the same work. (Published by K. Raghavan Pillai.[70]) 12 vss. Before acquired by the library, the ms. belonged to Budhanūr Aṭimuṭṭattu Illam.

Partial collation from the ms.

YY(51–99) designates collections of refrain vss., all of which have the same line d as does a vs. (or vss.) which appear in the KK. The mss. of such collections are in both Devanāgarī and the Dravidian scripts. Only one, a Devanāgarī ms., is noted below. Many other YY(51–99) mss. are mentioned without the designation in the "Introduction" and in the "Notes on the Additional Verses" section.

YY51 Deccan College No. 6241. Devanāgarī script, paper, folios 2, $6\frac{2}{8}$ in. by $4\frac{1}{8}$ in., 5–6 lines to a side. Begins: śrīgaṇādhipāya namaḥ. Ends: iti śrīkṛṣṇalīlāśukaviracitaṃ gopālāṣṭakaṃ saṃpūrṇam. Ms. includes the following vss. arranged in the following order:

vss. 1–3 = KK st. 2.35–37
vs. 4 = KK st. 2.38
vss. 5, 6 = KK st. 2.39, 40
vss. 7, 8 = KKst. 2.41, 42

Collated from ms.

Z1 *Subhāṣitaratnabhāṇḍāgāra*, ed. Nārāyaṇ Rām Āchārya, Bombay: Nirnaya Sagar Press, 1952. 394 pp. KK vss. found in Z1:

o st. 2.1
o st. 2.3
o st. 2.4
o st. 2.60
st. 2.63 (Z4 vs. 115)
st. 2.72
o st. 292 (Z5 vs. 31)

70. *Ibid.*, p. iii.

st. 2.102
st. 2.107

Modern anthology.

Z2 *The Subhāṣitāvali of Vallabhadeva*, ed. Peter Peterson and Pandit Durgāprasāda, Bombay Sanskrit and Prakrit Series No. xxxi, Poona: R. N. Dandekar at the Bhandarkar Institute Press, 1961. 627 pp.
Manuscripts used for the edition (pp. i–ii):

A ms. from Kashmir purchased by Peterson
B ms. from Ulwar library borrowed by Peterson
C ms. borrowed by Peterson from Bühler through Aufrecht
D ms. borrowed by Peterson from Bühler through Aufrecht

KK vss. found in Z2:

st. 2.54 (Bhaṭṭacūlitaka)
st. 2.58
st. 2.61 (Jīvaka)
st. 2.63
st. 2.65
st. 2.92 (Bhāgavatāmṛtadatta, c.1352 A.D.—p.2)
st. 2.103
st. 2.109
st. 3.97

De[71] dates this anthology at about 1150 A.D. Peterson (p. 114) states that the compiler's date connot be before 1417 A.D.

oZ3 (Śukadeva's *Suktasudhākara*) According to Peterson[72] st. 3.97 is quoted by Śukadeva as composed by Bilvamañgala. Date of Śukadeva not known.

Z4 *The Paddhati of Sarngadhara*, Vol. I, ed. Peter Peterson, Bombay Sanskrit Series No. xxxvii, Bombay: Government Central Book Depot, 1888. 759 pp.

71. S. K. De, *Aspects of Sanskrit Literature* (Calcutta: Firma K. L. Mukhopadhyay, 1959), p. 156.

72. See "Description of the Manuscripts" section Z2, "Notes" No. 1041, p. 33.

KK vss. found in Z4:

st. 2.63 (Bilvamañgalaśrīcaraṇa)
st. 2.65
st. 2.72 (Vasuṃdhara)

De[73] dates this anthology at about 1363 A.D.

Z5 *Sadukti-karṇāmṛta of Śrīdharadāsa*, crit. ed. Sures Chandra Banerji, Calcutta: Firma K. L. Mukhopadhyay, 1965. 651 pp. Sources used for the edition (pp. ix–xi):

A ms. no. G 744 belonging to Asiatic Society, Calcutta (Bengali)
Ed Edition of the *Sadukti-karṇāmṛta* by Rāmāvatāra Śarmā, Lahore: 1933.
IO Aufrecht's transcript preserved in India Office Library, London
S Calcutta Sanskrit College ms. no. 178 (Bengali)
Sp Serampore College Library, District Hooghly [Case G, Shelf 8, No. 58]
ZDMG Portion of the text edited by Aufrecht and published in ZDMG, Vol. XXXVI

KK vss. found in Z5:

st. 1.106
st. 2.59 (Mayūra, c. 7th century A.D.[74])
st. 2.65
st. 2.70 (Śubhāñka)

Compiled about 1205 A.D.[75]

Z7 *The Sūktimuktāvalī of Bhagadatta Jahlaṇa*, ed. Embar Krishnamacharya, Gaekwad's Oriental Series No. LXXXII, Baroda: Oriental Institute, 1938. 463 pp.
Manuscripts used for the edition (p. 64):
K Yadugirisapatkumāraśrīyatirājasvāminām
Kh Madrās Oriental Library

73. S. K. De, "Kāvya," *A History of Sanskrit Literature*, Vol. I, ed. S. N. Dasgupta (Calcutta: University of Calcutta, 1962), p. 414.

74. Keith, *op. cit.*, p. 201.

75. See "Description of the Manuscripts" section Z5 (Banerji ed.), p. viii.

C Mahīśūra (Mysore) Rājakīyapustakālayastham
G Vaḍoda (Baroda) Rājakīyaprācyavidyālayastham (Gayakavāḍa Oriental Institute) sūktimuktāvalī saṃgrahākhyaṃ pustakam

KK vss. found in Z7:

st. 2.25 noted by Z7 (p.34) to be by Līlāśuka. Bhandarkar[76] does not list Līlāśuka (or Bilvamañgala) in his index of poets whose verses are given in Jahlaṇa's anthology.
st. 2.65
st. 2.72 (Vasuṃdhara)

According to De[77] and Bhandarkar the date of Jahlaṇa is c. 1247 A.D. There is a shorter and longer version of the *Sūktimuktāvalī*.

Z8 *The Rasārṇavasudhākara by Śrī Singa Bhūpāla*, ed. T. Ganapati Sastri, Trivandrum Sanskrit Series No. L, Trivandrum, 1916. 340 pp.
Manuscripts used for the edition (p.i.):

k Belonging to the Palace Library (Grantha)
kh Belonging to the Raja of Panthalam (Malayalam)
g Lent by Kailasapuram Govinda Pisharodi (Malayalam, 1580 A.D.)
gh Lent by Mr. Devan Parameswaran Numburi, Idappalli (Malayalam)
ñ Lent by Mr. Krishna Varyar, Chunakkara (Malayalam)
c Belonging to Kailasapuram Govind Pisharodi (Malayalam)

KK vs. found in Z8:

st. 2.72

According to Mr. Sastri (p. i) the date of the compiler is 1330 A.D.

Z9 Śṛṇgeri ms. of the *Subhāṣitasuradruma* of Keḷadī Vasavappa Nāyaka. D. D. Kosambi made a Devanāgarī copy of this Nan-

76. *Collected Works of Sir R. G. Bhandarkar*, Vol. II, ed. Narayan Bapuji Utgikar, Government Oriental Series Class B No. 2 (Poona: Bh.O.R.I., 1928), pp. 371–412.
77. S. K. De, "Kāvya," p. 414.

dināgarī ms. by dictation to Miss Shanta Kulkarni. The copy, in much disorder, is deposited in the Bh.O.R.I. The compiler, who lived according to P. K. Gode[78] c. 1697 A.D., seems to quote extensively from all three centuries of the KK.

Z11 *Padyāvalī compiled by Rūpa Gosvāmin*, ed. S. K. De, University of Dacca Oriental Publication Series No. 3, Dacca, 1934. Mss. used for edition:

D mss.	Dacca University mss.
P mss.	Bh.O.R.I. mss.
IO ms.	Eggling, IO ms.
TB ms.	Tübingen univ. ms.
SSP ms.	Saṃskṛta Sāhitya Pariṣad, Calcutta, ms.
AS mss.	As. Soc. Bengal mss.
VSP mss.	Vangīya Sāhita Pariṣad, Calcutta, mss.
PT	previous edition
AKG	previous edition
CC	Kṛṣṇadāsakavirāja, *Caitanyacaritāmṛta*, Calcutta, 1927.
CBh	*Caitanyabhāgavata*, ed. Amrita Bazar Patrika Office, Calcutta, 1926.

KK vss. found in Z11.

st. 2.59	(Mayūra; see Z5.)
st. 2.63	(Mañgala; this vs. is omitted in PB, AKG.)
st. 2.70	(Śubhāñka)
st. 2.72	
st. 2.102	(DB, DC, SSP, ASA, VSPA Nārada; Comm. Puruṣottamadeva; DD unassigned; all others anon.)
st. 2.107	(Mādhavendrapurī)
st. 2.108	(PA Śrīvatsa; all others Śrīvaiṣṇava.)
st. 3.84	(PB unassigned; all others Śāradākāra.)
st. 3.87	(This verse is omitted in PB; DB, DC, VSPA Śrīmad; PT Śrībhagavad; Comm. Śrībhagavad-śaśinandana; others anon.)

78. P. K. Gode, "Kavīndra Paramānanda and Keḷadi Bhasavabhūpāla," *Bhāratīya Vidyā*, Vol. III, Part 1 (November, 1941), p. 40.

st. 3.98 (DG unassigned; all others Vyāsa.)
st. 3.106

The compiler of this anthology died in 1591 A.D.[79]

Z12 *Haribhaktirasāmṛtasindhu* of Rūpa Gosvāmin. Information on verses listed below was from *The Kṛṣṇakarṇāmṛta,* ed. Sushil Kumar De, University of Dacca Oriental Publication Series No. 5, Dacca, 1938. 384 pp. For the complete information, given by De, see "Introduction," pp. 8–9.
KK vss. found in Z12:

o st. 1.30
o st. 1.32
o st. 1.41
o st. 1.54
o st. 1.65
o st. 1.99
o st. 2.25
o st. 3.97

Z13 *Haribhaktivilāsa* of Sanātana Gosvāmī (or Gopālabhaṭṭa[80]). Collation of vs. listed below was done from De's edition of the *Padyāvalī* (Z11).
KK vs. found in Z13:

st. 3.84

Both Sanātana Gosvāmi and Gopālabhaṭṭa were disciples of Caitanya.[81]

Z14 *Ujjvalanīlamaṇi* of Rūpa Gosvāmin. Information on verses listed below was from *The Kṛṣṇakarṇāmṛta,* ed. Sushil Kumar De, University of Dacca Oriental Series No. 5, Dacca, 1938. 384 pp. For the complete information, given by De, see "Introduction,"
KK vss. found in Z14:

o st. 1.21
o st. 2.11

79. J. N. Farquhar, *An Outline of the Religious Literature of India* (Oxford: Oxford University Press, 1920), p. 376.

80. *Ibid.*, p. 309.

81. *Ibid.*

Z22 "Mahākaviśrīkṣemendrakṛtā Aucityavicāracarcā," *Kāvyamālā*, Part I, ed. Paṇḍita Durgāprasāda and Kāshinātha Pāṇḍuranga Paraba, Bombay: Nirnaya Sagar Press, 1886. pp. 115–160. KK vs. found in Z22:

st. 2.65 (Candaka; Peterson has this to say about Candaka and the *Aucityavicāracarcā*:

Kalhaṇa mention this poet
Rāja. II. 16.
nāṭyaṃ sarvajanapṛekṣyaṃ
yaścakre sa mahākaviḥ /
dvaipāyanamuneraṃśas
tatkāle candrako 'bhavat //
Kṣemendra in his *Aucityavicāracarcā* quotes four verses by Candaka, of which two—kṛṣṇenāmba gatema and kṛśaḥ kāṇaḥ—...[82]

The first of these two verses is st. 2.65, the second is vs. 2 of Kosambi's critical edition of Bhartṛhari's *subhāṣitas*.[83])

Kṣemendra lived in the 11th century.[84] Kalhaṇa was born c. 1100.[85]

Z23 *The Subhāṣitaratnakoṣa compiled by Vidyākara*, eds. D. D. Kosambi and V. V. Gokhale, Harvard Oriental Series Volume 42, Cambridge: Harvard University Press, 1957. 341 pp. Ancillary Source used for edition:

P. *Prasanna-sāhitya-ratnākara* of Nandana

KK vs. found in Z23:

st. 2.70

The latest possible dates for Vidyākara, according to Kosambi,[86] are 1055 A.D.–1100 A.D.

---

82. See "Description of the Manuscripts" section Z2, p. 35.

83. Kosambi, *op. cit.*, p. 1 of the text.

84. Keith, *op. cit.*, p. 135.

85. *Ibid.*, p. 158.

86. *The Subhāṣitaratnakoṣa compiled by Vidyākara*, ed. D. D. Kosambi and V. V. Gokhale, Harvard Oriental Series Vol. 42 (Cambridge: Harvard University Press, 1957), p. xxxi.

Z25 *Kāvyānuśāsana* of Hemacandra. Collation of vs. listed below was done from De's edition of the *Padyāvalī* (Z11).
KK vs. found in Z25:

st. 2.70

Keith[87] gives Hemacandra's dates as 1088–1172 A.D.

Z26 *Alaṃkāramahodadhi* of Narendraprabhāsūri. Collation of vs. listed below was from H. G. Narahari, "On the Date of the Kṛṣṇakarṇāmṛta of Bilvamaṅgala," *The Indian Historical Quarterly*, Vol. 20, No. 1 (March, 1944), pp. 86–87. Narahari (p. 86) quotes the vs. below from the Gaekwad Oriental Series No. 95 edition of the *Alaṃkāramahodadhi.*
KK vs. found in Z26:

st. 2.65

The commentary according to Narahari (p. 86) was composed in 1226 A.D.

Z31 Otto Böhtlingk, *Indische Sprüche* Vol. I, St. Petersburg, 1870.
KK vs. found in Z31:

st. 2106 (Vṛddha-cāṇakya)

Z32 *Cānakya-Nīti-Text Tradition* Vol. I (Six Versions of Cāṇakya's Collection of Maxims), Part I (The Vṛddha-Cāṇakya Textus Ornatior Version) ed. Ludwik Sternbach, Hoshiarpur, 1963.
One of the sources used for edition:

Ah printed edition from Ahmedabad, 1913. Sternbach (p. 61) notes that Ah is a typical edition. It omits some aphorisms while adding quite a number of new well known aphorisms selected from the *Mānavadharmaśāstra*, the *Mahābhārata*, Bhartṛhari's *śatakas*, and the *Pañcatantra*:

KK vs. found in Z32:

o st. 2.106 (Omitted by Ah. Vs. st. 2.106 must be an interpolation into the Nīti text of Cāṇakya.)

Z41 *Kramadīpikā*. Three printed editions and three mss. were used. P. S. Subba Rama Pattar, who compiled the Naṭuvil Maṭham

87. Keith, *op. cit.*, p. 142.

catalogue (unpublished), told me that tradition attributes the *Kramadīpikā*, Z41(N), to Līlāśuka. M. Ramakrishna Kavi states that Bilvamaṅgala wrote the *Kramadīpikā*:

> ...a tantric work treating of Krishna's worship enumerating various rites. There is another work of the same name by a different author.[88]

Raja[89] gives the depository of Bilvamaṅgala's work as the Naṭuvil in Trichur.

KK vs. found in Z41:

add. vs. kalāttamāyā°

Z41(B) "Kramadīpikā," *Muṇḍamālā Tantra and Other Tantras*, ed. Rasikmohan Chatopādhyāya, (Title page is missing in the only available edition. Printed in Bengali script. Each *tantra* is separately numbered. The *Kramadīpikā* is the twenty third entry. There are 18 pages which contain 8 *paṭalas* of the *tantra*.) 641 pp.

Z41(Ch) Kasmirika Kesava Bhatta, *Kramadipika*, Chowkamba Sanskrit Series Nos. 233, 236, 254 (Benares, 1917, 1917, 1919). 248 pp.

Z41(S) *Kramadīpikā*, ed. Ram Chandra Kak and Harabhatta Shastri, Srinagar, 1929. 89 pp.

Z41(N) Naṭuvil Maṭham (Trichur) No. 172. Malayalam script, palm leaf, folios 50, 13¾ in. by 1 in., 5 lines to a side. No date. Text begins: add. kalāttamāyā° is vs. 1. Text ends: iti kramadīpikāyāṃ daśamaḥ paṭalaḥ. kramadīpikā samāptā. Commentary ends: iti paramahaṃsaparivrājakācāryapūrṇaprajñaśiṣyena... nityaprajñena puruṣottamavanāparanāmadheyena kṛtāyāṃ kramadīpikābhāvadīpikāyāṃ daśamaḥ paṭalaḥ. bhāvadīpikā samāptā. Collated from hand copy of ms. by unidentified copyist.

Z41(TPC) Trivandrum Palace Library No. 1246/1125. (The Trivandrum Palace Library collection is now in the University of Kerala Manuscripts Library.) Malayalam script, palm leaf, folios 58

---

88. M. Ramakrishna Kavi, "Literary Gleanings No. 9, Bilvamaṅgalasvāmin," *The Quarterly Journal of the Andhra Historical Research Society*, Vol. III, Part 1 (July, 1928), p. 67.

89. K. Kunjunni Raja, *The Contribution of Kerala to Sanskrit Literature* (Madras: University of Madras, 1958), p. 49, n. 103.

(incomplete), 9 in. by 2½ in., 9–11 lines to a side. Begins: add. kalāttamāyā° is vs. 1. Ends: missing.
Collated from description in *A Descriptive Catalogue of the Sanskrit Manuscripts in H.H. the Maharajah's Palace Library Trivandrum* Vol. IV, ed. K. Sāmbaśiva Śāstrī, Trivandrum, no date, p. 1533.

Z41(BORI) Bhandarkar Oriental Research Institute No. 648/1895–1902. (Commentary only) Devanāgarī script, paper, folios 54 (incomplete), 12 lines to a side. Begins: add. kalāttamāyā°. Ends: missing. Collated from ms.

Z42 *Mukundamālā*. Two printed editions.
KK vss. found in Z42:

o add. jayatu jayatu deva
add. prātar namāmi
add. prātar bhajāmi
add. prātar smarāmi

Z42(A) *Śrīmukundamālā*, ed. K. Rama Pisharoti, Annamalai University Sanskrit Series No. 1, Annamalainagar, 1933. pp. 68.

Z42(N) "Mukundamālāstotram," *Bṛhatstotraratnākaraḥ* Prathamo Bhagaḥ, Bombay: Nirnayasāgara Press, 1963, pp. 90–92.

Z43 *Bhāgavata Purāṇa*. Two printed editions.
KK vs. found in Z43:

add. barhāpīḍam

Z43(M) *Srimad Bhāgavatam* Two vols., Madras: V. Ramaswamy Sastrulu and Sons, 1937. 1992 pp.

Z43(G) *Śrīmadbhāgavatamahāpurāṇam*, Gorakhpur: Gita Press, 1943. pp. 765.

Interrelationships of the Manuscripts

In explaining the manuscript tradition of the Saundaryalaharī, W. Norman Brown describes very well the process of conflation between the traditions of a popular text.

> The interrelationships of the manuscripts used in preparing the text here published are not easy to determine. The principal diffi-

> culty comes from the fact that the Saundaryalaharī is so popular and so well known that many persons quote its stanzas from memory. Hence a reading in a manuscript may be erased or glossed by a user of the manuscript in favor of another reading which he knows and prefers. Such instances are copiously noted in the critical apparatus. When a copyist undertakes to copy a manuscript which has been so treated, the result is bound to be a mixture of traditions. There are, therefore, numerous cases in which a certain number of manuscripts will agree on a reading against a certain number of other manuscripts which agree on another reading. But on the next point of difference the alignment of manuscripts will be entirely different.[90]

If Kṛṣṇakarṇāmṛta is substituted for Saundaryalaharī in the above, the statement will be equally true. When such a user of a KK ms., as is described by Brown, makes an erasure, a gloss, or a correction, these can be noted in the original manuscript. In photographic copies and in even the best hand copies of mss. the evidence of this process, when it is present, tends to get blurred. Either the photograph does not record the original reading which is faintly discernable by eye under the yellow pigment, or the copyist, although aware of text critical methods, is defeated in trying to briefly convey the strata of evidence on a manuscript page.

In the KK there is a further problem with determining the interrelationships between manuscripts. This problem seems, at least among medieval stotra texts, peculiar to the KK. The problem is with the evidence of the Y mss. To restate their description: Y mss. are North Indian anthologies of devotional verses attributed to Bilvamañgala. These anthologies include a varying number of verses (100–537) in varying arrangements. There are six versions of this anthology if one considers it a single anthology with very varying versions. No manuscript includes less than 57 verses from the 328 standard verses of the KK; no manuscript includes more than 157 such verses. For the irregular sequence of the KK verses in Y mss. see "Synoptic Charts of Verse Sequences."

The following paragraphs will try to describe how the the aberrant Y mss. derived from the mainstream of the KK tradition.

---

90. *The Saundaryalaharī*, ed. W. Norman Brown, The Harvard Oriental Series Volume 43 (Cambridge: Harvard University Press, 1958), p. 43.

In South India the KK is a collection of about 330 vss. written by a South Indian and arranged into three centuries. It is possible that at an early period in the history of the KK these three centuries were closely associated with other devotional texts also written by a South Indian[91] or, alternatively, these three centuries were put together from a floating mass of South Indian devotional verses addressed to Kṛṣṇa. Thus we find that when one tradition of the KK becomes popular throughout the realms of the Vijayanagara kingdom-complex, its careful literary arrangement into 3 centuries is quickly obliterated by much use and recitation. Those who use the manuscripts as hymnals shuffle and reshuffle the verses which are written two or three together on a palm leaf. They insert those many other South Indian verses which they closely associate with the tradition they have at hand, and then, they pass on parts of these shuffled and extended manuscripts which find their way to devotional centers in North India where their copies are preserved to us in the manuscripts of the Y version, especially in those Devanāgarī manuscripts of Y(1–29).

Y1 is such a North Indian manuscript, dated 1418 A.D. (Since Y1 is fragmentary, reference is made to Y2 and Y3 mss. to supply evidence missing in the Y1 ms. All three mss. are from the same general tradition.) In Y1, then, we find the Vijayanagara version (DG, G1, G2, N1, N21) of the KK so much reduced, altered, diluted, pervaded by other, if similar, materials that its identity is, in fact, impossible to prove. All that can be said in proof of its identity are the following points.

1) The variant readings of the Vijayanagara version of the KK read more often with the Y1 and the other Y mss. than do the other versions. The Vijayanagara version (DG, G1, G2, N1, N21 mss.) reads more

91. Insistence that the KK tradition and the major part of the breakdown of the KK tradition took place in South India is due to the fact that both the KK vss. and the non-KK vss. in the Y mss. often demonstrate the initial assonance characteristic of Dravidian poetry; see Y. Proof of this will come when the non-KK vss. of the Y mss. are critically edited. (See J. Wilson, The Bilvamaṅgalastava, Leiden, 1973).

There is other evidence, not substantial however, which indicates that the non-KK Y vss. were originally South Indian: There are 10–12 non-KK vss. which appear in both the Dravidian mss. attributed to Kṛṣṇalīlāśuka (YY0) and in the Northern anthologies attributed to Bilvamaṅgala (Y). YY1 contains 10 such verses. Mention of these verses is made in the description of YY1, but they are not listed or described. YY10 contains 1½ non-KK Y vss. These are quoted at the end of the YY10 description.

often with the Y version than does the Caitanya version (A, B mss.) which is another differently aberrant version of the KK which, like the Vijayanagara version, has older testimony than other non-Y KK versions. The most significant variant reading which is shared by the Vijayanagara version (N1 and N21 only) and the Y version (Y31–69 mss. only) is st. 2.82 c and d.

2) The Vijayanagara version (DG, G1, G2, N1, N21 mss.) of the KK is quite out of the main stream of KK mss. There are many marked distortions in verse sequences aside from the major arrangement of centuries st. 1, st. 2, st. 3 thus: st. 2, st. 3, st. 1. This rearrangement would seem not to be a singular preservation of the authentic tradition but a part of a beginning breakdown of the tradition which culminates in the corrupt Y versions. An example of the corruption which the Vijayanagara version shares with the Y versions: Both include the Bhāgavata Purāṇa vs. X 21 5, add. barhāpīḍaṃ. In DG, G1, G2, add. barhāpīḍaṃ is vs. 1.103, in N1, N21 it is vs. 1.102, in Y11, Y12 it is vs. 180, and in Y21 it is vs. 231. This vs. occurs in non-Vijayanagara KK mss. which elsewhere reflect the Vijayanagara tradition.

3) If the Vijayanagara version shows evidence of belonging to a tradition which is beginning to undergo marked change and disorganization, the YO version has evidence which indicates that its form was once quite different and much more organized. The following colophonic verse is found as Y2 vs. 194 (Y11 vs. 231, Y21 vs. 180, Y31 vs. 378):

amībhir aṣṭābhir abhiṣṭutaḥ stavaiḥ
śatena devaḥ śatapatralocanaḥ /
kiśoraveṣeṇa kṛpāmbudaḥ svayaṃ
virājamāno hṛdi me vivardhatām //

May the god with the lotus eyes, who is praised in the above 108 vss.,
himself appear in the form of a body and come
into my heart.

The significance of this as a verse colophon has been lost in the Y mss. In Y11, Y13, and Y14, for example, a variant 'stavena' is given for 'śatena.'

In version YO, however, where verses of KK st. 3 are for the most part grouped together from st. 3.88 (Y2 vs. 89) to st. 3.69 (Y2 vs. 181), the above verse colophon pertains to these vss. of st. 3.

Diagram of Manuscript Relationships

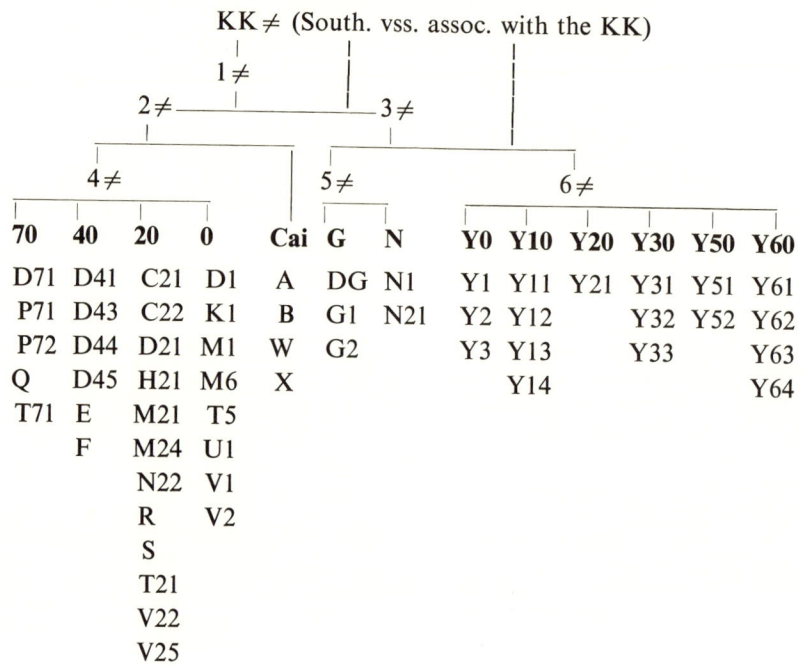

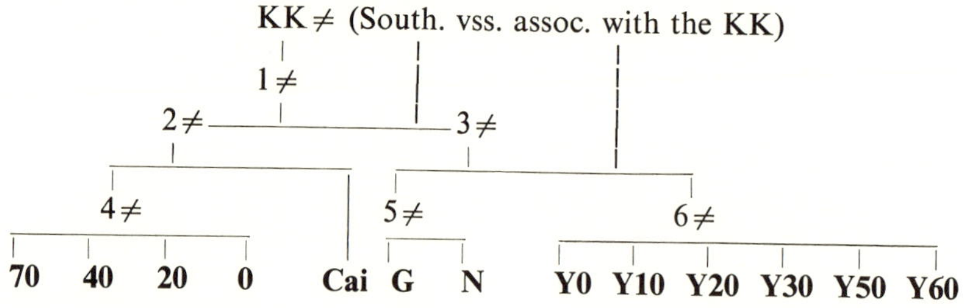

70	40	20	0	Cai	G	N	Y0	Y10	Y20	Y30	Y50	Y60
D71	D41	C21	D1	A	DG	N1	Y1	Y11	Y21	Y31	Y51	Y61
P71	D43	C22	K1	B	G1	N21	Y2	Y12		Y32	Y52	Y62
P72	D44	D21	M1	W	G2		Y3	Y13		Y33		Y63
Q	D45	H21	M6	X				Y14				Y64
T71	E	M21	T5									
	F	M24	U1									
		N22	V1									
		R	V2									
		S										
		T21										
		V22										
		V25										

(Mss. of mixed versions)

60	50	30	10
D64	C51	H31	D11
	C52		D12
			D14
			G11

1≠ represents the reconstruction of the KK text (KK≠) from 2≠ which is the reconstruction of the mainstream of the KK tradition and from 3≠ which represents the reconstruction of the aberrant Vijayanagara tradition. The history of this tradition is outlined in the paragraphs preceding the diagram.

2≠ represents the reconstruction of the mainstream of the KK tradition from the four Southern versions (70, 40, 20, and 0) and the Caitanyaite version (Cai).

Cai The Caitanyaite version is very important for it is the oldest datable version of the "mainstream" tradition (see A1 and B1-GA). A1 is dated 1573 A.D. which is probably some 65 years after Caitanya "joyfully made a copy" of the Kṛṣṇakarṇāmṛta which book the Brāham Vaishnavas were studying on the banks of the Krishnabinnā river. Caitanya walked to the undesignated banks after visiting the shrine of Viṭṭhala on the Bhīrmarathī.[92] Unfortunately Caitanya made a copy of only the first century. For the first century this is the authoritative version.

4≠ represents the reconstruction of the 4 versions of the Southern manuscripts of the KK. The oldest datable manuscripts are Devanāgarī manuscripts (D12 and D21) of the 18th century.

3≠ represents reconstruction of the aberrant Vijayanagara tradition. As already noted, the history of this tradition is outlined in the paragraphs preceding the diagram.

Methodological Principles for the Text Criticism of the Kṛṣṇakarṇāmṛta

Two principles or factors are basic to choosing the readings. The first principle is that the readings of the "mainstream" tradition (2≠) take precedence over those in the aberrant Vijayanagara tradition (3≠). The second principle is that the readings of the older versions take precedence over those of later versions.

The applications of these two principles often conflict with each other, because the Y version (6≠), which is the furthest, most aberrant development of the aberrant Vijayanagara tradition (3≠), includes subversions (Y0 and Y10) to which the oldest datable mss. belong.

Whenever these two principles are in conflict, the first principle is to be applied, not the second, because, according to the analysis in the "Interrelationships of the Manuscripts" section, the aberrant Vijayanagara tradition (3≠) underwent, very early, marked alteration from a prior tradition which was more like—if not the same as—the mainstream (2≠) tradition.

92. Jadunath Sarkar, *Caitanya's Pilgrimages and Teachings* (London, 1913), p. 119. (Material cited is from Sarkar's translation of Kṛṣṇadḥsa Kavirāja's "Caitanyacaritāmṛta.")

Thus in the first century, because the Caitanya version (Cai) includes the oldest datable mss. (A1–1573 A.D. and B1–1605 A.D.) in the "mainstream" tradition, the readings of this version take precedence over the readings in the versions (5≠ and 6≠) of the aberrant tradition (3≠) even though the Y0 and Y10 sub-versions of version 6≠ include mss. (Y1–1418 A.D. and Y11–c. 1450 A.D.) which are a good century and a half earlier.

In the second and third centuries, without the evidence of the Caitanya version, the situation is much more difficult. The early aberrant traditions (3≠ or 5≠) have to be balanced against a mainstream tradition so much later (4≠) that its corruption and leveling by popular commentaries, especially the long version of the P. Sūri commentary (70), is clearly revealed in the first century: 4≠ (and especially 70) read against the like readings of Cai and 3≠. Since 4≠ and 3≠ traditions seem equally dubious, in the second and third centuries a third principle is applied, that of the difficult reading. The difficult reading, if meaningful, is used rather than the easier reading. It should be further noted that in none of the 3 centuries is the science of the first two principles strictly adhered to. It is hoped that the few times when these first two principles are broken that it is done artfully with a true intuition. The third principle of choosing the difficult rather than the easy reading is too subjective to be called scientific. Here is an example of the difficulty of applying the principle of *lectio dificilior*: Many South Indian pandits and professors had convinced me of the meaninglessness of the lines c and d found in the Y version of the KK st. 2.82. One day, however, I found an Assamese play by Mādhavadeva based on the Y version of this very verse.[93]

93. Neog, *op. cit.*, pp. 46–51.

THE KṚṢṆAKARṆĀMṚTA TEXT AND TRANSLATION

CENTURY I

1.* All hail to Cintāmaṇi, to Somagiri, my religious
preceptor,
and to my teacher, the lord who bears a
peacock feather crest.
At the tips of tender shoots from the trees of wishes,
which are his feet,
Jayaśrī, the goddess of victory, realizes a
joy like that in a divine play-marriage
of her own choosing.

2. Behold the object which is showered by wish-tree
blossoms falling from the finger tips
of heavenly maidens
and which, although *nirvāṇa* calm,
produces a flood of sound from the famed flute.
It is the most high in the form of a boy who
gives final release into the hands of the
suppliant
as he did to the thousands of encircling, dancing
milkmaids whose hold on the garment wrapped
around them was constantly being loosened.

3. We here do reverence the dark blue boy, who has
unrestricted dominion over love's
sweetness,
the lover from the sandy courtyard of Kālindī
who became the father of
the love god's reincarnation;
whose eyes, bathed by nectar waves of beauty,
excite the regard of Lakṣmī's sidelong
glances
and become languid as a result of
these lively side glances which are the
chief cause and farthest end of love's
symptoms.

ŚATAKA I

1.* cintāmaṇir jayati somagirir gurur me
śikṣāguruś ca bhagavāñ chikhipicchamauliḥ /
yatpādakalpatarupallavaśekhareṣu
līlāsvayaṃvararasaṃ labhate jayaśrīḥ //

2. asti svastaruṇīkarāgravigalatkalpaprasūnāplutaṃ
vastu prastutaveṇunādalaharīnirvāṇanirvyākulam /
srastasrastaniruddhanīvivilasadgopīsahasrāvṛtaṃ
hastanyastanatāpavargam akhilodāraṃ kiśorākṛti //

3. cāturyaikanidānasīmacapalāpāṅgacchaṭāmantharaṃ
lāvaṇyāmṛtavīcilolitadṛśaṃ lakṣmīkaṭākṣādṛtam /
kālindīpulināṅgaṇapraṇayinaṃ kāmāvatārāṅkuraṃ
bālaṃ nīlam amī vayaṃ madhurimasvārājyam ārādhnumaḥ //

4. With a bright peacock plume hair ornament and
 a face as if dipped in sweet tenderness,
the Light takes life in that budding youth
 found where the nectar of full flute
 sounds swell
and, on all sides, the milkmaids of the
 full bud-like breasts adore.
The Light is the one wonder and the one
 delight of the world; let it shine in
 our heart.

5. His tender lotus face has the nectar of a
 very sweet smile;
a charming lock of his hair is fastened
 with the feather of the impassioned
 peacock.
In my mind, greedy to swallow the poisoned
 meat of sensual enjoyments,
let him, the Light, shine
 long—the indescribable Light with
 large eyes.

6.* Let the lotus face of the lord open in my heart—
with his lotus eyes half shut like buds
and the globes of his soft mirroring cheeks
puffed with the honey of flute sounds.

7. Let there open in my words—
just any particle of the sweetness of
 Murāri
in the artless form of a lovely child
with a moon face adored by soft flute music.

8. Decorated with only the feather of the
 impassioned peacock,
his artless lotus mouth languid with love
is darkened by mascara from the eyes of the
 young women of Vraja.
Let him, who is the soul of my poetry, be
 triumphant.

4. barhottaṃsavilāsakuntalabharaṃ mādhuryamagnānanaṃ
pronmīlannavayauvanaṃ pravilasadveṇupraṇādāmṛtam /
āpīnastanakuḍmalābhir abhito gopībhir ārādhitaṃ
jyotiś cetasi naś cakāstu jagatām ekābhirāmādbhutam //

5. madhuratarasmitāmṛtavimugdhamukhāmburuhaṃ
madaśikhipicchalāñchitamanojñakacapracayam /
viṣayaviṣāmiṣagrasanagṛdhnuni cetasi me
vipulavilocanaṃ kim api dhāma cakāstu ciram //

6.* mukulāyamānanayanāmbujaṃ vibhor
muralīninādamakarandanirbharam /
mukurāyamāṇamṛdugaṇḍamaṇḍalaṃ
mukhapaṅkajaṃ manasi me vijṛmbhatām //

7. kamanīyakiśoramugdhamūrteḥ
kalaveṇukvaṇitādṛtānanendoḥ
mama vāci vijṛmbhatāṃ murārer
madhurimṇaḥ kaṇikā 'pi kā 'pi kā 'pi //

8. madaśikhaṇḍiśikhaṇḍavibhūṣaṇaṃ
madanamantharamugdhamukhāmbujam /
vrajavadhūnayanāñjanarañjitaṃ
vijayatāṃ mama vāṅmayajīvitam //

9.* I seek refuge in the lord who is marked by
red paste from the jar-like breasts of
milkmaids.
In lotus hands, rosy like new shoots, he holds
his flute and ardently attends its music
while his lotus feet seem to fault the red of
the *pāṭalī* blossom and
the passionate essence of his face rises in
flowery sprigs of light from his
lower lip.

10. We seek the shelter of the lord who is the
object
of an unbroken line of glances
inscribed every moment by the milkmaids
and illumined by the emotions of the
unembodied love god's message.

11. Let it shine in my heart—the inexpressible
Light
which, embodied in the youth of Kṛṣṇa, moves to and
fro among the beautiful young women of Vraja
and is the source of the endearing
perturbation
which makes their eyes dance and widen with
joy.

12. Let my heart carry away the indescribable
bliss found at the lotus feet of Kṛṣṇa,
which are the only place in all the world where
Lakṣmī is found at her eternal play,
which uproot all of the pride from the clusters
of a lotus pond,
which, when freeing the suppliant from fear,
are excessively elevated over the haughty.

13. Let the lord of life come into our heart.
He is the boy
with eyes which are more sparkling every moment
and everyday are new with their totally artless
graces
and which, in the fullness of their love,
sustain his power.

9.* pallavāruṇapāṇipaṅkajasaṅgiveṇuravākulaṃ
phullapāṭalapāṭalīparivādipādasaroruham /
ullasanmadhurādharadyutimañjarīsarasānanaṃ
vallavīkucakumbhakuṅkumapaṅkilaṃ prabhum āśraye //

10. apāṅgarekhābhir abhaṅgurābhir
anaṅgalekhārasarañjitābhiḥ /
anukṣaṇaṃ vallavasundarībhir
abhyasyamānaṃ vibhum āśrayāmaḥ //

11. hṛdaye mama hṛdyavibhramāṇāṃ
hṛdayaṃ harṣaviśālalolanetram /
taruṇaṃ vrajabālasundarīṇāṃ
taralaṃ kiṃ cana dhāma saṃnidhattām //

12. nikhilabhuvanalakṣmīnityalīlāspadābhyāṃ
kamalavipinavīthīgarvasarvaṃkaṣābhyām /
praṇamadabhayadānapraudhigāḍhoddhatābhyāṃ
kim api vahatu cetaḥ kṛṣṇapādāmbujābhyām //

13. praṇayapariṇatābhyāṃ prābhavālambanābhyāṃ
pratipadalalitābhyāṃ pratyahaṃ nūtanābhyām /
pratimuhur adhikābhyāṃ prasphurallocanābhyāṃ
pravahatu hṛdaye naḥ prāṇanāthaḥ kiśoraḥ //

14. Let my mind float along with the
    flood of bliss
which is embodied in the boy who cools then
    agitates with an erotic play
which is the cresting sea of passion's tumult
    in the ocean of love's tender affection
where the reflection of his full moon face
    dances with faint smiles.

15. With the sounds piped by his own flute
    as if enjoyed
by the graceful expressions on
    his lotus face of natural beauty,
let that energy living in all creatures,
    incarnate as Kṛṣṇa, dance with
    rosy lotus feet as the life in my heart.

16. I do honour the lord's feet
whose jeweled anklets chatter
and whose footprints play
along the paths of Vraja.

17. Let the sweet jingling coming from the
    jeweled anklets
of the milkmaid's lord echo in my heart—
that sweet jingling which is acclaimed by
    melodious cries from the throat of
Kalinda's daughter's white swans which float
    on the lotus ponds of Kamalā.

18. Let him play in my fond heart—the Final Beatitude
    whose sweet lips
with flute notes flutter the lotus minds of
    silent sages,
whose long wide eyes are a tender red and
    filled with compassion,
whose hair bristles thickly when pressed to
    Kamalā's jar-like breasts.

14. mādhuryavāridhimadāndhataraṃgabhaṅgī-
śṛṅgārasaṃkulitaśītakiśoraveṣam /
āmandahāsalalitānanacandrabimbam
ānandasaṃplavam anu plavatāṃ mano me //

15. avyājamañjulamukhāmbujamugdhabhāvair
āsvādyamānanijaveṇuvinodanādam /
ākrīḍatām aruṇapādasaroruhābhyām
ārdre madīyahṛdaye bhuvanārdram ojaḥ //

16. maṇinūpuravācālaṃ
vande tac caraṇaṃ vibhoḥ /
lalitāni yadīyāni
lakṣmāṇi vrajavīthiṣu //

17. mama cetasi sphuratu vallavīvibhor
maṇinūpurapraṇayi mañju śiñjitam /
kamalāvanecarakalindakanyakā-
kalahaṃsakaṇṭhakalakūjitādṛam //

18. taruṇāruṇakuruṇāmayavipulāyatanayanaṃ
kamalākucakalaśībharakulakīṛtapulakam /
muralīravataralīkṛtamunimānasanalinaṃ
mama khelatu madacetasi madhurādharam amṛtam //

19. With half opened lotus eyes the primal
in the form of a boy kisses to confusion
the joyous sweet moon faces of the young
wives of Vraja.
Let some such of his moods be manifest in my
mind through the music of his flute.

20. Where tinkling bracelets sound softly and a
slipping yellow garment is held up by the hand,
where long tresses gradually fall loose
and a peacock feather ornament slips,
there the lord's form, whose every gesture
and aspect is fickle and wavering, is held
back by the arms of his fond consort
as he rises from the amorous couch. Let
his form be reflected in my mind.

21. We do reverence the lord's pretence at sleeping
with playfully closed eyes
where the conversational sallies between the
young wives of Vraja are so affecting to the
ear of the hearer that
a tender smile—although held back—as it were
oozes gently drop by drop
and hair begins to show standing straight on
end like sprouts of love.

22. Let us go to the woods of austerity
full of bright leaves and shoots,
or let us go within the milkmaids' breasts.
If we heed not the dancing feet in
Vṛndāvana,
we 'll find no other to worship.

23. When will I find the boy who is consecrated to the
kingship of all things with sweet forms?
He is accompanied by flute notes pouring out
rich like nectar.

19. āmugdham ardhanayanāmbujacumbyamāna-
harṣākulavrajavadhūmadhurānanendoḥ /
ārabdhaveṇuravam ādikiśoramūrter
āvirbhavantu mama cetasi ke 'pi bhāvāḥ //

20 kalakvaṇitakaṅkaṇaṃ karaniruddhapītāmbaraṃ
kramaprasṛtakuntalaṃ galitabarhabhūṣaṃ vibhoḥ /
vapuḥ prakṛticāpalaṃ praṇayinībhujāyantritaṃ
mama sphuratu mānase madanakeliśayyotthitam //

21. stokastokanirudhyamānamṛdulaprasyandimandasmitaṃ
premodbhedanirargalaprasṛmarapravyaktaromodgamam /
śrotuḥ śrotramanoharavrajavadhūlīlāmithojalpitaṃ
mithyāsvāpam upāsmahe bhagavataḥ krīḍānimīladdṛśaḥ //

22. vicitrapatrāṅkuraśāli bālā-
stanāntaraṃ yāma vanāntaraṃ vā /
apāsya vṛndāvanapādalāsyam
upāsyam anyan na vilokayāmaḥ //

23. sārdhaṃ samṛddhair amṛtāyamānair
ātāyamānair muralīninādaiḥ /
mūrdhābhiṣiktaṃ madhurākṛtīnāṃ
bālaṃ kadā nāma vilokayiṣye //

24. When will that child, adorned with a
peacock plume, soothe and cool our eyes
with a tender moon face marked by the
falling honey dew of gentle laughter?

25. O Kṛṣṇa-moon, soothe and cool my sight
by your wondrous play which supports
the world,
by the glory of a childhood touched with
first youth,
and by a sidelong gaze coloured with
tenderness.

26. When will he cast one glance on me from eyes blue like
Kālindī's lily petals and tremulous as
if on rising waves of compassion?
And the sounds of his flute's play which soothe
like the moon on the matted locks of
Kandarpa's opponent, Śiva—
when will they give my heart ineffable joy.

27. The milkmaids tell, O Lord,
how inconstant your gaze, how tender your talk,
how graceful and strong the slow measure of your
stride,
how deep your embrace, how intoxicating and
distracting your smile.

28. May I see your splendour, which is the most
magnificent in the three worlds,
which is in your many open smiles, your long wide
eyes,
which is closely embraced by the women of
Vraja,
which endlessly provides clusters of blossoms
which are streams of blue light.

24. śiśirīkurute kadā nu naḥ
śikhipicchābharaṇaḥ śiśur dṛśoḥ /
yugalaṃ vigalanmadhudrava-
smitamudrāmṛdunā mukhendunā //

25. kāruṇyakarburakaṭākṣanirīkṣaṇena
tāruṇyasaṃvalitaśaiśavavaibhavena /
āpuṣṇatā bhuvanam adbhutavibhrameṇa
śrīkṛṣṇacandra śiśirīkuru locanaṃ me //

26. kadā vā kālindīkuvalayadalaśyāmataralāḥ
kaṭākṣā lakṣyante kim api karuṇāvīcinicitāḥ /
kadā vā kandarpapratibhaṭajaṭācandraśiśirāḥ
kam apy antastoṣaṃ dadhati muralīkelininadāḥ //

27. adhīram ālokitam ārdrajalpitaṃ
gataṃ ca gambhīravilāsamantharam /
amandam āliṅgitam ākulonmada-
smitaṃ ca te nātha vadanti gopikāḥ //

28.* astokasmitabharam āyatāyatākṣaṃ
niḥśeṣastanamṛditaṃ vrajāṅganābhiḥ /
niḥsīmastabakitanīlakāntidhāraṃ
dṛśyāsaṃ tribhuvanasundaraṃ mahas te //

29. Bless me with your gentle eyes
which move to the music of the flute.
If blessed by you, I'll need no other;
if not, no other can help.

30. I place my trembling hands together and,
given voice by increase of a ceaseless
misery, I pray,
"O Lord, you who are the Ocean of Mercy, just
one time, anoint me with a drop of
the goodwill from your glance."

31. We have become anxious to see you as the boy
who bears well the peacock feather crest,
who is alluring to the lotus eyes of young women,
whose berry face is ready to subdue the lotus
moon.

32. If you would call to mind that your boyhood
is the wonder of the three worlds,
then you would come to know, as I do, my deep
desire
and would tell me how sometimes to see with
my very eyes your lovely lotus face graced by
the play of your flute.

33. The words you exchange with the impassioned
milkmaids—with your wide and
dancing accompaniment to the grace of their
wit—overflow with nectar and are
buoyant with youth.
They stir in the hearts of the good.

34. When, again, will the Ocean of Mercy
rise before me with the beneficent
power of a moon face
and interrupt my meditation with the nectar
of music from divine flute play?

29. mayi prasādaṃ madhuraiḥ kaṭākṣair
vaṃśīninādānucarair vidhehi /
tvayi prasanne kim ihā 'parair nas
tvayy aprasanne kim ihā 'parair naḥ //

30. nibaddhamugdhāñjalir eṣa yāce
nīrandhradainyonnatimuktakaṇṭhaḥ /
dayāmbudhe deva bhavatkaṭākṣa-
dākṣiṇyaleśena sakṛn niṣiñca //

31. picchāvataṃsaracanocitakeśapāśe
pīnastanīnayanapaṅkajalobhanīye /
candrāravingavijayodyatavaktrabimbe
cāpalyam eti nayanaṃ tava śaiśave naḥ //

32. tvacchaiśavaṃ tribhuvanādbhutam ity avaihi
maccāpalaṃ ca mama vā tava vā 'dhigamyam /
tat kiṃ karomi viralaṃ muralīvilāsi
mugdhaṃ mukhāmbujam udīkṣitum īkṣaṇābhyām //

33. paryācitāmṛtarasāni padārthabhaṅgī-
valgūni valgitaviśālavilocanāni /
bālyādhikāni madavallavabhāminībhir
bhāve luṭhanti sukṛtāṃ tava jalpitāni //

34. punaḥ prasannena mukhendutejasā
puro 'vatīrṇasya kṛpāmahāmbudheḥ /
tad eva līlāmuralīravāmṛtaṃ
samādhivighnāya kadā nu me bhavet //

35.* I long to hold in my restless gaze the
playful boy who is a balm to the sight;
he has roused in my mind an indescribable
agitation by his glances—tender,
innocent, and inconstant.

36. By the perturbation of your trembling
lower lip
and by the abundance of your tender
joyous flute notes:
by any such of your charms
you torment my heart—alas, alas.

37. Before some affliction comes to strike hard
let my limbs and unloose their joints,
let, O Lord, the stream of my consciousness
be made twofold by the moonlight
from your moon face.

38. Before the tenth age of man comes upon me from some
flaw to make all things dark,
let me attend your full moon face while it
sounds the flute and makes a playground
for your sweet expressions.

39. I give ear to the tinkling of jewelled
anklets
which is flooded by an echoing tide of
flute notes
from the Ocean of Compassion,
whose flooding tides are worshiped
by playful currents from the gaze of
rolling eyes.

40. O Lord, O Beloved, the only kin of all the world,
O Frisking One, O Kṛṣṇa, O only Ocean of compassion,
O Master, O Lover, the delight of all eyes.
Oh when will you come where I can see you?

35.* bālena mugdhacapalena vilokitena
manmānase kim api cāpalam udvahantam /
lolena locanarasāyanam īkṣaṇena
līlākiśoram upagūhitum utsuko 'smi //

36. adhīrabimbādharavibhrameṇa
harṣārdraveṇusvarasaṃpadā ca /
anena kenā 'pi manohareṇa
hā hanta hā hanta mano dunoṣi //

37. yāvan na me nikhilamarmadṛḍhābhighātaṃ
niḥsandhibandhanam udeti sa ko 'pi tāpaḥ /
tāvad vibho bhavatu tāvakavaktracandra-
candrātapadviguṇitā mama cittadhārā //

38. yāvan na me naradaśā daśamī kuto 'pi
randhrād udeti timirīkṛtasarvabhāvā /
lāvaṇyakelisadanaṃ tava tāvad eva
lakṣyāsam utkvaṇitaveṇu mukhendubimbam //

39. ālolalocanavilokitakelidhārā-
nīrājitāgrasaraṇeḥ karuṇāmburāśeḥ /
ārdrāṇi veṇuninadaiḥ pratinādapūrair
ākarṇayāmi maṇinūpuraśiñjitāni //

40. he deva he dayita he bhuvanaikabandho
he kṛṣṇa he capala he karuṇaikasindho /
he nātha he ramaṇa he nayanābhirāma
hā hā kadā bu bhavitā 'si padaṃ dṛśor me //

41. Oh how am I to get through
these empty wretched days
without seeing you, O Hari,
O kin of the unprotected,
    the only ocean of compassion.

42. What can we do about it? Whom can we tell all the things
    we have done on account of our longing?
Let the passion in our heart tell another
    more rewarding story.
It has continued too long—our wretched
    abject thirst for Kṛṣṇa
whose sweet smile, whose sweet stance
    rejoice the heart and eye.

43. Oh, luck is not with me
to catch him in my arms
or to hold in my gaze
his lively baby glances.

44. When shall I see your lotus face
with its always smiling dawn-red lips
joyously swelling the charming flute
    song
which is sweetly accompanied by
    half closed eyes that widen and dance?

45. When will the time come when that kind
    child
will look on me from his lotus eyes
long with delight and soothing like a
    balm?
His eyes roll wondrously with sapphire
    irises set in red.

41. amūny adhanyāni dināntarāṇi
hare tvadālokanam antareṇa /
anāthabandho karuṇaikasindho
hā hanta hā hanta kathaṃ nayāmi //

42. kim iha kṛṇumaḥ kasya brūmaḥ kṛtaṃ kṛtam āśayā
kathayatu kathām anyāṃ dhanyām aho hṛdayeśayaḥ /
madhuramadhurasmerākāre manonayanotsave
kṛpaṇakṛpaṇā kṛṣṇe tṛṣṇā ciraṃ bata lambate //

43. ābhyāṃ vilocanābhyām
ambhoruhalolalocanaṃ bālam /
dorbhyām api parirabdhuṃ
dūre mama hanta daivasāmagrī //

44. aśrāntasmitam aruṇāruṇādharoṣṭhaṃ
harṣārdradviguṇamanojñaveṇugītam /
vibhrāmyadvipulavilocanārdhamugdhaṃ
vīkṣiṣye tava vadanāmbujaṃ kadā nu //

45. līlāyatābhyāṃ rasaśītalābhyāṃ
nīlāruṇābhyāṃ nayanāmbujābhyām /
ālokayed adbhutavibhramābhyāṃ
kāle kadā kāruṇikaḥ kiśoraḥ //

46. My eyes search out the enchanting form of
Murāri
with his thick locks tied to a peacock
feather plume
with his happy dancing eyes and sweet
cherry lips
with his soft honied laugh—and his divine
play as a tortoise support to
Mt. Mandara's churning stick.

47. We are in search of the unfathomable excess
of perfected sweetness.
It has enchanted the world to stupefaction
by the overwhelming grace of its sidelong
lotus glances,
and its charming lotus face, which has stolen
for its complexion the dark rain cloud
colour, is languid after so much exertion,
and has only the play of the crest made of
an impassioned peacock's feather.

48. His face which charms the three worlds can
be seen at any time by the young
women of Vraja,
but the forest hermits must seek him always
further along their paths.
He is not even to be found in the eternal
words of the Vedas.
When can I hope to see the god who is
like the just opening bud of the blue
water lily?

49. When shall I see the god who is the
beloved
with rolling eyes which delight the
sight.
From his merry lotus face he looks out
timidly
and then through the holes of his flute he
sings a teasing song.

46. bahulacikurabhāraṃ baddhapicchāvataṃsaṃ
capalacapalanetraṃ cārubimbādharoṣṭham /
madhuramṛdulahāsaṃ mandaroddhāralīlaṃ
mṛgayati nayanaṃ me mugdhaveṣaṃ murāreḥ //

47. bahulajaladacchāyācoraṃ vilāsabharālasaṃ
madaśikhiśikhālīlottaṃsaṃ manojñamukhāmbujam /
kam api kamalāpāṅgodagraprasannajagajjaḍaṃ
madhurimaparīpākodrekaṃ vayaṃ mṛgayāmahe //

48. parāmṛśyaṃ dūre pathi pathi munīnāṃ vrajavadhū-
dṛśā dṛśyaṃ śaśvat tribhuvanamanohārivadanam /
anāmṛśyaṃ vācām anidamudayānām api kadā
darīdṛśye devaṃ daradalitanīlotpalanibham //

49. līlānanāmbujam adhīram udīkṣamāṇaṃ
narmāṇi veṇuvivareṣu niveśayantam /
ḍolāyamānanayanam nayanābhirāmaṃ
devam kadā nu dayitaṃ vyatilokayiṣye //

50. In this mind, ever fond of portraiture
from the libertine tradition,
the boyishness of Mukunda is delineated
constantly
with the form, which pleases the aesthete,
and the moon face—a light coming from the
lower lip wet with the honey of soft
sentimental smiles—cherished by
the full moon.

51. I am lost in the god whose eyes are like
lotuses: Their beauty is magnified when
they are gently pressed open by the rays
of the warming sun.
I am lost in the sweetness of his moon face
which is intoxicated with the excitements
of his own victorious sport at amorous
combat with the young women of Vraja.

59. I am lost in the god who is the viscid
lake where flows the nectar of melodious
sounds from a flute more lightly played
for the fingering of his lotus petal hands.
I am lost in the sweetness of the jewel,
his lower lip, ever carrying bursts
of gentle laughter expressing the excess
of his happy nature.

53. I am lost in the god whose chest shines with
saffron paint from the jar-like breasts
of ardent milkmaids roused to amorous
assault by the flowery arrows of the Love
God.
I am lost in the sweetness of his lotus face
which is ever magnified with a beauty stolen
from the moon by a soft smile
touched by passion.

50. lagnaṃ muhur manasi lampaṭasaṃpradāya-
lekhāvalehini rasajñamanojñaveṣam /
rajyanmṛdusmitamadhusnapitādharāṃśu
rākendulālitamukhendu mukundabālyam //

51. ahimakarakaranikaramṛdumṛditalakṣmī-
sarasatarasarasiruhasadṛśadṛśi deve /
vrajayuvatiratikalahavijayanijalīlā-
madamuditavadanaśaśimadhurimaṇi līye //

52. karakamaladalakalitalalitataravaṃśī-
kalaninadagaladamṛtaghanasarasi deve /
sahajarasabharabharitadarahasitavīthī-
satatavahadadharamaṇimadhurimaṇi līye //

53. kusumaśaraśarasamarakupitamadagopī-
kucakalaśaghusṛṇarasalasadurasi deve /
madalulitamṛduhasitamuṣitaśaśiśobhā-
muhuradhikamukhakamalamadhurimaṇi līye //

54. I crave to see the small person of Vraja who
bewitches all the world.
His black eyebrows are curved; his eyelashes are
not wanting in thickness.
His affectionate eyes are lively; his gentle
speech is tender.
His lower lip is red; His clear flute notes
sound softly.

55. That boyishness and that lotus face,
that compassion and those playful sidelong
glances
that beauty and that glory of his languid
smile—
truly, truly, these are hard to find
among the gods.

56. On every path we see Murāri's child form
with the very dark cheeks newly aglow.
It has come alive
for the one fixed purpose of quieting all
distresses
for those whose heart is full of faith.

57. His top-knot has a peacock plume and his body the
beauty of an emerald pillar.
His face is intensely sweet with dazzling smiles, and
his child's eye is lively.
His words are soothing with docile youth, but
his graceful stance is as formidable as that of a
mad elephant.
Who is this who thus enters with measured gait the lanes
of Mathurā?

54. ānamrām asitabhruvor upacitām akṣīṇapakṣmānkureṣv
ālolām anurāgiṇor nayanor ārdrāṃ mṛdau jalpite /
ātāmrām adharāmṛte madakalām amlānavaṃśīsvaneṣv
āśāste mama locanaṃ vrajaśiśor mūrtiṃ jaganmohinīm //

55. tat kaiśoraṃ tac ca vaktrāravindaṃ
tat kāruṇyaṃ te ca līlākaṭākṣāḥ /
tat saundaryaṃ sā ca mandasmitaśrīḥ
satyaṃ satyaṃ durlabhaṃ daivateṣu //

56. viśvopaplavaśamanaikabaddhadīkṣam
viśvāsastabakitacetasāṃ janānām /
praśyāmapratinavakāntikandalārdraṃ
paśyāmaḥ pathi pathi śaiśavaṃ murāreḥ //

57. mauliś candrakabhūṣaṇo marakatastambhābhirāmaṃ vapur
vaktraṃ citravimugdhahāsamadhuraṃ bāle vilole dṛśau /
vācaḥ śaiśavaśītalā madagajaślāghyā vilāsasthitir
mandaṃ mandam aye ka eṣa mathurāvīthīm ito gāhate //

58. His feet, which are sunbeams, defeat the light
of lotus ponds and are awarded Lakṣmī who
lives in the lotus.
His hands fondly play the flute and complete
the beauty of their art.
His arms make a vessel of love which pours
the waters of loving tenderness for the
fawn-eyed young women of Vraja.
His face is beyond the scope of speech. Oh what
is this childish splendour.

59. The peacock's tail feather is abundant ornament for his
costume. Nothing else is necessary.
His face needs only the bright marking of his own
lower lip which is the source of floods of
radiant beauty.
His glory is created of fashion and adornment by arts
whose manifestations are not heeded by
those of little understanding.
How bright it is! Oh how dazzling, oh how bright
and dazzling!

60. Mother, my three worlds are filled with the
child who is my desire.
Before me he makes full the indescribable glory
of his play.
In other directions my eye is witness to it.
Bu oh how can it be that he is so far away from
the grasp of my hand.

61. When the frisking adventures of the Lord?
When his thick locks and crowding curls?
When his soft words? When his large eyes?
When his sweet lips? When his sweet face?

62. If the Lord is surrounded by the beguiling
strains of his flute song,
when will he, who is friend to us the distressed,
be able to hear our repeated cry,
"Protect us, O Abode of Mercy."

58. pādau pādavinirjitāmbujavanau padmālayālambitau
pāṇī veṇuvinodanapraṇayiṇau paryāptaśilpaśriyau /
bāhū dauhṛdabhājanaṃ mṛgadṛśāṃ mādhuryadhārākirau
vaktraṃ vāgviṣayātilaṅghitam aho bālaṃ kim etan mahaḥ //

59. barhaṃ nāma vibhūṣaṇaṃ bahumataṃ veṣāya śeṣair alaṃ
vaktraṃ citraviṣeśakāntilaharīvinyāsadhanyādharam /
silpair alpadhiyām agamyavibhavaiḥ śṛṅgārabhaṅgīmayaṃ
citraṃ citram aho vicitram aha ho citraṃ vicitraṃ mahaḥ //

60. agre samagrayati kām api kelilakṣmīm
anyāsu dikṣv api vilocanam eva sākṣi /
hā hanta hastapathadūram aho kim etad
āśākiśoramayam amba jagattrayaṃ me //

61. cikuraṃ bahulaṃ viralaṃ bhramaraṃ
mṛdulaṃ vacanaṃ vipulaṃ nayanam /
adharaṃ madhuraṃ vadanaṃ madhuraṃ
capalaṃ caritaṃ ca kadā nu vibhoḥ //

62. paripālaya naḥ kṛpālaye 'ty
asakṛt kranditam ārtabāndhavaḥ /
muralīmṛdulasvanāntare
vibhur ākarṇayitā kadā nu naḥ //

63. When will he see me with his wide long eyes?
What disaster will focus the attention of him who
is the sea of mercy with the aroma of
childhood?

64.* Oh that I may see the boy who has the
deep green complexion of an emerald,
the sweetness of cherry lips and the charm
of a slow smile,
the cool balm of a nectar voice and the refreshing
fall of arrowy glances,
the magnitude of eyes like dawn and the fanfare
of a flute song?

65. The wondrous childhood of the Love God's
father is
sweeter than sweetness and
more inconstant than inconstancy.
Oh, it steals my heart away. What am I to do?

66. When will it be that I shall see the boy
who is a treasury of playful graces, who is
large of chest and lotus eye,
mild of slow smile and merry talk,
sweet of cherry lip and flute song?

67. It is those who have heaped up merit,
the fortunate, who see
the First Principle as a man crowned with
a peacock plume—
his eyes heavy with the burden of his
tender gaze and
his lower lip sweet with the nectar of an
open smile.

68. Is it the very god of love or a wheel of sweet
radiance?
Is it sweetness itself or the nectar of the
mind's eye?
Is it the joy of the flute or the beloved of
my life?
It is a child who rises before my eyes.

63. kadā nu kasyāṃ nu vipaddaśāyāṃ
kaiśoragandhiḥ karuṇāmbudhir naḥ /
vilocanābyāṃ vipulāyatābhyāṃ
ālokayiṣyan viṣayīkaroti //

64.* madhuram adharabimbe mañjulaṃ mandahāse
śiśiram amṛtanāde śītalaṃ dṛṣṭipāte /
vipulam aruṇanetre viśrutaṃ veṇunāde
marakatamaṇinīlaṃ bālam ālokaye nu //

65. mādhuryād api madhuraṃ
manmathatātasya kim api kaiśoram /
cāpalyād api capalaṃ
ceto bata harati hanta kiṃ kurmaḥ //

66. vakṣaḥsthale ca vipulaṃ nayanotpale ca
mandasmite ca mṛdulaṃ madajalpite ca /
bimbādhare ca madhuraṃ muralīrave ca
bālaṃ vilāsanidhim ākalaye kadā nu //

67. ārdrāvalokitadhurā pariṇaddhanetram
āviṣkṛtasmitasudhāmadhurādharoṣṭham /
ādyaṃ pumāṃsam avataṃsitabarhibarham
ālokayanti kṛtinaḥ kṛtapuṇyapuñjāḥ //

68. māraḥ svayaṃ madhuradyutimaṇḍalaṃ nu
mādhuryam eva nu manoayanāmṛtaṃ nu /
veṇor mudā nu mama jīvitavallabho nu
bālo 'yam abhyudayate mama locanābhyām //

69. It is a young boy whose face with dancing
eyes brightens the countenance of all
the quarters.
Dressed in the suitable trappings of the
cowpen,
he extracts the milk of joy for our eyes.

70. As a cool balm to the eyes he comes
with his peacock feather crest and the
tinkling of many ornaments,
with swinging arms and the play of lively
eyes
in the full moon of his lotus face tender
with a gentle smile.

71. With too many soft smiles from his tender moon
face
he intoxicates my heart and enters deep within
it—
this boy with the refreshing lively gaze
who is the ornament of the young assembly of
cowherds.

72. What is this where the paths of the earth
sound with flute notes?
Before our eyes it pours down what must be
streams of love.
This is he who has come from the paths of the
gods, the beloved who is so hard for us to
find,
the god who is adored by the three worlds,
the living god!

73. He is here! He has come to life for me:
deep blue like the *tamāla* tree,
friendly with twinkling star eyes,
the joy of his full moon face made real,
and the sportive music of his flute made to sound.

69. bālo 'yam ālolavilocanena
vaktreṇa citrīkṛtadiṅmukhena /
veṣeṇa ghoṣocitabhūṣaṇena
mugdhena dugdhe nayanotsavaṃ naḥ //

70. āndolitāgrabhujam ākulanetralīlaṃ
mandasmitārdravadanābujacandrabimbam /
śiñjānabhūṣaṇaśataṃ śikhipicchamauli
śītaṃ vilocanarasāyanam abhyupaiti //

71. paśupālabālapariṣadvibhūṣaṇaḥ
śiśur eṣa śītalavilolalocanaḥ /
mṛdulasmitārdravadanendusaṃpadā
madayan madīyahṛdayaṃ vigāhate //

72. kim idam adharavīthīkḷptavaṃśīnādaṃ
kirati nayanayor naḥ kām api premadhārām /
tad idam amaravīthīvallabhaṃ durlabhaṃ nas
tribhuvanakamanīyaṃ daivataṃ jīvitaṃ ca //

73. tad idam upanataṃ tamālanīlaṃ
taralavilocanatārakābhirāmam /
muditamuditavaktracandrabimbaṃ
mukharitaveṇuvilāsi jīvitaṃ me //

74. The far end of inconstancy, the only end of the
inconstant Lakṣmī's experience.
The far end of art, the artistic end of
Brahmā's endeavour.
The far end of fragrance, the far end of all
wondrous manifestations.
The far end of all auspicious lots. He is here
at the far end of Vraja's lot.

75. The culmination of my merit from good deeds—ah,
it comes to life before my eyes:
Wearing a moon face, which is doubly refreshing
with sweet tenderness,
and watering—with streams of nectar flowing
down the pathway of the flute—
the garden of my voice which thrives under the
stimulating benedicition.

76. All hail to the splendour which herds cows
and protects people,
which lies on the hips and breasts of Rādhā
and reclines on Śeṣa, the snake afloat in
the deluge.

77. It is here! Hail, all hail to the splendour
whose regal radiance is coloured by the
auspicious red paint
from the breasts of the cherished milkmaids.
Hail to the splendour, the primal spirit,
whose way is known by the flute song.

78. Before me it comes to life—engrossed in play:
A lovely flute song is played in time to
a youthful lotus petal foot
weighted with gently tinkling anklets.

79. He anoints my two ears with the nectar of
playful flute notes and rouses them to
passionate attention,
and then, with an abundance of playful side
glances overflowing with joy, he comes
to befriend my eyes. They will accept no
other.

74. cāpalyasīma capalānubhavaikasīma
cāturyasīma caturānanaśilpasīma /
saurabhyasīma sakalādbhutakelisīma
saubhāgyasīma tad idaṃ vrajabhāgyasīma //

75. mādhuryeṇa dviguṇaśiśiraṃ vaktracandraṃ vahantī
vaṃśīvīthīvigaladamṛtasrotasā secayantī /
madvāṇīnāṃ viharaṇapadaṃ mattasaubhāgyabhājāṃ
matpuṇyānāṃ pariṇatir aho netrayoḥ saṃnidhatte //

76. tejase 'stu namo dhenu-
pāline lokapāline /
rādhāpayodharotsaṅga-
śāyine śeṣaśāyine //

77. dhenupāladayitāstanasthalī-
dhanyakuṅkumasanāthakāntaye /
veṇugītagatimūlavedhase
tejase tad idam oṃ namo namaḥ //

78. mṛdukvaṇannūpuramanthareṇa
bālena pādāmbujapallavena /
anusvananmañjulaveṇugītam
āyāti me jīvitam āttakeli //

79. so 'yaṃ vilāsamuralīninadāmṛtena
siñcann udañcitam idaṃ madakarṇayugmam /
āyāti me nayanabandhur ananyabandhor
ānandakandalitakelikaṭākṣalakṣmīḥ //

80. The god who walks with the swinging grace
of an elephant looks on me from afar with
a gaze filled with Rādhā's sidelong glances.
He comes near—his mouth, ornamented by his teeth,
opens to a confluence of flute notes which
reach the heart.

81. Here he comes. Here comes the god whose flute
is accompanied by
his wondrous feet which are a refuge for the
unprotected,
which frisk in the most joyful divine play of all
three worlds,
and which sparkle over all the quaters with the
most intense of blazing ornaments.

82. It is he who stole the inward austerities of
great sages.
It is he who stole the clothes of the perturbed
young women of Vraja.
It is he who stole the pride of Indra, the lord of the
highest of the three worlds.
It is he who has stolen the lotus of my heart.

83. Oh, my eye beholds
this glory which is the whole world
of omniscience and innocence.
It has attained *nirvāṇa*.

84. Because his moon face has appeared,
that certain person called Kṛṣṇa
promotes the superfluous beauty
of the cool rayed moon
and divides the ocean of my thirst.

85. Again and again my mind kisses Murāri's
lotus face of the sweet lower lip.
It is that face which blesses all suppliants
with the benediction of his light red
eyes.

80. dūrād vilokayati vāraṇakhelagāmī
rādhākaṭākṣabharitena vilokitena /
ārād upaiti hṛdayaṃgamaveṇunāda-
veṇīmukhena daśanābharaṇena devaḥ //

81. tribhuvanasarasābhyāṃ divyalīlākulābhyāṃ
diśi diśi taralābhyāṃ dṛptabhūṣāparābhyām /
aśāraṇaśaraṇābhyām adbhutābhyāṃ padābhyām
ayam ayam anukūjadveṇur āyāti devaḥ //

82. so 'yaṃ munīndrajanamānasatāpahārī
so 'yaṃ madavrajavadhūvasanāpahārī /
so 'yaṃ tṛtīyabhuvaneśvaradarpahārī
so 'yaṃ madīyahṛdayāmburuhāpahārī //

83. sarvajñatve ca maugdhye ca
sārvabhaumam idaṃ mahaḥ /
nirviśan nayanaṃ hanta
nirvāṇapadam aśnute //

84. puṣṇānam etat punaruktaśobhām
uṣṇetarāṃśor udayān mukhendoḥ /
tṛṣṇāmburāśiṃ dviguṇīkaroti
kṛṣṇāhvayaṃ kiṃ cana jīvitaṃ me //

85. tad etad ātāmravilocanaśrī-
saṃbhāvitāśeṣavinamravargam /
muhur murārer madhurādharoṣṭhaṃ
mukhāmbujaṃ cumbati mānasaṃ me //

86. Behold Glory which has taken the form of a young
boy who is nectar for the eyes.
His hands teach a succession of graceful
gestures to the autumn lotus.
His feet jump over the first sprouts of the tree
of wishes,
and the brightness of his eyes destroys the
arrogance of their analogues in all three
worlds.

87. Manifesting itself in a priceless condition,
approved by the eye of the Love God,
Bliss takes the form of the lord whose dominion
includes the slopes which are the breasts of the
beautiful wives of Vraja.
Everyday he advances while playing charming
games,
and with the tender charm of a tender smile
he even reaches and dominates the heart of
Arundhatī, the faithful wife of Vasiṣṭha.

88. All hail to the lord, my life, who constantly
attends and lovingly drinks from the mouth
of the flute.
His new blooming youth is adorned with the last
flickering of childhood.
His eyes flash with passion, and the nectar of
his innocent smile intoxicates.
He infatuates the three worlds.

89. Those wondrous lotus feet are here.
Those wondrous lotus eyes are here.
That wondrous lotus face is here.
That wonder is here again. Oh mother,
the wonder!

86. karau śaradijāmbujakramavilāsaśikṣāgurū
padau vibudhapādapaprathamapallavollaṅghinau /
dṛśau dalitadurmadatribhuvanopamānaśriyau
vilokaya vilocanāmṛtam aho mahaḥ śaiśavam //

87. ācinvānam ahany ahany ahani sākārān vihārakramān
ārundhānam arundhatīhṛdayam apy ārdrasmitārdraśriyā /
ātanvānam ananyajanmanayanaślāghyām anarghyāṃ daśām
ānandaṃ vrajasundarīstanataṭīsāmrājyam ujjṛmbhate //

88. tad ucchvasitayauvanaṃ taralaśaiśavālaṃkṛtaṃ
madacchuritalocanaṃ madanamugdhahāsāmṛtam /
pratikṣaṇavilokanaṃ praṇayapītavaṃśīmukhaṃ
jagattrayavimohanaṃ jayati māmakaṃ jīvitam //

89. citraṃ tad etac caraṇāravindaṃ
citraṃ tad etan nayanāravindam /
citraṃ tad etad vadanāravindaṃ
citraṃ tad etat punar amba citram //

90. I do homage to the large emerald,
the central stone in the necklace of milkmaids
and the only ornament in the whole world
which adorns the jar-like breasts of Lakṣmī.

91. The lord Kṛṣṇa somehow keeps himself quite
neat although he has sprouts of heat
playing on his round mirror-like cheeks
and his beloved consort, Loveliness, is
smeared with bits of ruined make up,
gotten during a hair pulling fight, from another
beloved consort, Beauty.

92. Sweet, sweet, the body of this god.
Sweet, sweet, the face. Very sweet.
Oh, this gentle smile with the smell
of honey.
Sweet, sweet, sweet, sweet.

93. I seek the shelter of tee world, him,
who consented to assume a human form,
who is bedecked with a peacock feather,
whose entire property consists of the
erotic sentiment.

94. To this very day the thousands of Upaniṣadic
seers have never found you before their
eyes or in their heart.
O Master, why would you be merciful to me and
come within the sight of my eyes?

95. What is this brightness of your moon face,
O Keśava?
What is this wondrous figure which is
beyond description?
This is the brightness, this is the wondrous
figure for my delight. I fold my hands
and do reverence to you again and again
and again.

90. akhilabhuvanaikabhūṣaṇam
adhibhūṣitajaladhiduhitṛkucakumbham /
vrajayuvatihāravallī-
marakatanāyakamahāmaṇim //

91. kāntākacagrahaṇavigrahalabdhalakṣmī-
khaṇḍāṅgarāgalavarañjitamañjulaśrīḥ /
gaṇḍasthalīmukuramaṇḍalakhelamāna-
gharmāṅkuraḥ kim api gumphati kṛṣṇadevaḥ //

92. madhuraṃ madhuraṃ vapur asya vibhor
madhuraṃ madhuraṃ vadanaṃ madhuram /
madhugandhi mṛdusmitam etad aho
madhuraṃ madhuraṃ madhuraṃ madhuram //

93. śṛṅgārarasasarvasvaṃ
śikhipicchavibhūṣaṇam /
aṅgīkṛtanarākāram
āśraye bhuvanāśrayam //

94. nā 'dyā 'pi paśyati kadā 'pi na darśanāya
citte tatho 'paniṣadāṃ sudṛśām sahasram /
sa tvaṃ ciraṃ nayanayor anayoḥ padavyāṃ
svāmin kayā nu kṛpayā mama saṃnidhatse //

95. ke 'yaṃ kāntiḥ keśava tvanmukhendoḥ
ko 'yaṃ veṣaḥ ko 'pi vācām abhūmiḥ /
se 'yaṃ so 'yaṃ svādatām añjalis te
bhūyo bhūyo bhūyaśas tvāṃ namāmi //

96. The moon, subdued by your moon face,
has fallen ten times at your feet
and gains, in excessive amount, more
than its original brightness.
How vast is your compassion!

97. How can it be that your face is like a lotus?
When each of the phases of the moon is inferior to
words,
then what can I say? What other one lovely thing in
the world exists,
Kṛṣṇa, so that your face would be like it?

98. If you would be willing to be advised, listen carefully
about something which has not been seen even
by those incomparable poets of old:
The moon, like a lantern, ought for a long time clearly
to undertake the burden of the custom of waving
before your moon face.

99. All hail to your soothing smiles.
They are, as it were, an ocean of nectar
flowing without restraint
and destroying the essence of all other
joys
with unbroken streams of the elixir of
bliss.

100. It is admitted that there are thousands of eminent
aestheticians,
and there are those thousands who have vowed to
completely understand the subtleties of beauty.
We have no quarrel with these people, nor do we
flatter you, O Lord,
but, truly, the fulfillment of loveliness is
realized only in you.

96. vadanenduvinirjitaḥ śaśī
daśadhā deva padaṃ prapadya te /
adhikaṃ śriyaṃ aśnutetarāṃ
tava kāruṇyavijṛmbhitaṃ kiyat //

97. tat tvanmukhaṃ katham ivā 'mbujatulyakakṣyaṃ
vācām avāci nanu parvaṇi parvaṇīndoḥ /
tat kiṃ bruve kim aparaṃ bhuvanaikakāntaṃ
kṛṣṇa tvadānanam anena samaṃ nu yat syāt //

98. śuśrūṣase śṛṇu yadi praṇidhānapūrvaṃ
pūrvair apūrvakavibhir na kaṭākṣitaṃ yat /
nīrājanakramadhurāṃ bhavadānanendor
nirvyājam arhati cirāya śaśipradīpaḥ //

99. akhaṇḍanirvāṇarasapravāhair
vikhaṇḍitāśeṣarasāntarāṇi /
ayantritodvāntasudhārṇavāni
jayanti śītāni tava smitāni //

100. kāmaṃ santu sahasraśaḥ katipaye sārasyadhaureyakāḥ
kāmaṃ vā kamanīyatāparimalasvārājyabaddhavratāḥ /
nai 'vai 'tair vivadāmahe na ca vayaṃ deva priyaṃ brūmahe
yat satyaṃ ramaṇīyatāpariṇatis tvayy eva pāraṃ gatā //

101. When you came to earth, the milkmaids, humbled
by love and eager, lost all modesty and shame,
song seemed to fill with the wine of delight, and the
burden of desire became sweet.
Even from voices such as mine the swelling
melodic strains seem to scatter sweetness.
Unhappy birth had become beneficent.

102. The universe is your home, Lakṣmī your loving consort,
Brahmā and Kāma your sons,
the gods your full thronging attendants.
More wonderful than all this, O Lord, are your
adventures here.

103. Hail to the beneficent lord of
the three worlds
who has a forehead mark of musk
and whose amorous advances are
encouraged by the love play
of the Vraja women.

104. O Lord, there is no other god for me,
no other source of love or longing,
no other knowledge or power,
no other vital energy, no other life.

105. When describing your power,
let our words surge with sweetness.
When thinking of your childhood,
let our thoughts swell with enthusiasm.

106. Your nectar life: the mischievous misdeeds of
childhood, the longing of Rādhā in her
bower, and the sentimental strains of flute
music from your lovely lotus mouth—
let your nectar life, tasted by the tongue of
the fortunate, ever fill my heart.

101. galadvrīḍā lolā madanavinatā gopavanitā
madhusphītaṃ gītaṃ kim api madhurā cāpaladhurā /
samujjṛmbhā gumbhā madhurimakirāṃ mādṛśagirāṃ
tvayi sthāne jāte dadhati capalaṃ janma saphalam //

102. bhavanaṃ bhuvanaṃ vilāsinī śrīs
tanayas tāmarasāsanaḥ smaraś ca /
paricāraparaṃparāḥ surendrās
tad api tvaccaritaṃ vibho vicitram //

103. devas trilokīsaubhāgya-
kasturītilakāṅkuraḥ /
jīyād vrajāṅganānaṅga-
kelilālitavibhramaḥ //

104. premadaṃ ca me kāmadaṃ ca me
vedanaṃ ca me vaibhavaṃ ca me /
jīvanaṃ ca me jīvitaṃ ca me
daivataṃ ca me deva nā 'param //

105. mādhuryeṇa vivardhantāṃ
vāco nas tava vaibhave /
cāpalyena vijṛmbhantāṃ
cintā nas tava śaiśave //

106. yāni tvaccaritāmṛtāni rasanālehyāni dhanyātmanāṃ
ye vā śaiśavacāpalavyatikarā rādhāvarodhonmukhāḥ /
yā vā bhāvitaveṇugītagatayo līlā mukhāmbhoruhe
dhārāvāhikayā vahantu hṛdaye tāny eva tāny eva me //

107. If we have most firm faith in you, O Lord,
then your celestial child form will
bestow good fate on us,
and Mukti, herself, will fold, bud-like,
her hands and honour us;
Dharma, Artha, and Kāma will await our
command.

108. Hail, all hail to you, O Lord.
Your holy name is a benediction to the
three worlds.
Hail, all hail to you, O Lord Kṛṣṇa.
You are the avatar who is as nectar to
the mind, eye, and ear.

109. To you, who are revealed in those emotional states
of pious people which are accompanied by
repeated agitations which clearly become manifest as
uncontrollable possession by an overwhelming
deluge of joy,
to you, the ornament of glorious Gokula, the one
great ocean of loving tenderness shining in the
distance beyond words and thought,
to you, to whatever is that glory you embody,
we do homage.

110. With the production of this verse bouquet
which has the lasting fame of Kṛṣṇa
as its capital and which is the ornament
of Iśānadeva's feet,
Līlāsuka has written about you, O Lord Kṛṣṇa,
this nectar to the ears. May it continue
beyond one hundred aeons.

107. bhaktis tvayi sthiratarā bhagavan yadi syāt
daivena naḥ phalati divyakiśoraveṣaḥ /
muktiḥ svayaṃ mukulitāñjali sevate 'smān
dharmārthakāmagatayaḥ samayapratīkṣāḥ //

108. jaya jaya jaya deva deva deva
tribhuvanamaṅgaladivyanāmadheya /
jaya jaya jaya deva deva kṛṣṇa
śravaṇamanonayanāmṛtāvatāra //

109. tubhyaṃ nirbharaharṣavarṣavivaśāveśasphuṭāvirbhavad-
bhūyaścāpalabhūṣiteṣu sukṛtām bhāveṣu nirbhāsine /
śrīmadgokulamaṇḍanāya manasāṃ vācāṃ ca dūrasphuran-
mādhuryaikamahārṇavāya mahase kasmai cid asmai namaḥ //

110. īśānadevacaraṇābharaṇena nīvī-
dāmodarasthirayaśaḥstabakodgamena /
līlāśukena racitaṃ tava kṛṣṇa deva
karṇāmṛtaṃ vahatu kalpaśatāntare 'pi //

111. Constantly yielding an indescribable rain of nectar
in the openings of the ears
of the fortunate who multiply the sweet fragrance
by way of sweet repetition,
this nectar to the ears about Kṛṣṇa, the lord who
is sunk deep in the mind's eye of us, the
humble and keen-sighted, surges in voices and
ears.

112.* Whenever my eyes open wide in anticipation,
you should show your superhuman self
with the nectar of gentle flute sounds
accompanied
by eyes doubly wide with graciousness.

111. dhanyānāṃ sarasānulāpasaraṇīsaurabhyam abhyasyatāṃ
karṇānāṃ vivareṣu kām api sudhāvṛṣṭiṃ duhānaṃ muhuḥ /
vaśyānāṃ sudṛśāṃ manonayanor magnasya devasya naḥ
karṇānāṃ vacasāṃ vijṛmbhitaṃ aho kṛṣṇasya karṇāmṛtam //

112.* anugrahadviguṇaviśālalocanair
anusvanamṛdumuralīravāmṛtaiḥ /
yato yataḥ prasarati me vilocanaṃ
tatas tataḥ sphuratu tavai 'va vaibhavam //

CENTURY II

1. Daubed with fresh churned butter, gulping
 down milk, and smeared all over with curds,
 Murāri, childishly charming,
removes the misery of the world. Shining
 dark blue like clumps of *tamāla* bushes
 and decorated with a fresh peacock feather,
 may he grant our desire.

2. Seeing the blue beauty of his body, a thirsty herd
 of cows ever start to plunge into it
and a covey of blue throated peacocks call out
 their longing to see it so like a rain cloud.
Milkmaids think it *tamāla* shoots to put in their
 hair and start to cut at it.
May it protect us—the sanctifying beauty of his
 body as it downs and punishes Kāliya.

3. From deep in the pure waters of the Yamunā,
 milkmaids with cajoling word plead with the
 Lord Keśava for their clothes
while they honour him with their flower-like
 eyes which are tremulous with shame and no
 longer vivacious yet shining with love.
May the Lord Keśava protect us.

4. So that I might fill my hollow stomach, I was
 callous and made you dance before wicked men.
 There could be nothing worse than that.
Forgive it, Mother, kind Goddess of Speech, who
 are so pure in heart.
I shall expiate my sins by telling out all the
 glories of Viṣṇu when he came as a cowherd.

ŚATAKA II

1. abhinavanavanītasnigdham āpītadugdhaṃ
dadhikaṇaparidigdhaṃ mugdham aṅgaṃ murāreḥ /
diśatu bhuvanakṛcchracchedi tāpicchaguccha-
cchavi navaśikhipicchālāñchitaṃ vāñchitaṃ naḥ //

2. yāṃ dṛṣṭvā yamunāṃ pipāsur aniśaṃ vyūho gavāṃ gāhate
vidyutvān iti nīlakaṇṭhanivaho yāṃ draṣṭum utkaṇṭhate /
uttaṃsāya tamālapallavam iti cchindanti yāṃ gopikāḥ
kāntiḥ kāliyaśāsanasya vapuṣaḥ sā pāvanī pātu naḥ //

3. devaḥ pāyāt payasi vimale yāmune majjatīnāṃ
yācantīnām anunayapadair vañcitāny aṃśukāni /
lajjālolair alasavilasair unmiṣatpañcabāṇair
gopastrīṇāṃ nayanakusumair arcitaḥ keśavo naḥ //

4. mātar nā 'taḥ param anucitaṃ yat khalānāṃ purastād
astāśaṅkaṃ jaṭharapiṭharīpūrtaye nartitā 'si /
tat kṣantavyaṃ sahajasarale vatsale vāṇi kuryāṃ
prāyaścittaṃ guṇagaṇanayā gopaveṣasya viṣṇoḥ //

5. I do homage to the cowherd, Nanda's son, whose wide eyes
are, as it were, reflections of the blooming red
lotus, and to his happy life in Vṛndāvana.
With one foot crossed in front of the other, he
stands
and keeps filling the flute with his breath while he
opens and closes its holes with the dawn red
rays of his finger tips.

6. He fills his flute with sweet music and goes
along slowly grazing his cattle on the
pastures of Vṛndāvana.
In the Vedas he is reported to be the slayer
of the demons who were ruining Indra's
sacrifices. Tell all about him, O tongue—
this paramour of the milkmaids.

7. In dream I saw the cloud-dark god wreathed
with fresh leaves of sacred basil.
A pendent peacock plume was fastened to the
base of his braided hair,
and in his shimmering yellow clothes he seemed
to be girt by streaks of lightning.
He held me closely in arms like emerald
pillars.

8. Once, Kṛṣṇa took some clothes left on the bank of
a river and got on top of a bower of jasmine
creepers there.
The bewildered girl, caught thus, kept pleading,
"What shall I do?"
Then with frowns and small smiles, with bashfulness
and forthright love, she tried to snatch the clothes
held in the hand of Kṛṣṇa's reflection on the water.

9. In some future life may I earn enough merit
to be born on the banks of the Yamunā as
the sort of bamboo shoot
which would come to know the happiness found
on the lower lip of the good cowherd's
son.

5. aṅgulyagrair aruṇakiraṇair muktasaṃruddharandhraṃ
vāraṃ vāraṃ vadanamarutā veṇum āpūrayantam /
vyatyastāṅghriṃ vikacakamalacchāyavistāranetraṃ
vande vṛndāvanasucaritaṃ nandagopālasūnum //

6. mandaṃ mandaṃ madhuraninadair veṇum āpūrayantaṃ
vṛndaṃ vṛndāvanabhuvi gavāṃ cārayantaṃ carantam /
chandobhāge śatamakhamakhadhvaṃsināṃ dānavānāṃ
hantāraṃ taṃ kathaya rasane gopakanyābhujaṃgam //

7. veṇīmūle viracitaghanaśyāmapicchāvacūḍo
vidyullekhāvalayita iva snigdhapītāmbareṇa /
māṃ āliṅgan marakatamaṇistambhagambhīrabāhuḥ
svapne dṛṣṭas taruṇatulasībhūṣaṇo nīlameghaḥ //

8. kṛṣṇe hṛtvā sicayanicayaṃ kūlakundādhirūḍhe
mugdhā kā cin muhur anunayaiḥ kiṃ nu iti vyāharantī /
sabhrūbhaṅgaṃ sadarahasitaṃ satrapaṃ sānurāgaṃ
chāyāśaureḥ karatalagatāny ambarāṇy ācakarṣa //

9. api januṣi parasminn āttapuṇyo bhaveyaṃ
taṭabhuvi yamunāyās tādṛśo vaṃśanālaḥ /
anubhavati ya eṣa śrīmadābhīrasūnor
adharamaṇisamīpanyāsadhanyām avasthām //

10. O my heart! find Mukunda of the morning lotus
eyes,
who is beautiful with the shimmering peacock
plume fastened to his braid.
He is the sapphire-blue good fortune of the milkmaids.
He is the large root of all the creepers
called the Vedas.

11. O Lady Flute, who have tasted the honey breath
from the smiling lotus face of Mukunda, I salute
you and ask of you today,
"When you reach the jewel lips of Nanda's son,
whisper in his ear and tell him how wretched
I am."

12. I sing praise to the young cowherd who makes an
end to whole tribes of demons,
who is dark like the water filled rain cloud,
who frisks and plays with milkmaids,
whose place is under the wishing tree, whose yellow
clothes are like flashing lightning,
to whom multitudes of god and sages bow, whose
reflection plays in the minds of the good.

13. We serve that singular young cowherd
of the lotus face, lovely and lotus soft,
who delights in playing sweet flute notes
while his lower cherry lip scorns coral.

14. Mādhava puts the mouth of the flute to his lips,
and ever opening and closing
its holes with his light quick fingers,
he pipes sweetly in the forest.

15. See the boy who carries the smell of fresh butter
about his face,
whose words are loaded with the geniality
of a thief,
in whose eyes are false tears,
and who has a gentle dancing about the feet.

10. ayi paricinu cetaḥ prātarambhojanetraṃ
kabarakalitacañcatpicchadāmābhirāmam /
balabhidupalanīlaṃ vallavībhāgadheyaṃ
nikhilanigamavallīmūlakandaṃ mukundam //

11. ayi murali mukundasmeravaktrāravinda-
śvasanamadhurasajñe tvāṃ praṇamyā 'dya yāce /
adharamaṇisamīpaṃ prāptavatyāṃ bhavatyāṃ
kathaya rahasi karṇe maddaśāṃ nandasūnoḥ //

12. sajalajaladanīlaṃ vallavīkelilolaṃ
śritasuratarumūlaṃ vidyudullāsicelam /
natasuramunijālaṃ sanmanobimbalīlaṃ
suraripukulakālaṃ naumi gopālabālam //

13. adharabimbaviḍambitavidrumaṃ
madhuraveṇuninādavinodinam /
kamalakomalakamramukhāmbujaṃ
kam api gopakumāram upāsmahe //

14. adhare viniveśya vaṃśanālaṃ
vivarāṇy asya salīlam aṅgulībhiḥ /
muhur antarayan muhur vivṛṇvan
madhuraṃ gāyati mādhavo vanānte //

15. vadane navanītagandhavāhaṃ
vacane taskaracāturīdhurīṇam /
nayane kuhanāśrum āśrayethāś
caraṇe komalatāṇḍavaṃ kumāram //

16. They say that he, Nanda's son, to protect the
 cowherds on the banks of the Yamunā
drank down a forest fire.
Only such as he can be the protector of us
 who seek protection.

17. That glory, which has a sapphire beauty, is
 incarnate
in the paramour who is respected by the whole
 world
and who can be found in the speculations on
 the Vedas as revealed by Brahmā.
May he lessen all our afflictions.

18. May it be conducive to our pleasure—
 that indescribable form of the young cowherd which
 is the pleasantest thing in all the world,
which is found on the highest peaks of Vedic
 lore and in the hearts of yogis, but is
 easiest to meet among the lotus feet of the
 beautiful women of Vraja.

19. I bow my head to the son of Vasudeva, the baby
 Kṛṣṇa
of the flowing locks, dawn red lips, long eyes,
 and the blue beauty of the flax flower.
He is clothed with the sky and adorned with
 golden ornaments.

20. We do reverence, good fortune incarnate, the son of
 Vasudeva who lived in Vraja.
Circlets of bells sound on his hands and feet;
a golden thread is hung around his hips,
and the side locks of his hair are tied into
 a bud-like knot with pearl strands.

21. I am always thinking of the Oversoul incarnate in
 the flute player with lotus eyes, cloud blue
 complexion, and a peacock feather plume.
He can be found in the Vedāntas and amid the cows
 under the trees of Vṛndāvana.

16. amunā kila gopagopanārthaṃ
yamunārodhasi nandanandanena /
damunā vanasaṃbhavaḥ pape naḥ
kim u nā 'sau śaraṇārthināṃ śaraṇyaḥ //

17. jagadādaraṇīyajārabhāvaṃ
jalajāpatyavacovicāragamyam /
tanutāṃ tanutāṃ śivetarāṇāṃ
suranāthopalasundaraṃ maho naḥ //

18. sā kā 'pi sarvajagatām abhirāmasīmā
kāmāya no bhavatu gopakiśoramūrtiḥ /
yā śekhare śrutigirāṃ hṛdi yogabhājāṃ
pādāmbuje ca sulabhā vrajasundarīṇām //

19. atyantabālam atasīkusumāvabhāsaṃ
digvāsasaṃ kanakabhūṣaṇabhūṣitāṅgam /
visrastakeśam aruṇādharam āyatākṣaṃ
kṛṣṇaṃ namāmi śirasā vasudevasūnum //

20. hastāṅghrinikvaṇitakaṅkaṇakiṅkiṇīkaṃ
madhyenitambam avalambitahemasūtram /
muktākalāpamukulīkṛtakākapakṣaṃ
vandāmahe vrajacaraṃ vasudevabhāgyam //

21. vṛndāvanadrumataleṣu gavāṃ gaṇesu
vedāvasānasamayeṣu ca dṛśyate yat /
tad veṇuvādanaparaṃ śikhipicchacūḍaṃ
brahma smarāmi kamalekṣaṇam abhranīlam //

22. One foot crossed in front of the other and a
peacock plume atop his head,
the mouth of the flute placed at the tilted face—
Just thus may the almight glory, supremely
compassionate, appear for me when life departs.

23. To quiet the loud complaint in the cowherd
village, the mother of the butter thief bound
him by the waist with a churning rope,
and, oh, how that bondage was the entire cause
of a great outcry throughout all the three
worlds which are tucked in the three folds
of his belly.

24. I am a Shaivite and conscientiously say the
Shaivite prayer regularly. I must remind
you that none of this is to be questioned—
yet my thoughts are always on the milkmaid's
child with the smiling face and the blue
beauty of the flax flower.

25. May Rādhā purify the world who, all her thoughts
given up to the Eternal Lord, Kṛṣṇa, kept
churning in a vessel empty of curds.
May the Lord purify the world who, intending to
milk a cow, ropes a bull while he looks with
impatient ardor at Rādhā's breasts fluttering
like a bouquet.

26. We take refuge in Govinda of the moon face,
whose soft front curls are tinged with dust
raised by cows,
whose body is marked by the saffron from the
bosoms of milkmaids,
and who, with playful effort, raises aloft
Govardhana mountain.

22. vyatyastapādam avataṃsitabarhibarhaṃ
sācīkṛtānananiveśitavaṃśanālam /
tejaḥ paraṃ paramakāruṇikaṃ purastāt
prāṇaprayāṇasamaye mama saṃnidhattām //

23. ghoṣapraghoṣaśamanāya matho guṇena
madhye babandha jananī navanītacoram /
tad bandhanaṃ trijagatām udarāśrayāṇām
ākrośakāraṇam aho nitarāṃ babhūva //

24. śaivā vayaṃ na khalu tatra vicāraṇīyaṃ
pañcākṣarījapaparā nitarāṃ tathā 'pi /
ceto madīyam atasīkusumāvabhāsaṃ
smerānanaṃ smarati gopavadhūkiśoram //

25. rādhā punātu jagad acyutadattacittā
manthānam ākalayatī dadhiriktapātre /
tasyāḥ stanastabakacañcalaloladṛṣṭir
devo 'pi dohanadhiyā vṛṣabhaṃ nirundhan //

26. godhūlidhūsaritakomalakuntalāgraṃ
govardhanoddharaṇakelikṛtaprayāsam /
gopījanasya kucakuñkumamudritāñgaṃ
govindam induvadanaṃ śaraṇaṃ bhajāmaḥ //

27 When the lord of the lotus eyes took birth
as Varāha, the boar, the oceans of this
world were unable to fill his hair
follicles,
yet Yaśodā bathed this very lord with the
water held in her two hands.

28 You, who are wearied with much wandering in the
forests of the Vedāntas,
hear these other and better directions:
Seek for the goal of the Upaniṣads in the homes
of the milkmaids where, as Kṛṣṇa, it can be
found tied to a wooden mortar.

29. If I, who am purified by worshiping Devakī's
son
and am cleansed by water from the feet of Pūtana's
enemy,
shall remember Arjuna's charioteer,
then what can the messenger of Death do to me?

30. May some part of the cheerfulness of the lord, who has
of his own accord taken the form of a cowherd,
brighten my heart forever and ever. It is the one
cure for the ills of life.

31. We see a bright darkness
with round cheeks reddened by filaments
from clusters of *kadamba* flowers hanging from
each ear.
It is beyond the ken of Vedāntic expression.

32. We adore the flute player
of the sidelong lotus glances,
the tender lower lip like a half shut bud
and swiftly moving finger tips.

27. yadromarandhraparipūrtividhāv adakṣā
vārāhajanmani babhūvur amī samudrāḥ /
taṃ nāma nātham aravindadṛśaṃ yaśodā
pāṇidvayāntarajalaiḥ snapayāṃ babhūva //

28. param imam upadeśam ādriyadhvaṃ
nigamavaneṣu nitāntacārakhinnāḥ /
vicinuta bhavaneṣu vallavīnām
upaniṣadartham ulūkhale nibaddham //

29. devakītanayapūjanapūtaḥ
pūtanāricaraṇodakadhautaḥ /
yady ahaṃ smṛtadhanaṃjayasūtaḥ
kiṃ kariṣyati sa me yamadūtaḥ //

30. bhāsatāṃ bhavabhayaikabheṣajaṃ
mānase mama muhur muhur muhuḥ /
gopaveṣam upaseduṣaḥ svayaṃ
yā 'pi kā 'pi ramaṇīyatā vibhoḥ //

31. karṇalambitakadambamañjarī-
kesarāruṇakapolamaṇḍalam /
nirmalaṃ nigamavāgagocaraṃ
nīlimānam avalokayāmahe //

32. sācisaṃcalitalocanotpalaṃ
sāmikuḍmalitakomalādharam /
vegavalgitakarāṅgulīmukhaṃ
veṇunādarasikaṃ bhajāmahe //

33. Some man with the soft dark complexion of a young
tamāla tree
has put Rukminī, the daughter of the Kuṇḍina
king,
in a chariot, bearing the banner of Garuḍa
and taken her away.

34. Travellers, don't go along the road of the
Bhīmarathī river.
There is someone there who is clothed by the sky
and dark like the *tamāla* tree—
with arms akimbo on his hips.
He is a thief who takes away everything in your
heart.

35. Between each young woman was Mādhava;
between each Mādhava was a young woman.
In the middle of a circle so arranged,
the son of Devakī played his flute.

36.* He, who is the forest fire burning the forest of
bamboos which are Kaṃsa and his line,
who is the son of Devakī, played the flute
which became the bringer of happiness for rows of
swans found among
many lotus flowers and which was honoured by peacocks
with the cry, *keka*

37.* When the lutes with their strumming inspired him to keep time,
when the lutes inspired him to dance with the
sounding of small bells,
when the lute inspired him to sing so tenderly,
then he, the son of Devakī, played the flute.

38.* Kissed by their eyes like a line of lovely
moons,
the beloved of cowherds, herds of cows, and
milkmaids,
the lover and leader of crowds of milkmaids,
the son of Devakī, played the flute.

33. syandane garuḍamaṇḍitadhvaje
kuṇḍineśatanayā 'dhiropitā /
kena cin navatamālakomala-
śyāmalena puruṣeṇa nīyate //

34. mā yāta pānthāḥ pathi bhīmarathyā
digambaraḥ ko 'pi tamālanīlaḥ
vinyastahasto 'pi nitambabimbe
dhūrtaḥ samākarṣati cittavittam //

35. aṅganām aṅganām antare mādhavo
mādhavaṃ mādhavaṃ cā 'ntareṇā 'ṅganā /
ittham ākalpite maṇḍale madhyagaḥ
saṃjagau veṇunā devakīnandanaḥ //

36.* kekikekādṛtānekapaṅkeruhā-
līnahaṃsāvalīhṛdyatāhṛdyatā /
kaṃsavaṃśāṭavīdāhadāvānalaḥ
saṃjagau veṇunā devakīnandanaḥ //

37.* kvā 'pi vīṇābhir ārāviṇā kampitaḥ
kvā 'pi vīṇābhir ākiṅkiṇīnartitaḥ /
kvā 'pi vīṇābhir āmāntaraṃ gāpitaḥ
saṃjagau veṇunā devakīnandanaḥ //

38.* cārucandrāvalīlocanaiś cumbito
gopagovṛndagopālikāvallabhaḥ /
vallavīvṛndavṛndārakaḥ kāmukaḥ
saṃjagau veṇunā devakīnandanaḥ //

39.* Embraced in a flutter by the infatuated women
afraid, as it were,
of the line of angry bees appearing in the garland
of flowers on his head,
and pressed to the unclothed full bosoms of these
milkmaids,
the son of Devakī played on his flute.

40.* In the middle of the women who live in
Nanda's village, Vṛndāvana,
his chest shining with the garland of
victory,
the lord and husband to Bhāmā of the precious
golden complexion,
the son of Devakī, played the flute.

41.* With his dancing eyebrows marking the joining
beat of the measures clapped out by young
girls keeping time,
and giving his own attention to the singing of the
milkmaids,
the son of Devakī played the flute.

42.* The lover of Rādhā uprooted Indra's Pārijāta
tree
and planted it in the courtyard of Bhāmā's
home.
On the bank of the Yamunā under a cool
banyan tree
he, who is the son of Devakī, played
the flute.

43. Just ahead is a tall *arjuna* tree, and in front of
that is a path.
This goes to a cowherd's village and near that is
the Kālindī river.
In a grove of *tamāla* trees on its bank, grazing
a herd of cows,
a cowherd plays. He will show you, O friend, the
unimpeded path.

39.* maulimālāmilanmattabhṛṅgīlatā-
bhītabhītapriyāvibhramāliṅgitaḥ /
srastagopīkucābhogasaṃmelitaḥ
saṃjagau veṇunā devakīnandanaḥ //

40.* cārucāmīkarābhāsabhāmāvibhur
vaijayantīlatābhāsitoraḥsthalaḥ /
nandavṛndāvane vāsitāmadhyagaḥ
saṃjagau veṇunā devakīnandanaḥ //

41.* bālikātālikātālalīlālayā-
saṃgasaṃdarśitabhrūlatāvibhramaḥ /
gopikāgītadattāvadhānaḥ svayaṃ
saṃjagau veṇunā devakīnandanaḥ //

42.* pārijātaṃ samuddhṛtya rādhāvaro
ropayām āsa bhāmāgṛhasyā 'ṅgaṇe /
śītaśīte vaṭe yāmunīye taṭe
saṃjagau veṇunā devakīnandanaḥ //

43. agre dīrghataro 'yam arjunatarus tasyā 'grato vartanī
sā ghoṣaṃ samupaiti tatparisare deśe kalindātmajā /
tasyās tīratamālakānanatale cakraṃ gavāṃ cārayan
gopaḥ krīḍati darśayiṣyati sakhe panthānam avyāhatam //

44.* Ever do I bow to the eternal come as a child,
a tender cowherd covered by the dust raised by
cows.
Followed by crowds of boy cowherds,
he goes from house to house in the evening to
tether the cows.

45. I take refuge with him who is the highest good, the presiding
deity of the wise,
the treasury of felicities, the storehouse of all the
wonders in the world,
light's own home, the essence of infinite bliss,
the elixir of streams of nectar, the fruition of good
deeds for fawn eyed damsels.

46. May it protect us—that primal glory, the
ornament of Arjuna's chariot, Kṛṣṇa.
A whip is placed in his red lotus hand,
and dangling necklace, earrings, and golden
thread
are on his cloud blue body on which show drops
of sweat.

47. May he, who is born on earth as the fruit of
Devakī's merit, protect us.
His limbs are outstretched. In his turban is
tucked his whip, and between his teeth he holds
the reins.
Everyday with handfuls of water he washes the
horses of Pāṇḍava's chariot and stops their
itching with his nails.

48. May my mind approach his feet and live
with the cowherd Nanda's son, whose body is
bright with youth,
whose every action expresses the good, whose
smile, as it were, is made of jasmine and
mandāra flowers.
He is the friend of the young women of Vraja
and the sun of lotus sages.

44.* godhūlidhūsaritakomalagopaveṣaṃ
gopālabālakaśatair anugamyamānam /
sāyantane pratigṛhaṃ paśubandhanārthaṃ
gacchantam acyutaśiśuṃ praṇato 'smi nityam //

45. nidhiṃ lāvaṇyānāṃ nikhilajagadāścaryanicayaṃ
nijāvāsaṃ bhāsāṃ niravadhikaniḥśreyasarasam /
sudhādhārāsāraṃ sukṛtaparipākaṃ mṛgadṛśāṃ
prapadye māṅgalyaṃ prathamam adhidaivaṃ kṛtadhiyām //

46. ātāmrapāṇikamalapraṇayipratodam
ālolahāramaṇikuṇḍalahemasūtram /
āviḥśramāmbukaṇam ambudanīlam avyād
ādyaṃ dhanaṃjayarathābharaṇaṃ maho naḥ //

47. nakhaniyamitakaṇḍūn pāṇḍavasyandanāśvān
anudinam abhiṣiñcann añjalisthaiḥ payobhiḥ /
avatu vitatagātras totrasaṃsyūtamaulir
daśanavidhṛtaraśmir devakīpuṇyarāśiḥ //

48. vrajayuvatisahāye yauvanollāsikāye
śubhasakalavilāse kundamandārahāse /
nivasatu mama cittaṃ tatpadāya pravṛttaṃ
munisarasijabhānau nandagopasya sūnau //

49. All hail to sweetness incarnate, the foremost
of protectors.
The notes of his flute mix with streams of nectar from
the sweet cherry lips of his tender smile
and at once cause the great forest to rejoice.
It is as if his lotus feet are embraced by Mother Earth—
her hair standing on end with joy.

50. May it ever live in our hearts—Glory incarnate
as the dark lover of the milkmaids
who fills Gokula with the sweet, steady notes
of the flute to beguile and soothe and to
subdue the organs of action.
It must be admitted, however, that when he
incarnates as Infatuation, he stirs and
confuses the minds of youth.

51. I take refuge with Brahman come to earth as the
sinless thief of fresh butter,
who is beyond the ken of the Vedas,
whose limbs everywhere bear the marks of
enjoyment with the skilled and sportive
wives of the cowherds.

52. May the enemy of Murāri protect us—who was watched
raising Govardhana mountain aloft.
Yaśodā watched him with joy. The milkmaids watched him
throughout with fond attention.
Indra watched with alarm while the *siddhas* filled the
paths with flowers.
The boy cowherds watched with jealousy, the people
of his village with sympathy and the world with
wonder.

53. A woman caught Kṛṣṇa stealing in her house.
So she locked the door on him and went straight
to his mother
where she was astounded to see him tied with a
rope to the wooden mortar.

49. araṇyānīm ārdrasmitamadhurabimbādharasudhā-
saraṇyā saṃkrāntaiḥ sapadi madayan veṇuninadaiḥ /
dharaṇyā sānandotpulakam upagūḍhāṅghrikamalaḥ
śaraṇyānām ādyaḥ sa jayati śarīrī madhurimā //

50. mugdhaṃ snigdhaṃ madhuramuralīmādhurīdhīranādaiḥ
kāraṃ kāraṃ karaṇavivaśaṃ gokulaṃ vyākulatvam /
śyāmaṃ kāmaṃ yuvajanamanomohanaṃ mohanatvaṃ
citte nityaṃ nivasatu maho vallavīvallabhaṃ naḥ //

51. vidagdhagopālavilāsinīnāṃ
saṃbhogacihnāṅkitasarvagātram /
pavitram āmnāyagirām agamyaṃ
brahma prapadye navanītacoram //

52. ānandena yaśodayā samadanaṃ gopāṅganābhiś ciraṃ
sāśaṅkaṃ balavidviṣā sakusumaiḥ siddhaiḥ pathi vyākulam /
serṣyaṃ gopakumārakaiḥ sakaruṇaṃ paurair janiḥ sasmitaṃ
yo dṛṣṭaḥ sa punātu no muraripuḥ protkṣiptagovardhanaḥ //

53. antargṛhe kṛṣṇam avekṣya coraṃ
baddhvā kavāṭaṃ jananīṃ gatai 'kā /
ulūkhale dāmanibaddham enaṃ
tatrā 'pi dṛṣṭvā stimitā babhūva //

54. One day the baby was crawling across some
inlaid jewels and met his own lotus face
reflected there.
He tried to get it, and vexed at not obtaining
it, he looked to his mother's face and
cried.

55. Let the seers of old, who knew the nature of the
soul,
worship the supreme being placed deep in the
cave of the Vedas.
We shall dive deep into the nectar ocean of
stories about the boyish pranks of
Yaśodā's son.

56. They say that once a milkmaid, intending
to sell yogurt and so forth,
had all her thoughts on Murāri.
Because of this abstraction, she called
out,
"Govinda, Dāmodara, Mādhava!"

57. On earth there are in all probability only three
hitching posts for the elephant called Murāri:
the wooden mortar, the mind of ascetics, and the
bud-like breasts of milkmaids.

58. Gladly do I think of the baby Mukunda
lying in his nest of fig tree leaves,
thrusting with his lotus hand his lotus
foot into his lotus mouth.

59. "Welcome, Śiva. Please sit right here on my left, Brahmā.
How do you do, Kārttikeya? Greetings, Indra. We haven't
been seeing you, Kubera, O God of Wealth."
When Yaśodā heard Kṛṣṇa, the enemy of Kaiṭabha,
talking like this in his sleep, she cried,
"Whatever are you saying, child. Get away, evil eye!"
May the saying of these words protect us.

54. ratnasthale jānucaraḥ kumāraḥ
saṃkrāntam ātmīyamukhāravindam /
ādātukāmas tad alābhakhedād
vilokya dhātrīvadanaṃ ruroda //

55. upāsatām ātmavidaḥ purāṇāḥ
paraṃ parastān nihitaṃ guhāyām /
vayaṃ yaśodāśiśubālalīlā-
kathāsudhāsindhuṣu majjayāmaḥ //

56. vikretukāmā kila gopakanyā
murāripādārpitacittavṛttiḥ /
dadhyādikaṃ mohavaśād avocad
govinda dāmodara mādhave 'ti //

57. ulūkhalaṃ vā yamināṃ mano vā
gopāṅganānāṃ kucakuḍmalaṃ vā /
murārināmnaḥ kalabhasya nūnam
ālānam āsīt trayam eva bhūmau //

58. karāravindena padāravindaṃ
mukhāravinde viniveśayantam /
vaṭasya patrasya puṭe śayānaṃ
bālaṃ mukundaṃ manasā smarāmi //

59. śambho svāgatam āsyatām ita ito vāmena padmāsana
krauñcāre kuśalaṃ sukhaṃ surapate vitteśa no dṛśyase /
itthaṃ svapnagatasya kaiṭabharipoḥ śrutvā yaśodāgiraḥ
kiṃ kiṃ bālaka jalpasī 'ti racitaṃ dhūdhūkṛtaṃ pātu naḥ //

60. "Mother!" "What is it, Prince of Yadus?" "Give me a drinking cup." "What for?" "For drinking milk."
"There is no milk now." "When will there be?" "Tonight." "What is night?" "When darkness comes."
Then Kṛṣṇa closed his eyes and said, "Night has come; give me some milk,"
while with his raised hand he kept pulling at the garment across his mother's bosom. May he protect us.

61. "Your older brother, Musalī, has gone to play on the sandy islands of the Kālindī river.
While he is away, Hari, drink the milk of the dappled cow so that your topknot will grow."
Hari listened to these coaxing words of Yaśodā, and when he had taken half the milk, with childish anticipation he felt his topknot. May he protect us.

62. Once, when Hari's mouth was opened wide in laughter, there appeared butter, become Mount Kailāsa, and mud, swallowed previously, become this earth. A drink of milk had become the Ocean of Milk.
When his mother saw this, she became greatly alarmed with concern about his digestion and said, "I am undone. Someone has cast an eye on my boy. Get away evil eye. Live long, my child." May Hari, thus spoken to, save us.

63. While his mother with one finger chucks him under the chin, the just appearing radiance of Śauri's first teeth mixes with drops of milk on the lower lip of his smiling face
after, with half-opened eyes, nursing a time from one of his mother's breasts while his hand kept brushing the drops of milk coming from the other.
May that radiance protect us.

60. māotaḥ kiṃ yadunātha dehi caṣakaṃ kiṃ tena pātuṃ payas
tan nā 'sty adya kadā 'sti vā niśi niśā kā vā 'ndhakārodaye /
āmīlyā 'kṣiyugaṃ niśā 'py upagatā dehī 'ti mātur muhur
vakṣojāmbarakarṣaṇodyatakaraḥ kṛṣṇaḥ sa puṣṇātu naḥ //

61. kālindīpulinodareṣu musalī yāvad gataḥ khelituṃ
tāvat karburikāpayaḥ piba hare vardhiṣyate te śikhā /
itthaṃ bālatayā pratāraṇaparāḥ śrutvā yaśodāgiraḥ
pāyān naḥ svaśikhāṃ spṛśan pramuditaḥ kṣīre 'rdhapīte hariḥ //

62. kailāso navanītati kṣitir iyaṃ prāgjagdhamṛlloṣṭati
kṣīrodo 'pi nipītadugdhati lasatsmerapraphulle mukhe /
mātrā 'jīrṇadhiyā dṛḍhaṃ cakitayā naṣṭā 'smi dṛṣṭaḥ kayā
dhūdhū vatsaka jīva jīva ciram ity ukto 'vatān no hariḥ //

63. kiṃcitkuñcitalocanasya pibataḥ paryāyam ekaṃ stanaṃ
sadyaḥ prasnutadugdhabindum aparaṃ hastena saṃmārjataḥ /
mātraikāṅgulilālitasya cubuke smerānanasyā 'dhare
śaureḥ kṣīrakaṇānvitā nipatitā dantadyutiḥ pātu naḥ //

64. During her wedding celebration Lakṣmī resorted to the
stratagem of modesty and bent her head so that she
could see the form of Murāri—with a splendour
like that cast by an aggregation of sapphires—
which was reflected within the pendant pearl
glowing above her high breasts.
May Lakṣmī delighted by her vision give you delight.

65. "other, when Kṛṣṇa went to play today, he ate all
the mud he wanted."
"Is this true, Kṛṣṇa?" "Who said so?" "Musalī"
"It isn't true, mother. Look in my mouth."
Then Kṛṣṇa's mother told him to open his mouth.
In the open mouth she saw the whole world and
was amazed. May Keśava whose mother was amazed,
protect us.

66. Among the star wives of the Moon, Arcturus is known
as the wife who is the mother of pearls.
Aldebaran, jealous of this, brought forth a blue
jewel which is found at the bosoms of cowherd's
wives.

67. In a jewelled pillar Yaśodā saw the endlessly lovely
reflection of the dancing Kṛṣṇa.
She took it to be a second Kṛṣṇa and divided a lump of
butter into two parts.

68. "Wake up my child; dawn has come.
Live for hundreds of autumns, Kṛṣṇa."
After saying this Yaśodā gazed at
his face for a long time.
We serve Glory whose face is watched
by Yaśodā.

69. Kissed by the milkmaids, who thought him a child,
he enjoyed their lips.
Closely held by them, he reddened their neck with
his embrace.
Placed on their laps, he touched their private
parts with his hand.
May this foremost person of the wicked, the baby
Kṛṣṇa, take our sins far away.

64. uttuṅgastanamaṇḍaloparilasatprālambamuktāmaṇer
antarbimbitam indranīlanikaracchāyānukāridyuti /
lajjāvyājam upetya namravadanā spaṣṭam murārer vapuḥ
paśyantī muditā mude 'stu bhavatāṃ lakṣmīr vivāhotsave //

65. kṛṣṇenā 'mba gatena rantum adhunā mṛd bhakṣitā svecchayā
satyaṃ kṛṣṇa ka evam āha musalī mithyā 'mba paśyā 'nanam /
vyādehī 'ti vidārite 'tha vadane dṛṣṭvā samastaṃ jagan

66. svātī sapatnī kila tārakāṇāṃ
muktāphalānāṃ jananī 'ti roṣāt /
sā rohiṇī nīlam asūta ratnaṃ
kṛtāspadaṃ gopavadhūkuceṣu //

67. nṛtyantam atyantavilokanīyaṃ
kṛṣṇaṃ maṇistambhagataṃ mṛgākṣī /
nirīkṣya sākṣād iva kṛṣṇam agre
dvidhā vitene navanītam ekam //

68. vatsa jāgṛhi vibhātam āgataṃ
jīva kṛṣṇa śaradāṃ śataṃ śatam /
ity udīrya suciraṃ yaśodayā
dṛśyamānavadanaṃ bhaje mahaḥ //

69. oṣṭhaṃ gṛhṇañ chiśur iti dhiyā cumbito vallavībhiḥ
kaṇṭhaṃ gṛhṇann aruṇitapadaṃ gāḍham āliṅgitāṅgaḥ /
doṣṇā lajjāpadam abhimṛśann aṅkam āropitā 'tmā
dhūrtasvāmī haratu duritaṃ dūrato bālakṛṣṇaḥ //

70. "O Lakṣmaṇa, these clouds distress me who have lost
my Sītā.
The cruel *kadamba*-scented breezes cut me to the quick."
So speaking, in his sleep, of an event suffered in a
former birth, may Hari, glanced at jealously by
the suspicious Rādhā, bring us joy.[1]

71. "Release my lips, O Hari. I am frightened; it was you
who sucked Pūtanā to death.
Stop embracing me so; the Arjuna twin demon trees were
torn up by your embrace.
Don't amorously cut me with your nails. Incarnated
as a man-lion, you tore Hiraṇyakaśipu to death."
May Hari, whose night's love-play was thus put off by
the playful mockery of Lakṣmī, save us.

72. "Once there was a man named Rāma." "Yes." "His
wife was called Sītā." "Yes." "Rāvaṇa
abducted her from Rāma during his stay in the
Pañcavaṭī forest in obedience to his father's
command."
Hari, indicating with yeses that he was listening to
his mother's bedtime story, said,
"My bow, my bow, where is my bow, Lakṣmaṇa?"
May these alarmed words protect us.

73. Although but a boy, you hold a mountain aloft
with a finger tip.
Although dark, you are a light in the deep darkness.
Although immovable, you are drawn by the eyes of
Rādhā.
Although an adulterer, you destroy the inevitability of
rebirth. How are you all this?

74. Salutations to you, O son of Nanda, thief of butter,
child of dark beauty, who are clothed by the sky,
whose hips are beautiful with a net of new bells,
who is adorned with a necklace of bright tiger
claws.

---

1. Adapted from a translation by D. H. H. Ingalls. See notes on Z23 in the "Manuscripts Used" section.

70. ete lakṣmaṇa jānakīvirahitaṃ mām khedayanty ambudā
marmāṇī 'va ca ghaṭṭayanty alam amī krūrāḥ kadambānilāḥ /
itthaṃ vyāhṛtapūrvajanmacarito yo rādhayā vīkṣitaḥ
serṣyaṃ śaṅkitayā sa naḥ sukhayatu svapnāyamāno hariḥ //

71. oṣṭhaṃ muñca hare bibhemi bhavatāṃ pānair hatā pūtanā
kaṇṭhāśleṣam amuṃ jahīhi dalitā vā 'liṅganenā 'rjunau /
mā dehi cchuritaṃ hiraṇyakaśipur nīto nakhaiḥ pañcatām
itthaṃ vāritarātrikelir avatāl lakṣmyā 'phāsād dhariḥ //

72. rāmo nāma babhūva huṃ tadabalā sīte 'ti huṃ tāṃ pitur
vācā pañcavaṭīvane viharatas tasyā 'harad rāvaṇaḥ /
nidrārthaṃ janakīkathām iti harer huṃkārataḥ śṛṇvataḥ
saumitre kva dhanur dhanur dhanur iti vyagrā giraḥ pāntu naḥ //

73. bālo 'pi śailoddharaṇāgrapāṇir
nīlo 'pi nīrandhratamaḥpradīpaḥ /
dhīro 'pi rādhānayanāvabaddho
jāro 'pi saṃsāraharaḥ kutas tvam //

74. bālāya nīlavapuṣe navakiṅkiṇīka-
jālābhirāmajaghanāya digambarāya /
śārdūladivyanakhabhūṣaṇabhūṣitāya
nandātmajāya navanītamuṣe namas te //

75. May he grant us happiness—the god, born as Yaśodā's
child, clothed in the shining sky.
In his right hand he holds a tasty milk-rice sweet.
In his left hand he keeps a lump of butter like the
full autumn moon.
Arranged around his neck he wears extraordinarily bright
tiger claws.

76. I do homage to Hari going across the ground of the
courtyard with a crawling motion so active
that his bells go "kiṇi, kiṇi".
From his feet comes the sound "kuñkuṇu kuṇu".
On his arms and hands are bracelets and rings.

77. I take refuge with the child with the flowing curls
whose body is caked with mud,
who wearies his mother running after him among the
cows.

78. Ever do I take refuge with the boy cowherd
with a curving peacock feather crest
and a flute placed on his jewel-like lower lip
who beguiles circles of good milkmaids.

79. The object of my contemplation should be he
who is the good fortune of Prahlāda, named for
his function as a man-lion,
who is the wise man's necessity, found deep in
the great cave of the Vedas.

80. What is the important thing in life?
The worship of the lotus feet of Kaṃsa's enemy .
What is a light in the darkness?
The contemplation of the enemy of the demon
called the blind one.

81. May my mind delight in the son of Nanda,
the paramour of beautiful milkmaids,
the thief who steals butter from butter pots,
the full moon to the lily eyes of Kamalā.

75. pāṇau pāyasabhaktam āhitarasaṃ bibhran mudā dakṣiṇe
savye śāradacandramaṇḍalanibhaṃ haiyaṃgavīnaṃ dadhat /
kaṇṭhe kalpitapuṇḍarīkanakham apy uddāmadīptiṃ vahan
devo divyadigambaro diśatu naḥ saukhyaṃ yaśodāśiśuḥ //

76. kiṅkiṇikiṇikiṇirabhasair
aṅgaṇabhuvi riṅkhaṇaiḥ sadā 'ṭantam /
kuṅkuṇukuṇupadayugalaṃ
kaṅkaṇakarabhūṣaṇaṃ hariṃ vande //

77. saṃbādhe surabhīṇām
ambām āyāsayantam anuyāntīm /
lambālakam avalambe
taṃ bālaṃ tanuvilagnajambālam //

78. añcitapicchācūḍaṃ
vañcitasaujanyavallavīvalayam /
adharamaṇinihitaveṇuṃ
bālaṃ gopālam aniśam avalambe //

79. prahlādabhāgadheyaṃ
nigamamahāguhāntarādheyam /
naraharipadābhidheyaṃ
vibudhavidheyaṃ mamā 'nusaṃdheyam //

80. saṃsāre kiṃ sāraṃ
kaṃsāreś caraṇakamalaparivasanam /
jyotiḥ kim andhakāre
yad andhakārer anusmaraṇam //

81. kalaśanavanītacore
kamalādṛkkumudacandrikāpūre /
viharatu nandakumāre
ceto mama gopasundarījāre //

82. "Who are you boy?" "The younger brother of Bala."
"What are you doing here?" "I mistook this for my house."
"Tell me this: Why have you put your hand into the butter pot?"
"Kind lady, to find a certain calf. Don't for a moment be upset."
May Kṛṣṇa's answer to the blessed milkmaid prosper us.

83. O Kṛṣṇa, you delight in the mud of the cowherds' courtyards but are shy of the Brahman's sacrifice.
You answer to the "huhs" and "uh huhs" spoken by the cow village people but keep silent when extensively praised by the pious.
You serve the wayward women of Gokula but will not rule the self controlled.
It is known that your graceful lotus feet are stayed only by love.

84. Hail to you, O Spendour, embodied as the son of Yaśodā.
You enjoy the lotus face of Rādhā and are gladdened.

85. There may be other avatars of the lotus eyed god, Viṣṇu—all of them beneficent.
But aside from Kṛṣṇa who of them came to save cows, cowherds, and milkmaids?

86. When, at the early morning milking time, the lowing of the cows begins everywhere in the cowpens of Gokula, then Glory is seen incarnate as Kṛṣṇa, who is dark blue like clouds just forming,
who has jingling anklets, a child's ornament on his forehead, a belt of true tinkling little bells on his hips, and tiger claws around his neck, and who is the perfection of the beauty and happiness of childhood.

82. kas tvaṃ bāla balānujaḥ kim iha te manmandirāśaṅkayā
brūhy etan navanītapātravivare hastaṃ kimarthaṃ nyaseḥ /
mātaḥ kaṃ cana vatsakaṃ mṛgayituṃ mā gā viṣādaṃ kṣaṇād
ity evaṃ varavallavīprativacaḥ kṛṣṇasya puṣṇātu naḥ //

83. gopālājirakardame viharase viprādhvare lajjase
brūṣe godhanahuṃkṛtaiḥ stutiśatair maunaṃ vidhatse satām /
dāsyaṃ gokulapuṃścalīṣu kuruṣe svāmyaṃ na dāntātmasu
jñātaṃ kṛṣṇa tavā 'ṅghripaṅkajayugaṃ premācalaṃ mañjulam //

84. namas tasmai yaśodāyā
dāyādāyā 'stu tejase /
yad dhi rādhāmukhāmbhojaṃ
bhojaṃ bhojaṃ vyavardhata //

85. avatārāḥ santv anye
sarasijanayanasya sarvatobhadrāḥ /
kṛṣṇād anyaḥ ko vā
prabhavati gogopagopikāmuktyai //

86. madhyegokulamaṇḍalaṃ pratidiśaṃ hambhāravair jṛmbhite
prātardohamahotsave navaghanaśyāmaṃ raṇannūpuram /
bhāle bālavibhūṣaṇaṃ kaṭiraṭatsatkiṅkiṇīmekhalaṃ
kaṇṭhe vyāghranakhaṃ ca śaiśavakalākalyāṇakārtsnyaṃ mahaḥ //

87. I sing praise of the boy cowherd who wears an exquisite
garland,
who is the blue color of a rain cloud, whose great
divine play has been witnessed by men,
who held a mountain aloft on the palm of his hand, who
gives delight with the music of the flute,
who is the protector of the people of Vraja, who
delights in amorous play with loving women.

88. I sing praise of the boy cowherd who is the dark
color of a blue water lily petal,
whose cheeks are dimpled with smiles, who is
intent on his soothing flute song,
who has a cap of clustering curls, whose divine
play includes skill in theft,
who is death to the enemies of Indra, who wears
a garment of golden color.

89.* I sing praise of the boy cowherd who is the blue
color of a just forming rain cloud,
who is intent on the music of the flute, who is
adorned with the charming peacock's garment,
who has destroyed hordes of demons, whose divine
play is kind and benevolent,
whose ever new pastimes are for the welfare of
his parthers, who always defers to Lakṣmī.

90. I sing praise of the cowherd king who is
merciful to people of goodwill,
who brings together all delightful qualities, who is
the embodiment of life, consciousness, and bliss,
who removes worldly illusion, who is the consort
of Satyabhāmā,
who is the source of inner and outer control,
who subdues all obstacles.

91. I do homage to the pure and holy son of Vasudeva
who is the consort of Lakṣmī, who has caressing
lotus eyes,
who has a full moon face, who is a friend to Indra,
who is a vessel of compassion, whose limbs are lovely.

87. sajalajaladanīlaṃ darśitodāralīlaṃ
karataladhṛtaśailaṃ veṇuvādyai rasālam /
vrajajanakulapālaṃ kāminīkelilolaṃ
kalitalalitamālaṃ naumi gopālabālam //

88. smitalalitakapolaṃ snigdhasaṃgītalolaṃ
lalitacikurajālaṃ cauryacāturyalīlam /
śatamakharipukālaṃ śātakumbhābhacelaṃ
kuvalayadalanīlaṃ naumi gopālabālam //

89.* muralininadalolaṃ mugdhamāyūracelaṃ
dalitadanujajālaṃ dhanyasaujanyalīlam /
parahitanavahelaṃ padmasadmānukūlaṃ
navajaladharanīlaṃ naumi gopālabālam //

90. sarasaguṇanikāyaṃ saccidānandakāyaṃ
śamitasakalamāyaṃ satyalakṣmīsahāyam /
śamadamasamudāyaṃ śāntasarvāntarāyaṃ
suhṛdayajanadāyaṃ naumi gopālarāyam //

91. lakṣmīkalatraṃ lalitābjanetraṃ
pūrṇenduvaktraṃ puruhūtamitram /
kāruṇyapātraṃ kamanīyagātraṃ
vande pavitraṃ vasudevaputram //

92. May Kṛṣṇa of much courage, who went down to the
Yamunā river and subdued the furious serpent,
who is intent on removing the neglect of the gods,
help me be attentive.

93. May the yellow clad person with a flute in his hands,
who stands in the midst of the young Vraja women,
protect us.
In his crest there is a peacock feather and on his
lovely forehead a dot of musk.
In his two ears there are two very tender palm
leaves and in his nose a pearl.
On his neck, heavy with the scent of a *mandāra* flower
garland, is a necklace with the Kaustubha gem.

94. When Murāri stole the clothes of the deer-eyed
women while they were playing in the water,
their cloak was their two hands, their long thick
hair, and their closed eyes.

95. May the yellow clad one protect us.
In the celestial Gañga-like streams of bright beams
from the lovely pearl in his nose, there is the
play of sportive side long glances from the
rolling black eyes of milkmaids.
Among the lotuses which are his feet the milkmaids'
lovely black ringlets move quickly about like
fish and bees.

96.* May the yellow clad one protect us.
When set free by the notes blown by his mouth through
the row of holes in his flute,
the deer-eyed women broke the bonds of love for
their own lord and husband,
their ringlets became disordered, their lips,
breasts, and navels throbbed,
their hair so stood on end that their subjection to
love was quite evident.

92. madamayam adamayad uragaṃ
yamunām avatīrya vīryaśālī yaḥ /
mama ratim amaratiraskṛti-
śamanaparaḥ sa kriyāt kṛṣṇaḥ //

93. maulau māyūrabarhaṃ mṛgamadatilakaṃ cārulālāṭapaṭṭe
karṇadvaṃdve ca tālīdalam atimṛdulaṃ mauktikaṃ nāsikāyām /
hāro mandāramālāparimalabharite kaustubhasyo 'pakaṇṭhe
pāṇau veṇuś ca yasya vrajayuvatiyutaḥ pātu pītāmbaro naḥ //

94. murāriṇā vārivihārakāle
mṛgekṣaṇānāṃ muṣitāṃśukānām /
karadvayaṃ vā kacasaṃhatir vā
pramīlanaṃ vā paridhānam āsīt //

95. yāsāṃ gopāṅganānāṃ lasadasitatarālolalīlākaṭākṣā
yannāsācārumuktāmaṇirucinikaravyomagaṅgāpravāhe /
mīnāyante 'pi tāsām atirabhasacalaccārunīlālakāntā
bhṛṅgāyante yadaṅghridvayasarasiruhe pātu pītāmbaro naḥ //

96.* yadveṇuśreṇirūpasthitasuṣiramukhodgīrṇanādaprabhinnā
eṇākṣyas tatkṣaṇena truṭitanijapatipremabandhā babhūvuḥ /
astavyastālakāntāḥ sphuradadharakucadvaṃdvanābhipradeśāḥ
kāmāveśaprakalpyaprakaṭitapulakāḥ pātu pītāmbaro naḥ //

97. May it stay ever in our heart—that certain lovely sapphire,
which was carried in the abdomen-mine by Devakī and bought by the cowherd
of great merit, Nanda, from Vasudeva by the barter of his own daughter,
which sparkled on the charming necklace made of a row of cowherds and which was the decoration of the milkmaids.

98. May he keep watch over us—that boy cowherd who stood on the shoulders of a boy seated on a stool placed on top of another,
who silenced the ringing of the bell and broke open the milk pot placed in the net bag,
who, then, cupped his hands to make a funnel next his mouth, shook his head for joy, and drank the milk,
who, then, spit the drink of milk in the eyes of the milkmaid who came in.

99. In past births we surely must have performed sacrifices and given gifts to worthy people.
We must have honoured our elders and performed difficult austerities,
because to you, who are the enemy of the demon, Cāṇūra, who steal away the sins of your devotees, who prosper devotees with many benefits, who are devoted to Śrī,
love and devotion, which is not easy for others to obtain and is inimical to transmigration,
is ours.

100. If you become gracious, what use have I for any excellence? And if you do not become gracious, what use (then also) of any of my excellences? Whether their lovers love or not, equally are the saffron designs futile for the damsels.[2]

2. Translation by V. Raghavan, *Prayers, Praises and Psalms* (Madras, n.d.). p. 329.

97. devakyā jaṭharākare samuditaḥ krīto gavāṃ pālinā
nandenā 'nakadundubher nijasutāpaṇyena puṇyātmanā /
gopālāvalimugdhahārataralo gopījanālaṃkṛtiḥ
stheyān no hṛdi saṃtataṃ samadhuraḥ ko 'pi 'ndranīlo maṇiḥ //

98. pīṭhe pīṭhaniṣaṇṇabālakagale tiṣṭhan sa gopālako
yantrāntaḥsthitadugdhabhāṇḍam avabhidyā 'cchādya
ghaṇṭāravam /
vaktropāntakṛtāñjaliḥ kṛtaśiraḥkampaṃ piban yaḥ payaḥ
pāyād āgatagopikānayanayor gaṇḍūṣaphūtkārakṛt //

99. yajñair ījimahe dhanaṃ dadimahe pātreṣu nūnaṃ vayaṃ
vṛddhān bhejimahe tapaś cakṛmahe janmāntare duścaram /
yenā 'smākam abhūd ananyasulabhā bhaktir bhavadveṣiṇī
cāṇūradviṣi bhaktakalmaṣamuṣi śreyaḥpuṣi śrījuṣi //

100. tvayi prasanne mama kiṃ guṇena
tvayy aprasanne mama kiṃ guṇena /
rakte virakte ca vare vadhūnāṃ
nirarthakaḥ kuṅkumapatrabhaṅgaḥ //

101. May he ever protect us—the yellow clad one
to whom the milkmaids in Gokula at the end of night
joyfully sing praises so that by the abundance of
lustre from their own teeth they repel the rays
of the moon
while they quickly churn the curd so that the jingling
of the bangles on their wrists keeps time to their
singing, and the ends of their upper garments
dance.

102. I contemplate him who infatuates the whole world,
who has the grace of three curves (delineated by
his stance) under the tree of wishes,
who holds his pendent left earring at his left
shoulder, whose eyebrow creeper is slightly
raised,
whose soft lips are slightly parted, who looks
obliquely,
who merrily plays his flute with lively shoot-like
fingers.

103. May Hari, who delights hosts of immortals, protect you.
When he came into the wrestling ring, he seemed
to wrestlers like a mighty mountain, to other people
a child, to women the God of Love,
to cowherds an ordinary mortal, to Indra in heaven
the immeasurable body of the universe,
to Kaṃsa, whose eyes oscillated with fear, the
wrathful God of Death, to yogis the object for
contemplation.

104. May the world infatuating King of the Yadus, surrounded
by cowherds and milkmaids, protect us.
He sits upon a jewelled throne, gladly putting a
dot of musk on the forehead and joyfully touching
the bosom of Lakṣmī seated in his lap,
and honours the God of Love with moonbeam sprouts
from their mutual smile.

101. gāyanti kṣaṇadāvirāmasamaye sānandam induprabhāṃ
rundhantyo nijadantakāntinivahair gopāṅganā gokule /
mathnantyo dadhi pāṇikaṅkaṇajhaṇatkārānurūpaṃ javād
vyāvalgadvasanāñcalā yam aniśaṃ pītāmbaro 'vyāt sa naḥ //

102. aṃsālambitavāmakuṇḍaladharaṃ mandonnatabhrūlataṃ
kiṃcitkuñcitakomalādharapuṭaṃ sāciprasārekṣaṇam /
ālolāṅgulipallavair muralikām āpūrayantaṃ mudā
mūle kalpataros tribhaṅgilalitaṃ dhyāye jaganmohanam /

103. mallaiḥ śailendrakalpaḥ śiśur itarajanaiḥ puṣpacāpo 'ṅganābhir
gopais tu prākṛtātmā divi kuliśabhṛtā viśvakāyo 'prameyaḥ /
kruddhaḥ kaṃsena kālo bhayacakitadṛśā yogibhir dhyeyamūrtir
dṛṣṭo raṅgāvatāre harir amaragaṇānandakṛt pātu yuṣmān //

104. saṃviṣṭo maṇiviṣṭare 'ṅkatalamadhyāsīnalakṣmīmukhe
kastūrītilakaṃ mudā viracayan harṣāt kucau saṃspṛśan /
anyo'nyasmitacandrikākisalayair ārādhayan manmathaṃ
gopīgopaparīvṛto yadupatiḥ pāyāj jaganmohanaḥ //

105. Kṛṣṇa pulled the end of Rukmiṇī's upper garment so that her gaze like a blue water lily was embarrassedly turned downwards and mixed with the light of her bright golden breasts,
and became, as it were, a tender mango shoot. Then, Kṛṣṇa embraced Rukmṇī with her lowered face shining with a confused smile. May he prosper us.

106. You playfully raise with your two arms some little hill placed on the ground.
For this you are always called Govardhana in heaven and on earth.
It is counted as nothing that I bear you, who hold the three worlds, on the tips of my two breasts.
But what is the use of talking so much about it, O Keśava. Fame is gotten by good luck.

107. O Celebration of Sandhyā, well be it with you. O Bath, salutations to you.
O Gods and Manes, I am unable to refresh you with libations of water. Forgive me.
Sitting somewhere, I shall spend my time contemplating the enemy of Kaṃsa, the topmost ornament of the Yādava people, and remove my sin. That I hold enough. Of what use is the rest.

108.* O Cowherd, O Ocean of Mercy. O Lord of the Princess of Sindhu,
O Killer of Kaṃsa, O Compassionate Saviour of the King of Elephants, O Enemy of Madhu,
O Younger Brother of Rāma, O Teacher of the Three Worlds, O Lotus-eyed One,
O Lord of the Milkmaids, save me. I know of no one other than you who can.

105. ākṛṣṭe vasanāñcale kuvalayaśyāmā trapādhaḥkṛtā
dṛṣṭiḥ saṃvalitā rucā kucayuge svarṇaprabhe śrīmati /
bālaḥ kaś cana cūtapallava iti bhrāntasmitāsyaśriyaṃ
śliṣyaṃs tām atha rukmiṇīṃ natamukhīṃ kṛṣṇaḥ sa puṣṇātu
naḥ //

106. urvyāṃ ko 'pi mahīdharo laghutaro dorbhyāṃ dhṛto līlayā
tena tvaṃ divi bhūtale ca satataṃ govardhano gīyase /
tvāṃ trailokyadharaṃ vahāmi kucayor agre na tad gaṇyate
kiṃ vā keśava bhāṣaṇena bahunā puṇyair yaśo labhyate //

107. sandhyāvandana bhadram astu bhavate bhoḥ snāna tubhyaṃ
namo
bho devāḥ pitaraś ca tarpaṇavidhau nā 'haṃ kṣamaḥ
kṣamyatām /
yatra kvā 'pi niṣadya yādavakulottaṃsasya kaṃsadviṣaḥ
smāraṃ smāraṃ aghaṃ harāmi tad alaṃ manye kim anyena
me //

108.* he gopālaka he kṛpājalanidhe he sindhukanyāpate
he kaṃsāntaka he gajendrakaruṇāpārīṇa he mādhava /
he rāmānuja he jagattrayaguro he puṇḍarīkākṣa māṃ
he gopījananātha pālaya paraṃ jānāmi na tvāṃ vinā //

109.* All hail to the crown jewel of the cowherds who is
surrounded by milkmaids.
He wears a mark made of musk on his forehead and on
his chest the Kaustubha jewel,
on his nose a new pearl, in his hand a flute, and
on his wrists bracelets,
over his whole body sandal paste and around his
neck pearls.

110.* All hail to the child's flute notes coming forth so
that *Om* might sound.
The fiute notes cause the worlds to exult, the Vedas to
sound, trees to rejoice,
mountains to fly, deer to be tame, cows blissful,
and cowherds bewildered, ascetics' flesh to
rise and the seven basic notes to sound.

109.* kastūrītilakaṃ lalāṭaphalake vakṣaḥsthale kaustubhaṃ
nāsāgre navamauktikaṃ karatale veṇuṃ kare kaṅkaṇam /
sarvāṅge haricandanaṃ ca kalayan kaṇṭhe ca muktāvaliṃ
gopastrīpariveṣṭito vijayate gopālacūḍāmaṇiḥ //

110.* lokān unmadayan śrutīr mukharayan kṣoṇīruhān harṣayan
śailān vidravayan mṛgān vivaśayan govṛndam ānandayan /
gopān saṃbhramayan munīn mukulayan saptasvarān
jṛmbhayann
oṃkārārtham udīrayan vijayate vaṃśīninādaḥ śiśoḥ //

CENTURY III

1. Behold the object which is the way of welfare for the
whole world. It is Kṛṣṇa, who frequents Lakṣmī's
bosom,
whom those who have dispelled ignorance and passion
always keep before them, as it were,
who is praised by Rādhā, whose entry is marked
by carpets of flowers fallen from heaven
and added to by layers from the trees atop the great
mountain raised aloft on his hand.

2. I take refuge in Glory incarnate as the enchantingly
sweet boy crowned king of flute players,
who elicits the feeling of wonder by the
amours enjoyed by Rādhā, who is a treasury of
graces,
whose lotus face with natural smiles is beyond
the ordinary,
who shatters the proud importance of the emerald.

3. I serve the supreme glory who incarnated as
a boy because of compassion,
whose dignity of stride is not attained by
the elephant,
who ever lives in the minds of the self-controlled,
who delights in the woods of the Yamunā.

4. May supreme glory, incarnate as Kṛṣṇa, exceedingly
delightful and all pervading,
ever permeate my heart.
Although his three worlds are independent,
he is subdued by Vraja women with
command in their large eyes.

ŚATAKA III

1. asti svastyayanaṃ samastajagatām abhyastalakṣmīstanaṃ
vastu dhavastarajastamobhir aniśaṃ nyastaṃ purastād iva /
hastodastagirīndramastakataruprastāravistārita-
srastasvastarusūnasaṃstaralasatprastāvi rādhāstutam //

2. rādhārādhitavibhramādbhutarasaṃ lālityaratnākāraṃ
sādhāraṇyapadavyatītasahajasmerānanāmbhoruham /
ālambe harinīlagarvagurutāsarvasvanirvāpaṇaṃ
bālaṃ vaiṇavikeṣu mugdhamadhuraṃ mūrdhābhiṣiktaṃ mahaḥ //

3. kariṇām alaṅghyagativaibhavaṃ bhaje
karuṇāvalambitakiśoravigraham /
yaminām anāratavihāri mānase
yamunāvanāntarasikaṃ paraṃ mahaḥ //

4. atantritatrijagad api vrajāṅganā-
niyantritaṃ vipulavilocanājñayā /
nirantaraṃ mama hṛdaye vijṛmbhatāṃ
samantataḥ sarasataraṃ paraṃ mahaḥ //

5. I salute the archer god as a boy who is putting
 forth the first tender sprouts of the forest of
 of youth,
whose power of beauty is a wrestling opponent to
 the God of Love, who is a kinsman to the dark
 clouds,
who is adorned with closely attached ornaments,
 the graceful women of Vṛndāvana,
whose lotus face has a slight smile, whose
 cherry lips erase sweetness.

6. Somehow it revels in my soul—the primal glory,
 incarnate as the Kṛṣṇa,
who is free from the human condition but represents
 himself as not free,
who has attained an incarnation but has not
attained a grown up life as lover and
 politician,
who has touched youth but has not yet rubbed off the
 condition of childhood.

7. May those several majestic qualities, so compelling
 to the whole world,
spontaneously manifest themselves in my heart which
 is a friend to so many desires.
I know nothing sweeter than the ocean of Nanda's
 merit, Kṛṣṇa,
whose lotus face smiles when his flute makes music
 with the lute.

8. When will this heart of mine plunge deep in the great
 lake of the oversoul, incarnate as Kṛṣṇa,
whose cranes are the lotus faces of the very beautiful
 women of Vraja,
who is honoured by those of good deeds with their
 ears open to the play of floods of sweet nectar
 sounds from his flute?

5. kandarpapratimallakāntivibhavaṃ kādambinībāndhavaṃ
vṛndāraṇyavilāsinīvyasaninā veṣeṇa bhūṣāmayam /
mandasmeramukhāmbujaṃ madhurimavyāmṛṣṭabimbādharaṃ
vande kandalitārdrayauvanavanaṃ kaiśorikaṃ śārṅgiṇaḥ //

6. āmuktamānuṣam amuktanijānubhāvam
ārūḍhavigraham arūḍhavidagdhalīlam /
āmṛṣṭayauvanam amṛṣṭakiśorabhāvam
ādyaṃ mahaḥ kim api mādyati mānasaṃ me //

7. te te bhāvāḥ sakalajagatīlobhanīyaprabhāvā
nānātṛṣṇāsuhṛdi hṛdi me kāmam āvirbhavantu /
vīṇāveṇukvaṇitalasitasmeravaktrāravindān
nā 'haṃ jāne madhuram aparaṃ nandapuṇyāmbupūrāt /

8. sukṛtibhir ādṛte sarasaveṇuninādasudhā-
rasalaharīvihāraniravagrahakarṇapuṭaiḥ /
vrajavarasundarīmukhasaroruhasārasike
mahasi kadā nu majjati madīyam idaṃ hṛdayam //

9. May the play of compassionate side long glances
from Kṛṣṇa,
the main ocean of compassion and virtue,
prosper us
while ever stealing away the deep darkness of delusion
which permeates our heart sick with desire.

10. Venerated in the Upaniṣads, which are the culmination
of all the Vedas,
the lotus foot of the supreme splendour,
when it came to Vraja as the lotus foot of Kṛṣṇa,
was very highly honoured
by distinguished decorations of wet cow dung.

11. When shall I see that boy, so strange, with the lotus eyes
whose face is enjoyed by the eyes, languid with
intoxication, of the young wives of Vraja,
whose charming face, overspread with gentle open
smiles,
joyfully reflects itself again and again with increasing
intensity in the lotus mind of sages?

12. When shall we just once be able to drink with both
our longing eyes from the flood of your
radiance, blue like the water lily petal—
even though the flood has been made into the leavings
of a drink, because it has been drunk by the
eyes of the intoxicated women of Vraja?

13. I serve the Splendour with the lotus eyes,
who is the essence of the excellence of the lovely,
whose glory is celebrated in the song of the young
women of the cowherd village,
who plays on the soft sounding flute.

9. tṛṣṇāture cetasi jṛmbhamāṇaṃ
muṣṇan muhur mohamahāndhakāram /
puṣṇātu naḥ puṇyadayaikasindhoḥ
kṛṣṇasya kāruṇyakaṭākṣakelih //

10. nikhilanigamamaulilālitaṃ
padakamalaṃ paramasya tejasaḥ /
vrajabhuvi bahuman mahetarāṃ
sarasakarīṣaviśeṣabhūṣitam //

11. udāramṛdulasmitavyatikarābhirāmānanaṃ
mudā muhur udīrṇayā munimano'mbujāmreḍitam /
madālasavilocanavrajavadhūmukhāsvāditaṃ
kadā nu kamalekṣaṇaṃ kam api bālam ālokaye //

12. vrajajanamadayoṣillocanoccheṣaśeṣī-
kṛtam api capalābhyāṃ locanābhyām ubhābhyām /
sakṛd api paripātuṃ te vayaṃ pārayāmaḥ
kuvalayadalanīlaṃ kāntipūraṃ kadā nu //

13. ghoṣayoṣidanugītavaibhavaṃ
komalasvanitaveṇunisvanam /
sārabhūtam abhirāmasaṃpadāṃ
dhāma tāmarasalocanaṃ bhaje //

14. We honour only the boy
who is always engaged in charming games,
who is the original home of excellence in
bodily form,
whose blue beauty increases like that of a
rain cloud.

15. I do homage to the two lotus feet of
Murāri
whose childhood has been given us by his mercy,
which are in danger of being crushed by garlands, made
of blossoms from the tree of wishes,
on the heads of hosts of gods bowing in reverence.

16. I serve that boy and that forest of Vṛndāvana where
the wishing trees grow,
where Kārttikeya's peacock dances with a multitude
of the boy's peacock plume crown,
where Śiva's bull, getting scent of the boy's cow in
the cowpen, becomes wild and mighty,
where the elephant of Indra, wishing for the boy's
charming gait, stands rooted.

17. I take refuge in that very boy who is the home of
pity,
whose smile is marked by the red nectar of his
lower lip,
whose glory is colored after the ocean,
whose long eyes are like just opening lotus petals.

18. I serve him who is the youthful good Fortune of the
cowherd people,
whose body ornamentation is accomplished by waves of
loveliness,
who has put a sacred peacock plume in the place for
an ornament,
whose garland is of sidelong glances overflowing
with compassion.

14. līlayā lalitayā 'valambitaṃ
mūlageham iva mūrtisaṃpadām /
nīlanīradavikāsavibhramaṃ
bālam eva vayam ādriyāmahe //

15. vande murāreś caraṇāravinda-
dvaṃdvaṃ dayādarśitaśaiśavasya /
vandāruvṛndārakavṛndamauli-
mandāramālāvinimardabhīru //

16. yasmin nṛtyati yasya śekharabharaiḥ krauñcadviṣaś candrakī
yasmin dṛpyati yasya ghoṣasurabhiṃ jighran vṛṣo dhūrjaṭeḥ /
yasmin sajjati yasya vibhramagatiṃ vāñchan hareḥ sindhuras
tad vṛndāvanakalpakadrumavanaṃ taṃ vā kiśoraṃ bhaje //

17. aruṇādharāmṛtaviśeṣitasmitaṃ
varuṇālayānugatavarṇavaibhavam /
taruṇāravindadaladīrghalocanaṃ
karuṇālayaṃ kam api bālam āśraye //

18. lāvaṇyavīcīracitāṅgabhūṣāṃ
bhūṣāpadāropitapuṇyabarhām /
kāruṇyadhārālakaṭākṣamālāṃ
bālāṃ bhaje vallavavaṃśalakṣmīm //

19. We serve the lord's body, which evokes only
sweet feelings, as it moves along the streets
of Mathurā
where it is rained upon by a shower of blue lotus
glances from the eyes of the fawn eyed
ladies in the city.

20. Oh, Nanda's son agitates my heart
by casting a flurry of sidelong glances,
by the charming perturbation of a gentle
rapturous smile,
by low and very pleasing talk.

21. We do homage to the honoured rogue of the
cowherds,
whose lotus face has a slight smile,
whose lotus eyes, when they appear,
are imprisoned by side long glances
excited by love.

22. My mind joyfully dives deep in Murāri's moon lotus
face which evokes only the feeling of sweetness,
which has a voluptuous smile caressed by the eyes
of Rādhā,
which sends forth the nectar of flute sounds brightened
by a counter play between many styles and moods,
which deeply delights in chance sidelong glance embraces—
deep and very playful.

23. When the power of the archer god,
which is a diamond cage refuge for those who
come for protection,
has been incarnated out of pity as a cowherd,
why should we seek for something else?

24. May it ever abide in my heart—
the power incarnate which finds enjoyment at the
full bosom of Rādhā,
whose tenderness is fully tasted by Ramā,
which is the most solitary and charming land
in the three worlds.

19. madhuraikarasaṃ vapur vibhor
mathurāvīthicaraṃ bhajāmahe /
nagarīmṛgaśāvalocanā-
nayanendīvaravarṣavarṣitam //

20. paryākulena nayanāntavijṛmbhitena
kamreṇa komalamadasmitavibhrameṇa /
mandreṇa mañjulatareṇa ca jalpitena
nandasya hanta tanayo hṛdayaṃ dhunoti //

21. kandarpakaṇḍūlakaṭākṣabandīr
indīvarākṣīr abhilakṣyamāṇān /
mandasmitādhāramukhāravindān
vandāmahe vallavadhūrtapādān //

22. līlāṭopakaṭākṣanirbharapariṣvaṅgaprasaṅgādhika-
prīte rītivibhaṅgasaṃgaralasadveṇupraṇādāmṛte /
rādhālocanalālitasya lalitasmere murārer mudā
mādhuryaikarase mukhendukamale magnaṃ madīyaṃ manaḥ //

23. śaraṇāgatavajrapañjare
śaraṇe śārṅgadharasya vaibhave /
kṛpayā dhṛtagopavigrahe
kiyad anyam mṛgayāmahe vayam //

24. jagattrayaikāntamanojñabhūmiś
cetasy ajasraṃ mama saṃnidhattām /
ramāsamāsvāditasaukumāryaṃ
rādhāstanābhogarasajñam ojaḥ //

25. We here believe in what the songs say about
you as a mine of pity,
and our hearts are overwrought about your
charming childhood, O Lord.

26. My eyes yearn for the time when a certain
little boy, who tends the calf pen and
who is marked with a white curl of hair
on his chest, will appear to gladden them.

27. We long for the Glory who came to earth in Vraja,
who is full of sweetness and pleasant to think
about,
whose moon face is marked with a very gentle
smile,
who is the most alluring thing to the eyes of
the three worlds.

28. We long for your lotus face
which has lively flute notes flowing like
drops of honey and
which is a battlefield with waves of bee
glances from Vraja women.

29. I see the special glory, incarnate as Kṛṣṇa, who is
well worth seeing,
who is lovely with a light movement of his lotus feet
and smiling face adorned with drops of sweat
and who is magnified by the women of Vraja who
fully express the celestial dance and repeat its
rhythm and mood in their singing and who are refreshed
by the nectar play from the flood of glances from
Kṛṣṇa's long reddish eyes.

25. vayam ete viśvasimaḥ
karuṇākarakīrtikiṃvadantyā te /
api ca vibho tava lalite
capalatarā matir iyaṃ bālye //

26. vatsavāṭacaraḥ ko 'pi
vatsaḥ śrīvatasalāñchanaḥ /
utsavāya kadā bhāvī 'ty
utsuke mama locane //

27. madhurimabharite mano'bhirāme
mṛdulatarasmitamudritānanendau /
tribhuvananayanaikalobhanīye
mahasi vayaṃ vrajabhāji lālasāḥ smaḥ //

28. mukhāravinde makarandabindu-
niṣyandalīlāmuralīnināde /
vrajāñganāpāñgataraṃgabhṛñga-
saṃgrāmabhūmau tava lālasāḥ smaḥ //

29. ātāmrāyatalocanāṃśulaharīlīlāsudhāpyāyitaiḥ
gītāmreḍitadivyakelibharitaiḥ sphītaṃ vrajastrījanaiḥ /
svedāmbhaḥkaṇabhūṣaṇena kim api smereṇa vaktrendunā
pādāmbhojamṛdupracārasubhagaṃ paśyāmi dṛśyaṃ mahaḥ //

30. We are searching for the special illusive radiance
whose living form is as follows:
In his hands, formed in a naturally tender fashion,
is a flute which fully expresses a child's
feeling.
At his side are girls who behold with loving delight
his sidelong glances.
On his head is a peacock feather and on his
sweet lotus face an expression of sweet
naīvete.

31. O tree gods, how can your trunks compare?
Behold
the indescribable trunk of light incarnate
as a boy
who bears a lotus face of much sweetness
with the added charm of a flute placed on his
slightly opened lips.

32. Because I have completed the necessary good deeds,
I shall behold
the modern manifestation of the ancient spirit
which shines with such a radiance, never shared by
another,
that it overwhelms the oltus eyes of the
milkmaids.

33. I do homage to the whole essembly of the gods
with a complete prostaration of my body and
with my whole heart ask for just this.
Let my love and devotion be towards the incarnation
of Nanda's accumulated merit, Kṛṣṇa,
whose sweet full moon face is animated by a slight
smile.

34. In these streams which are the lives of men
I believe the instant which is to be counted
is just that in which the life of the blue hued
child is intimately experienced by some
insight.

30. pāṇau veṇuḥ prakṛtisukumārākṛtau bālyalakṣmīḥ
pārśve bālāḥ praṇayasarasālokitāpāṅgalīlāḥ /
maulau barhaṃ madhuravadanāmbhoruhe maugdhyamudre
'ty ārdrākāraṃ kim api kitavaṃ jyotir anveṣayāmaḥ //

31. ārūḍhaveṇutaruṇādharavibhrameṇa
mādhuryaśālivadanāmbujam udvahantī /
ālokyatāṃ kim anayā vanadevatā vaḥ
kaiśorake vayasi kā cana kāntiyaṣṭiḥ //

32. ananyasādhāraṇakāntikāntam
ākrāntagopīnayanāravindam /
puṃsaḥ purāṇasya navaṃ vilāsaṃ
puṇyena pūrṇena vilokayiṣye //

33. sāṣṭāṅgapātam abhivandya samastabhāvaiḥ
sarvān surendranikarān idam eva yāce /
mandasmitārdramadhurānanacandrabimbe
nandasya puṇyanicaye mama bhaktir astu //

34. eṣu pravāheṣu sa eva manye
kṣaṇo 'pi gaṇyaḥ puruṣāyuṣeṣu /
āsvādyate yatra kayā 'pi vṛttyā
nīlasya bālasya nijaṃ caritram //

35. Again and again we do homage to the Glory which
dazzles the world,
whose lower lip is naturally lovely, whose bright
gaze is poignant with innate compassion,
whose lotus face is captivating, whose slight
smile is tender with sweetness,
whose home is the heart of those who know true
joy, who delights the eyes of milkmaids.

36. In my heart amid its repeated delusions may
these two things constantly appear:
the special boy with the lotus eyes and
the dust from the feet of the women of
Vraja.

37. When death is near, may that naughty boy at
the bosom of the milkmaids
appear before me in his charming costume gently
playing flute notes.

38. We do homage to the glory which is the best remedy—
with no other taste than sweetness—for the
heart,
which is the best subject for speech or no subject
at all, which is found at the bosom of milkmaids.

39. In some future birth may all my faculties delight
in the chief adornment of the world,
in the enchanting light incarnated in the lord
with the long lotus eyes
who is as nectar to the eyes of the beautiful women
of Vraja.

40. I worship the wonderful Glory which embodied itself
in the charming form of the cloud-dark god,
who is the aupicious one whose eyes are fixed on
the rows of berry-like bosoms
of the milkmaids who appear to be under the influence
of the passion of love, who is worshipped by rows
of silent ascetics,
who is the subject for repeated praise by rapturous
hearts and by the songs of the Vedas.

35. nisargasarasādharaṃ nijadayārdradivyekṣaṇaṃ
manojñnamukhapaṅkajaṃ madhurasārdramandasmitam /
rasajñahṛdayāspadaṃ ramitavallavīlocanaṃ
punaḥ punar upāsmahe bhuvanalobhanīyaṃ mahaḥ //

36. sa ko 'pi bālaḥ sarasīruhākṣaḥ
sā ca vrajastrījanapādadhūliḥ /
muhus tad etad yugalaṃ madīye
momuhyamāne 'pi manasy udetu //

37. mayi prayāṇābhimukhe ca vallavī-
stanadvayīdurlalitaḥ sa bālakaḥ /
śanaiḥ śanaiḥ śrāvitaveṇunisvano
vilāsaveṣeṇa puraḥ pratīyatām //

38. atibhūmim abhūmim eva vā
vacasāṃ vāsitavallavīstanam /
manasām aparaṃ rasāyanaṃ
madhurādvaitam upāsmahe mahaḥ //

39. jananāntare 'pi jagadekamaṇḍane
kamanīyadhāmni kamalāyatekṣaṇe /
vrajasundarījanavilocanāmṛte
capalāni santu sakalendriyāṇi me //

40. muniśreṇīvandyaṃ madabharalasadvallavavadhū-
stanaśreṇībimbastimitanayanāmbhojasubhagam /
punaḥślāghābhūmiṃ pulakitahṛdāṃ naigamagirāṃ
ghanaśyāmaṃ vande kim api kamanīyākṛti mahaḥ //

41. As it is for them who experience the sweet glory of the
lord in human form even with wavering minds,
so might it be for us also who call out, "O Lord,
O Kṛṣṇa, O Beloved."

42. When shall I see—rising from the modern ocean of
fame obtained by Yaśodā—the blue moon
with the wide eyes, dressed in the clothes of
a boy
and considered by the thin waisted women to be
especially worthy to be seen.

43. May it save us—the power which is the original
form of the treasure of beauty and grace,
which is naturally unaware of the series of
faults by devotees,
which, in the form of a boy, is approached by
the good,
which is a vessel which holds the hearts of the
good.

44. May it delight us—the Splendour which is the
home of Lakṣmī,
which completely captivates the heart by smiles
gentle with tenderness,
which mock the proud arrogance of nectar,
which is watched by the eyes of the young women of
Vraja.

45. May it play in our hearts the Glory which blesses
the auspicious bosom of milkmaids and
which rains for the eyes an unfailing nectar of joy
which is marked by just sprouting smiles.

46. Do you worship the unconquered chest which has been
smeared when pressed to the saffron on the jarlike
bosoms of milkmaids and
which is coloured coral by thick drops made of red dust
from the cheek-like slopes of a great forested
mountain added to a mixture of the mud and musk of
the musk deer.

41. anucumbatām api calena cetasā
manujākṛter madhurimaśriyaṃ vibhoḥ /
ayi deva kṛṣṇa dayite 'ti jalpitām
api no bhaveyur api nāma tādṛśāḥ //

42. kiśoraveṣeṇa kṛśodarīdṛśāṃ
viśeṣadṛśyena viśālalocanam /
yaśodayā labdhayaśonavāmbudher
niśāmaye nīlaniśākaraṃ kadā //

43. prakṛtir avatu no vilāsalakṣmyāḥ
prakṛtijaḍaṃ praṇatāparādhavīthyām /
sukṛtikṛtapadaṃ kiśorabhāve
sukṛtimanaḥpraṇidhānapātram ojaḥ //

44. apahasitasudhāmadāvalepair
atisumanoharam ārdramandahāsaiḥ /
vrajayuvativilocanāvalehyaṃ
ramayatu dhāma ramāvarodhanaṃ naḥ //

45. aṅkūritasmeradaśāviśeṣair
aśrāntaharṣāmṛtavarṣam akṣṇām /
saṃkrīḍatāṃ cetasi gopakanyā-
dhanyastanasvastyayanaṃ maho naḥ //

46. mṛgamadapaṅkasaṃkaraviśeṣitavanyamahā-
giritaṭagaṇḍagairikaghanadravavidrumitam /
ajitabhujāntaraṃ bhajata hā bata gopavadhū-
stanakalaśasthalīghusṛṇamardanakardamitam //

47. May he protect us—the god in the form of a
child with a tender and charming full moon
face who is the culmination of sweetness and
the enemy of Madhu, the demon,
who has consented to take the guise of a cowherd,
who anoints the world, in an action which includes
both root and branch, with a net of sidelong
glances.

48. If, in Vraja, you worship the archer god's lotus
feet which make the jewelled anklets tinkle,
it is as if you worship a beautiful lotus which
is in a well filled lake echoing with swans.

49. May it save us—the oversoul, which has embodied
itself in the beautiful blue body of infinite
sweetness,
which is the refuge of those without refuge, which
has the eyes of the autumn lotus.
which is surrounded by the young women of Vraja
whose smiling lotus eyes are subdued by the
arrows of the god of love.

50. May he protect us—he who embodies the power which
rules the universe, who is lovely without
artifice,
who is well trained in the method of herding cows,
whose boyhood is giving way to a youthfulness never
previously manifest.
whose celestial limbs, with their excess of well
manifest splendour, are the sun.

51. May he protect us—the god who came as a boy, the
most tender in all three worlds,
who is watched by the immortal women, who stay in the
sky,
who are foremost in creating pleasure by the beauty
and sweetness of their eyes,
while he directs his sidelong glances to the lovely
activities of the young women of Vraja.

47. āmūlapallavitalīlam apāṅgajālair
āsiñcatī bhuvanam ādṛtagopaveṣā /
bālyākṛtir mṛdulamugdhamukhendubimbā
mādhuryasiddhir avatān madhuvidviṣo naḥ //

48. viraṇanmaṇinūpuraṃ vraje
caraṇāmbhojam upāssva śārṅgiṇaḥ /
sarase sarasi śriyā 'śritaṃ
kamalaṃ vā kalahaṃsanāditam //

49. śaraṇam aśaraṇānāṃ śāradāmbhojanetraṃ
niravadhimadhurimnā nīlaveṣeṇa ramyam /
smaraśaraparatantrasmeranetrāmbujābhir
vrajayuvatibhir avyād brahma saṃveṣṭitaḥ naḥ //

50. suvyaktakāntibharasaurabhadivyagātram
avyaktayauvanaparītakiśorabhāvam /
gavyānupālanavidhāv anuśiṣṭam avyād
avyājaramyam akhileśvaravaibhavaṃ naḥ //

51. anugatam amarīṇām ambarālambinīnāṃ
nayanamadhurimaśrīnarmanirmāṇasīmnām /
vrajayuvativilāsavyāpṛtāpāṅgam avyāt
tribhuvanasukumāraṃ devakaiśorakaṃ naḥ //

52. May he protect us—the lord who incarnated as the
son of a cowherd king,
who is zealously drunk from head to foot by the
minds of ascetics,
whose sweetness the milkmaids know.

53. May it grant our desires—the radiance incarnate
in Kṛṣṇa who is blue like the petals of the
water lily where Lakṣmī lives and who is
distinguished by buds of rising flesh, the
ornaments of enjoyment,
who, with diverse waves of lively and affectionate
sidelong glances, comes close at hand to the deer-eyed
women of Vraja afflicted by separation from him.

54. Hail to the prince whose hair is bathed with a
shower of flowers scattered by celestial
maidens,
whose body is coloured by the red metal dust of the
mountains of the gods,
whose peacock plume is that of Skanda's king peacock.

55. Hail to the lord's lotus face vibrant with love,
charming with smiles—sweet, gently, and bright,
and with eyes which rove to the bosom of the
young women of Vraja.

56. Hail to the Glory, incarnate as Kṛṣṇa, who inspires
series of triumphs for deer-eyed women, whose
lips, bathed with smiles containing all the red
light of dawn, are like the just risen sun,
whose naive affectionate smile appears languid, whose
sweat from subduing the love of the beautiful women
of Vraja is aupicious, whose lotus face is
dignified.

52. āpādam ācūḍam atiprasaktair
āpīyamānā yamināṃ manobhiḥ /
gopījanajñātarasā 'vatān no
gopālabhūpālakumāramūrtiḥ //

53. diṣṭyā vṛndāvanamṛgadṛśāṃ viprayogākulānāṃ
pratyāsannaṃ praṇayacapalāpāṅgavīcītaraṃgaiḥ /
lakṣmīlīlākuvalayadalaśyāmalaṃ dhāma kāmān
puṣṇīyān naḥ pulakamukulābhogabhūṣāviśeṣam //

54. jayati guhaśikhīndrapicchamauliḥ
suragirigairikakalpitāṅgarāgaḥ /
surayuvativikīrṇasūnavarṣa-
snapitavibhūṣitakuntalaḥ kumāraḥ //

55. madhuramandaśucismitamañjulaṃ
vadanapaṅkajam aṅgajavellitam /
vijayatāṃ vrajabālavadhūjana-
stanataṭīviluṭhannayanaṃ vibhoḥ //

56. alasavilasan mugdhasnigdhasmitaṃ vrajasundarī-
madanakadanasvinnaṃ dhanyaṃ mahad vadanāmbujam /
taruṇam aruṇajyotsnākārtsnyasmitasnapitādharaṃ
jayati vijayaśreṇīm eṇīdṛśāṃ madayan mahaḥ //

57. Hail to the hair thrill of the radiance which became
incarnate as Kṛṣṇa for the pleasure of the three worlds.
The sprouts of thrilled hair decorate his great chest
when Rādhā watches with playful sidelong glances,
and the dense wealth of their dominion becomes
impenetrable from the deep embrace given in fear
(of separation)
by Lakṣmī during the moment of her confused awakening
after sleep at the end of love making.

58. The imaginings and impressions of my mind which have
long been contemplated now triumph taking shape as
Kṛṣṇa
whose lower lip has the nectar distilled from its
smile, who bears the insignia of the impassioned
peacock's plume,
whose lotus eyes are large, who is found together with
the graceful women of Vraja,
whose lotus face captivates the heart, whose flute
notes are sweet.

59. May it conquer—that natural abundance of full
nectar like radiance which is incarnated as Kṛṣṇa
whose crest is fashioned from a peacock's feather.
From the good fortune resulting from the smallest
part of a drop, the five-arrowed love god reaches
the summit of good fortune.

60. May it prevail—the Glory embodied in the boy who
supports the burden of impassioned milkmaids'
bosoms,
who is constantly enjoyed by aesthetes who have shaken
off all other concerns,
who, although with all a child's instability, is
indestructible by the extent of his great eyes
subduing the charm of the autumn moon by the beauty of
his tender smile.

57. rādhākelikaṭākṣavīkṣitamahāvakṣaḥsthalīmaṇḍanā
jīyāsuḥ pulakāṅkurās tribhuvanasvādīyasas tejasaḥ /
krīḍāntapratisuptadugdhatanayāmugdhāvabodhakṣaṇa-
trāsārūḍhadṛḍhopagūḍhagahanāḥ sāmrājyasāndraśriyaḥ //

58. smitasnutasudhādharā madaśikhaṇḍibarhāṅkitā
viśālanayanāmbujā vrajavilāsinīvāsitāḥ /
manojñamukhapaṅkajā madhuraveṇunādadravā
jayanti mama cetasaś ciram upāsitā vāsanāḥ //

59. jīyād asau śikhiśikhaṇḍakṛtāvataṃsā
sāṃsiddhikī sarasakāntisudhāsamṛddhiḥ /
yadbinduleśakaṇikāpariṇāmabhāgyāt
saubhāgyasīmapadam añcati pañcabāṇaḥ //

60. āyāmena dṛśor viśālatarayor akṣayyam ārdrasmita-
cchāyādharṣitaśāradendulalitaṃ cāpalyamātraṃ śiśoḥ /
āyāsān aparān vidhūya rasikair āsvādyamānaṃ muhur
jīyād unmadavallavīkucabharādhāraṃ kiśoraṃ mahaḥ //

61. The cowpen is his royal camp, some cowherds his
lieutenants,
the offering of tributes fulfilled by hanging
cowropes on his shoulders, his harem the
milkmaids,
his adornments the red metal dust and—the wonder
of it—peacock plumes.
Even so, people boldly assert that this person is
the lord of the three worlds.

62. Who does not indeed long for the Glory which is incarnated
as the lover of the milkmaids,
who chooses a glorious peacock plume for an ornament,
who has a dark and pleasing brilliance,
whose body has been anointed with only the essence of
beauty, who is a monsoon to the lake of Lakṣmī,
who is the spring of divine play nectar to the pious
hearts of aesthetes dedicated to that play.

63. How sweet is the very immature face of Murāri
which has deep red lips and fluttering eager
eyes,
which is full of joy and wondrous radiance,
which has the nectar of an open smile, and
which beguiles the memory.

64. Awake, awake, O Mind. You have reached your
goal at last.
Enjoy this full beatitude standing right here
before you.

65. Sweet is the Glory incarnate who is a baby in
age,
who is red of feet tender with compassion,
who is abundant of hair and wide of eye,
who is charming of body mascara black.

61. skandhāvārapadaṃ vrajaḥ katipaye gopāḥ sahāyādayaḥ
skandhālambini vatsadāmni dhanadā gopāṅganāḥ svāṅganāḥ /
śṛṅgārā girigairikaṃ śiva śiva śrīmanti barhāṇi vā
śṛṅgagrāhikayā tathā 'pi tam imaṃ prāhus trilokeśvaram //

62. śrīmadbarhiśikhaṇḍamaṇḍanajuṣe śyāmābhirāmatviṣe
lāvaṇyaikarasāvasiktavapuṣe lakṣmīsaraḥpravṛṣe /
līlākṛṣṭarasajñadharmamanase līlāmṛtasrotase
ke vā na spṛhayanti hanta mahase gopījanapreyase //

63. āpāṭalādharam adhīravilolanetram
āmodanirbharitam adbhutakāntipūram /
āviḥsmitāmṛtam anusmṛtilobhanīyam
āmudritānanam aho madhuraṃ murāreḥ //

64. jāgṛhi jāgṛhi cetaś
cirāya caritārthatā bhavataḥ /
anubhūyatām idam idaṃ
puraḥ sthitaṃ pūrṇanirvāṇam //

65. caraṇayor aruṇaṃ karuṇārdrayoḥ
kacabhare bahulaṃ vipulaṃ dṛśoḥ /
vapuṣi mañjulam añjanamecake
vayasi bālam aho madhuraṃ mahaḥ //

66. I salute the supreme divinity incarnate in the child
whose body is blue like the young *tamāla* tree,
whose abundant locks are entrancing with a peacock plume
as a crown, who is showered with wild flowers,
whose bright forehead mark is made from mountain
minerals, who is always charming,
whose chief delight is the nectar of music from his
happy flute, who has a wealth of beauty.

67. Heavy of tender foot, slim of ankle, massive of
buttocks,
lotus like of abdomen, mighty of arms, broad of
chest,
sweet of lower lip, charming of face, lively of
eye,
abundant of hair, sylvan of dress—oh, the
charming Glory!

68. Homage to that one who is the whole of great bliss,
who with his human birth always achieves great charm,
who always yields nectar with his flute notes,
who always looks with long sidelong glances.

69. I do homage to the highest god, who is blended with
the essence of boyishness,
who has a glittering peacock feather crest, whose face
has a caressing smile,
who has playful sidelong glances roving wherein
suppliant people find bliss,
who is dark like new clouds, who is filled with the
enjoyment of his own sweetness.

70. This, incarnate in Kṛṣṇa, is the result of my eyes'
longing.
By his face he is, as it were, the totality of
delight,
by his smile, the charm of sweetness,
by his gaze, the tenderness of compassion.

66. mālābarhamanojñakuntalabharāṃ vanyaprasūnokṣitāṃ
śaileyadravakḷptacitratilakāṃ śaśvanmanohāriṇīm /
līlāveṇuravāmṛtaikarasikāṃ lāvaṇyalakṣmīmayīṃ
bālaṃ bālatamālanīlavapuṣaṃ vande parāṃ devatām //

67. guru mṛdupade gūḍhaṃ gulphe ghanaṃ jaghanasthale
nalinam udare vīraṃ bāhvor viśālam uraḥsthale /
madhuram adhare mugdhaṃ vaktre vilāsi vilocane
bahu kacabhare vanyaṃ veṣe manojñam aho mahaḥ //

68. jihānaṃ jihānaṃ nu jānena maughdyaṃ
duhānaṃ duhānaṃ sudhāṃ veṇunādaiḥ /
lihānaṃ lihānaṃ nu dīrghair apāṅgair
mahānandasarvasvam ekaṃ namet tam //

69. lasadbarhapīḍaṃ lalitalalitasmeravadanaṃ
bhramatkrīḍāpāṅgaṃ praṇatajanatānirvṛtipadam /
navāmbhodaśyāmaṃ nijamadhurimābhogabharitaṃ
paraṃ devaṃ vande parimilitakaiśorakarasam //

70. sārasyasāmagryam ivā 'nanena
mādhuryacāturyam iva smitena /
kāruṇyatāruṇyam ive 'kṣaṇena
cāpalyasāphalyam idaṃ dṛśor me //

71. O Lord, if ever we should place our faith in you,
there would be no missing perfect bliss—
how much less lesser benefits![3]

72. O Master, this folding of my hands in prayer is to
your lotus feet
which look like red lotuses,
which are worshipped by milkmaids blind with passion,
which are swarmed to by bee-like yogīs.

73. We invoke that youth who sympathetically gives
ear
to the prayers of the beautiful women of Vraja
and to the guileless Sarasvatīs.

74. May he abide in my heart—
that certain boy who is, as it were, a flood
of pity,
whose face is sweet and glances languid,
whose hand plays a melodious flute.

75. May all those things which are connected with
the child protect us: all the well-trained
herding of the cows, the peacock plume crests,
the famous music of the flute so pleasing to
creatures,
the milkmaids calmed by his soothing gaze.

76. May he protect us—the presiding deity of the world
who came to earth as the boy
whose lips blossom in smiles and soothe with
the nectar of flute notes,
whose eyes ever sparkle, who is covered with a
garland of impassioned sidelong glances,
who is embraced by Kamalā clinging closely to
his chest.

---

3. Linus c and d of the Sanskrit verse were translated by M. B. Emeneau.

71. yatra vā tatra vā deva
yadi viśvasimas tvayi /
nirvāṇam api durvāram
arvācīnāni kiṃ punaḥ //

72. rāgāndhagopījanavanditābhyāṃ
yogīndrabhṛṅgendraniṣevitābhyām /
ātāmrapaṅkeruhavibhramābhyāṃ
svāmin padābhyām añjalis te //

73. arthānulāpān vrajasundarīṇām
akṛtrimāṇāṃ ca sarasvatīnām /
ārdrāśayena śravaṇāñcalena
saṃbhāvayantaṃ taruṇaṃ gṛṇīmaḥ //

74. manasi mama saṃnidhattāṃ
madhuramukhā mantharāpāṅgā /
karakalitalalitavaṃśā
kā 'pi kiśorā kṛpālaharī //

75. rakṣantu naḥ śikṣitapāśupālyā
bālāvṛtā barhiśikhāvataṃsāḥ /
prāṇapriyaprastutaveṇugītāḥ
śītādṛśoḥ śītalagopakanyāḥ //

76. smitastabakitādharaṃ śiśiraveṇunādāmṛtaṃ
muhus taralalocanaṃ madakaṭākṣamālākulam /
uraḥsthalavilīnayā kamalāsamāliṅgitaṃ
bhuvastalam upāgataṃ bhuvanadaivataṃ pātu naḥ //

77. Serve him whose lotus eyes grant wishes,
whose lotus heart is compassionate,
whose lotus feet are the chief wealth of ascetics,
whose lotus face holds sway over the young wives of
Vraja.

78. May he protect us—the patron deity of cow pens,
who drives out all other delights,
who is the kingdom of bliss come to earth,
who is the great treasure of natural sweetness.

79. May it protect us—the supreme glory incarnate
in the person who roamed the sands of the
Kālindī River,
who is worshipped by the delights of play,
who is closely pressed to the full bosoms
of the milkmaids out of joy at his dear
flute and costume.

80. Let it play in my heart—the Glory
who carried on a quarrel with the black
clouds,
who somehow made a home in the forest,
whose flute notes enchant the sylphs.

81. May he protect us—the king of the cowherd community,
who is in no way a subject which can be expressed
in words,
who is surrounded by fawn-eyed women—mature women
languid with the burden of their hips—who make
a line around him by the confluence of their
nectar steps,
who causes the love god's hands to discharge the
arrows lying in his quiver.

82. I behold that boy who constantly watches over the cows,
whose sweet flute is placed in his left hand and whose
horn is at his hip,
who, under the thick shade of the *tamāla* tree on the
sands of the Kālindī river where the water flows
close by, eats the sweet rice and yogurt food put
on a lotus leaf plate.

77. nayanāmbuje bhajata kāmadughaṃ
hṛdayāmbuje kim api kāruṇikam /
caraṇāmbuje munikulaikadhanaṃ
vadanāmbuje vrajavadhūvibhavam //

78. nirvāsanaṃ hanta rasāntarāṇāṃ
nirvāṇasāmrājyam ivā 'vatīrṇam /
avyājamādhuryamahānidhānam
avyād vrajānām adhidaivataṃ naḥ //

79. gopīnām abhimatagītaveṣaharṣād
āpīnastanabharanirbharopagūḍham /
kelīnām avatu rasair upāsyamānaṃ
kālindīpulinacaraṃ paraṃ maho naḥ //

80. khelatāṃ manasi khecarāṅganā-
mānanīyamṛduveṇunisvanaiḥ /
kānane kim api naḥ kṛtāspadaṃ
kālameghakalahodvahaṃ mahaḥ //

81. eṇīśābavilocanābhir alasaśroṇībharapraudhibhir
veṇībhūtarasakramābhir abhitaḥ śreṇīkṛtābhir vṛtaḥ /
pāṇī nāma vinodayan ratipates tūṇīśayaiḥ sāyakair
vāṇīnām apadaṃ paraṃ vrajajanakṣoṇīpatiḥ pātu naḥ //

82. kālindīpuline tamālanibiḍacchāye puraḥsaṃcarat-
toye toyajapatrapātranihitaṃ dadhyannam aśnāti yaḥ /
vāme pāṇitale nidhāya madhuraṃ veṇuṃ viṣāṇaṃ kaṭi-
prānte gāś ca vilokayan pratikalaṃ taṃ bālam ālokaye //

83. May it appear in our heart—that dark Glory known as Kṛṣṇa,
who is the forehead mark of musk decorating the moon faces of the milkmaids,
who is the blue lily blossoming above the golden jar-like bosom of Lakṣmī,
who is the magic mascara for *yogins* in their exercises to attain the buried treasure which is *nirvāṇa*.

84. I worship Govinda whose body ornaments are celestial, who concentrates on the gentle music of the flute,
whose moon face has the lovely colour of the opened blue water lily blossom, who is fond of the peacock feather crest,
who has the divine white curl of hair on his chest, who wears the noble Kaustubha jewel, who is handsome clothed in yellow,
whose form is saluted by the lotus eyes of milkmaids, who is surrounded by crowds of cows and cowherds.

85. May that Keśava protect us—the remembrance of whose name dispels evil,
from whose lotus feet the celestial Gaṅga river
issues and adorns the head of Śiva,
whose chest is the playhouse of Kamalā, whose eyes are the sun and the moon,
in the interior of whose lotus navel Brahmā looks like a bee.

86. May they protect you— the glances of the milkmaids which are a prayerful handful of dark lotuses at Murāri's feet,
which are fish in his lake-like navel, which are the love god's arrows to his heart,
which are an emerald necklace at his throat, which are bees at his lotus face,
which are peacock feather crests on his topknot.

83. yad gopīvadanendumaṇḍanam abhūt kastūrikāpatrakaṃ
yal lakṣmīkucaśātakumbhakalaśavyākocam indīvaram /
yan nirvāṇanidhānasādhanavidhau siddhāñjanaṃ yogināṃ
tan naḥ śyāmalam āvir astu hṛdaye kṛṣṇābhidhānaṃ mahaḥ

84. phullendīvarakāntim induvadanaṃ barhāvataṃsapriyaṃ
śrīvatsāṅkam udārakaustubhadharaṃ pītāmbaraṃ sundaram /
gopīnāṃ nayanotpalārcitatanuṃ gogopasaṃghāvṛtaṃ
govindaṃ kalaveṇunādaniratam divyāṅgabhūṣaṃ bhaje //

85. yannābhīsarasīruhāntarapuṭe bhṛṅgāyamāṇo vidhir
yadvakṣaḥ kamalāvilāsasadanaṃ yaccakṣuṣī ce 'ndvinau /
yatpādābjaviniḥsṛtā suranadī śambhoḥ śirobhūṣaṇaṃ
yannāmasmaraṇaṃ dhunoti duritaṃ pāyāt sa naḥ keśavaḥ //

86. rakṣantu tvām asitajalajair añjaliḥ pādamūle
mīnā nābhīsarasi hṛdaye mārabāṇā murāreḥ /
hārāḥ kaṇṭhe harimaṇimayā vaktrapadme dvirephāḥ
picchācūḍāś cikuranicaye ghoṣayoṣitkaṭākṣāḥ //

87. May he be protective—the young cowherd
who, at the sound of the early morning churning
of curds, awoke
and went with silent step into the milkmaids'
homes,
quickly blew out the lamps with his lotus breath
and swallowed the fresh butter.

88. In the early morning I think of the thief of fresh
butter,
who shakes off sleep at the sound of buttermilk making,
who opens his lotus eyes,
whose praiseworthy body is enchanting, who is
a delight to the eyes,
whose lotus face, still close to sleep, gives delight.

89. The god I worship is a certain cowherd whose
tender shoot-like
fingers are perfumed by the milkmaid's hair,
whose cheeks are adorned with red lotus blossoms
placed at his ear,
who is to be looked for among the cow-like words
of the Āgamas.

90. May he prosper us—the thief whose theft of
fresh butter takes away the sin of stealing,
whose adultery takes away the sin of offending
the marriage bed of the *guru*,
whose slaying of Rāvaṇa takes away the sin of
murder,
whose sucking of Pūtanā, the witch, to death takes
away the sin of drinking intoxicating liquor.

91. O Love God, do not abide in my heart.
It is really only a home for the husband of
Mā.
O husband of Ramā, keep him out.
Who can tolerate trespass of his own home?

87. dadhimathananinādais tyaktanidraḥ prabhāte
nibhṛtapadam agāraṃ vallavīnāṃ praviṣṭaḥ /
mukhakamalasamīrair āśu nirvāpya dīpān
kavalitanavanītaḥ pātu gopālabālaḥ //

88. prātaḥ smarāmi dadhighoṣavidhūtanidraṃ
nidrāvasānaramaṇīyamukhāravindam /
hṛdyānavadyavapuṣaṃ nayanābhirāmam
unnidrapadmanayanaṃ navanītacoram //

89. phullahallakavataṃsakollasad-
gallam āgamagavīgaveṣitam /
vallavīcikuravāsitāṅguli-
pallavaṃ kam api vallavaṃ bhaje //

90. steyaṃ harer harati yannavanītacauryaṃ
jāratvam asya gurutalpakṛtāparādham /
hatyāṃ daśānanahatir madhupānadoṣaṃ
yatpūtanāstanapayaḥ sa punātu kṛṣṇaḥ //

91. māra mā 'rama madīyamānase
mādhavaikanilaye yadṛcchayā /
he ramāramaṇa vāryatām asau
kaḥ saheta nijaveśmalaṅghanam //

92. I worship the baby Kṛṣṇa, his left hand and bent
knee placed on the ground, his body outstretched
while he watches the lump of fresh butter in
his right lotus hand.

93. I worship the cowherd, who is the full moon of Gokula,
who stands in the middle of cows, cowherds,
and milkmaids
at the foot of the coral tree, delightful like
Madana, the Love God,
his berry lips sounding the song of the flute.

94. At dawn one should contemplate the baby cowherd
adorned with ear rings and curls,
very prettily scampering on his hands and
knees.

95. O husband of Sītā, the moment you abandon your
bow and arrows,
take into your hand the jewel-precious flute,
and put the peacock plume on the top of your
head,
I shall bow to you.

96. We resort to the cowherd's son, thinking he
will lead us to milk since it is he who is
a cowherd as well as the lord of the ocean
of milk,
and he always creates an obstacle to this because
he at once makes it difficult to obtain milk
from a mother's breast.

97.* You forcibly shake off my hand and go away.
What is the wonder in that, Kṛṣṇa?
If you can get out of my heart,
then I shall consider you as strong as a man.

92. ākuñcitaṃ jānu karaṃ ca vāmaṃ
nyasya kṣitau kṣitau dakṣiṇahastapadme /
ālokayantaṃ navanītakhaṇḍaṃ
bālaṃ bhaje kṛṣṇam upānatāñgam //

93. mandāramūle madanābhirāmaṃ
bimbādharāpūritaveṇunādam /
gogopagopījanamadhyasaṃsthaṃ
gopaṃ bhaje gokulapūrṇacandram //

94. jānubhyām abhidhāvantaṃ
bāhubhyām atisundaram /
sukuṇḍalālakaṃ bālaṃ
gopālaṃ cintayed uṣaḥ //

95. vihāya kodaṇḍaśarān muhūrtaṃ
gṛhāṇa pāṇau maṇicāruveṇum /
māyūrabarhaṃ ca nijottamāñge
sītāpate tvāṃ praṇamāmi paścāt //

96. ayaṃ kṣīrāmbhodheḥ patir iti gavāṃ pālaka iti
śrito 'smābhiḥ kṣīropanayanadhiyā gopatanayaḥ /
anena pratyūho vyaraci satataṃ yena jananī-
stanād apy asmākaṃ sakṛd api payo durlabham abhūt //

97.* hastam ākṣipya yāto 'si
balāt kṛṣṇa kim adbhutam /
hṛdayād yadi niryāsi
pauruṣaṃ gaṇayāmi te //

98.* May Kṛṣṇa come to give us help, like a physician
to those with chronic and advanced disease, like
a treasure to the poor,
like the sun rising in the darkness, like a boat
to those drowning in the ocean,
like a sweet-raining cloud to the thirsty.

99.* I have worshipped that cowherd who is a jewel amulet for
the three worlds and the Lord of Love,
who is more beautiful than the God of Love, whose face is
smiling, who is surrounded by milkmaids,
who is red like a heap of red lead powder, who
holds in his many hands the golden flute-creeper,
the tender bow and fragrant shafts, and the disc,
lotus, noose, and hook.

100.* I salute the compliant cowherd, Kṛṣṇa, very handsome,
intent on his circle dance, surrounded by thousands
of milkmaids whose loving condition is filled with
fresh feeling,
an embodiment of love who infatuates celestial and human
courtesans, a form—seen at evening, in the forest,
when the flowers bloom, on the sandy river beaches,
in the moonlight—which charms the three worlds.

101.* I salute the eternal god who stands on a lotus
and plays the flute,
who goes to Vṛndāvana forest and plays
under a *kadamba* tree.

102.* At the beginning of day one should do worshipful service
to the eternal Govinda, the best of the worshipful
immortals who include Indra etc.,
the child who looks like a blue cloud, whose throat
glitters with tigers' claws,
whose hips and ankles are tied with a band of bells
shining with bright jewels,
whose face shines like an opened lotus, who, out of grace,
slew the demons incarnate in the cart and the
wet nurse, Pūtanā.

98.* tamasi ravir ivo 'dyan majjatām amburāśau
plava iva tṛṣitānāṃ svāduvarṣī 'va meghaḥ /
nidhir iva vidhanānāṃ dīrghatīvrāmayānāṃ
bhiṣag iva kuśalaṃ no dātum āyātu śauriḥ //

99.* kodaṇḍaṃ masṛṇaṃ sugandhi viśikhaṃ cakrābjapāśāṅkuśaṃ
haimīṃ veṇulatāṃ karaiś ca dadhataṃ sindūrapuñjāruṇam /
kandarpādhikasundaraṃ smitamukhaṃ gopāṅganāveṣṭitaṃ
gopālaṃ madanādhipaṃ tam abhajaṃ trailokyarakṣāmaṇim //

100.* sāyaṃkāle vanānte kusumitasamaye saikate candrikāyāṃ
trailokyākarṣaṇāṅgaṃ suranaragaṇikāmohanāpāṅgamūrtim /
sevyaṃ śṛṅgārabhāvair navarasabharitair gopakanyāsahasrair
vande 'haṃ rāsakelīratam atisubhagaṃ vaśyagopālakṛṣṇam //

101.* kadambamūle krīḍantaṃ
vṛndāvanaiveśitam /
padmoparisthitaṃ vande
veṇuṃ gāyantam acyutam //

102.* bālaṃ nīlāmbudābhaṃ navamaṇivilasatkiṅkiṇījālabaddha-
śroṇījaṅghāntayugmaṃ vipularurunakhaprollasatkaṇṭhabhūṣam /
phullāmbhojābhavaktraṃ hataśakaṭapatatpūtanādyaṃ
prasannaṃ
govindaṃ vanditendrādyamaravaram ajaṃ pūjayed vāsarādau //

103.* For good fortune do worshipful service at mid-day
everyday to the god who is richly clad in yellow,
who is radiant with brightly shining locks fastened with
the best feathers of the blue throated bird,
whom the gods worship as the giver of salvation, whose
blue water lily eyes look like the blossoming blue
kuruvinda,
who is approached by milkmaids and cows, who conquers
multitudes of enemies, who has a jasmine and
mandāra flower smile.

104.* At evening one should chant and contemplate Vāsudeva
who gives final release and performs the function of
creating, preserving, and destroying. His body is
pure, his brightness incomparable, and his color
blue.
He is approached by the gods and praised by ascetics,
such as Nārada, for the sake of determining reality.
He, the invincible, has rid the earth of her load
by scattering hosts of her enemies with the edge
of his disc.

105.* One should contemplate Hari with the complexion of the
sun in the guise of a cowherd who looks like the
God of Love with eight hands holding
the unbroken sugar cane bow and the flowery arrow,
the discus, the conch, the noose, the spear head,
and the golden flute.

106.* O Murāri, take delight in these verses even as you took
delight in the devotion of sages' wives,
in the offering of Vidura and in the offering of
Kunti,
in the summit of Govardhana, in the rice offering,
in the mother's milk offered by Yaśodā,
in the offering of Bhāradvāja, in the offering of
Śabarikā, in the lips of the young women.

103.* vandyaṃ devair mukundaṃ vikasitakuruvindābham
indīvarākṣaṃ
gopīgovṛndavītaṃ jitaripunivahaṃ kundamandārahāsam /
nīlagrīvāgryapicchagrathanasuvilasatkuntalaṃ bhānumantaṃ
devaṃ pītāmbarāḍhyaṃ yaja yaja dinaśo madhyamāhne
ramāyai //

104.* cakrāntadhvastavairivrajam ajitam apāstāvanībharam ādyair
āvītaṃ nāradādyair munibhir abhinutaṃ tattvanirṇītihetoḥ /
sāyāhne nirmalāṅgaṃ nirupamaruciraṃ cintayen nīlabhāsaṃ
mantrī viśvodayasthityapaharaṇapadaṃ muktidaṃ vāsudevam //

105.* kodaṇḍam aikṣavam akhaṇḍam iṣuṃ ca pauṣpaṃ
cakrābjapāśasṛṇikāñcanavaṃśanālam /
bibhrāṇam aṣṭavidhabāhubhir arkavarṇaṃ
dhyāyed dhariṃ madanagopālavilāsaveṣam //

106.* yā prītir vidurārpite muraripo kuntyarpite yādṛśī
yā govardhanamūrdhni yā ca pṛthuke stanye yaśodārpite /
bhāradvājasamarpite śabarikādatte 'dhare yoṣitāṃ
yā prītir munipatnibhaktiracite 'py atrā 'pi tāṃ tāṃ kuru //

By just putting in the pot the handful of his means—
grain fallen on the path, which he had gleaned—
Mukunda pleased the girl selling fruit more than if he
had given (good) grain.

Till death I shall hear the cowherd boy
with the sound of bracelets on his wrists,
golden bells sounding at his hips,
and the Gañga at his feet.

The aesthete, who everyday attentively listens
and reads the three hundred and three verses which
are nectar to the ears about the life of the Lord,
is like a perfected being: He partakes of the
supreme bliss whose embodiment has the whole world
for a playground.

May he dwell in our hearts and bless us—the beloved of
the milkmaids,
whose lovely form is a fragment of his artful illusion,
who delights with his softly sounding flute,
who enraptures the three worlds.

Why do you fill yourself with milk under the cow's tail
with the wind in your face to relieve
the full udder?
Perform this treatment, Mukunda, on my breasts so that
they will be without milk.

May he protect us—the Lord Kṛṣṇa who saw the moon
reflected in a pot of water and, thinking it to be
butter, put his fingers in to take some and was much
bewildered when he got none.

May this god, who is the son of Devakī, prevail.
May Kṛṣṇa, the light of the Vṛṣṇi line, prevail.
May he, who is cloud dark and charming of body, prevail.
May Mukunda, who destroys the troubles of the earth, prevail.

āttaṃ padavyāṃ vigalāyyadhānyaṃ
pātre diśan kevalam eva pāṇim /
priyaṃkaro 'bhūt phalavikrayiṇyā
dhānyārpaṇād apy adhikaṃ mukundaḥ //

karayoḥ kaṅkaṇarāvaṃ
kaṭivilasatkāñcikiṅkiṇīrāvam /
caraṇe jāhnavirāvaṃ
kalaye gopālabālam āmaraṇam //

karṇāmṛtaṃ bhagavataś caritaṃ rasajñaḥ
ślokatrayādhikaśatatrayam ādareṇa /
śṛṇvan paṭhann anudinaṃ samupaiti siddhiṃ
siddho yathā sakalalokavihārarūpām //

kalāttamāyālavakāntamūrtiḥ
kalakvaṇadveṇuninādaramyaḥ /
śrito hṛdi vyākulayaṃs trilokīṃ
śriye 'stu gopījanavallabho naḥ //

govālamūle vadanānilena
kiṃ pūryase vatsapayodharārtham /
kucau madīyau payasā vihīnau
etāṃ cikitsāṃ kuru me mukunda //

ghaṭodakeṣu pratimāśaśāṅkaṃ
vilokya kṛṣṇo navanītabuddhyā /
ādātum antar nihitāgrahastaḥ
pāyāt tadaprāptisamākulo naḥ //

jayatu jayatu devo devakīnandano 'yaṃ
jayatu jayatu kṛṣṇo vṛṣṇivaṃśapradīpaḥ /
jayatu jayatu meghaśyāmalaḥ komalāṅgo
jayatu jayatu pṛthvībhāranāśo mukundaḥ //

Everyday early in the morning the home of Nanda can be
identified
by the sound of the churning of curds, by the cries of
the swans in the pond,
by the lowing of the precious cows, by the sounds of
the songs of beautiful women,
by the sounds of Hari's flute, by the sounds of prayers
which know the soul.

The oversoul, which everyday the sages search for in
every branch of the Vedas,
is now found on the laps of the lotus eyed women of
Gokula.

An impression of an image, which is associated with a flute,
often comes into my mind.
Its pair of feet are crossed; its hands are rosy.
Its limbs are like lotuses; its buttocks are clothed in yellow.
Its lotus face is tilted sidewyas; its shoulders are
somewhat bent.

In the early morning I bow with heart, word, and head
to the pair of lotus feet of the supreme soul,
Nārāyaṇa, who saves from the ocean of hell,
who is the chief object of Brahmans engaged in
meditation.

In the early morning I worship him who frees from danger
those who ask for
the removal of the danger of the evils accruing from all
former births,
who raised his hand with the discus to make an end to the
terrible affliction of the elephant king whose foot
had fallen into the mouth of an crocodile.

In the early morning to quiet the evils and great pain
of existence I call to mind
Nārāyaṇa, who is the color of black mascara, whose
chariot is Garuḍa,
who caused the release of the great elephant overcome by
the crocodile
whose weapon is the discus, whose lotus eyes sparkle.

dadhimathananinādair dīrghikāhaṃsanādaiḥ
surabhimaṇininādaiḥ sundarīgītanādaiḥ /
harimuralininādair ātmavidbrahmanādair
anudinam anubhāvyaṃ nandagehaṃ prabhāte //

nigamataroḥ pratiśākhaṃ
pratidinam ṛṣibhir gaveṣitaṃ brahma /
militam idānīm aṅke
gokulapaṅkeruhākṣīṇām //

pādadvaṃdve vinimayavatī pāṭalā pāṇipadme
pāthovāhadyutir apaghane pītavāsā nitambe /
sācībhūtā vadanakamale saṃnatā kiṃ cid aṃse
vāraṃ vāraṃ manasi valate vaṃśinī vāsanā me //

prātar namāmi manasā vacasā ca mūrdhnā
pādāravindayugalaṃ paramasya puṃsaḥ /
nārāyaṇasya narakārṇavatāraṇasya
pārāyaṇapravaṇavipraparāyaṇasya //

prātar bhajāmi bhajatām abhayaṃkaraṃ taṃ
prākṣarvajanmakṛtapāpabhayāpahatyai /
yo grāhavaktrapatitāṅghrigajendraghora-
śokapraṇāśakaraṇodyatacakrapāṇiḥ //

prātaḥ smarāmi bhavapāpamahārtiśāntyai
nārāyaṇaṃ garuḍavāhanam añjanābham /
grāhābhibhūtavaravāraṇamuktihetuṃ
cakrāyudhaṃ taralavārijapatranetram //

He, who has a peacock plume, the form of a fine
dancer, and the *karṇikāra* flower in his
ears,
who wears clothes the red color of gold and the
Vaijayantī garland,
who fills the holes of his flute with the nectar of
his lower lip, and by groups of cowherds
whose praise is sung, enters Vṛndāvana which is
delightful as is appropriate for his home.

What use is there in further chewing
the rags of so many stories and instructions?
The heart of enlightenment must be sought
with effort by knowers of the truth.

Multitudes of ascetics, whose minds are
deeply immersed in the captivating body
of the jewel-like lord,
utter quiet prayers, offer oblations,
perform vows, and release the gods.

"Dear girl, what are you thinking of? Pick
beforehand the jasmine which is about to bloom.
What is the use of that jasmine for me?" "What sort of
flowers are pleasing to you?"
"I seek the elephant-among-men flower, O friend, known as
the crown jewel of the Vedas.
Even the cows ever leave the meadow grass alone when flowers
are about to fragrantly bloom."

I worship Mukunda whose eyes are like the dark lotus
petal,
who is the sapphire set in the golden *tilaka* of Lakṣmī,
who is the eager bee at the lotus faces of the milkmaids,
who is a wave of the Yamunā in destroying multitudes of
sins.

When the clothes thief, who wears a forest
garland of creepers which are encircling arms
and lotuses which are eyes, walks on the very
paths along the Yamunā, then the yellow
clothed Viṣṇu appears again.

barhāpīḍaṃ naṭavaravapuḥ karṇayoḥ karṇikāraṃ
bibhrad vāsaḥ kanakakapiśaṃ vaijayantīṃ ca mālām /
randhrān veṇor adharasudhayā 'pūrayan gopavṛndair
vṛndāraṇyaṃ svapadaramaṇaṃ prāviśad gītakīrtiḥ //

bahuśāstrakathākanthā-
romanthena vṛddhena kim /
anveṣṭavyaṃ prayatnena
tattvajñair jyotirāntaram //

maṇiviḍambitatasya manohare
vapuṣi magnamanomunimaṇḍalāḥ /
japam amuñcata homam amuñcata
vratam amuñcata devam amuñcata //

mugdhe dhyāyasi kiṃ gṛhāṇa purataḥ kundaṃ vikāsonmukhaṃ
kiṃ kundena mamā 'munā sumanasaḥ kīdṛgvidhās te priyāḥ /
puṃnāgaṃ mṛgaye sakhi śrutiśirobhūṣāviśeṣāyitaṃ
gāvo 'py ujjhitaghāsam āsata yadā modaprakāśonmukhāḥ //

lakṣmīsuvarṇatilakākhacitendranīlaṃ
gopāṅganāvadanapaṅkajalolabhṛṅgam /
duṣkarmakulakaṣaṇe yamunātaraṃgaṃ
vande mukundam asitotpalapatranetram //

vanamālini yāti vastracore
paridhānīkṛtabāhupallavānām /
udabhūt punar utpalekṣaṇānāṃ
yamunāpāthasi vā sa pītavāsāḥ //

APPENDIX

CRITICAL APPARATUS

In this Critical Apparatus the manuscripts are cited by the sigla indicated in the section entitled "Manuscripts Used." Where all manuscripts from a single group agree the citation is of the symbol used for that group. For example, Y refers to all the Y manuscripts in which the verse occurs. DG refers to all six DG manuscripts in which the verse occurs, but DG1 refers to only one manuscript of the DG group, DG2 to another, and DG3 to another.

To determine whether a verse occurs in a manuscript which is not specifically or explicitly cited in the critical apparatus, see the chart entitled "Synoptic Chart of Verse Sequences."

For further explanation of the sigla and other abbreviations used in the Critical Apparatus see below.

Abbreviations Used in the "Critical Apparatus"

st. standard. When prefixed to a verse number (e.g. st. 1.1), st. indicates that this is the usual position of the verse in more than fifty per cent of the mss. For further explanation see "General Abbreviations."

* When an asterisk is affixed to a standard verse (e.g. st. 1.1 *), the asterisk indicates some doubt as to whether this position of the verse is valid for a critical sequence. For further explanation see "General Abbreviations."

t text. When added after a ms. [e.g. C21 (t)], t indicates that the reading is found in the text of a ms. but not in the commentary or marginal gloss.

c commentary. When c occurs in the critical apparatus after a ms. [e.g. P71 (c)], it indicates that the reading is found in the commentary but not in the text of the ms. Also it indicates that the reading is found everywhere it occurs in the commentary.

i introductory tag. When i occurs in the critical apparatus after a ms. [e.g. R21 (i)], it indicates that the reading is found in the introductory tag which identifies the commentary, but not in the text or in any other part of the commentary unless that other part is specifically designated, e.g. R21 (ig).

e entry. When e occurs in the critical apparatus after a ms. [e.g. S21 (e)], it indicates that the reading is found entered within the commentary, but the gloss on the entry is of another reading.

g gloss. When g occurs in the critical apparatus after a ms. [e.g. H31 (g)], it indicates that the reading is not found entered within the commentary, but the gloss on the entry, whatever the entry may be, indicates the reading. The reading indicated by the gloss does not occur in any other part of the commentary or in the text unless the other part or the text is specifically designated, e.g. H31 (tg).

g-1 first gloss. When g-1 occurs in the critical apparatus after a ms. [e.g. H31 (g-1)], it indicates that the reading is not found entered within the commentary, but the first two or more glosses on the entry, whatever the entry may be, indicates the reading. The reading indicated by the first gloss does not occur in any other part of the commentary or in the text unless the other part or the text is specifically indicated, e.g. H31 (tg-1).

p pāṭhe. When p occurs in the critical apparatus after a ms. [e.g. C51 (p)], it indicates that the commentator has noted the reading to be a variant reading to the one given in the text. Because of the conflation of traditions, however, it is possible to find the same reading in the text and in the variant reading, e.g. C51 (tp).

To illustrate the use of the above abbreviations and the symbols, described in the "Manuscripts Used" section, the following example is given: C21 (t). (C21 identifies a ms. deposited in the Asiatic Society, Calcutta [see p. 36].)

C, according to the information given on p. 29, indicates that the ms. is written in the Devanāgarī script and includes a commentary by Pāpayallaya Sūri.

21, according to the information given on pp. 30 and 31, indicates that the verse sequence 1.66 and 1.67 of the standard version is reversed. This single reversal is found in mss. with the short version of the Pāpayallaya Sūri commentary (see p. 31). One can conclude, then, that this is a ms. with the short version of the Pāpayallaya Sūri commentary.

(t), according to information given on p. 235, indicates that the reading in question is found in only the text (not the commentary) of the C21 ms.

Śataka I

1 a V2 V22 V25 jayatu; N21 (vs. 1.1) lokagurur (for somagirir), D1 N21 (vs. 3.10) somagurur

b Y13 sikhyā guruś (incorrect for śikhyā guruś, śiṣyā guruś, śikṣāguruś?), Y14 śiṣyo guruś, Y21 śiṣyā guruś; all mss. except B D11 D21 D45 N1 Y °piñcha° (this variant form of °piccha° will not be noted hereafter); Y °picchacūḍaḥ

c D1 M21 Y14 tatpāda°; G2 °pallavakomaleṣu

d Y līlāmayaṃ vararasaṃ

2 a Y14 Y21 astu; D11 G1 G2 N1 N21 V1 Y °karāgravilasat°; G11 H31 M1 Y3 Y21 Z9 °āvṛtaṃ (for °āplutaṃ), Y2 Y13 °āmṛtaṃ

b DG1 DG4 °laharīsaṃmugdhadhenuvrajam; Y2 Y21 °laharīnirmāṇa°

c D1 svastaprasta° (for srastasrasta°), DG srastaprasta° (°prasta° incorrect for °prāsta°?), N21 srastasvasta°, Y2 Y3 Y14 srastavyasta°, Y21 srastadhvasta°, Y13 srastadhyasta°; N1 °viruddha°; T21 °nīvivigalad°; Y3 °sahasrāmṛtaṃ

d K1 akhilaṃ dāraṃ (for akhilodāraṃ), N21 Y2 akhilādhāraṃ; DG4 D1 G11 T21 Y3 Y14 Y21 °ākṛtiḥ (for °ākṛti), D64 G1 K1 M1 Y2 °ākṛtiṃ

3 D12 no evidence except for line d beginning with °lam amī vayaṃ)

a all mss. except B D71 G1 N1 R21 (te) °nidhānasīma°; G2 °chavīmādhuraṃ (for °chaṭāmantharaṃ), X1 chaṭaṃ mantharaṃ; K1 N22 °mandaraṃ (for °mantharaṃ), D1 maṇḍitaṃ

b all mss. except B DG G1 G2 °vīcilālita°; D1 °kaṭākṣād vṛtaṃ; D71 M1 M23 P72 °āvṛtam (for °ādṛtam), G2 M21 °āmṛtam

c D71 G1 G11 H21 (e) H31 (te) M1 M21 N1 N21 X1 °āñkaṇa° (añkaṇa- variant form of añkana-?) (for °āñgaṇa°), B D1 °āñgana° (añgana- variant form of añgaṇa-); D71 °praṇayanaṃ kāmā° (for praṇayinaṃ kāmā°), N1 °praṇayitā-kāmā

d N1 bālaṃ nīlasamuccayaṃ

4 a Z9 barhottamsi°; all mass. except B C21 (t) DG1 DG4 D1 D11 D12 G1 G2 G11 K1 M1 M21 N21 °vilāsi°; G11 D71 °kuntaladharaṃ; N1 °mughānanaṃ

b DG1 DG4 pronmīlannayanadvayapravilasad°; Z9 pratilasad° (for pravilasad°), G2 pravisarad°; D12 °praṇādāvṛtam

c M21 āpītastana°

d Z9 vaś (for naś); all mss. except B DG D11 D12 D21 G2 N1 N21 S21 Z9 cakāsti

5 a N1 N21 R21 T71 omit °tara°; D11 D64 M1 P72 °vidagdha° (for °vimugdha°), D21 °vimṛgya°

b G2 °picchavāñchita°; N21 manojñaruci°

c C21 (t) D64 viṣayamiṣāmiṣa°

d all mss. except B DG D11 D21 G2 N1 N21 R21 Z9 cakāsti

6 a N21 °nayanāñcalaṃ; C21 (t) C52 (t) D64 M1 vibho

b X1 °ninādam aravindanirbharam; N21 °makarandavibhramam

c C51 (e) C52 (e) D1 P72 (t) R21 (e) Y13 Y14 mukulāyamāna°; Y2 Y13 °galla-maṇḍalaṃ;

d N1 vijṛmbhaṇam (for vijṛmbhatām), Y2 vijṛmbhitam

7 a DG omits °mugdha°, G2 kamanīyamugdhakiśora°

b U1 °āvṛta° (for °ādṛta°), M1 M21 M22 Q71 (c vs. 1.30b [c vs.1.31d reads °ādara° which presupposes °ādṛta° in the text]) X1 Z9 °āmṛta°

c C21 (t) vāri (for vāci); C21 (t) D1 P72 (t) U1 murāre

d D1 kvaṇitā 'pi (for kaṇikā 'pi)

8 a G11 madaśikhaṇḍiśikhaṇḍi°

b D1 K1 N1 N22 R21 °mandara° (for °manthara°), N21 °mandana°

c D21 °āñcalacumbitaṃ (for °āñjanarañjitaṃ), all mss. except the preceding and B D11 D12 °āñcalavañcitaṃ)

d D21 vāci nirantaraṃ (for vāñmayajīvitaṃ), N21 vāñmayijīvitaṃ

9 a Y °pāṇipallava°; C52 (t) °sañga° (for °sañgi°); N1 Y2 Y13 Y21 °rasākulaṃ (for ravākulaṃ), Y14 °rasāmalaṃ

b C21 (t) °padi vādipāda° (for parivādipāda°), G1 °paripāṭapāda°, G2 N1 X1 °parivāripāda° U1 °parivādapāda°, DG2 °parivādipādi°

c G1 °smitamañjarī; N21 madhurānanaṃ

d D11 vibhum āśraye; Y2 Y13 Y14 prabhum ādriye

10 (D1 has line order a b d c)
a B1 D12 apāṅgalekhābhir (for apāṅgarekhābhir) D71 apāṅgarevābhir
b D71 abhaṅgarekhārasa°; DG D1 G1 G11 U1 °līlā° (for °lekhā°), all mss. except preceding and B1 C21 C51(g) C52(g) D12 H21(g) H31(g) P71(g) S21 °rekhā°, P72(c) is omitted
c D1 anukvaṇaṃ; D1 K1 pallavasundarībhir
d C51(t) C52(t) D44 H31(e) T21 U1 abhyarcamānaṃ (for abhyasyamānaṃ) all mss. except preceding and B D11 D12 G1 G2 N1 abhyarcyamānaṃ; D1 D12 N1 N21 prabhum

11 a no variant readings
b N1 °vilolalolanetram
c D45 taraṇaṃ; DG vrajapāla°;
d C52(t) saṃnidhānām (incorrect for saṃnidhānam, saṃnidhattām?)

12 (D64 omits line b; its line order is a d c)
a DG °lakṣmīr niya°; C21(t) °nityalolā
b DG4 vimala° (for kamala°), M21 M22 nigama°; DG °vimalavīthī°; N1 °garvakūlaṃ kaṣābhyām
c N1 pramadabhayanidāna° (for praṇamadabhayadāna°), N21 pramadaharanidāna, Z9 praṇamadabhayanānā°; B C21(t) D12 °gāḍhādṛtābhyāṃ (for °gāḍhoddhatābhyāṃ, D11 F41° gāḍhoddhṛtābhyāṃ, B1(p) °gāḍhodyatābhyāṃ, B3(p) as in text
d N1 kam api; DG kim api viharatu (unmetrical for kim api vahatu), DG1 corrects to mama viharatu

13 a R21(t) °parigatābhyāṃ (for °pariṇatābhyāṃ), D44 °pariṇatibhyāṃ; B D11 D12 C21(te) śrībharā (for prābhavā°), D1 bhāvanā°, M1 pāvanā°; DG N1 N21 °ālaṃkṛtābhyāṃ (for °ālambanābhyāṃ), D1 °ālambitābhyāṃ
b N1 pratipadalikhitābhyāṃ; P72(t) yātanābhyāṃ (for nūtanābhyāṃ)
c DG U1 uditābhyāṃ (for adhikābyāṃ), N1 N21 asitābhyāṃ; F41 prasraval° (for prasphural°), C51(te) C52(te) D1 H31(e) praśnuval° (incorrect for prasnuval°?), all mss. except preceding and B C21(t) DG D11 D12 D64 G1 N1 N21 U1 prasnuval°
d all mss. except B C21(t) DG D12 G2 N21 prabhavatu; D64 prāṇināthaḥ

14 a B D11 °madāmbutaraṃga° (for madāndhataraṃga°), D12 °madāmbujaraṅga°; C21(c) C51(c) D44 D64 P72 R21 S21 °bhaṅgi (for °bhaṅgī), DG N1 °bhaṅga, N21 reads both bhṛṅgi and bhṛṅgī (incorrect for?)
b DG G2 N1 bhṛṅgāra°; all mss. except B DG D12 G2 N1 N21 S21 °saṃkalita° (for °saṃkulita°), S21(p) °saṃkalita°; U1 UV °gopa° (for °śita°), D1 °hāsya°; D1 N1 °veṣaḥ
c N1 N21 ānandahāsa°; S21(t) °hāsamilitā°; R21(t) °lalitāsana°
d D12 ānandasaṃstavam; C21 C51 C52 H21 H31 P71 P72 S21 anuplavatāṃ

15 a no variant readings

b Z9 °kalaveṇu°; G11 H31 (t) °nādaḥ
c no variant readings
d Z9 ārdraṃ madīya; DG bhuvanādyam (for bhuvanārdram), D12 bhuvanārham, N1 bhuvanāḍhyam

16 a no variant readings
b C51 C52 D45 N1 N21 taṃ caraṇaṃ (for tac caraṇaṃ), D44 tac caritaṃ D1 P72 (te) vibho
c N1 madīyāni
d D1 lakṣmīṇāṃ (for lakṣmāṇi), K1 lakṣyāṇi

17 a D12 D72 G2 sphurati; H21 (t) °vibho
b D1 D44 G1 K1 Y13 Y14 °praṇayamañju (for °praṇayi mañju), N1 N21 °praṇatamañju, G2 omits °yi; Y14 saṃjitam
c N1 N21 vṛndāvane° (metrically incorrect for kamalāvane°); Y2 kamalāpaṭe kila kalinda°; Y14 °vana° (for °cara°)
d D1 kalahāsya°; N1 N21 °haṃsarāji°; DG4 °pūjita° (for °kūjita°), D1 °mārjita°; C52 (t) N1 N21 Y11 UV °ādṛśam (for °ādṛtam) D12 °āhatam, K1 °ādhṛtam, M24 °āvṛtam, M1 °āmṛtam, Y2 °ācitam, Y13 (perhaps °āvṛtam or °ādhṛtam; it is difficult to make out), Y21 °ādṛḍham

18 a K1 karuṇā° (for taruṇā°), Z9 aruṇā°; Y14 °varuṇāyita° (for °karuṇāmaya°), Y21 °kamalāyita°, Y2 N21° karuṇāyita°, Y13 °karuṇāyate° (metrically incorrect), N1 °karuṇālaya°; D1 °vipulāyati° (for °vipulāyata°), Y13 Y14 °vipulāyita°
b Z9 °kalaśāhati°; C21 C51 (p) C52 (p) D1 D21 D44 D64 G1 G2 G11 H21 H31 (p) K1 M1 M23 M24 N1 P71 (p) P72 (p) R21 S21 U1 °pulakīkṛta° (for kulakīkṛta°), B C51 C52 D11 D12 D45 D71 F41 H31 M21 M22 P71 P72 T21 T71 Y2 Y13 Y21 Z9 °vipulīkṛta°, N21 °mukulīkṛta°, DG °kulakīkṛta° (only mss. to read as in text), Y14 °vipulākṣata°; M24 °vapuṣam
c N21 muralīkṛta°; Y13 °taralā °; C21 (t) (corrects to °nalinam) D11 °nayanam (for °nalinam), G1 omits °li°
d D21 pari° (for mama); K1 khedasi (incorrect for khelasi?) (for khelatu), all mss. except preceding and B C21 (t) DG D12 D21 M24 N1 N21 R21 Z9 khelati; G1 M22 mama (for mada°), K1 M24 Y21 mṛdu°, Y13 tad eva (metrically incorrect)

19 a C52 (t) āmugdhadharma° (for āmugdham ardha°), DG āmugdhamudgha°, D1 C21 (t) āmugdham arda° (incorrect for?), D12 āmugdhamūrdha°, M1 āmugdhamagdha° (incorrect for?); P72 °nayanāñjana°; C21 (t) C51 (te) C52 (te) D1 D21 D45 H21 (e) H31 (e) K1 M1 N1 R21 (te) S21 (e) °cumbamāna-
b G2 °vadhūnayanā°
c D1 °veṇunavam; B D12 āttakiśora°
d all mss. except B C21 (t) C51 C52 DG D11 D12 D21 D45 F41 G1 K1 M24 N1 N21 R21 S21 U1 āvirbhavanti; DG1 D1 ko 'pi bhāvāḥ

20 a Y11 Y13 Y14 kvaṇatkanakakaṅkaṇaṃ; H21 (t) karanibaddha°
b C51 (te) C52 (te) D45 F41 Y2 śrama° (for krama°), B D12 klama°, D11 suma°;

N1 °prahṛta° (for °prasṛta°), D1 °praśruta; P72(t) U1 °kuṇḍalaṃ; V1 kalitabarha°; Y14 °barhi°; V1 vibho

c T21 textual evidence destroyed (for vapuḥ), D1 upana (metrically and otherwise incorrect for?), all mss except the preceding and DG G1 N1 N21 Z9 punaḥ; C21(c) C51(g) C52(g) D44 D64 H21 H31 P71 P72 R21 S21(t) T71 UV V1 prasṛti° (for prakṛti°), M21 C21(t) prasṛta°, S21(c) omitted

d Y3 Y11 Y13 Y14 Y21 B3(p) mahaḥ (for mama); G2 spurati

21 a D71 °nirudhyamānam atula°; C51(te) D11 D45 F41 R21(p) °praspandi° (for °prasyandi°), N21 °prasyanda°

b C52(t) DG F41 °romodbhavam

c B C21(t) D12 śrotuṃ śrota° (for śrotuḥ śrotra°), D1 M24 U1 śrotuśrotra°, D71 śrotraśrotra°, C51(t) C52(t) śrotṛśotṛ°, all mss. except preceeding and DG T21 D11 D64 K1 śrotṛśrotra°; N1 °manoramavraja° (for °manoharavraja°), N21 °manoramaṃ vraja°, B C21(t) DG D1 D11 D12 D21 D64 G1 G11 H21(t) K1 M1 M24 T21 U1 °manoharaṃ vraja°

d N1 N21 mithyasvādam; M24 °bhagavato līlānimīlad°; D1 °nimīlā° (for °nimīlad°); C21 C51(c) C52(c) D64 H21(c) H31(c) M1 P71(c) P72(c) R21(c) S21(p) T71 °dṛśoḥ (for °dṛśaḥ), U1 °dṛśam, C21(p) C51(p) C52(p) H21(p) H31(p) P71(p) P72(p) R21(p) °dṛśaḥ (as in text)

22 a all mss. except for B DG G1 G2 N1 N21 Y3 Y14 Y21 °śālibālā- (for °śāli bālā-)

b DG G1 G2 dhāmavanāntaraṃ (for yāma vanāntaraṃ), Y3 Y21 vā 'tha vanāntaraṃ, Y13 nāthavanāntaraṃ, Y14 vyāpyavanāntaraṃ, all mss. except preceding and B D12 N1 N21 Y2 maunimano'ntaraṃ)

c DG G2 °vātavāsyam (for °pādalāsyam), Y13 Y14 °jānapāsyam, D11 °pādabhāvyam, Y21 °jānupadmam, all mss. except preceding and B D12 Y2 °pādapāsyam

d G11 U1 upāsyamānaṃ (for upāsyam anyan), K1 upāsmahe 'nyaṃ, B(except B1) C21(t) C51(t) C52(t) D1 D11 D21 D45 N21 S21(t) Y3 Y13 Y14 Y21 upāsyam anyaṃ, Y2 upāsyam anye; B vilokayāma

23 a C52(i) H21(i) P71(ti) T71 sādhyaṃ (for sārdhaṃ), D1 sādyaṃ, VI sārthaṃ; C51(c) C52(c) H21(c) H31(c) P71 P72(c) T71 samṛddher (for samṛddhair), C51(p) C52(p) H31(p) P71(p) P72(p) samṛddhair (as in text), C21 omits c to this part of the text, D71 samudrair

b M1 M21 M24 āmnāyamānair (for ātāyamānair), D1 U1 āsvādyamānair, C21(e) ādāyamānair, G1 ārdrāyamāṇair, G11 āpyāyamānair, K1 ādhyāyamānair, S21(t) sāmābhirāmair, S21 omits c to this part of the text, all mss. except preceding and B DG D12 G2 N1 R21(p) ādhmāyamānair

c C52(t) G11 °abhiṣaktaṃ

d S21(c) vilokayāmi

24 a DG °kuruṣe

b no variants

c DG yugalīṃ (incorrect for?); G1 vigamaṃ (for vigalan°), G11 vikalaṃ; R21(t) °mṛdudrava°; G11 °dviṣa- (for °drava-), M1 °smita°

d M1 °dravamūdrā°; N1 °mudrāmadhunā

25 a Y14 kāruṇyabarbara°
b Y lāvaṇya° (for tāruṇya°), N1 ms. destroyed here; DG °saṃdalita° (for °saṃvalita°), D11 °saṃkalita°, Y13 Y21 °saṃcalita°, C21 (t) omits °va° of saṃvalita°; DG1 °yauvanaśaiśavena (for °śaiśavavaibhavena), DG2 DG4° śaiśavena (omits °vavaibha°)
c G1 āpuṣyatā (for āpuṣṇatā), C51 (te) C52 (t) D45 V2 āpluṣṇatā, D11 ākṛṣyatā, D12 āpuṣṇatām (the following are incorrect forms) DG1 DG4 āyuṣmatā, DG2 āpuṣpatā, Y13 āpuplutā; Y14 āpodbhutaṃ, Y21 āpaplutā; C51 (t) C52 (t) bhuvanasadbhuta°; G2 acyuta vibhrameṇa; B1 adbhuta vibhrameṇa; D1 M1 °adbhutavikrameṇa
d Y13 Y14 Y21 śiśirīkṛta°; G11 bhojanaṃ me (for locanaṃ me), Y2 Y13 Y14 mānasaṃ me, Y21 mānasena, DG1 DG4 M24 S21 locane me, DG2 locanena me (one extra syllable), K1 N1 locanena

26 a N1 °śyāmalatanoḥ (for °śyāmataralāḥ), N21 °śyāmatalanāḥ (incorrect for?), all mss. except preceding and B1 B2 B3 (p) D11 D12 UV °śyāmalatarāḥ
b M24 kaṭākṣau; N1 °nicayāḥ (for °nicitāḥ), M1 °nirmitāḥ, K1 °ninatāḥ
c DG °jataścandra° (incorrect for °jatācandra°); R21 (t) S21 (t) °candraśikharāḥ
d C51 C52 D11 D44 D45 D71 F41 T21 V1 kam apy; N21 ante toṣaṃ; M1 M24 T21 antaḥkṣobhaṃ; N1 kim api (for dadhati), C21 (g) C51 C52 D45 F41 H21 H31 M21 P71 P72 R21 (c) S21 (g) T71 V1 dadati; D1 °ninadeḥ

27 a no variant readings
b C21 (t) ca gataṃ gambhīra°; C51 (t) C52 (t) °gambhīraviśāla°; D1 °mandiram (for °mantharam), N1 N21 °maṇḍanam
c C21 (t) C51 (te) C52 (te) D45 M1 N1 P72 (te) S21 (e) āmandam (for amandam), N21 ānandam; N1 °āliṅgatam (incorrect for?), N21 omits °ṅgi° (of °āliṅgitam); D71 attamanmathaṃ (for ākulonmada-)
d M24 he nātha; B1 B2 B3 (p) F41 vidanti

28 a N1 °stimita° (metrically incorrect for °smita°; G11 °kānta° (metrically incorrect for °bhara°), D11 omits °bhara°; N21 ākulāyatākṣaṃ (for āyatāyatākṣaṃ), S21 (t) āyatākulākṣaṃ, D11 āyatāmbujākṣaṃ; C21 (t) G11 M1 M24 P72 (t) T71 omit °tāya°; N1 omits the second °ya°
b G2 °stanamathitaṃ; N1 mṛgāṅganābhiḥ
c B °stavakita° (this variant form of °stabakita° will not be noted hereafter); G2 K1 °bhāraṃ (for °dhāraṃ), R21 (te) °pūraṃ
d N1 N21 S21 (p) U1 paśyāmas (for dṛśyāsaṃ), K1 dṛśyāmas, D44 dṛśyāsu; G11 maho 'sti (for mahas te), D1 G2 H21 (t) N1 N21 mahas tat

29 a Y13 prasādaiḥ
b H31 (t) tvaṃ vaṃśanādā° (for vaṃśīninādā°), T21 Y11 Y13 Y14 vaṃśair ninādā°; C21 (t) D1 K1 P72 (t) videhi
c Y21 mayi prasanne; Y14 prapanne kim
d D1 omits line d; turyaprasanne

30 a a C52 (t) niṣiddhamugdhā°; B D12 °mūrdhāñjalir
b C21 (t) DG2 D1 K1 M1 nirandhra°; N1 °dainyena vimukta° (for °dainyon-

natimukta°), N21 °daityo na vimukta°; all mss. except preceding (N1 N21) and B DG D1 D12 D71 G1 G2 M24 °onnata°; R21 °ruddha° (for °mukta°), G11 evidence for °kta° destroyed, all mss. except preceding and B D11 D12 D44 D45 D71 F41 N1 N21 V1 °mugdha°; all mss. except DG D11 D71 G1 G2 G11 H31(t) M1 N1 N21 R21(t) S21(eg[p reads with unexcepted ms.]) U1 Z9 °kaṇṭhaṃ (for kaṇṭhaḥ)

c B3 D71 M21 dayānidhe; Z9 kṛṣṇa (for deva); U1 bhavatprasāda-

d no variant readings

31 a no variant readings

b N21 pītastanī°; all mss. except DG G1 G2 N1 N21 °pūjanīye

c M1 °vinayo° (for vijayo°), N1 °nayano°; U1 °vastrabimbe

d DG4 cāpalya ne 'ti nayanaṃ; N1 navaśaiśavena (for tava śaiśave naḥ), K1 bhavaśaiśavena (or bhava śaiśavena), D1 tapaśaiśaveniḥ (or tapa śaiśaveniḥ) (incorrect for?), N21 tava śaiśave me, DG D64 G1 G2 G11 U1 tava śaiśavena (DG4 omits °va of tava)

32 a D1 M24 tacchaiśavaṃ; DG D11 D12 G11 avehi (for avaihi), K1 aveni (incorrect for?), all mss. except preceding and B G1 G2 avaimi

b C21(c) N21 R21(t) S21 tac° (for mac°), C21(t) tvac°, D12 muc°, all mss. except preceding and B DG D1 D11 G1 G2 N1 S21(p) yac°; G2 N1 N21 tava (for mama); G2 vā mama vā 'dhigamyam (for vā tava vā 'dhigamyam), N1 vāstranasāvagamyam (incorrect for?), N21 vāmanasoragamyam (incorrect for?), D1 D71 vāgbhir avādagamyam, D11 vāgavicāragamyam, C52(te) vādavivādagamyam, G11 vā tava vā 'py agamyam (or vā tava vā 'pyagamyam), all mss. except preceding and B DG D12 G1 vāgavivādagamyam

c K1 yat (for tat), N1 tvatkiṃkaro 'smi (for tat kiṃ karomi, N21 tat kiṃ karo 'smi; N1 N21 bhagavan (for viralaṃ), D21 G2 vigalan°, D1 viraman° C21(t) G1 U1 viralan° (incorrect for viralaṃ) all mss. except preceding and B D11 D12 D44 G11 M24 viraṇan°; D1 D71 H21(t) Q71 S21(t) T21 U1 UV °ninādа-(for °vilāsi), D21 °nivāda-, G11 vilāsaṃ, all mss. except preceding and B D11 D12 G2 N1 N21 °vilāsa-

d no variant readings

33 a N1 āsītāmṛta° (incorrect for āsitāmṛta°?); C21(t) D64 M24 P72(t) °bhañgi-(for °bhañgī-)

b K1 pālgūni (incorrect for valgūni, phalgūni?), U1 palgūni (also incorrect), M24 pratgūni (also incorrect), all mss. except preceding and B DG D1 D12 V1 phalgūni; N1 vellitaviśāla° (for valgitaviśāla°), N21 vegitaviśāla°, U1 pallavitaśāla°; U1 °vilopanāni

c DG bālyāmṛtāni (for bālyādhikāni), C51(t) C52(t) G2 G11 bālyādikāni, N1 bramidikāni (incorrect for?); D1 D71 G11 P72(te) U1 °pallava° (for °vallava°), R21(t) °vallabha°, D21 D45 F41 °ballava° (this variant form °vallava° will not be noted hereafter); C52(c) H21(t) H31 P71 T71 °bhāṣitāni (for °bhāminībhir), D1 °jīvitāni, B D12 °bhāvinībhir, K1 °vallabhānir (incorrect for?), all mss. except preceding and DG D21 D45 F41 G1 G2 N1 bhāvitāni d DG bhāvair; M1 M24 suhṛdāṃ (for sukṛtāṃ), D12 suvṛtāṃ, D1 sadṛśām, all mss. except preceding and B DG G1 G2 G11 N1 sudṛśāṃ

34 a DG F41 G2 V1 puraḥ; B D12 prasannendumukhena (for prasannena mukhendu°), U1 prasannendumukhābja°); D1 cetasā
b DG N1 N21 purā 'va°; DG 'vatīrṇaḥ sa°; (for 'vatīrṇasya), D1 'vatīrṇaṃ sa°; N21 mahākṛpāmbudheḥ
c N1 N21 gambhīralīlā; N1 °muralīravat (metrically incorrect for °muralīravāmṛtaṃ), N21 °muralīravaḥ saḥ (metrically and other wise incorrect)
d H31(t) te (for me); DG4 D44 D71 M1 me 'bhavat (or me bhavat?)

35 a (A1 no evidence for line a except the last three syllables); all mss. except B DG D12 D71 G1 G2 G11 M21 (vs. 3.84) T21 bhāvena; M21 (vs. 3.84) V1 vilokanena
b D1 aticāpalam; K1 M1 udvahanti (for udvahantam), D1 udyahanti (incorrect for?)
c N1 °rasāyanapūritena; G11 īkṣitena (for īkṣaṇena), A1 īkṣinena (incorrect for?)
d N1 upagantum ahā kadā syām (ahā incorrect for aha?); G1 utsuko 'si (for utsuko 'smi), Al utsukāḥ sma, all mss. except preceding and Q71 R21(p) T21 UV V1 utsukāḥ smaḥ

36 a B2 adhīra bimbā; G1 °vidrumeṇa
b M1 varṣārdra°; C21(t) D21 D71 F41 G1 K1 M21 M24 N1 N21 P72 R21(t) S21(c[tp read with critical text]) T21 °svana° (for °svara°), H21(t) °dhvana°, D1 °śuna°
c N21 rūpeṇa kenā 'pi
d G1 dunoti (for dunoṣi), G2 dhunoṣi, N1 evidence for first letter destroyed (°unoti), V1 dhinoti, all mss. except preceding and A1 B D12 dhunoti

37 a D11 °abhighātaḥ (for °abhighātaṃ), D21 °abhidhāna-, P72(c) abhibhūta-, all mss. except preceding and A1 B DG D12 D64 °abhighāta-
b B D12 upaiti (for udeti), N1 udetu; A1 B1 B2 D12 na ko 'pi tāpaḥ (for sa ko 'pi tāpaḥ), D1 sa kopatāpaḥ, D11 navoḍhatāpaḥ, D64 K1 U1 navo 'pi tāpaḥ, R21 naropatāpaḥ, M1 nṛpopatāpaḥ, all mss. except preceding and B2 DG G1 G2 G11 N1 navopatāpaḥ
c DG4 vibhor; G1 U1 bhavati; C21(t) tāvakacāruvaktra-; K1 °bimba- (for °candra-), C52(t) D1 G11 M21 °candrā, N1 omits °candra-
d DG4 candrātapād viguṇitā

38 a D21 G1 smara° (for nara°), B1 D12 N1 P72(t) nava°, B1(p) reads with text; N21 ca dīrgha- (for kuto 'pi), N1 kutau 'pi (incorrect for kuto 'pi?) G11 kṣito 'pi (incorrect for?), all mss. except preceding and A1 B D12 G2 M24 dṛśo 'pi
b N21 nidrā hy (for randhrād), N1 tandrā hy; A1 B upaiti; A1 C52(t) P72(t) °bhāvāḥ (incorrect for °bhāvā), G11 U1 °bhāvaḥ (slso incorrect)
c N21 omits °keli°; C51(t[no c on this part of the t]) C52(t[no c on this part of the t]) D45 F41 G2 R21(t) U1 °bhavanaṃ (for sadanaṃ), N21 sadṛśaṃ; all mss. except A1 B D1 D11 D12 D44 D71 G2 G11 K1 M24 N1 U1 etu (for eva)
d D1 lakṣye samut° (for lakṣyāsam ut°), G11 lakṣe samut°, V1 lakṣmyāḥ samut°,

G2 lakṣmyā samaṃ, K1 lakṣmyā lasat°, all mss. except preceding and B lakṣmyā samut°

39 a K1 śrīlola°; G2 ālokalocana°; U1 °vilokanakeli°; K1 °vilokitavalli°; N1 °kelidhānī-

b DG gītājitā; U1 °ārdra° (for °āgra°), C51 (t) °āpra°; M24 °saraṇaiḥ (for °saraṇeḥ), M1 °saraṇoḥ, C51 (t) C52 (t) °saraṇe, G11 °saraṇīṃ, D44 °saraṇiḥ,D71 °saraṇīḥ, B D11 D12 °caraṇaiḥ

c D1 ardhāni veṇu°; M24 °ninadaprati°

d D44 R21 (t) ākarṣayāmi (for ākarṇayāmi), B1 B3 (p) D12 D71 H21 (e) M21 P72 (te) ākarṇayāni

40 (G2 the line order is a c b d)

a D11 kṛṣṇa (for deva), N1 daiva; P72 (t) jagadaika° (for bhuvanaika°), C21 C51 C52 H21 H31 P71 P72 (c) T71 V1 jakadeka°

b D11 deva (for kṛṣṇa); G2 nalinalocana he dayālo (for capala... sindho)

c Z9 karuṇa (for ramaṇa)

d DG2 DG4 dṛśo me

41 a D1 amūlyadhanyāni (for amūny adhanyāni), C21 (t) DG1 DG4 G2 amūni dhanyāni, DG2 amunāṃnyadhanyāni (incorrect for?); DG1 DG4 vinā 'ntarāṇi

b Z9 kṛṣṇa (for hare), M24 hire

c no variants

d no variants

42 (H21 (t) text missing for line a; A1 text missing for line a b)

a U1 aha (for iha), V1 iva; D12 kṛpaṇaḥ (for kṛṇumaḥ), all mss. except preceding and B DG D11 D71 G1 G2 N1 Q71 (c vs. 1.117 [c vs. 1.116 reads with the unexcepted mss.]) R21 S21 śṛṇumaḥ; all mss. except B DG D11 D12 D21 G1 G2 G11 K1 N1 R21 (t) kathaṃ kṛtaṃ; U1 āśayaṃ (for āśayā), DG4 āśaya, M24 āśayāḥ

b D1 U1 kathayati (for kathayatu), K1 kathayatha, G11 (ms. is destroyed here), all mss. except preceding and B1 B3 (p) C21 (t) C51 (p) C52 (p) D11 D12 G2 G2 H31 (p) M24 P71 (p) P72 (p) T21 kathayata; C21 DG1 DG4 D1 D11 D44 D64 D71 F41 G1 H21 (c) M1 M24 N1 N21 R21 S21 T21 kathāṃ (for kathām), all mss. except preceding and B D12 G2 kathaṃ; D1 D21 very incorrect for anyāṃ dhanyām aho; DG1 DG4 dhanyāṃ (for anyāṃ), C21 (c) D11 D44 D64 F41 G11 H21 (c) K1 N1 R21 S21 dhanyām, M24 dham (one syllable missing), all mss. except preceding and B D12 G2 dhanyā; C21 (c) D11 D44 D64 F41 G11 H21 (c) K1 N1 R21 S21 anyām aho (for dhanyām aho) M1 asyāmahe, G2 dhanyām ahe, all mss. except preceding and B12 manyāmahe; D11 hṛdayāśayaḥ (for hṛdayesayaḥ), G1 hṛdaye mayā, DG4 hṛdaye dvaye, N1 hṛdaye mama, C51 C52 D45 H21 (t) H31 M21 P71 P72 T71 V1 hṛdayeśayam, DG1 DG2 D1 D21 hṛdayeśaye, U1 hṛdayeśaya, M1 hṛdayeśayā, D64 hṛdayeśayām, N21 hṛdayeśayāḥ, B C21 D12 D44 D71 F41 G2 G11 H21 (c) K1 R21 S21 T21 hṛdayeśayaḥ (as in text)

c A1 text missing for madhuramadhurasmerākāre; N21 madhuramṛdula°

d M21 kṛpaṇakṛpaṇaṃ; C21 D64 D71 H31 K1 M21 M24 P71 P72 T21 T71 tṛṣṇā kṛṣṇe (for kṛṣṇe tṛṣṇā), M1 kṛṣṇaḥ kṛṣṇe, D21 kṛṣṇe kṛṣṇe, G11 śliṣṭā kṛṣṇā, D1 kṛṣṇe (two syllables omitted), D44 kṛṣṇā kṛṣṇā; N1 ciraṃ tvayi; G11 bata lambitā

43 a K1 śrībhyāṃ (for ābhyāṃ)
b A1 B D11 D12 N1 amburuhavi° (for ambhoruhalola°, D1 G2 amburuha° (metrically incorrect), C21 (t) G11 K1 amburuhaviśāla°, R21 (t) ambhojadaladalita° (metrically incorrect), H31 (t) ambujadaladalita°, T21 ambujadalalālita° (metrically incorrect), U1 ambujadala°, all mss. except preceding and DG G1 ambujadalalalita°; Z9 devam (for bālam) D1 bālā
c all mss. except DG G1 K1 N1 U1 UV dvābhyām api; G11 parirabdhaṃ (for parirabdhuṃ), D21 parihartuṃ N21 pari bandhu-
d D21 hare (for dūre), G11 dūre dūre, C21 (t) D1 mahanta° (for mama hanta), C52 (t) daivā (for daiva°), Z9 sukṛta°; R21 U1 °samāgrīm, N1 ms. destroyed here (Neither the reading of the critical text nor any of the variant readings are metrically correct for the half verse c d.)

44 a K1 śrīśrānta°; P72 (t) āśrāntasthitam; U1 madhurāruṇā° (for aruṇāruṇā), Z9 masṛṇāruṇā°; DG1 DG4 aruṇādharoṣṭhaharṣād (for aruṇāruṇādharoṣṭhaṃ), N1 aruṇādharoṣṭhabimbaṃ, K1 aruṇāruṇādharābjaṃ
b U1 harṣāśru°
c D1 D11 G11 viśrāmyadvipula° (for vibhrāmyadvipula°), M1 vibhrāmyan vipula°, D12 G2 vibhrāmyadviguṇa°; B3 (p) D1 D11 S21 (t) °ārdra°; C21 (te) P72 (te) R21 (te) °ārtha°; D11 °yugmaṃ (for °mugdhaṃ)
d no variants

45 a A1 B1 D12 R21 (t) līlāyitābhyāṃ (for līlāyatābhyāṃ), N21 lolāyatābhyāṃ; R21 (t) śaśiśītalā°
b D45 līlāruṇābhyāṃ
c M1 D71 °vikrmābhyāṃ (for °vibhramābhyāṃ), D1 °viśramābhyāṃ
d M1 loke (for kāle), V1 bālaḥ; D1 M1 kāruṇikaṃ

46 a A1 B D12 M24 Z9 bahala°; F41 °bhāre (for °bhāraṃ), R21 (t) °bhāvaṃ
b DG śapharacapala° (for capalacapala°), N21 vipulacapala°, C51 (t) capala° (3 syllables are missing)
c M24 madhuravidula°; A1 B M21 Q71 U1 V1 mantharodāra° (for mandaroddhāra°), D11 sundarodāra°, mandakedāra°, all mss. except preceding and DG D44 G1 N1 N21 T21 Z9 mandarodāra°; C21 (t) °śīlaṃ (for °līlaṃ)
d D1 mṛdayati; A1 tanayaṃ (for nayanaṃ), T21 vadanaṃ; DG °veṇuṃ; C52 (t) D21 murāre (for murāreḥ), Z9 murārim

47 a A1 B DG4 M1 M24 N1 bahala° (for bahula°), N21 sajala°; G2 °jaladāc chāyā°; M1 omits °jalada°; N1 U1 °kāraṃ (for °coraṃ), C21 (t) °cāraṃ, A1 B D12 °cauraṃ; G2 °harā° (for °bharā°), M24 °darā°
b N1 °vadanāmbujam (metrically incorrect for mukhāmbujam)
c UV V1 karuṇā (for kamalā°), M24 kamanī°; M24 °lolāpāṅga° (for °pāṅgodagra°; A1 B D11 D12 M24 °prasaṅga° (for °prasanna°), G2 ms. destroyed

here; A1 B D11 D12 °jaḍaṃ jagan- (for °jagajjaḍaṃ), M24 °niketanaṃ,D1 °jagajjaraṃ, G11 °padāmbujaṃ, N1 °jagathitaṃ (incorrect for?)

d no variant readings.

48 a C52(t) H21(t) H31 M21 P71 T71 parāmṛgyaṃ (for parāmṛśyaṃ), N1 parāmṛgyad°, DG Z9 parāmṛśyan, M25 varāmṛśyan; D12 pathi rama (for pathi pathi), all mss. except preceding and A1 B DG G1 G2 G11 N1 pariṣadi; D12 omits mu° of munīnāṃ

b N1 omits dṛśā, all mss. except preceding and A1 B D1 G2 G11 K1 M1 N21 dṛśāṃ; D1 G2 omit dṛśyaṃ; P72(t) °veṣam (metrically incorrect for°vadanam), all mss. except preceding and A1 B C21 DG D11 D12 D21 D44 D64 G1 G2 G11 H21(c) H31 M1 M24 N1 N21 Q71 (c vs. 1.127, 128 [c vs. 1.126 reads with the unexcepted mss.]) R21 S21 Z9 °vapuṣam

c D11 H21(t) H31 M21 N1 P71 T71 anāmṛgyaṃ (for anāmṛśyaṃ), G11 M1 M24 N21 T21 anādṛśyaṃ; N1 vācam (for vācām), B2 B3 (p reads with text, in one ms. only) vācā; A1 B2 B3 munisamudāyānām (metrically incorrect for aniśam udayānām), Z9 udayam udayānām, B2 D1 D11 D12 D21 G11 N1 T21 aniśam; U1 kathā (for kadā)

d N1 darīdṛg yad dūre vidaralitanīlo° (incorrect for?); D44 dari° (for dara°); B1 B2 D11 D71 H21(t) M21 P71 P72(t) T71 °rucim (for °nibham), B3 °rucam, A1 reads with text, D21 G2 °dṛśam, B1(p) °daśam, M1 °nibhā

49 a G2 H31(t) M1 N1 nīlā (for līlā), D21 G1 G11 K1 S21(p) T21 U1 UV smerā°; D44 H31 M1 °āmbujānanam

b G11 M24 Z9 °ninadeṣu; C21(t) C52(t) D45 viveśayantam

c A1 B C51 C52 D12 D45 D64 F41 R21 S21 sa dolāyamāna° (for ḍolāyamāna) DG D21 G1 N1 N21 lolāyamāna°, M1 dholāyamāna°, līlābhirāma°, D1 tolāyamāna°

d D11 D64 G11 H31 K1 M1 M21 N21 P71 R21 S21 T71 U1 vande (for devaṃ), N1 bālaṃ; Z9 mathitaṃ; G11 hṛdi lokayiṣye (for vyatilokayiṣye), N21 navanītacoram

50 a N1 laṅghana° (for lampaṭa°); C51(t) C52(t) DG D45 °saṃpradāyaṃ (for °saṃpradāya-), G11 M24 °saṃpradāyī, F41 °saṃpradāye, all mss. except preceding and A1 B D11 D12 G1 N1 P72(t) T21 °saṃpradāyi

b C21(t) G11 N1 rekhā° (for lekhā°); DG °āvalekhana° (for °āvalehini), G1 G2 °āvalehana°, D44 T21 °āvalehani C21(t) D64 °āvilekhini, G11 N1 °āvayonava°, V1 °āvilekhana°, all mss. except preceding and A1 B °āvalekhini;

c N1 udyan° (for rajyan°), G11 rājño C21(t) T21 lajjā, all mss. except preceding and A1 B C51(p) C52(p) DG D11 D12 G1 G2 M24 P71(p) P72(p) lajjan°; A1 B D11 D12 °mṛdūllasitādharāṃśu-

d M24 mukundaḥ (for mukunda°), A1 mukanda° (incorrect for mukunda°) A1 °bālam (for °bālyam)

51 a Z9 °karanikalalita° (for °karanikaramṛdu°); A1 B D1 D11 D12 F41 G2 H21(t) H31 M24 N1 P71 T71 °mudita° (for °mṛdita°), Z9 °tarala°

b M1 omits °tara°; H21(t) omits °ruha°; T71 °rasa° (for °dṛśa°), D12 D64 omit °dṛśa°; C51(t) C52(t) deva

c C51 (t) D12 D45 omit °rati°; B2 B3 G11 N1 V1 °vijayi°
d M1 mudamudita°; C52 (t) DG2 °madhuramaṇi

52 a G11 T21 V1 °daradalita° (for °dalakalita°), Z9 °madanadala°, D1 D64 °dalita° (metrically incorrect); N1 °lalirava° (metrically incorrect for °lalitatara°); G2 °mṛdu° (metrically incorrect for °taravaṃśī-)
b DG4 °galadamṛdu°
c G1 °rasahara°; D64 °sahitavīthī-
d Z9 vahadadharamaṇiruciramadhurimaṇi; D12 G2 M1 omit madhurimaṇi, M24 omits °maṇi

53 a DG1 kusumaśarasamaraparikupita°, DG2 kusumaśaraśaparaparikupita° (incorrect for preceding reading of DG1?), DG4 G1 omit one °śara°; D45 omits °mada°; F41 has °kupitagomadapī (incorrect for?)
b B °kalasa° (for °kalaśa°)
c D45 F41 mṛdu° (for mada°); A1 B D12 °mudita° (for °lulita°), G2 M1 R21 (t) S21 (c) T21 T71 U1 Z9 °lalita°; G2 omits °hasi°; M21 °tulita° (for °muṣita°), G2 °mathita°
d D45 omits °ka°; K1 °madhuramaṇi

54 a DG D21 G1 G11 K1 N1 U1 akṣayya° (for akṣīṇa°) DG °pakṣmāṃkuruṣv (incorrect for °pakṣmāñkureṣv), N21 patrāñkureṣv
b C52 (t) ākālām (for ālolām), G1 ālokām; DG G1 G2 G11 anurāgiṇīṃ; G1 G11 H31 (t) N1 ārdrāmṛtāṃ
c K1 śrītāmrām (for ātāmrām), M1 ākamrām; D1 D12 D64 K1 N1 U1 °madhurā (for °m adharā°); N1 °ādhare (for °āmṛte), G11 °āyate; D21 G2 madhurkalām (for madakalām), G11 'mṛtakalām, K1 madakarām; D1 āmnāta° (for amlāna°), D12 āmnāna°, N1 āmnāya°, C21 D64 āmlāna°; C21 (t) T21 °vaṃśa°, (for °vaṃśī°), G11 M1 °vaṃśi°; DG G1 K1 N1 U1 V1 °rave (for °svane), D1 °śune
d N21 āśāstāṃ; B1 (p reads with text) °pater

55 a no variant readings
b D44 G11 M1 tac ca līlākaṭākṣam
c B1 D12 tan mādhuryaṃ; A1 mañju° (for manda°), B D11 D12 sāndra°
d A1 B D12 daivate 'pi

56 a A1 °śamanāyabaddha°
b A1 B °stavakita° (variant form of °stabakita°)
c A1 D12 M1 paśyāma (for praśyāma°), U1 paśyāmi, D21 praśyāmaṃ, all mss. except preceding and B D11 N1 paśyāmaḥ; DG4 °patīkṣakānti° (for °pratinava°), DG1 DG2 °pratibhava°; M1 °kāntikuntalāgraṃ; DG2 °ārtaṃ (for °ārdraṃ)
d C21 (t) dṛśyāmaḥ (for paśyāmaḥ), M1 paśyāma, U1 paśyāmi, N21 suśyāmaṃ; U1 paśyāmi tribhuvanasundaraṃ mahas te

57 a D1 M24 maulau (for mauliś), G11 mauliṃ; R21 (p) °lāñchanā (for °bhūṣaṇo), H31 (t) N1 T21 bhūṣaṇaṃ, all mss. except preceding and A1 B D11 D12 G11

M21 °bhūṣaṇā; DG1 DG2 G1 G2 G11 H31 M1 M24 N1 N21 marataka° (variant form of marakata°)

b K1 dvitrivimugdha°; N21 °vimugdhabhāsa° D21 °madhurārambhaṃ vilole; D1 bhāve (for bāle), N1 līlā°, G1 bālye; G1 'pi lole (for vilole), T21 viśāle, G11 vilolaṃ; G11 vibhuḥ (for dṛśau)

c G11 bālaḥ (for vācaḥ), G1 H31 (t) vācā; R21 S21 candana° (for śaiśava°), N1 śaiśira°; C21 (t) G11 °śitalo; N21 mara° (for mada°), D1 vada°; N1 evidence for °ślāghyā destroyed; U1 vilāsodgatir

d R21 (t) aye ca kṛṣṇa (for aye ka eṣa), N21 aye kaṭākṣa; D21 madhurāṃ (for mathurā°) K1 madhuro, all mss. except preceding and B D12 madhura° (variant form of mathurā°); DG N1 aho (for mitho), C21 (t) G1 ato, D21 imāṃ, A1 B D11 D12 K1 mitho

58 a A1 B D12 K1 vāda° (for pāda°), D71 kānti°; all mss. except A1 B C21 (p) C51 (p) C52 (p) DG D11 D12 D71 G1 G2 G11 H21 (p) H31 (p) M1 N1 N21 P71 (p) P72 (p) R21 S21 (tp) U1 °ālaṃkṛtau

b D12 °śilpi°; D71 N21 °śilpakriyau

c D1 D11 G11 M1 dohana° (for dauhṛda°), all mss. except preceding and DG G2 K1 M1 M24 N1 dohada°; D21 °bhājane (for °bhājanaṃ), C21 (t) G1 R21 (t) °bhājanau; G2 °dhārāṃ (for °dhārā°); D1 G2 H31 (t) °girau (for °kirau), N1 °girāṃ, DG4 °karau, G1 °ṅkitau, P72 (t) °śiro, all mss. except preceding and A1 B DG1 DG2 D12 °giro

d V1 °vibhavā° (for °viṣayā°), H31 (t) M21 °ādi° (for °āti°); A1 B D11 D12 °laṅghanam (for °laṅghitam), G11 U1 °lambitam; N21 suramyaṃ mahaḥ; M21 ekaṃ (for etan; D1 kim etaṃ namaḥ

59 a A1 B D11 (vs. 1.59) etan nāma (for barhaṃ nāma), D11 M24 N1 barhāṇām a°; M24 °pi (for vi°); M1 bahuratam; R21 (p) veṣair aśeṣair (for veṣāya śeṣair), U1 veṣām āśeṣair, G11 veṣād aśeṣair, C21 D11 (vs. 1.60) H31 S21 veṣāya veṣair, N21 veṣāya vanyair, D64 veṣāya vaivair (incorrect for?)

b D21 vaktra° (for vaktraṃ), F41 vaktre; B C21 (t) D1 D11 (vs. 1.60) D12 M1 N1 N21 R21 U1 dvitri° (for citra°) all mss. except preceding and A1 B1 (p) DG D11 (vs. 1.59) G11 K1 M21 M24 T21 dvitra°; D11 (vs. 1.59) °kāntikalanā

c DG1 DG2 śīrer (for śilpair), DG4 kṣīrer, G11 śītair, D21 śīlyair (incorrect for?) all mss. except preceding and A1 B C21 (t) C51 (t) C52 (t) D11 (vs. 1.50), D12 G1 H21 (t) H31 (te) M24 P72 (t) R21 (p reads with the unexcepted mss.) S21 śīlair; DG1 elpa° (incorrect for alpa°), DG4 etya° (also incorrect); N21 alpavidhām; G11 N1 °vibhavaṃ

d P71 (t) T71 vaktraṃ citram aho; N21 aho dhunoti hṛdayaṃ citrāṅgarāgaṃ mahaḥ; D11 (vss. 1.59, 1.60) G11 M1 M21 P71 vicitritam aho (for vicitram aha ho), C21 T71 U1 vicitratam aho, R21 vicitravad aho, D64 H21 H31 K1 P72 vicitram aha hā, C52 vicitra aha ha (metrically incorrect)

60 a C21 (t) kelisamagralakṣmīm (for kām api kelilakṣmīm), N1 kāntir adhīralakṣmīm; N21 kṣām (for kām), R21 (t) veṇu° (for keli°), R21 (p) kānti°; D1 K1 N1 °lakṣmī

b N1 vanyāsu (for anyāsu), K1 vinyāsu (incorrect for?); all mss. except A1 B

C21 (t) D11 D12 D21 D44 F41 P72 (t) V1 sākṣī (for sākṣi)

c N21 hantastāthamāram (incorrect for hastapathadūram); N1 masta° (for hasta°), G11 hanta, C21 (t) omits hasta°, D45 T21 V1 hastam; D45 T21 V1 atha (for patha°), D1 N1 R21 (t) pada°, G11 pathi°, C21 (t) vadha°; G2 omits °dūram aho, D1 °dūraṃ mayā

d M1 āśāṃ (for āśā°), G2 āsīd āśā° (metrically incorrect), all mss. except preceding and A1 B DG D1 D11 D12 G1 G11 N1 N21 āsīt; N21 °kiśoram avalambagajatrayaṃ me; D11 adya (for amba), C51 (t) D11 G11 ambu°

61 a A1 B D12 G1 N1 M24 Z9 bahalaṃ (for bahulaṃ), G2 viralaṃ; G2 bahulaṃ (for viralaṃ), G1 śiśiraṃ, M24 lalitaṃ, N21 vipulaṃ, N1 bhramaṇaṃ, DG mṛdulaṃ, C52 (t) vimalaṃ; G1 hasitaṃ, N21 bhramalaṃ (incorrect for?) N1 viralaṃ, DG vacanaṃ

b DG vipulaṃ (for mṛdulaṃ); DG nayanaṃ (for vacanaṃ), C21 (t) racanaṃ, P72 (t) vasanaṃ; DG śiśiraṃ hasitam (for vipulaṃ nayanam)

c C51 C52 D21 H21 P71 P72 S21 T71 lalitaṃ vadanaṃ (for vadanaṃ madhuraṃ), N1 madhuraṃ vadanaṃ M24 madanaṃ vadanaṃ, T21 vadanaṃ capalaṃ, G2 madhuraṃ (metrically incorrect), all mss. except preceding and A1 B DG D12 G1 vadanaṃ lalitaṃ

d G2 omits capalaṃ, D1 H31 (t) caritaṃ (for capalaṃ); D1 H31 (t) capalaṃ (for caritaṃ), DG calitaṃ; V1 nu for ca; DG cakāstu vibhoḥ

62 a DG1 DG2 Y11 Y12 Y13 paripālayataḥ (for paripālaya naḥ), Y2 paripālayamaḥ

b M24 asakṛc śrannitam (incorrect for asakṛt kranditam), all mss. except preceding and G2 Y2 Y11 Y12 Y13 Y14 Y21 asakṛj jalpitam; all mss. except A1 B C51 (p) C52 (p) DG D11 D12 G1 M1 P71 (p) P72 (p) Q71 (vs. 1.158d [158b reads with the unexcepted mss.]) R21 (p) Y2 Y11 Y12 Y13 Y14 Y21 ātma° (for ārta°); Y12 °mādhavaḥ (for °bāndhavaḥ), B2 D71 Y2 Y13 °bāndhava

c S21 °svarāntare; Y2 °āntare corrected to °āntaraṃ

d D71 Y21 prabhur (for vibhur), G2 muhur, Y2 Y11 Y12 Y13 Y14; Y2 balānuja (for kadā nu naḥ), Y11 Y12 Y14 balānujaḥ, Y13 balānuje

63 a N1 kasyāṃ (for kasyām), C51 (t) C52 (t) DG D1 D11 D64 kasyā; N1 a° (for nu), G11 na, H21 (te), H31 (te), M21 tu; C21 (t) viruddhaśāyāṃ; DG °śāyāḥ

b M24 °bandhiḥ (for gandhiḥ), Z9 °śobhi (metrically incorrect), N1 M1 °sandhiḥ

c B2 (p reads with text), D12 rasaśītalā° (for vipulāyatā°)

d H31 M21 T21 vilokayiṣyan (for ālokayiṣyan), D44 vyālokayiṣye, M1 vālokayiṣyan (incorrect for?), D1 yā lokayiṣyan, N21 vyālolaniṣyan (incorrect for?), all mss. except preceding and A1 B DG D11 D12 vyālokayiṣyan; T71 vipulaḥ (for viṣayī°)

64 a C21 (t) C51 (t) D1 D12 D21 D44 K1 P72 (t) madhuramadhurabimbe

b N21 mṛdulam amṛta°; N21 V1 °vākye (for °nāde), C51 C52 D45 F41 °vāde, H21 (t) °dhāre

c S21 (t) vimalam aruṇa°; D1 karuṇanetre; M1 viśritaṃ; B veṇuvāde

d D71 H21 H31 M1 M21 (vss.1.64, 3.83) M24 (vss. 1.64, 3.84) R21 S21 marataka° (variant form of marakata°) N21 makarata° (incorrect for marakata°); D1 °maṇilīlāṃ; G11 K1 M1 M21 (vs. 3.83) M24 (vs. 3.84) ālokayāmaḥ

65 (G1 omits lines c and d)
a D12 atimadhuraṃ
b N1 °vārasya (for tātasya), G11 °pātasya, C21(t) D1 °tāpasya
c no variant readings
d D11 T21 omit bata, all mss. except preceding and A1 B DG D11 G2 N1 mama; D21 R21(t) omit hanta

66 (G1 omits lines a and b)
a M24 vakṣastale
b D1 G2 madhuraṃ (for mṛdulaṃ); G2 Z9 mṛdu° (for mada°)
c G11 mṛdulaṃ (for madhuraṃ), D64 madhure; Z9 muralīninādе
d G1 mugdaṃ vilāsa°; B1 ālokaye (metrically incorrect for ākalaye)

67 a V1 °dayā (for °dhurā), D1 °madā, D64 °dhare, all mss. except preceding and A1 B DG D11 D12 G1 G2 G11 M1 N1 °dharā; G11 °netre
b G2 āviḥsmita° (for āviṣkṛta°), DG1 DG2 G11 M1 N1 āvismita°, DG4 second syllable of āvismita° is destroyed; DG1 °snuta° (for °smita°), DG 2 °suta (metrically incorrect), DG4 °stuta°; DG2 dhurā (for °sudhā°)
c D1 M1 °barhibarhām
d C51(t) kṛtapuñja°; M1 °puñjām (for °puñjāḥ), D1 G11 M24 °pūjāḥ

68 a C21(t) D1 D21 M1 M24 U1 māra svayaṃ; C52(t) na (for nu); D12 vidhura° (for madhura°), N21 sakala°, C51(t) C52(t) madhuraṃ; M24 °dviti° (for °dyuti°). N1 °jjata° (incorrect for?)
b A1 D12 tu (for nu), C21(t) D11 D64 K1 M1 N1 N21 R21(t) T71 U1 su°, DG4 na; C21(t) °nayasaumyataṃ (for °nayasaumyatvaṃ?); D12 ca (for nu), K1 omits
c A1 B C21(p) C51(p) C52(p) D1 D11 D12 G1 G2 G11 H21(p) H31(p) K1 M24 P71(p) P72(p) R21(p) veṇī° (for veṇor), N21 gopī° V1 vīṇā°, all mss. except preceding and DG N1 vāṇī; B C21(te) D12 K1 °mṛjo (for °muḍā), A1 °mṛtojo (incorrect for °mṛjo?), M24 °mṛdo, C51(p) C52(p) D21 G2 P71(p) P72(p) R21(t) °sudhā, N21 °jana (metrically incorrect), all mss. except preceding and DG G1 N1 °mṛjā; N21 khalu ma (incorrect for nu mama), T71 nu nanu
d B1(p) ambudayate; DG D12 G1 locanābhyām

69 a A1 B1 D12 °vilokitena
b A1 citrīyita° (for citrīkṛta°), G2 vikrīdhita° (incorrect for?)
c D64 °bhūṣaṇe naḥ
d D12 G1 M24 mugdhe nayanotsavaṃ (for dugdhe nayanotsavaṃ), G11 bālena mahotsavaṃ, N21 bhūyāṃ (incorrect for?) nayanotsave, DG dugdhe nu mahotsave, V1 dugdhe nayanotsukaṃ G2 dugdhe nayanotsave, N1 ms. destroyed here

70 (T71 omits portion between °vadanā° in 1.70.b and °vadane° in 1.71.c)
a A1 B D12 °lolanetram (for °netralīlaṃ), D11 °lolanetra-, M24 °nīlanetram, G11 °netralīlā-, all mss. except preceding and DG N1 N21 °netralīlam
b D11 līlā (for manda°), C51(p) C52(p) P71(p) P72(p) āviḥ°, all mss. except preceding and DG D21 G11 N1 N21 Z9 ārdra°; P71 T71 °smitaṃ ca (for

°smitārdra°); D21 °nayanāmbuja° (for °vadanāmbuja°), D1 °madhurānana°, T21 °madurāmbuja°, Z9 °vadanojjvala°

c C52(t) D1 S21(t) śiñjānubhūṣaṇa°; A1 B D12 °citaṃ (for °śataṃ), D1 °śitaṃ; C52(t) C52(t) D1 D21 D44 D45 F41 G11 H31(t) M21 M24 N21 R21(t) T21 U1 V1 °picchamaulim

d DG abhyupaimi (for abhyupaiti), N21 abhyupaitu

71 (T71 see st. 1.70)

a C51 C52 D1 D45 F41 H21 H31 M21 P71 P72 R21 S21 (p reads with text) śiśupāla° (for paśupāla°), N21 vrajapāla°; N1 °jālapariṣad°; D1 °vibhūṣayāḥ (incorrect for °vibhūṣaṇaḥ?), all mss. except preceding and A1 B C21 (p) C51 (p) C52(p) DG D12 D21 G1 G2 G11 H21 (p) H31 (p) K1 M1 M24 N1 N21 P71 (p) P72(p) R21 (p) S21 (p) °vibhūṣaṇaṃ

b D44 veṣa° (for eṣa), K1 eṣu, N1 eti; G1 H21 (t) H31 (t) P71(t) °locanam

c DG °saṃpadām (for °saṃpadā), D64 °saṃpadāṃ

d DG ayanaṃ (for madayan), G11 madanaṃ; M24 hi (for vi°); T21 vigūhate

72 a DG1 DG4 G1 yad idam; DG D1 G1 adhuravīthī°; C51 (t) C52(t) °vīthīkṛtya°; G2 °ninādaḥ (for °ninādaṃ), C51 (t) C52(t) °nināda

b U1 kim api (for kirati), K1 kiyati; N1 kām api trīpyamārāt (incorrect for?)

c D21 adhara° (for amara°), T71 apara°; N1 °vallavīdurlabhaṃ (for °vallabhaṃ durlabhaṃ), all mss. except preceding and A1 B1 C51 C52 DG1 DG4 D1 D12 G1 G2 G11 M1 T21 °durabhaṃ vallabhaṃ

d N1 °jananīyaṃ (for kamanīyaṃ), all mss. except preceding and A1 B DG D11 D12 S21 °bhajanīyaṃ; M1 M24 daivata; D12 jīvite; C21 (t) me (for ca), R21 yat, A1 ya (incorrect for?)

73 a K1 upagataṃ (for upanataṃ), Z9 upanayan

b N21 calanayanāmbujatārakā°

c N1 uditamudita° (for muditamudita°), T21 mṛditamṛdita°, Z9 muditamṛdula°; C21 C51 C52 D1 D21 D64 G11 M1 °vaktraṃ; G11 candrabimbaṃ murāreḥ (metrically incorrect)

d all mss. except the following A1 B C51 (t) C52(t) DG D11 D12 D71 Z9°vilāsajīvitaṃ

74 (D1 line order: a d b c)

a K1 N1 cāturya° (for cāpalya°); G11 M1 N1 caturānubhavair (for capalānubhavair), N21 sukṛtāvibhavair, Z9 kamalānubhavair

b N1 ms. destroyed cāturya ... śilpa

c D21 Y54 saundarya° (for saurabhya°) K1 saubhāgya°; T71 °ādbhutakolisīma;

d D21 saurabhya° (for saubhāgya°); S21 (c [tp read with text]) yad (for tad); Z9 °bhoga° (for °bhāgya°)

75 a D71 vaktrabimbaṃ; DG2 D71 U1 vahanti (for vahantī)

b C51 (t) C52(t) K1 °vīthir (for °vīthī°), DG2 °vīthiṃ, DG1 DG4 °vīthīṃ A1 DG2 D1 D12 °śrotasā (for °srotasā), T21 U1 °srotasāṃ; K1 cintayantī (for secayantī), C21 (t) DG1 DG4 M1 U1 secayanti

c D21 tadvāṇīnāṃ; D12 U1 virahaṇapadaṃ; M24 °vadaṃ (for °padaṃ), N21

°padām; K1 yatta° (for matta°), N21 ukti°, G1 M24 mukta°, G2 vastu°, M1 mañju°, P71 T71 masta°, N1 mastu°, T21 mantra°, D1 G11 manta°(incorrect for?)

d DG G1 N21 saṃnidhattām

76 a D44 tejaso

b D64 pāle dayitāstanasthāline loka° (metrically incorrect for pāline loka°); C21(t) D1 M24 pālane lokapālane

c N1 °payodharotsedha-

d no variant readings

77 a N1 °dayitākuca°; U1 standadvayī-

b no variant readings

c D64 °gīti° (for °gīta°), N1 °nāda°, U1 °mūla°, M1 omits; G2 omits °gati°;

d A1 B D11 D12 brahmarāśimahase (for tejase tad idam oṃ); N21 astu te (for oṃ namo); A1 omission of namaḥ corrected

78 a U1 °nūpuramandareṇa (for °nūpuramanthareṇa), K1 °nūpuram antareṇa, N1 reads with K1 except the °ram a° portion of the ms. is destroyed, D1 °nūpuramandireṇa

b D1 bhāvena (for bālena), D64 jālena; T71 °āmbujavallabhena

c DG1 D64 G11 M24 anusvanaṃ (for anusvanan°), D11 anusmayan°, K1 anukṣaṇan°, A1 B D12 anusmaran°, N21 anusvanan° (incorrect for?), N1 anusvana° (metrically incorrect), T21 anukvaṇa° (metrically incorrect), all mss. except preceding and C21(t) DG2 DG4 D1 D21 D44 G1 G2 M1 U1 Z9 anukvaṇan°

d DG D21 āyātu; N21 me mānasam; P72(t) R21(g) ātma° (for ātta°) DG4 D11 H21(t) K1 N21 R21(t) T21 °keliḥ (for °keli), C52(t) D71 G1 G11 M1 P72(t) U1 °kelī, C21(t) °kelīḥ, D1 °keśiḥ

79 (D1 omits all of vs. after so 'yaṃ vilāsa°)

a no variant readings

b N21 saṃcimnu (incorrect for?); DG2 G2 udañcitamadaṃ; DG4 tad a° (for mada°), M1 manu°, all mss. except the preceding and B1 DG1 DG2 G2 D12 mama; C51(t) °karmayugmam

c DG1 DG4 āyātu (for āyāti), K1 śrī yāti, DG2 ayāta; DG1 DG4 amanyabandhor; all mss. except A1 B D12 G2 M1 M24 N1 ananyabandhur

d D11 D64 G11 H21(t) P72(t) T21 °lakṣyaḥ (for °lakṣmīḥ), A1 D21 G2 M1 °lakṣmī, N21 °lakṣmyaḥ, all mss. except preceding and B DG D12 K1 M24 N1 °lakṣaḥ

80 a H31(t) N21 ārād vilokayati; M1 °velagāmi (for kheligāmī), A1 B D11 D12 G2 °keligāmī

b all mss. except B1 (p reads with unexcepted mss.) DG D11 D12 D64 G1 G2 H31(t) M1 dhārākaṭākṣa°; C21(t) H21(t) H31(t) U1 vilokanena (for vilokitena), all mss. except preceding and A1 B C51(t) C52(t) D11 D12 G2 G11 K1 vilocanena

c no variant readings

d U1 veṇe (for veṇī°); DG1 DG4 °makhena (for °mukhena), K1 °duhena, C21 (t) °dukhena (incorrect for?, DG2 °nakhena, H31 (t) illegible, U1 mukhena; all mss. except the preceding and A1 B D11 D12 G1 G11 T21 U1 UV °dughena; A1 B D11 D12 daśanāṃśubhareṇa (for daśanābharaṇena), C52 (t) M21 P71 (te) T71 UV VI dasanāvaraṇena, G11 raśanāvaraṇena, M1 omits

81 a N21 tribhuvanamahitābhāṃ; C51 (c2) C52 (c2) D71 H21 (t) H31 (c) P71 T71 VI dīpta° (for divya°), C21 C51 (tcl) C52 (tcl) D45 F41 H21 (c) P72 R21 (c) dṛpta°, G11 dīpya°, M1 diva° (metrically incorrect); all mss. except A1 B DG D11 D12 D21 D44 D64 G1 G2 G11 H31 (t) K1 M1 M24 N21 R21 (t) S21 T21 U1 Z9 °bhūṣā° (for °līlā°); C21 (c) C51 C52 D45 D71 H21 H31 (c) P71 P72 R21 (c) T71 °āparā° (for °ākulā°), F41 °āvarā°, V1 °āpadā°, M24 °ākarā, C21 (t) K1 °āṅkurā°, D44 G11 N21 °ākucā°, G1 °āspadā°, T21 °āśu° (metrically incorrect)

b all mss. except A1 B (B3p reads with unexcepted mss.) DG D11 D12 G1 H31 (te) N21 dṛśi dṛśi; B3 (p) sarasābhyāṃ (for taralābhyāṃ), N1 śikharābhyāṃ, all mss. except preceding and A1 B D12 śiśirābhyāṃ; B3 DG D44 H31 (t) U1 dīpta° (for dṛpta°), G11 tṛpta°, all mss. except preceding and A1 B C21 (t) D11 D12 D21 D44 D64 G1 G2 K1 M1 M21 M24 R21 S21 T21 divya°; D11 °bhūṣo° (for °bhūṣā°), D44 °veṣā°, all mss. except preceding and A1 B C21 (t) DG D12 D21 D64 G1 G2 G11 H31 (t) K1 M1 M21 M24 N21 R21 S21 T21 U1 Z9 °līlā°; D44 M21 R21 (t) S21 T21 °āvarā° (for °āparā°), A1 B D12 °ādarā°, B1 (p) G11 M1 °ādharā°, DG D21 G1 °āpadā°, M24 °āravā°, D11 °ottarā°, R21 (p) °āspadā°, all mss. except preceding and C21 (t) D64 G2 H31 (t) K1 N1 U1 Z9 °ākulā

c G2 akaraṇaśaraṇā°; D64 G11 P72 (t) °śaraṇābhyāṃ mad°; D71 parābhām (for padābhyām), DG4 ms. destroyed here

d N21 vrajamayam anu°; G11 āyāti vedaḥ

82 a no variant readings

b T21 omits entire line; M1 ne 'yaṃ; T71 °vadhūjanatāpa°

c N21 so 'yaṃ madāndha? anujeśvara°; DG1 DG4 tṛtīyabhavane°

d H31 (t) yo 'yaṃ; G1 H31 P71 T71 °āmbujatāpahārī

83 a M21 °jñatvaṃ (for °jñatve), D12 °jñate; B2 °jñatvena; D71 M1 maugdhe; B2 maugdhyena

b DG2 sārvavemam; H31 (t) imaṃ mahaḥ; V1 idaṃ mama

c Z9 niviśan; D12 K1 hanti (for hanta), V1 tejo

d H31 (e) nirmāṇasukham; C52 (t) ucyate (for aśnute), K1 astu te, M24 anyate

84 a V1 kṛṣṇānam etat (for puṣṇānam etat), C51 C52 D21 D45 F41 muṣṇānam etat, N21 puṣṇātu me tat, Z9 puṣṇāt tad etat; all mss. except A1 B C51 (t) D12 G1 K1 Z9 °śobham

b K1 N21 M1 udayan (for udayān), all mss. except preceding and A1 B D12 Z9 udayaṃ

c all mss. except A1 B DG D12 D21 G1 U1 UV V1 triguṇī°; M21 °karotu

d U1 kṛṣṇābhidaṃ (for kṛṣṇāhvayaṃ), D71 G11 kṛṣṇādvayaṃ; N21 mānase me

85 a G11 ātālavilocana°; D44 °śrīḥ
b Z9 saṃtoṣatāśeṣa°; C21 (t) °mārgam (for °vargam), G11 °vargaḥ, B D12 T71 °garvam, A1 (? corrected to °garvam)
c D71 M1 R21 (te) murāre; D11 adhurādharo°; H21 (t) °oṣṭhe
d no variant readings

86 (D1 omits all of vs. before °śriyau)
a N21 kadā (for karau), all mss. except A1 B DG D11 D12 G1 G2 G11 M24 N21 S21 śaradudañcitāmbujavilāsa°; P72 (t) °vilāpa° (for °vilāsa°), D64 °vilāsam; F41 °dīkṣā° (for °śikṣā), D64 °īkṣā°, N21 °śikhā°; DG2 DG4 °gurau
b D21 pade; D21 °ollaṅghinī (for °ollaṅghinau), D71 °ollaṅghanau, Z9 °ollaṅghitau
c D71 °bhuvanaikamāna°; C21 (t) °kriyau
d DG vilokayati locanā° (for vilokaya vilocanā°), G11 vilokaya trilocanā; S21 muhuḥ śaiśavam (for mahaḥ śaiśavam), all mss. except preceding and A1 B C21 (t) DG D11 D12 D21 D71 G1 G2 G11 K1 R21 (t) S21 (p) U1 mahac chaiśavam

87 a DG H31 (t) ācinvānam uṣasy; D11 niḥsārān (for sākārān), C21 (t) D44 nā 'kārān; G1 vikāra° (for vihāra°) U1 vihāraṃ; D11 vihāraśramān
b āmanthānam arundhatī°; N21 °smitajyotsnayā (for °smitārdraśriyā), G2 °smitādyaśriyau, C21 (t) °smitārdrakriyā, all mss. except preceding and A1 B C21 (c) C51 (p) C52 (p) D1 D11 D12 D64 G11 H21 H31 M24 P71 (p) P72 (p) R21 S21 °smitāsyaśriyā
c C51 (t) D45 F41 G11 °janya (for °janma°) A1 anarthyāṃ (anarghyāṃ), C52 (t) D71 G11 H21 (t) H31 M21 M24 anarghaṃ; D12 diśām
d all mss. except A1 B DG D1 D12 G11 K1 N21 āmandaṃ vraja°; G1 °taṭe (for °taṭī°), G2 °taṭā° (incorrect for?)

88 a H21 (t) P71 (t) tam ucchvasita° (for tad ucchvasita°), G2 ms. destroyed here, all mss. except preceding and A1 B2 B3 samucchvasita°
b C51 (c) C52 (c) D45 D71 G2 H21 H31 M21 P71 P72 (c) R21 T21 U1 madavimugdha° (for madanamugdha°), P72 (t) madavidagdha°, C51 (t) C52 (c) padavimugdha°, N21 madhuramugdha°, D1 madanamudra°; M21 °mugdhahārā°; M1 °mlātam
c C21 (c) D1 D44 G2 H21 (te) K1 M1 R21 (t) S21 (t) T21 °vilocanaṃ (for vilokanaṃ), N21 °viśobhanaṃ, all mss. except preceding and C21 (t) DG °vilobhanaṃ; U1 praṇayanīta°
d K1 °vimocanaṃ (for °vimohanaṃ), all mss. except preceding and DG D12 G1 M1 U1 V1 °manoharaṃ; DG G1 °jīvanam

89 (G2 lines c d destroyed; N1 lines a b destroyed)
a no variant readings
b A1 D11 D12 N21 vadanāravindam (for nayanāravindam
c A1 D12 D44 N21 nayanāravindam (for vadanāravindam), D11 nadanāravindam, D1 vayanāravindam
d D44 nayanāravindam (for punar amba citram), A1 B2 B3 (p reads with text)

D11 D12 vapur asya citram, C51(t) C52(t) D45 F41 G11 K1 M24 Z9 punar eva citram

90 a no variant readings

b DG G1 M21 ati° (for adhi°); DG °bhūṣaṇam abdhi° (for °bhūṣitajaladhi°), G2 °bhūṣaṇaṃ jaladhi° (metriclly incorrect); DG G1 °kumbhe

c D45 F41 V1 °yuvatīhārāvali- (for °yuvatihāravallī-), N1 ms. destroyed for °hāravallī-, P72(t) °yuvativihāravallī- (metrically incorrect), D21 °yuvativihārāvallī- (metrically incorrect), C51(t) C52(t) °yuvatihārāvalī- (metrically incorrect)

d N1 ms, destroyed for entire line; DG1 DG4 D71 G1 G11 H21 H31 M1 M21 M24 R21(c) marataka° (variant form of marakata°), A1 makarata° (incorrect for marakata°); M1 maratakamaṇināyakamahaṃ vande (entire line—metrically incorrect)

91 a D21 K1 M1 kāntākuca°; N21 °kacagrahakutūhala°; H21(t) °sagraha° (for °vigraha°), N1 °lālasa°, M1 ms. destroyed here, G2 ms. destroyed here to °mañjulaśrīḥ; Z9 °saṃgataśrī; D1 M1 N21 °bandha°, all mss. except preceding and A1 B DG D11 D12 D21 G1 G11 N1 U1 °baddha°; T71 °lakṣyaiḥ (for °lakṣmī-), B1 DG D12 D21 G1 G11 T21 °lakṣmīḥ

b M1 N1 kaṇṭhā° (for khaṇḍa°), G11 karṇā°, K1 caṇḍā°, N21 citrā°; C51(t)°āṅgaroga°; all mss. except A1 B DG D12 G11 D64 °rāgarasa°; D71 °mañjulāṅgaiḥ; C51(t) D1 M24 Z9 °śrīḥ), C21(c) C51(c) C52(c) D44 H21(c) H31(c) N21 P71(c) P72(c) R21(c) S21(c[p reads with text]) V1 °śri

c DG4 ms. destroyed here; DG1 DG2 °mukula° (for °mukura°), M1 °makara°; C52(t) M1 °kuṇḍala° (for °maṇḍala°); D11 D12 G11 M1 °lekhamāna- (for °khelamāna-), DG1 DG2 °khelavaktra-, Z9 °lolamāna- D71 °sevyamāna-

d N21 marmā° (for gharmā°), M1 karmā° G11 narmā°, D1 kharmā°, D64 dharmā°, T71 barhā°; G1 °āṅkurā (for °āṅkuraḥ), A1 °āṅkura corrected to °āṅkuraḥ, all mss. except B DG D11 G11 M1 S21(p) °āṅkuraṃ; G1 kam api; D71 H21 V1 khelati (for gumphati), Z9 rājati, G1 kuñcati, R21 jṛmbhati, P72(c) madhūyati, M1 cumbita°, C21(t) DG D11 G1 G11 H31 N1 S21(t) T21 U1 UV cumbati, all mss. except preceding and A1 B D12 S21(p) śumbhati; D11 devakṛṣṇaḥ(for kṛṣṇadevaḥ), N1 kṛṣñadevam, all mss. except preceding and A1 B DG D1 D12 D21 G1 G2 G11 S21(p) U1 kṛṣṇatejaḥ

92 a T21 adharaṃ madhuraṃ; G2 madhrasya; Y2 Y14 Y21 śiśor (for vibhor), C21(t) vibho

b DG1 G1 K1 adharaṃ (for the first madhuraṃ); D21 vadanaṃ after the first madhuraṃ; Y2 Y21 vadanaṃ after the third madhuraṃ; M24 vadanaṃ madanam; D71 vadanāmburuham

c M1 mṛdugandhi (for madhugandhi), DG G1 madhuraṃ ca, Y2 madhugandha°, A1 madhugandha° corrected to madhugandhi; Y2 °śuci° (for mṛdu°), Y21 śuci°, Y14 suvi°; Y2 °smitam eva tadā; T71 etad ahe

d no variant readings

93 a D1 D64 °sarvajñaṃ (for °sarvasvaṃ), A1 °sarvaśvaṃ (incorrect for?)

b no variant readings

c D45 °nirākāram (for °narākāram), G1 °narārāmam, B3(p) °navākāram

d D1 āśrayed; U1 jadadāśrayam; D1 M1 °āśraye

94 a K1 T71 adyā 'pi; all mss. except A1 B DG D11 D12 G1 G2 G11 K1 M24 N1 S21 ca (for 'pi); A1 B D12 nidarśanāya (for na darśanāya), D11 vimarśanāya, all mss. except preceding and DG G1 G2 G11 M24 N1 na darśanena

b M24 yat tat pato 'paniṣad° (for citte tatho 'paniṣad°), N1 cittena vo 'pariṣad°, N1 citte tadā 'pi niṣad°, G2 citte tado 'paniṣad°, R21(t) T21 U1 V1 cittena co 'paniṣad°, all mss. except preceding and A1 B DG D11 D12 G1 G11 citte vo 'paniṣad°; all mss. except A1 B DG D1 D11 D12 D64 G2 G11 M1 M24 °ṣadā (for ṣadaṃ); D12 G1 suhṛdāṃ (for sudṛśāṃ), N1 suhṛśam

c U1 na tvaṃ (for sa tvaṃ), DG G1 G2 tattvaṃ DG caraṃ (for ciraṃ), B2 B3 cirān, N1 cirā? (last syllable is destroyed)

d H21(t) svāmī; DG D64 G1 G11 K1 M24 N21 T21 U1 UV V1 Z9 kadā (for kayā), G2 nayā°; D12 M1 'pi (for nu); D11 mayi (for mama); N1 saṃnidhehi (for saṃnidhatse), C21(t) D1 G2 H21(e) K1 P72(te) saṃnidhatte

95 a H21(te) se 'yaṃ (for ke 'yaṃ), N1 kā 'sau

b M24 ke 'yaṃ (for ko 'yaṃ), N21 ko vā; D21 K1 M24 N1 kvā 'pi (for ko 'pi), D1 kvo 'pi (incorrect for?), all mss. except preceding and DG G1 M1 T21 U1 V1 kā 'pi

c M24 ke 'yaṃ (for se 'yaṃ), A1 so 'yaṃ (this and the other A1 variants in line c have been corrected to read with critical text version); N21 mugdha° (for so 'yaṃ), all mss. except preceding and B DG D1 D11 D12 N1 V1 se 'yaṃ; DG G1 svādyatām (for svādatām), T21 svādyatā, D64 śyāmatā, G2 svāgatām, D1 svādutāṃ, all mss. except preceding and B D11 D12 N1 svādutā; DG añjalisthe (añjalis te), D71 mañjulaśrī, M1 mañjulaśri, D11 añjalisrī (incorrect for?), N1 añjulas te (incorrect for?) all mss. except preceding and B D12 G1 G2 mañjulaśrīḥ

d R21(t) bhūyaḥ prāyaśas tvāṃ; A1 DG D71 H21 H31 K1 M21 P71 T71 bhūyasas; D12 te (for tvāṃ), D1 tvaṃ, K1 °tiṃ (incorrect for?), G11 tān, C21(t) C52(t) D45 D64 F41 G1 N1 N21 S21(p) taṃ, all mss. except preceding and A1 B DG R21 U1 V1 tan

96 a N21 vadanena; G11 °virājitaḥ śaśī

b N21 dayādivyapadam (metrically incorrect for daśadhā deva padaṃ); B3(p) devapadaṃ (for deva padaṃ); B3 prapadyate (for prapadya te)

c A1 āndhakāṃ (for adhikaṃ); G11 tadā (for °tarāṃ), D1 tadā 'ttaḥ (different meter—aupacchandasika)

d C52(t) H21(t) P71(t) T71 tāruṇya°; G11 kāruṇyanirmitaṃ; C21(t) hi yat (for kiyat), K1 kiyat tat (different meter—aupacchandasika), D1 kiyat tati (incorrect for K1 reading?)

97 a M21 'bjasaroja° (for 'mbujatulya°), A1 'mbuja° (corrected to 'mbujatulya°), all mss. except preceding and B C21(p) C51(p) C52(p) DG D11 D12 D21 G1 G2 G11 H21(p) H31(p) M1 N1 N21 P71(p) P72(p) R21(p) S21(S21p reads with the unexcepted mss.) U1 'bjasamāna°; H31(t) °kakṣyāṃ (for °kakṣyaṃ),

A1 B C51(t) D1 D11 D12 D21 D45 D64 F41 G2 H21(t) U1 °kakṣaṃ

b[1] as in critical text. This line found in A1 B DG D11 D12 G1 G2 G11 N1 U1. Variants are: U1 vācām abhūmir a?śārada°; G1 vācāṃ gocaram anuparvaṇi (metrically incorrect); DG G1 °īnduḥ (for °īndoḥ)

b[2] occurs in all texts except those which have line b[1]: vāñmādhurībahulaparvakalā-samṛddham Varients are: M21 M24 °bahala°; M1 R21(tp) S21 °sarva° (for °parva°), P72(t) °pakṣa°, D64 °parya°; N21 °samṛddhim (for °samṛddham), D1 °samṛddhiḥ, D64 °samudram

c C21(t) D64 H31(t) M1 M21 M24 N21 yad (for kim); D12 °kānte (for °kāntam), N1 °kānt? (ms. destroyed after t), D1 °kānti, A1 B G2 K1 °kānta-

d G11 etat (for kṛṣṇa), A1 kiṃ tat (corrected to kṛṣṇa), M1 yat yat, G2 veṣa°, A1 B D12 veṇu, all mss. except preceding and DG D11 G1 N1 U1 yasya; the last half of line d has two basically different readings: A1 B DG D11 D12 G1 G2 G11 N1 read with the critical text[1] (°ānanam anena samaṃ nu yat syāt) with the following minor variant readings: D11 amuṣya samaṃ kathaṃ syāt; DG G2 samunnayat syāt; G11 yadi syāt; N1 n?yi syāt (ms. somewhat destroyed here; the second reading (°ānanasamā suṣamā sadā syāt) occurs in all texts not listed above (before superscript 1). The minor vairants to the second reading are: R21(t) suṣamaṃ (for suṣamā), C51 C52 D21 D45 F41 H31 M1 suṣumā, N21 'dhyupamā; D1 M1 S21(t) samā (for sadā), D11 U1 kathaṃ

98 (U1 line order c d a b)

a U1 śṛṇu vaco yadi māmakīnaṃ; DG D12 M24 yadi śṛṇu praṇi°; C51(p) C52(p) P72(p) read with text praṇidhānapūrvaṃ; all mss. except preceding and A1 B D11 D21 G1 G2 G11 N1 S21 śuśrūṣase yadi vacaḥ śṛṇu māmakīnaṃ

b M21 M24 °vibhinnakaṭākṣitaṃ; D21 N1 yat (for tat)

c B2 C51 C52 D45 F41 N21 V1 °dhuraṃ (for °dhurāṃ), D11 D64 G1 G11 °dhurā, C21(t) °dhutaṃ; D12(p) G2 °endau (for endoḥ), C51(t) D12 D71 G11 N21 °endo

d DG nivyājam; M24 añcati cirāya

99 a DG2 G1 ākhaṇḍa°; D71 G2 M21 P71(t) P72(t) R21(t) S21(t) T71 pravāha- (for pravāhair), G1 pravāher

b K1 °vibhūṣaṇāni (for °rasāntarāṇi), G2 rathāntarāṇi

c DG2 āyantrito° (for ayantrito°), G2 ayantrita°; D64 °orrdhvānta° (for °odvānta°), D44 H21(t) M1 °oddhvānta°, G2 °adhvānta°, DG G1 N1 °odātta°; N1 °rasāntarāṇi (for °sudhārṇavāni)

d M1 dhyāyanti; Z9 kṛṣṇasya śucismitāni

100 a K1 tubhyaṃ santu; G2 santi; G11 sahasraśaṃ; D1 K1 katipayo; D12 M1 N21 svārasya (for sārasya°), N1 bhārasya; G11 °dhaureyakān (for °dhaureyakāḥ), D12 N21 °dhaureyakā

b M1 vaḥ (for vā); N21 °parigama° (for °parimala°; C51 C52 D21 D45 F41 H21(t) P71 P72 T21 T71 U1 V1 °pariṇati°; N1 °pariṇatiḥ; G1 °labdhavratāḥ

c A1 B D12 K1 nai 'vai 'vaṃ (for nai 'vai 'tair), H21(t) devai 'tair, V1 tair nai 'vaṃ, G11 tair evaṃ, N1 ms. destroyed here; D11 D21 M21 vividāmahe (for vivadāmahe), D11 na ca punar, Z9 kṛṣṇa priyaṃ d DG G1 Z9 tat (for yat); R21 yat sarvaṃ; K1 U1 kamanīyatā°; M1 °parimalas; K1 sāraṃ; D1 K1 M1 gataḥ (for gatā), A1 gatāḥ (corrected to gatā),C51 (t) C52(t) D44 H21 (t) P72(t) S21 (t) gatāḥ, DG4 gataṃ

101 a G11 T21 °krīḍā (for °vrīḍā), DG G1 M1 M21 M24 R21 (e) T71 °vrīḷā (variant form of °vrīḍā); DG GL ḍolā° (for lolā); G1 °vinutā (for °vinatā), N1 °lalitā, D1 T21 °kalitā, D11 °vimatā, all mss. except preceding and A1 B DG D12 G11 UV °vanitā; D44 gopavijitā

b A1 B D12 G1 S21 madasphītaṃ; A1 B D11 D12 vītaṃ; DG4 kām api (for kim api), G11 kam api, N1 omits; H31 (t) °dharā (for °dhurā), T71 °vadhūḥ, D1 °durā, N21 S21 (t) °dhurāḥ

c P71 T71 samujjṛmbho gumbho; N1 kumbhā (for gumbhā), A1 B C52 D11 D12 D45 F41 U1 gumphā (variant form of gumbhā); D1 D11 D21 G1 H31 (t) M1 N1 R21 S21 T21 V1 °girāṃ (for °kirāṃ), C21 (t) DG M1 °kirā, G11 ms. destroyed here; N1 naigama° (for māddṛśa°), DG nāgama° (incorrect for N1 reading?), M24 māmaka°; D1 D12 °girā

d N1 ms. destroyed for line d; A1 B D12 yāte (for jāte), DG G1 M24 U1 jāne; V1 dharati capalaṃ janma ca phalam

102 a C51 (t) C52(t) D11 D45 H31 (t) K1 bhuvanaṃ bhavanaṃ (for bhavanaṃ bhuvanaṃ) C21 (te) D1 D21 F41 U1 bhuvanaṃ bhuvanaṃ D44 bhuvanaṃ bhuvanaṃ corrected to text reading

b T71 munayas tāmaruhāsanaṃ; DG tvām arasāsana; A1 C21 (t) D1 D71 G1 G11 H21 (t) H31 (t) K1 M21 N21 P72(t) R21 (t) tāmarasāsana; DG D21 D44 G1 G11 K11 K1 S21 smaro vā (for smaraś ca), T71 karasya, M1 smarasya, P72(t) svaraś ca, D1 smitaś ca

c C51 C52 DG D45 F41 M24 parivāra° (for paricāra°), Z9 paricāri°; all mss. except A1 B C21 (t) DG D11 D12 F41 H31 (t) K1 M24 N21 R21 (t) S21 U1 Z9 °paraṃparā

d U1 vibhor

103 a C21 (t) D1 G11 H21 (t) P72(t) trilokasaubhāgya-

b A1 B D12 °makarāñkuraḥ; G2 M1 °āñkuraṃ

c Z9 bhāti vrajā°; G1 vrajajanāpaṅga-; S21 °saṅga- (for °naṅga-), N21 °saṃga-, D44 °liṅga-, M24 °nāga

d DG kelir (for keli°), all mss. except preceding and A1 B D1 D11 D12 D45 D71 M1 kelī°; N21 °talita° (for °lālita°), G1 S21 (e) T71 °lulita°, all mss. except preceding and A1 B D11 D12 D45 D71 F41 G11 H31 (e) °lalita°; T71 °vaibhavaḥ (for °vibhramaḥ), H31 (t) °vigrahaḥ

104 a DG2 vāma° (for kāma°)

b DG1 vedhadaṃ (for vedanaṃ), DG2 vedhaṃ (incorrect for DG1 reading?), DG4 vedhaidaṃ (incorrect for DG1 reading?), M1 vadanaṃ (metrically incorrect for?)

c K1 S21 jīvitaṃ (for jīvanaṃ), K1 daivataṃ (for jīvitaṃ), S21 jīvanaṃ

d D44 tvatpadāmbujā (for daivataṃ ca me); D64 M1 vedanāparam, K1 jīvanāparam

105 M25 omits lines c and d)
a all mss. except A1 B DG D11 D12 D21 D44 G2 S21 vijṛmdhantām̧
b Z9 kṛṣṇa (for tava), DG4 D1 D71 K1 U1 tana°; D1 D64 G1 G11 K1 N1 U1 Z9 śaiśave
c H31(t) cāpalye nai 'va; DG D44 G1 G11 S21(t[c destroyed here])
d K1 stana° (for tava), D1 tāna°; D64 G11 M24 N1 vaibhave (for śaiśave), D1 °vaibhave

106 a Z5 raśanā°; Z5 (p found only in S and 10) dhanyātmanā
b D1 M1 yā (for ye); G11 ye ye (for ye vā), Z9 yad vā; D45 V1 cāpalaśaiśava°; N1 dhārāvarodhon° (for rādhāvarodhon°), M24 rāseṣṭarādhon°, T71 dhārāparādhon°, Z5 (p found only in Ed) rādhānubandhon°, D64 D71 rādhāparodhon°, all mss. except preceding and A1 B DG D12 G1 Z5 rādhāparādhon°
c C52(t) S21(t) ye (for yā), DG sā (for vā), G2 yā; G2 R21 bhāvukaveṇu°; M21 ratayo (for °gatayo), M1 °gataye; C52(t) D64 līlām̧; S21 °ruhair (for °ruhe), D1 G1 P72(t) °ruho
d N1 dhārā°... °tu (ms. destroyed); D1 DG4 rādhā° (for dhārā°), M1 līlā°; D11 Z5 (p found only in Ed) °vāhitayā (for °vāhikayā), Z5 (p found only in Sp) °vāhatayā, Z5 (p found only in A) °vāhikatayā (metrically incorrect), Z9 vāhikatām̧; G1 bhavanti (for vahantu), U1 vahanti, Z5 (except Ed which reads with critical text) harantu; S21(t) tu (for me)

107 a N21 bhakṣi (for bhaktis); D11 priyatarā (for sthiratarā), C51(t) H21(t) P71(t) T71 sthiratayā
b D1 D44 M24 S21(t) devena (for daivena), N1 deve 'pi, N21 deveśa; M1 N1 S21 sā (for naḥ); DG N1 phalatu (for phalati), all mss. except preceding and A1 B C21(t) D11 D12 G1 G2 G11 H31(t) K1 S21 phalita°; D12 bhāgya° (for divya°), K1 daiva°; A1 B2 B3 G11 °mūrtiḥ (for °veṣaḥ), D11 °mūrtau, D12 °veṣaḥ, D44 °veṣam, M1 °veṣa
c DG muktis tv ayam̧ (for muktiḥ svayam̧), M1 muktis tvayi, D44 bhakti svayam̧, C21(t) C51(t) D1 D71 K1 M24 N1 U1 mukti svayam̧; N21 °añjalir āśritā °smān (for °añjali sevate 'smān), DG °añjaline 'va te 'smād, N1 °añjalir eva cā 'smān, M1 añjalir etasmāt; S21(P) sevate 'smin (for sevate 'smān), R21(t) sevanena
d M1 dharmātma; C21(t) C52(t) D1 M1 samayaḥ; K1 N1 T21 °pratīkṣyāḥ

108 (P71 R21 T71 line order a d c b)
a no variant readings
b Z9 °dhāma° (for °nāma°), D1 °tāma°; C51(t) DG1 DG4 D64 D71 °dheyam (for dheya), A1 °dheyā (corrected to °dheya), K1 (vs. 1.108) K1 (vs. after colophon to century 3) °dheyā (both K1 readings uncorrected), D1 °dheyāḥ
c A1 B C51 C52 D12 D21 G1 G2 S21 deva kṛṣṇa deva (for deva deva kṛṣṇa), C21 D44 D64 D71 M1 M21 M24 N21 T21 U1 bālakṛṣṇa kṛṣṇa, P71 R21 T71 deva deva deva, H21 K1 (vs. 1.108) P72 V1 bālakṛṣṇa deva H31 bālakṛṣṇa mūrte, Z9 deva bālakṛṣṇa, D1 bālakṛṣṇa (metrically incorrect), K1 (vs. after colophon to century 3) jaya jaya bālakṛṣṇa deva deva (entire line), DG D45 F41 N1 read as in text

d DG D44 P72(t) omit °mṛtā; N1 °āmṛtāvṛtā° (metrically incorrect for °āmṛtā°); H21(t) Z9 °āvatāraḥ (for °āvatāra), M1 °āvatāram, K1 (vs. 1.108 °āvatārā, K1 (vs. after colophon to century 3) °āvatā (both K1 readings incorrect), D1 °āvatārāḥ

109 a M1 tulyanirbhara°; D11 °marṣa° (for °varṣa°), C51(t) N21 omit these two syllables; D64 °varṣati; DG °varṣaviśadāveśastuvadvedhase; D64 H21(t) S21(e) °ādeśa° (for °āveśa°), C21(te) °āleśa°; C21(t) °spurāvir°; DG M1 °āvirbhava- (N1 ms. destroyed from °āveśa... sukṛtāṃ)

b DG °sauhṛdeṣu (for bhūṣiteṣu), D21 S21 °veṣṭiteṣu, P72(t) °dūṣiteṣu, H21(t) °bhāṣiteṣu); R21(p) S21 sudṛśāṃ, DG sukṛtā; A1 °nirbhāsane (for °nirbhāsine), S21 °nirbhāvine, D11 K1 °nirbhāṣate, M24 °nirbhāsi me, all mss. except preceding and B DG D12 G1 N1 °nirbhāsate

c D12 viduṣāṃ (for manasāṃ), D1 maṇirāṃ (incorrect for?), H21(e) H31(e) mahase C51(e) C52(e) mahatve, all mss. except the preceding and A1 B DG D11 G1 K1 N21 S21 mahate; DG2 D21 vācā (for vācāṃ), D64 vācaṃ; all mss. except A1 B DG D12 G1 K1 S21 vi° (for ca); D11 S21 °dūre sphuran- (for dūrasphuran-), G2 °bhūmisphuran-, all mss. except A1 B DG D12 D21 G1 K1 N1 V1 °dūrāyate

d all mss. except A1 B DG D11 D12 D21 G1 G2 K1 S21 rasārṇavāya; D64 mahate

110 a M24 īśānam eva; D21 deva (for nīvī-), K1 sevi-, N21 tena, M24 nīla-, A1 nīmī (incorrect for?), D1 vindā, DG4 K1 S21(t) nīvi-

b M1 °stabakād gamena (for °stabakodgamena, DG1 N1 mss destroyed here, DG2 DG4 °stabakāṅgamena, D44 °stabakodyamena, A1 B D12 °stabakodbhavena, D1 °stabakodramena

c all mss. except A1 B DG D11 D12 G1 G11 R21 kṛṣṇa deva

d C21(t) kṛṣṇāmṛtaṃ

111 a C21(t) rasanā° (for sarasā°), DG2 rasasā°; N1 °rāga° (for °lāpa°), N22 °pāpa°, M24 °lepa°; B2 B3 (2 mss. as in text) D11 (vs, 1.111) °laharī° (fors °saraṇi°), D64 °karaṇe; all mss. except A1 B D1 D12 G11 (vs. 1.110) K1 N22 S21 °saubhāgyam (for °saurabhyam)

b D71 H21(t) N1 °dṛṣṭiṃ (for °vṛṣṭiṃ), D64 °vṛddhiṃ, S21 °puṣṭiṃ; DG1 DG4 duhānī (for duhānaṃ), DG2 duhānā D11 (vs. 1.111) duhānāṃ; K1 N22 mahat (for muhuḥ)

c D21 lokānāṃ (vanyānāṃ), G11 (vs. 2.112) vaṃśānāṃ, D12 H21(t) K1 N22 S21 dhanyānāṃ, A1 B DG G1 G11 (vs. 1.110) vanyānāṃ; DG G2 mṛgasya devasya

d G11 (vs. 1.110) kṛṣṇānāṃ; D11 (both vss.) G11 (vs. 1.110) M24 vacasā (for vacasāṃ), D1 vacanāṃ; D11 (vs. 2.2) karṇasya (for kṛṣṇasya), B1 C51 C52 D12 D21 D45 F41 V1 śrīkṛṣṇa°; D11 (vs. 2.2) kṛṣṇāmṛtam

112 a D11 (vs. 2.5) anugrīvā; D1 H31(t) °dviguṇavilola

b F41 °svana° (for °svanan°), T21 °svanaṃ, A1 B D12 D21 S21 °smaran°; B45 F41 V1 °dviguṇagalad° (foı °mṛdumuralī°), M21 °muralīgalad° (metrically incorrect), N21 °veṇukalad° (metrically incorrect), all mss. except preceding and A1 B DG D11 (vs. 2.5) D12 D21 G11 S21 °veṇugalad° (metrically incorrect)

c DG yatas tataḥ (for yato yataḥ) T21 tayor yataḥ; D11 (vs. 2.5) he (for me), A1 mad°

d D1 H21(t) T21 tadai 'va; DG G2 śaiśavam (for vaibhavam), D11 (vs. 1.112) M21 vaibhavaḥ, D21 vaibhavaiḥ

Śataka II

1 a G2 ms. destroyed for entire line

b G11 dadhigaṇa°; D21 °madidigdhaṃ (for °paridigdhaṃ) D1 °parimugdhaṃ

c H31(t) viśatu; D14 N21 P72(t) bhavana°; D12 °cchedinā piccha°; all mss. except D12 D21 D41 D43 D45 D64 tāpiñcha° (variant form of tāpiccha°)

d YY1 śiti° (for nava°), T21 nakha°; D41 D43 D45 °picchair lāñchitaṃ;

2 a D43 vyūḍho

b no variant readings

c no variant readings

d D12 sā pātanī; D12 D41 D43 vaḥ

3 a R22(t) vimate

b K1 yācantīnāṃ manu°; V1 anunatapadair

c S21(t) abjālolair; D14 atasavilasair (for alasavilasair), D43 alasavalitair, D41 alasavilitair (incorrect for D43 reading?)

d no variant readings

4 a D12 mātas tātaḥ; U1 phalānāṃ (for khalānāṃ), C51(t) balānāṃ, D1 kalānāṃ,

b M6 °vṛttaye (for °pūrtaye), Y21 °mūrtaye, DG6 M1 āsīt

c R22(t) vatsate, D45 E41 kurve (for kuryāṃ), D43 ms. destroyed here

d no variant readings.

5 a E41 (E41p reads with text) °randhraiḥ

b T21 pāraṃ pāraṃ; D12 veṇunā 'pūrayantam (for veṇum āpūrayantam), K1 veṇīm āhārayantam

c N1 vima... mala° (for vikacakamala°—ms. destroyed here); D43 D45 E41 S21(p) V1 °vistāri° (for °vistāra°), G11 ms. destroyed here, N1 N21 °vistīrṇa°

d N1 vṛndāvanabhuvicaraṃ; G2 °bālam (for °sūnum), D12 °vṛndam, D14 D21 °sūnuḥ

6 a Y11 Y12 mandānudati pavanaṃ (for mandaṃ madhuraninadair), Y2 Y14 Y21 mandaṃ nudati pavanaṃ, Y13 mandam mṛdati pavane; YY1 °ninadaṃ (for °ninadair, M1 °ninade; YY1 veṇunā 'pūrayantaṃ

b Y13 Y14 vṛdaṃ vṛndaṃ vanabhuvi; D12 gataṃ (for gavāṃ): Y12 corayantaṃ

c Y12 vṛndobhāge (for chandobhāge), D45 chandobhāgyaṃ; DG2 DG3 DG5 DG6 D41 D43 D71 N21 °mukhamakha° (for °makahmakha°), Y13 °makha° (metrically incorrect), D1 °mūrkhamukha° (metrically incorrect), K1 Y14 °mukhamukha°, G11 N1 mss. destroyed here, all mss. except preceding and

DG1 E41 T21 V1 Y11 Y12 Y21 Y31 Y32 YY1 °makhamukha°; H31(t) Y2 Y14 Y31 Y32 °dhvaṃsinaṃ (for °dhvaṃsināṃ), DG6 °dhvaṃsinā, N1 ms. destroyed here, Y13 °dhvaṃsitāṃ

d Y13 katham arasane; Y11 Y12 rasano; Y2 Y11 Y12 Y13 Y14 Y21 gopakanyākiśoram

7 a K1 veṇīmāle; Y12 Y14 Y21 Y31 Y32 vinihita° (for viracita°), Y12 Y14 Y21 °karaḥ śyāmalaḥ komalāṅgo; D21 °ghanaḥ śyāma°; YY1 °āvataṃso

b Y31 Y32 vidyunmālā; Y31 iha (for iva); Y11 Y13 Y21 °pītāṃśukena (for °pītāmbareṇa), YY1 °pītāmbaraṃ ca

c M24 ārāliṅgan (for māṃ āliṅgan), D1 D12 D21 K1 māṃ āliṅgaṃ; C51(t) DG1 K1 M1 M24 S21(t) T71 °bāhu

d Y12 Y14 Y21 dṛṣṭaḥ svapne; D12 Y14 Y32 °bhūṣaṇe; D41 D43 D64 meghanīlaḥ

8 a D64 kṛṣṭo; D12 dattā; D41 D43 tīravṛkṣādhirūḍhe (for kūlakundādhirūḍhe), D1 kuṅkumājyādhinūdhe (incorrect for?), N1 kūlakuntādhirūḍhe, all mss. except preceding and DG1 DG2 DG6 G1 G2 H31(t) M1 M6 M21 M24 N21 kūlakuñjādhirūḍhe

b M1 M6 kā cin mugdhā (for mugdhā kā cin), G2 mūḍhā kā cin; DG6 kiṃ ca (for kiṃ nu), C21(t) C51(t) D1 D11 D21 D45 D71 K1 M1 M6 P72(t) R22 S21(t) kiṃ v, T71 nanv, C22 D12 D64 kiṃ tv, D14 N21 kiṃ ci (incorrect for?); C21(te) C51(te) DG2 DG3 DG5 D12 K1 R22(te) U1 vyāharanti (for vyāharantī), D71 vyāharantīm

c T21 sarasahasitaṃ

d N1 P71(t) T71 aṃśukāny ācakarṣa

9 a T21 Y12 ayi; D12 D21 D41 D43 D45 E41 G1 M1 M6 M24 R22 U1 Y12 Y14 Y21 Y31 Y32 āpta° (for ātta°), G11 ārta°, D1 ānta°, N1 ms. destroyed; C51(t) D1 puṇye

b Y31 yādṛśo; Y12 Y21 veṇunālaḥ

c C52(t) D71 H31(t) P71(t) T71 yad (for ya); Y12 eka° (for eṣa), Y14 ekaḥ

d E41(p) °dala° (for °maṇi°), Y12 Y21 °madhu°; C51(t) DG4 D1 D12 D64 K1 M6 Y32 °samīpaṃ (for °samīpa°), Y12 °samīpe; D12 prāpya° (for °nyāsa°), Y12 °dharmām (for °dhanyām); Y21 abaddham (for avasthām)

10 a D14 Y32 api (for ayi), G2 atha, Y21 ari°; Y21 paricaya° (for paricinu), Y14 paricita°; Y31 °netre

b Y2 kabaradalita° (for kabarakalita°), P72(t) karakabalita°, Y13 kavarakalita°); D1 P72(t) °dhāmā° (for °dāmā), M1 °tāmā°, DG2 Y21 °mādā; Y31 °ābhiśāmam

c C51(te) C52(te) balibhidupala° (for balabhidupala°), N21 balabhir apala°; K1 °upalanetraṃ; D1 Z9 vallabhī° (for vallavī°), K1 pallavī°; G2 °kelilolaṃ

d D1 D71 Y13 °mūlakundaṃ

11 (Y11 Y14 Y21 line order c d a b)

a D12 D14 api murali; U1 °mukundaḥ; U1 °āravindaḥ (for °āravinda-), C21(t) C22(t) D1 D14 D71 °āravindaṃ, Y11 °āravindāt, Y21 °āravinde, Y14 °āravindā

b¹ occurs only in Y11 Y14 Y21:
śravaṇanicayadhūmre sāmprāptaṃ prāṇanāthe; variants are: Y21 smaraṇanivadadhūmre; Y11 prāṇanāye
b² as in text. variants are: D12 D71 H31(t) M24 R22(t) °madhurasaṃjñe; C21(c) C22(c) C51 C52 H21(c) H31(c) P71(p) P72(p) S21(p) Y31 Y32 namaskṛtya
c Y11 Y14 Y21 Y31 Y32 madhuram adhara° (for adharamaṇisa°), Y11 Y14 Y21 Y31 °bimbaṃ (for °mīpaṃ), Y32 °bimbe, D41 YY1 °mīpe; Y11 Y14 Y21 prāpnuvatyām Y21 karṣe (for karṇe), Y11 karṇai (incorrect for?), Y11 maddiśāṃ (for maddaśām), DG6 D1 D21 D71 U1 Y14 maddaśā; D64 mandasūno
d no variant readings

12 a R22(t) navajala° (metrically incorrect for sajalajala°); D1 °jaladhinīlaṃ
a¹ N1 and N21 read sajalajaladanīlaṃ darśitodāralīlaṃ (this is st. 2.87.a) N1 text for °lajaladanīlaṃ darśi° is destroyed; N1 °nīlaṃ for °līlaṃ
b DG6 śruta° (for śrita°), K1 sṛta°; C22 DG6 D1 D12 E41 K1 P72(t) S21(t) U1 °ullāsa°; C22 D14 D41 D43 D45 D64 E41 °cailam (for °celam), P72(t) °khelam
c D45 V1 suraripukulakālaṃ (for natasuramunijālaṃ), M24 natamunisurajālaṃ; E41(p) manmano°; N1 N21 °vṛndalīlaṃ
d D45 V1 natasuramunijālaṃ (for suraripukulakālaṃ), M24 suraripukacakālaṃ

13 (Y1 ms. destroyed from beginning to °pakumāram)
a M21 °vilambita°
b M21 °vinoda° (for °nināda°), M24 °vināda°; E41 G11 M24 R22(t) Y2 Y12 Y14 Y21 Y31 Y32 °vinoditam (for °vinodinam), D12 °manoharam, R22(c) °vinodanam, Y13 °vinodinam corrected to vinoditam
c Y11 ms.destroyed for lines c and d; Y2 kanaka° (for kamala°), Y51 Y52 amala°; D41 D43 Y51 °komalakānta° (for °komalakamra°), D45 °komalanamra°, D14 °komalacāru°, Y2 Y13 Y21 °komalakaṃ pra°, C51(t) °komalakaṃbra° (incorrect for?), Y32 °komalakaṃja°, °komalakunda°; Y52 °mukhadvijaṃ (for °mukhāmbujaṃ), Y12 °sukhāmbujāṃ
d D1 kim (for kam), Y2 kim corrected to kam; Y12 omits °kumara°; C21(c) C51(c) C52(c) D64 H21(c) H31(c) R22 S21(c) āśraye

14 a Y11 veṇutālaṃ (for vaṃśanālaṃ), Y21 Y31 Y32 veṇunālaṃ
b no variant readings
c N21 antanayaṃ (for antarayan)
d no variant readings

15 a Y51 vadane sarojasukumāraṃ (metrically incorrect)
b C51(t) DG6 D1 G11 °dhurīṇām
c D43 D45 Y21 Y32 Y51 kuhakā° (for kuhanā°), E41 K1 kuhanā° (incorrect for?); D21 D64 °āśram (incorrect for °āśrum), P72(t) Y51 °śārayam (metrically incorrect); Y21 śāraye 'haṃ
d N1 murārim corrected to kumāram (as in text)

16 a D1 yamunākhilagopa°; D21 D45 N1 UV V1 'khilagopa
b no variant readings

c M6 jvalano (for damunā), R22(t) yamunā; M1 U1 papau
d no variant readings

17 a D1 K1 U1 jagadādharaṇīya°
b M24 jalajāvatyavaco 'pi cāragamyam
c D41 tanutāttanutāṃ
d D1 suranātho phala°

18 (D45 V1 Y2 Y14 Y31 Y32 Y51 Y52 have the line order c d a b; R21(t) omits c d)
a M1 yā (for sā)
b Y2 Y14 Y21 Y31 Y32 Y51 Y52 kṣemāya (for kāmāya), Y2 Y21 Y31 Y32 Y51 Y52 vo (for no); D43 G11 bhavati
c R22 omits hṛdi
d Y2 Y14 Y21 Y31 Y32 Y51 pādāmbujeṣu (for pādāmbuje ca), DG2 DG3 pādāmbujena, D12 pādāmbuje 'va

19 a M6 °ābhirāmaṃ (for °āvabhāsaṃ), H21(t) °aprakāmaṃ, all mss. except preceding and C21(t) DG1 DG2 DG3 D14 D43 (corrected to read with the unexcepted mss.) D71 M1 N1 °aprakāśaṃ
b C51 P72 R22 °vāsanaṃ (for °vāsasaṃ), N21 °vāsataṃ; D1 kalita° (for kanaka°); G2 °āṅgaḥ
c no variant readings
d C21 C22(c) C51 C52 D14 D21 D45 H21(c) H31 K1 P71(p) P72(p) Q71 R22 V1 namāmi manasā; M24 °sūnuḥ

20 a D64 °kiṅkiṇīnāṃ (for °kiṅkiṇīkaṃ), DG6 °kiṅkiṇīyaṃ
b P72(t) °vāmasūtram; M21 °sūtre
c no variant readings
d D12 vasudevasūnam (incorrect for vasudevasūnum?)

21 a C22 °drumalateṣu (for °drumataleṣu), Y2 °drumatale ca; Y2 Y13 Y14 Y21 Y31 Y32 vrajeṣu (for gaṇeṣu), N21 kaṇeṣu
b Y2 Y13 Y14 Y21 Y31 Y32 ca mṛgyate; C21(t) U1 yaḥ
c C22(t) yad; N1 N21 °nādaninadaṃ (for °vādanaparaṃ), all mss. except preceding and C22 C52(t) DG1 D11 D12 D64 G11 H31(t) M24 P71 T71 Y2 Y13 Y14 Y21 Y31 Y32 °nādanaparaṃ
d D14 atra nīlam

22 a Y2 Y11 Y14 Y21 vinyasta° (for vyatyasta°), Y31 Y32 vinyasya°; Y11 avataṃ śatabarhi°
b Y2 Y11 Y14 Y21 Y31 Y32 °veṇunālam (for °vaṃśanālam), N1 veṇunānam (incorrect for?), all mss. except preceding and DG1 DG5 DG6 G1 G2 G11 M6 M21 M24 N21 YY1 °veṇurandhram
c D21 kim api kāruṇikaṃ; Y11 °kāraṇikaṃ; K1 parastāt
d N21 saṃnidhatāt (for saṃnidhattāt?) (for saṃnidhattām), C51(t) M1 Y32 saṃnidhattam (incorrect for?)

23 a Y2 Y11 Y12 Y13 Y14 Y21 Y32 ghoṣasya ghoṣa°; Y13 °sāmamāya° (for °śamanāya), D45 E41 N1 °śamanārtham; C21 (t) D14 gavāṃ (for matho), Y2 Y11 Y12 Y13 Y14 Y21 Y31 Y32 mitho, D45 E41 N1 atho, D64 M24 P72 (t) madho, E41 (p) adho, D43 mudā°, D1 ado°
b Y2 Y11 Y12 Y13 Y14 Y21 Y31 Y32 °cauram
c M6 tad yad dhanaṃ tri°; Y11 °jagatīm
d M21 ākrānta° (for ākrośa°), Y32 āśoka°, Y13 ākośa°

24 a no variant readings
b Y2 Y13 Y31 Y32 °japaratāḥ sutarāṃ (for °japaparā nitarāṃ), Y21 japaratā nitarāṃ
c Y2 Y13 Y14 Y21 Y31 Y32 ceto 'smadīyam (for ceto madīyam); R22 (t) °āvabhāvaṃ
d K1 gopi°; Y14 gopakiśorabhāram

25 a Y2 Y14 Y21 Y31 Y32 Z7 (Z7-K ms. reads with text) °dṛṣṭir (for °cittā), D41 N1 mss. destroyed here
b Y2 Y14 Y21 Y31 Y32 manthānakaṃ (for manthānam ā°), Z7 (Z7-K Kh mss. read with text) manthānikāṃ, D71 panthānaṃ ā°; Y2 Y14 Y21 Y31 Y32 Z7 (except K Kh mss.) vidadhatī (for °kalayatī), DG2 DG3 DG5 DG6 D11 D71 G11 U1 Z7 (K Kh mss.) °kalayate
c D14 G1 Z7 (Z7-G ms. reads with text) °stabakacūcuka°; Y14 Y21 Y31 Z7 (G ms.) °locanālir (for °loladṛṣṭir), Y2 °locanena, Y32 °locanāni (corrected to °locanāliṃ), D1 °lobhadṛṣṭer
d Y14 dohada° (for dohana°), N21 dehana° D41 godhana°; Y2 Y14 Y21 Y31 Z7 (G ms.) dhavalaṃ (for vṛṣabhaṃ), Y32 śavalaṃ (corrected to dhavalaṃ); Y31 nyayuñjat (for nirundhan), Y2 Y32 niyuñjat (incorrect for?), Y14 Y21 viyuñjan, C22 (t) nyarundhan, D12 D41 D64 dudoha

26 a Y2 Y12 Y14 Y21 Y31 Y32 Y51 Y52 °bhāsura° (for °komala°), D1 omits these these syllables, K1 °lomala° (incorrect for?); U1 °kuṇḍalā (for °kuntalā°), G2 °kundalā° (incorrect for?)
b Y12 Y14 °oddharaṇa (for °oddharaṇa°) Y51 Y52 °oddharaṇaṃ; Y12 Y14 Y51 Y52 uddhṛtabāhudaṇḍam (for °kelikṛtaprayāsam), G2 °kelikaraprayāsam, D11 °kelikṛtaprayatnam
c Y2 Y12 Y14 Y21 Y31 Y32 Y51 Y52 gopīstanastabakakuṅkuma°; Y2 Y21 Y51 Y52 °piṅgalāṅgaṃ (for °mudritāṅgaṃ), Y14 Y32 °piṅgarāṅgaṃ, Y12 Y31 °paṅkilāṅgaṃ
d Y2 Y12 Y14 Y21 Y31 Y32 Y51 Y52 bhaja sādhu cetaḥ (for śaraṇaṃ bhajāmaḥ); D14 prapadye (for bhajāmaḥ), C21 (t) prapadye (corrected to bhajāmaḥ), D1 M6 N1 N21 bhajāmi, DG1 DG3 DG5 G1 vrajāmaḥ, DG6 T21 bhajāmahe (metrically incorrect)

27 a C51 (t) C52 (t) °paripūrṇa°
b G1 ime (for amī), G2 ms. destroyed here
c C22 (t) C51 (t) DG1 DG2 DG3 DG5 D1 D11 D12 D21 D41 D43 D64 D71 G2 K1 M1 M6 M21 R22 (t) tan nāma

d DG3 P71(t) T71 °jale (for °jalaiḥ), H21(t) H31(t) °tale, D64 °nalaiḥ, G11 ms. destroyed here; C51(t) C52(t) M1 M24 N21 °jalai (incorrect for?)

28 a R22(e) T21 V1 varam imam; C51(e) C52(te) āśrayadhvaṃ (for ādriyadhvaṃ), C51(t) āśriyadhvaṃ (incorrect for?)
b C51(t) D11 K1 U1 YY1 cāru° (for cāra°) D11 U1 °bhinnāḥ (for khinnāḥ)
c Y21 kamaleṣu
d no variant readins

29 a no variant readings
b C22(te) D12 D45 D64 H21(t)Y2 Y14 Y31 °dhūtaḥ (for °dhautaḥ), Y21 °pūtaḥ
c D12 Y14 śritadhanaṃjaya°
d N1 mā (for me); D1 D41 D43 yamadhūtaḥ

30 no variant readings
b H21(t) bhṛśaṃ muhur muhuḥ (for muhur muhur muhuḥ), D11 sadā muhur muhuḥ, Y14 Y21 muhur muhur mahaḥ
c no variant readings
D12 pāyikā 'pi (for yā 'pi kā 'pi) Y2 prāpikā 'pi; M6 kamanīyatā (for ramaṇīyata), N21 maraṇīyatā, D1 Y14 ramaṇīyatāṃ; D1 G11 vibho

31 a D71 °kapola° (for °kadamba°), Y51 °hṛdaye (metrically incorrect)
b Y51 Y52 keśara° (variant form of kesara°)
c no variant readings
d G11 iva (for ava°)

32 a M6 sāmi° (for sāci°), Y2 sāca° (incorrect for?), Y14 sāva°, DG6 sauci°; C22 (te D12 E41 N21 Y21 °saṃvalita° (for °saṃcalita°), D12 °saṃbālita° (incorrect for?), G1 H21(te) Y1 Y2 °saṃcarita°, D41 °cañcalita°; C52(t) G11 P72(t) T71 Y31 °āntaraṃ (for °otpalaṃ), D64 °otpale, DG1 DG2 DG3 DG6 D21 D41 D43 G1 M6 N1 N21 S21 UV Y1 Y2 Y14 Y21 Y32 °āñcalaṃ
b N21 °kuḍmalitapallava°
c Y1 Y2 Y14 Y21 Y31 Y32 vaṃśa° (for vega°); M6 vegavellita°; DG1 D41 D43 °āṅgulīyakam (for °āṅgulīmukhaṃ), N21 °āṅgulīnakhaṃ, DG3 °āṅgulīmakhaṃ
d Y1 Y2 veṇuvāda°; D64 °sarikaṃ; N1 Y1 Y2 Y14 Y21 Y31 Y32 bhaje mahaḥ (for bhajāmahe), G2 bhaje mahe, N21 bhajemaḥ (incorrect for?)

33 a C22(t) Y21 Y31 °ketumaṇḍane (for °maṇḍitadhvaje), Y32 °ketumaṇḍale, D1 °ketumaṇḍitadhvaje (metrically incorrect)
b Y31 Y32 °endra° (for °eśa°); Y21 Y31 Y32 °duhitā (for °tanayā°); D11 Y21 °ādhirohitā
c DG D41 D43 G1 G2 G11 Y31 Y32 °komala° (for °pallava°), Y21 °kandala°, C22 °kāntinā
d D12 līyate (for nīyate), Y31 dhīyate

34 a Z9 āyāta (for mā yāta), Y21 mayā 'pi; C51(t) C52(t) D1 G11 H21(t) H31(t) Y14 panthāḥ (for pānthāḥ), Y31 pathyāḥ, Y2 panthin (incorrect for?); Y14 pathibhīramatyā (incorrect for pathi bhīmarathyā), Y2 pathibhiḥ pramathya (incorrect for?)

b Y14 Y21 Y31 Y32 pitāmbaraḥ (for digambaraḥ), Y2 pitāmbaraṃ; D1 kvā 'pi
c Y2 visrastahasto; N1 °hasto vanitānitambe
d C21(t) D1 dhūrtasya mā karṣati; DG1 DG3 DG5 D41 E41 G1 G11 H21(t) M1 M21 N1 T21 T71 Y2 Y14 Y32 Z9 cittavṛttim (for cittavittam), Y31 hanta cittam, D12 D21 S21(t) cittavṛttam, D14 cinnavṛtim (metrically incorrect), D1 citradhṛttīḥ (incorrect for?)

35 a C21(c) C22(c) C51(c) C52 D21 E41 H21 H31(c) P71(c) P72 U1 Y51 Y52 antarā (for antare), YY1 antako; Y11 bālakaṃ (for mādhavo), YY51 mādhavaṃ
b YY1 bālakaṃ cā 'ntare (for mādhavaṃ mādhavaṃ); U1 Y14 Y32 YY1 'ṅganāḥ
c D11 madare (for maṇḍale), Y2 maṇḍalī°
d no variant readings

36 (Y2 omits line a and b)
a YY51 kelikelā° (for kekikekā°), R22(t) kekakekā°; M21 °āmṛtā° (for °ādṛtā°), D1 °ādhṛtā°, D12 °āhṛtā, N1 N21 Y14 Y21 Y31 Y32 YY51 °ākṛtā°; N21 °ārāva° (for °āneka°), Y14 Y21 Y31 Y32 °ātaṃka°; YY51 °saṃkāhalā- (for °paṅkeruhā-) N21 °śaṅkṅkākulā-, N1 °ṣaṅkārhayā
b Y21 entire line: līlayaā yena haṃsāvalihlāditā; M1 °haṃso (for °haṃsā); Y31 °hrādanirhrādite (for °hṛdyatāhṛdyatā), Y14 °hrādanihrāditā, Y32 °hrādanihrādite, M24 °hṛdyayā vidyayā, N21 °hṛdy anāhṛdyatā, N1 reads with N21 with first two syllables destroyed, P72(p) °hṛdyatām āhṛtaḥ, DG6 °hṛdy anādodyatā
c S21(t) °vāha° (for °dāha°), D71 M21 °dāva°, D71 M21 S21(t) U1 °dāhā° (for °dāvā°)
d no variant readings

37 a D12 M21 Y2 Y21 Y31 Y32 kā 'pi; Y2 Y14 Y21 Y31 Y32 āmasvanaṃ (for ārāviṇā), N1 N21 āmāravā°, YY51 ātriṇā, D12 ārāviṇāṃ, H21(t) ārāviṇī; H21(t) M1 M6 M21 N1 N21 S21(p) YY51 rañjitaḥ (for kampitaḥ), Y14 Y21 gāyati, Y2 Y31 Y32 gāyatī
b D64 M21 Y2 Y21 Y31 Y32 kā 'pi; N21 veṇīdṛśā (for vīṇābhir ā°), N1 vīṇādṛśā; Y31 Y32 vīṇāraṇatkaṅkaṇaṃ (vīṇābhir ākiṅkiṇī), Y2 Y14 vīṇāravāt kaṅkaṇaṃ, Y21 viṇāraṅkaṇaṅkanaṃ (incorrect for?), YY51 vīṇābharākiṅkiṇī; C21(p) C22(p) C51(tp) C52(tp) D1 D12 H21(p) H31(p) M6 N1 N21 P71(p) P72(p) R22(p) S21(p) U1 °nṛtyataḥ (for °nartitaḥ), Y2 Y21 Y31 Y32 °nṛtyatī, Y14 °nṛtyati, T21 °nartitam
c[1] Y2 Y14 Y21 Y31 Y32 have the following line: kā 'pi bhṛṅgāravārāviṇī rañjitā with the following variant readings: Y14 kvā 'pi; Y31 śṛṅgārahārāvalī (for bhṛṅgāravārāviṇī), Y32 śṛṅgāravīrāvaṇī, Y14 bhṛṅgāravārāgiṇī
c[2] all mss. except those listed uder c[1] read as in text with the following variants: D64 M21 kā 'pi; YY51 vīṇābharā°; M24 āmāntarā (for āmāntaraṃ), D12 āmāntare; C21(p) C22(p) C51(p) C52(p) D1 D21 G11 H21(p) H31(tp) K1 M1 M6 M24 N21 P71(p) P72(p) R22(p) S21(tp) U1 gāyataḥ (for gāpitaḥ), C22(e) D45 T21 gāyitaḥ, D64 gāthitaḥ, C51(te) C52(t) gopitaḥ
d no variant readings

38 a N21 °candrānanā; E41 (E41p reads with text) M6 M24 N1 N21 S21 Y2 Y14 Y21 Y31 Y32 °locanācumb° (for °locanaiḥ cumb°), YY51 locanaḥ cumb°; D1 śumbhitā (for cumbito), N1 U1 cumbitā

b N1 N21 °gogopikā° (for °gopālikā°)

c Y32 omits line c; G11 H31(t) M1 M24 Y2 Y14 Y21 Y31 °vṛnārikā° (for °vṛndārakaḥ), E41 (E41p reads with text) °vṛndārakā°; D71 peśalaḥ (for kāmukaḥ)

d no variant readings

39 a[1] M6 M24 N1 N21 Y2 Y14 Y21 Y31 Y32 YY51 have the following line: maulimandāramālāmiladbhṛṅgikā- with the following variant readings. YY51 °lānalad° (metrically incorrect for °mālāmilad°; M24 °valat° (for °milad°); M6 °bhṛṅganīlālakā- (metrically incorrect for °bhṛṅgikā-)

a[2] all mss. except those listed under a[1] read as in text with the following variant readings: P71 T71 °lasanmatta°; M1 °milanmukta°; D11 °bhṛṅgāvalā- (incorrect for?)

b N1 N21 gītabhīta°

c D45 E41 Y2 Y14 Y31 Y32 trasta° (for srasta°), N1 supta°; N21 °gopaṃ (for °gopī); Y14 °bhujābhoga°; M6 °kucābhāra°; C22 D12 Y2 Y14 Y21 Y31 Y32 °saṃmīlitaḥ (for °saṃmelitaḥ), T21 V1 °saṃmelitaṃ

d no variant readings

40 a Y14 Y21 Y31 Y32 °ābhāsi°; Y2 Y31 Y32 °vāsā vibhur (for °bhāmāvibhur), Y21 °bhāsāvibhur, D12 T21 YY51 °māno vibhur, M6 °mānaprabhā, D14 D45 E41 °mānāmbaro, D11 °pītāmbaro, H31(t) °bhāmābhuvi, D1 °mānāviḥbhor (incorrect for?)

b G11 H31(t) M1 M6 M21 M24 N1 N21 T21 U1 YY51 °milad° (for °latā°), Y2 Y14 Y31 Y32 °bharā°, Y21 °rucā°, C22(t) °lasad°; C21 D11 D21 H21(c) H31(c) K1 P71(p) P72(p) R22 S21(c) U1 V1 Y21 Y31 Y32 °vāsito (for °bhāsito), D14 °bhūṣito, D64 °vāsino, H31(t) °bhāsino, M1 °bhāsite, C22(c is omitted for this part of the text); Y21 Y23 °orusthalaḥ

c M24 °vṛndāvanāvasito; R22(t) YY51 vāsito (vāsitā°), D21 D64 vāsināṃ, D1 M21 vāsinā, P72(t) vāsitaṃ, N1 N21 vāsite, Y32 kāmukī (corrected to trāsitā°)

41 a D1 bhāvikā° (for bālikā°); Y14 °nālika° (for °tālika°); M24 °pālitāla° (metrically incorrect for °tālikātāla°); Y31 Y32 °tālasaṃlīlayā (for °tālalīlālayā-), D12 °tālasaṃlīlālayā- (metrically incorrect)

b D21 nanda° (for saṃga°), D12 Y31 Y32 manda°; YY51 °saṃdṛśyato (for °saṃdarśita°), C51(t) D64 Y21 °saṃdarśitā°)

c D12 °dattagītā°; Y14 sadā (for svayaṃ)

d no variant readings

42 (E41 gives no commentary for this verse)

a D12 rādhāṅgaṇe (for rādhāvaro), M24 R22(t) rādhāpayo, D1 rādhāvaraṃ yo (metrically incorrect), YY51 rādhāvarayo (metrically incorrect), all mss. except preceding and D11 D12 D45 T21 V1 Y2 Y14 Y21 Y31 rādhāvayo

b C21 C22 C51 C52 D1 D21 D64 D71 G11 H21 H31 K1 M1 M6 M21 N1 P71

P72 R22 S21 T71 U1 rūpayā māsabhā (for ropayām āsa bhā°), M24 ropayām āsa mā°, D11 ropayām āsataṃ, Y31 rodhayāṃ āsa; C21 C22 C51 C52 D1 D14 D64 D71 H21 K1 P71 P72 R22 S21 T71 U1 UV YY51 sā guṇair aṅgaṇe (for °māgṛhasyā 'ṅgaṇe), G11 H31(te) M1 M21 N21 sā guṇair aṅkaṇe; M24 °bhā guṇair aṅkaṇe, D21 S21 sā kayā cā 'ṅgaṇe, D11 satyabhāmāṅgaṇe, D12 Y14 Y21 Y31 °mā bhayād aṅgaṇe, Y2 °gā bhayād aṅgaṇe, M6 sā mayād aṅkaṇe N1 reads with M6 with syllables for °ā ma° destroyed, D45 T21 V1 UV read with text

c Y2 omits entire line; U1 sītanīle (for śītaśīte), D71 śītaśītaṃ, D64 śītasīte M6; śītasīte; M6 Y14 Y21 YY51 taṭe (for vaṭe), D14 vade; C22(t) D14 N1 C22(t) D14 N1 yāmuneye (for yāmunīye), YY51 yāmune ya; Y14 sadā (for taṭe)

d no variant readings

43 a YY1 agre tiṣṭhati so'yam; M6 taros; M6 tatpārśvato (for tasyā 'grato), YY1 tadvāmano; C22 D45 D64 G1 G2 M21 N1 N21 Y32 vartinī (for vartanī), C51(e) C52(e) D12 M1 P72 R22 S21(t) U1 vartmani, C21 E41 YY1 vartmanī

b D11 sā poṣaṃ; Y51 śāradanabhonīlā (for tatparisare deśe), C51(e) R22 YY1 tatparisaroddeśe, Y31 Y32 tatparisare puṇyā

c M6 YY1 °tamālakomala°; M6 YY1 °vane (for °tale), N21 °taṭe; M6 Y31 Y32 vṛndaṃ gavāṃ; M6 YY1 pālayan (for cārayan), C21(t) N1 Z9 cālayan

d Y31 Y51 gopas tiṣṭhati (for gopaḥ krīḍati), Y32 gopyaḥ tiṣṭhati; N1 Y31 Y32 Y51 YY1 Z9 sate (for sakhe)

44 a M6 °gopakumāraveśaṃ; K1 °komalaveśagopaṃ

b D1 anuramyamānam

c D12 sāyantaṃ C22(t) D1 D11 D64 M6 R22(p) U1 pratidinaṃ (for pratigṛhaṃ), D43 pratidinaṃ corrected to pratigṛhaṃ

d D64 praṇate

45 a D14 Y12 Y14 nidhir lāvaṇyānāṃ (for nidhiṃ lāvaṇyānāṃ), D41 D43 sakalavaṇyānāṃ (metrically and otherwise incorrect); Y14 °niścayaṃ (for °nicayaṃ), all mss. except preceding and DG1 DG2 DG5 DG6 D1 G1 G2 Y2 (vs. 186) Y2 (vs. 228) Y12 Y21 Y31 Y32 °nilayaṃ

b Y32 niravadhikave stotravacasām; Y14 °niḥśreyasaparam

c Y2 (vs. 186) °sāraḥ; T21 sukṛti°; Y2 (vs. 186) Y12 Y14 Y21 Y31 Y32 vrajadṛśāṃ

d P72(t) Y14 Y21 adhidevaṃ; D14 T71 mṛgadṛśām (for kṛtadhiyām): D1 adhidaivāṅkuraśriyaḥ

46 a M6 ātāmrapāli°; Y32 °prathita° (for °praṇayi°), D12 °praṇata°, all mss. except preceding and C22 DG1 DG2 DG3 DG5 D45 E41 G1 G2 G11 M1 Y51 Y52 YY1 °praṇaya°; N21 °pramodam

b G1 °nūpura° (for °kuṇḍala°), D1 °maṇḍala°, D71 °kuḍmala°; YY1 °kuṇḍalakarṇapāśam

c YY1 ambhojapatradṛśam ambuda°; Y51 Y52 āvibhradambukaṇam; Y14 ambujanīlam āḍhyam

d Y14 avyād (for ādyaṃ), Y31 āḍhyam; Y14 Y32 Y52 YY1 maho vaḥ

47 a M6 navaniyamita°
b M1 abhiṣiñjann
c M21 °gotras (for °gātras), D1 D12 °gātraṃ; UV V1 totraniṣṭyūtamaulier
d D1 vidhṛtadaśanaraśmir

48 (D45 has the line order a b d c)
a Z9 varayuvati°; T21 °ollāsakāye
b G11 sakalaguṇa° (for śubhasakala°), all mss. except preceding and DG G1 G2 M6 N1 T71 Z9 sakalaśubha°
c Z9 sammadāya pravṛttaṃ (for tatpadāya pravṛttaṃ), H31 (t) M21 P72 (t) tvatpadāyattavṛttaṃ, D1 D71 tatpadāyattavittaṃ, DG2 tatpadāya pradattaṃ, all mss. except preceding and DG1 DG3 DG5 D12 N1 N21 M6 tatpadāyattavṛttaṃ
d all mss. except C51 C52 DG1 DG2 DG3 DG5 D21 D64 D71 G1 G11 M21 N1 N21 P71 P72 R22 T71 gopālasūnau

49 a D1 D11 D41 D43 R22 (t) Y2 Y14 Y21 Y31 araṇyānām; Y2 Y14 Y21 Y31 Y32 °smitasarasa°; Y2 Y14 °sudhām
b Y2 Y14 araṇyāt (for saraṇyā); M24 sākrāntaiḥ (for saṃkrāntaiḥ), U1 saṃkrānte, Y21 saṃkrāntiḥ; E41 has a variant reading for first half of line b, but unable to determine what it is; D11 ninadan (for madayan), D12 sadayan, N21 padayan (the two preceding incorrect for?); Y14 daṇḍe (for veṇu°)
c Y2 śaraṇyā sānandaṃ sadayam upagūḍhā°; Y31 °otpalakam (for °otpulakam), Y14 °otphalam, C21 (t) °otpalakim; M1 °kamala- (for °kamalaḥ), U1 °kamalaṃ, Y21 °kamalaiḥ
d U1 ādyaṃ sa; P71 (t) U1 UV V1 jayatu; R22 (t) U1 śarīrī), M1 śarīraṃ

50 a P72 (t) °veṇu° (for °dhīra°)
b N1 N21 vivaśahṛdayaṃ (for karaṇavivaśaṃ), DG6 D1 D12 D41 D43 E41 G2 N22 U1 karuṇavivaśaṃ; DG6 D12 D45 E41 (p) G2 N22 T21 U1 gokula° (for gokulaṃ), G11 ms. destroyed here
c D14 M24 P72 (t) śyāmaṃ śyāmaṃ (for śyāmaṃ kāmaṃ), C21 C51 C52 kāmaṃ śyāmaṃ, N1 N21 kāmaṃ kāmaṃ; C22 (t) D1 K1 N21 yuvati° (metrically incorrect for yuva°); D41 D43 D45 mohanāṅgaṃ (for mohanatvaṃ), M6 mohananta (incorrect for?)
d no variant readings

51 a G2 sadagdhagopāla°; D1 D64 Y51 Y52 °vilāsanīnāṃ (for °vilāsinīnāṃ), Y21 °vilāsitānāṃ
b Y52 saṃbhogaviddhā°; P72 (t) °āñcitasarva°; D1 °gotraṃ
c M1 āmnāyaśirām
d K1 brahmāḥ (incorrect for?); D11 D12 Y2 Y14 Y21 Y31 Y32 Y51 Y52 °cauram (for °coram), K1 °coraḥ

52 a D21 sānandena (for ānandena), G2 sānandaṃ tu; D12 samathanaṃ
b D64 sukusumaiḥ (for sakusumaiḥ), DG1 DG2 DG3 D14 G1 G2 M6 N1 N21 Z2 sakusumaṃ; G11 svīye (for siddhaiḥ), M6 snigdhaiḥ, M24 siddyaiḥ, M1

svīyaiḥ, DG2 omits these two syllables; G2 siddhaiḥ parivyākulaiḥ; C21 (t) DG1 DG2 DG3 DG5 D64 U1 UV V1 Z2 pṛthi vyākulam, (C21 omits c for this part of the text)

c M24 śleṣaṃ (for serṣyaṃ), G2 sedhā°, D41 savyaṃ, D43 D71 M6 N1 N21 U1 sevyaṃ; Z2 pauraiḥ suraiḥ; D14 saṃsmitaṃ

d G11 yo (for no), Z2 vo; D45 suraripuḥ (for muraripuḥ, P72(t) muradviṣaḥ; DG1 DG2 DG3 Z2 (p in A and C mss.) prakṣipta°

53 a P72(t) antargṛhaṃ D11 cauraṃ

b C22 D12 D14 D41 D43 D45 D64 E41 kapāṭaṃ (variant form of kavāṭaṃ), DG1 DG2 DG5 R22(t) jananīgatai 'kā (for jananīṃ gatai 'kā), D12 jananīyaśodā

c M24 ulūkhalaṃ; D12 °nibandham

d DG1 DG2 DG3 sthimitā (incorrect for?), M21 smimita (also incorrect)

54 a Y21 jānucaro murāriḥ; Y52 Y61 Y62 Y63 Y64 kadā cit (for kumāraḥ)

b G11 saṃkrāntabhātmīya°

c Y63 Y64 anāptikhedād

d DG1 DG2 DG3 DG5 G1 G2 M21 Y21 ālokya; Y62 Y63 Y64 dhātrīmukham ā° (for dhātrīvadanaṃ), Y31 mātur mukham ā°, Y32 Y61 mātur vadanaṃ; G2 N1 N21 dhātrīvadanāny arodīt; Y31 āruroha; Y21 ruroha

55 a D14 E41 G11 upāsyatām; N1 Y12 Y14 Y21 Y31 Y32 Y51 Y52 brahmavidaḥ (for ātmavidaḥ), U1 ātmanibaddhaḥ (metrically incorrect); D14 M24 T21 Y32 purāṇaṃ (for purāṇāḥ), DG1 DG2 purāṇaḥ, M6 purogāḥ

b[1] Y12 Y14 Y21 Y31 Y32 Y51 Y52 have the following line; sanātanaṃ brahmaniruddhacittāḥ with the following variant reading: Y51 Y52 nibaddhacittāḥ

b all other mss. read with the text with the following variants; DG6 paramaṃ pradhānaṃ nihitaṃ; DG1 DG2 DG3 DG5 M1 U1 purastāt (for parastāt), D45 V1 pumāṃsaṃ, S21 (S21p reads with text) parasyāṃ, M6 parasyā? (ms. destroyed here)

c DG6 D41 D43 G2 Y12 Y14 Y21 Y31 Y32 Y51 Y52 YY1 yaśodāsuta°; D12 M21 °śiśupāla° (for °śiśubāla°), M6 °śiśughoṣa°; Y12 Y14 Y21 Y31 Y32 YY1 °bālakeli-

d Y12 pramajjayāmaḥ (for °ṣu majjayāmaḥ), all mss. except preceding and DG1 DG2 DG3 DG5 DG6 G1 G2 G11 M6 N1 N22 Y14 Y21 Y31 Y32 Y51 Y52 (°ṣu līlayāmaḥ), M6 °ṣu lālayāmaḥ

56 a C21 C51 C52 DG D11 D12 D41 D43 D71 E41 G1 G2 G11 K1 M1 M24 N21 U1 vikrītu° (variant form of vikretu°); C51 C52 D12 khila (for kila)

b Y14 Y21 mukundapādā; D14 °cittakṛttiḥ

c U1 mohadaśād

d no variants

57 (C22 M21 YY1 have the line order c d a b)

a no variant readings

b Y2 Y11 Y14 Y21 Y31 Y32 Y51 Y52 vrajāṅganānāṃ

c Y21 kamalasya (for kalabhasya); Y2 Y11 Y14 Y21 Y31 Y32 Y51 Y52 viṣṇor (for nūnam)

d D45 āsīt tritayaṃ hi loke; C22(t) D14 Q71 S21(t) Y2 Y11 Y14 Y21 Y31 Y32 Y51 Y52 eva loke

58 a no variant readings

b D1 padāravindena niveśayantam; Y21 mukhāravindena (for mukhāravinde ni°), K1 mukhāravindena vi° (metrically incorrect); D64 viniveśayante

c C21(t) varasya (for vaṭasya), Z2 aśvattha°; D11 parṇasya (for patrasya), Y21 mukhe (for puṭe); Y2 vrajeśvarasya śayane śayānaṃ

d Z2 satataṃ smarāmi

59 (T21 text destroyed after surapate)

a R22(t) śambhoḥ; Z5 Z11 padmodbhava (for padmāsana), D45 padmāsane, T21 U1 padmāsanaḥ

b D64 Z11 (p found only in PB PT Comm VSPB) kroñcāre; D1 D64 mukhaṃ; D1 purapate; C51(t) D64 citteśa; C51(t) D1 D12 D64 E41 H21(t) M6 S21 (S21p reads with text) U1 dṛśyate (for dṛśyase)

c D1 °midhā (incorrect variant for °ripoḥ), all mss. except preceding and D21 G1 G2 H31(t) M21 N1 N21 Z11 (PB reads with text) °jitaḥ; R22(t) yaśo vā (for yaśodā), D41 D43 Z11 (PB reads with text) jananyā °śiraḥ (for °giraḥ), M1 °śiśiraḥ (metrically incorrect)

d Z11 (p found only in SSP ASA) jalpasi (for bālaka); Z11 'ty anucitaṃ (for 'ti racitaṃ), Z5 'ty anucita; G11 'ti satataṃ D12 'ti caritaṃ, N1 'ti suciraṃ, N21 'ti cacitaṃ (incorrect for?); D21 D41 D43 D45 D64 E41 P72 U1 Z5 Z11 thūthū° (for dhūdhū°), Z11 (p found only in SSP ASA) thyūthyū°; D64 °kṛṭaḥ; Z5 Z11 vaḥ (for naḥ)

60 a DG6 pātuḥ (for pātuṃ)

b C21(p) C22(p) C51(p) C52(p) D64 H21(p) H31(p) P71(p) P72(p) R22(p) S21(p) 'stī 'ha; DG1 DG2 astu vā; R22(t) kālā° (for kā vā), N1 N21 kutrā; C21(t) C51(c) C52(c) D41 D45 D64 M6 Q71 R22(t) S21(c[tp read with text]) V1 'ndhakārodayaḥ (for 'ndhakārodaye), 'ndhakārāgame

c C51(t) DG1 DG2 DG3 DG5 D1 D14 D21 M24 N1 N21 U1 'bhyupagatā; C22(t) D1 G1 G2 M1 M6 M21 M24 N1 N21 S21(t) punar (for muhur), C21(c) C22(c) C51(c) C52(c) D12 D71 G11 H21 H31(c) P71(c) P72(c) R22 S21(c) payo

d D1 °karaṃ; D41 P72(t) S21(t) V1 °āmśuka° (for °āmbara°), U1 °āmbuja°; C21(t) D1 M6 T71 kṛṣṇasya; E41 vaḥ

61 a D11 °dakeṣu; D12 Y2 Y14 Y21 muśalī (variant form of musalī); N1 N21 Z2 krīḍituṃ

b P72(t) UV V1 kārparikaṃ (for karburikā°), D12 karburakaṃ, R22(t) karjurakā (incorrect for?), S21(t) karburakaṃ

c D11 bāladhiyā; Y2 pratārita° (for pratāraṇa°), Y14 pravartita°, Y21 pravardhita°, Y32 pravardhana°; Y2 Y14 Y21 °dhiyā (for °parāḥ), Y32 °hriyā, Y31 °paraṃ, G11 R22(t) U1 °parā; Y2 Y14 Y21 Y31 Y32 śṛṇvan yaśodāgiraḥ

d N1 pāṇibhyāṃ svaśikhāṃ; D12 naṣṭaśikhāṃ (for nas svaśikhāṃ), Y31 Y32 svasya śikhāṃ, Y2 Y14 vas svaśikhāṃ; Y21 °śikhāṃ kareṇa vimṛśan pīte 'rdhadugdhe hariḥ; N1 ms. somewhat destroyed for last half of line d; Y14 pīte 'rdhadugdhe hariḥ (for kṣīre 'rdhapīte hariḥ), D1 he nandasūnaścayam (incorrect for?), Y32 kṣīrārdhapīto hariḥ; M24 haraḥ (for hariḥ)

62 a C52(t) DG5 D11 D71 E41(p) G1 G11 H21(t) H31(t) M1 M6 M21 P71 R22 U1 kailāse (for kailāso), R22(p) entry reads kailāse but gloss reads with text; D12 D14 navanītanikṣitir (for navanītati kṣitir),D1 navanītavikṣitir, G11 navanītavakṣitir (incorrect for?); D11 G11 M1 M21 P71 R22 kṣititale (for kṣitir iyaṃ), M24 kṣitir ayaṃ, D1 kṣitiramyaṃ, R22 (p[gloss on entry not given]) kṣititalaṃ; G2 ājagdha° (for prāgjagdha°), DG1 DG2 DG3 DG5 tv ājagdha°, G1 S21 cā 'jagdha°, D43 N1 cā 'dagdha°, N21 tajjagdha°, D41 cā 'dakṣa° M1 prājñada°, M21 prāgjanma; D11 D45 S21(t) °mṛlloṣṭhati (variant form of °mṛlloṣṭati), G11 °mṛlloṣṭavat

b C52(t) D11 D21 E41(p) G11 H31(t) M1 M21 P71 R22 kṣīrode (for kṣīrodo), R22(p) entry reads kṣīrode, no gloss given; DG1 DG2 DG3 DG5 D12 D14 D71 G11 M6 M21 °dugdhavilasat° (for °dugdhati lasat°), D64 °dugdhavilasaṃ; S21 V1 smere (for smera°), D64 smeraṃ, K1 smeraḥ, N1 text destroyed here, E41(p) unable to determine D41 D43 °praphullānane

c U1 naṣṭo 'sti; N21 dṛṣṭāṃ (for dṛṣṭaḥ), D1 duṣṭa°, N1 ms. destroyed here; DG1 DG2 DG3 DG6 G1 tayā (for kayā), D1 °kriyā, D41 D43 kathaṃ, D64 kathya

d D12 G11 H21(t) M21 P72(t) bālaka; DG1 DG2 DG3 śatam (for ciram); N21 'varāṃ (for 'vatān), D41 'vatāṃ; C21 C22(c) D11 D12 D71 G11 H21 H31 K1 M21 M24 P71 P72 S21(p) T71 vo (for no)

63 a Y2 Z1 Z4 Z11 ardhonmīlita° (for kiṃcitkuñcita°), D21 ardhāṃ kuñcita°; D11 D21 Y2 Z1 Z2 Z4 Z11 paryāptam (for paryāyam), D12 paryāsam, C21 C22 C51 C52 D45 D64 E41 G1 G11 H21(c) H31(c) K1 M21 P71 P72(c) R22 S21 T71 V1 paryāya°, DG6 paryāpta; D1 D12 D14 D21 H21(t) H31(t) P72(t) eka° (for ekaṃ), C51(t) D64 R22(t) V1 °pīta°, C21 C22 C51(c) C52 D45 E41 G1 G11 H21(c) H31(c) K1 M21 P71 P72(c) R22(c) S21 °pītaṃ, Q71 °pīna°; DG6 ekau stanau

b D12 D21 D41 M24 YY1 Z11 (only in DF VSPB) prastuta° (for prasnuta°), Z2 Z11 (only in PA PB) prasruta°, D64 praśruta°, DG1 DG2 DG3 R22(t) prasṛta° (metrically incorrect), D1 prasmṛta°, N1 ms. destroyed here; Y2 Z1 Z4 Z11 (except ASC IO which omit these two syllables), °digdham (for °bindum); D14 D21 saṃmārjanaḥ (for saṃmārjataḥ), C21(t) C22(t) C51(te) C52(e) DG6 D41 D64 G11 K1 M6 R22(te) S21(te) saṃmārjitaḥ, U1 saṃmārjitam, YY1 saṃmārjataṃ, Y2 saṃmārjayan, Z11 (ASB only) saṃmārdataḥ

c Y2 Z1 Z4 Z11 (except PT) mātrā cā (for mātraikā°), Z11 (only PT) mātā cā YY1 lālitasva°; Z11 vadane (for cubuke), G11 cubuka°, C22(t) D11 D12 D14 D41 G1 H31 M1 M6 M21 M24 Y2 YY1 Z1 Z4 cibuke (variant form of cubuke); Y2 Z11 smerāyamāṇe (for smerānanasyā), Z4 smerāyamāne; Y2 Z11 muhur (for 'dhare), Z1 Z4 mukhe, Z2 YY1 'nanāc, D1 'dadhe, M21 'pāre

d Y2 Z1 Z4 Z11 viṣṇoḥ (for śaureḥ), C21(t) H31(t) K1 U1 śaure; Y2 Z11 °kaṇorudhāmadhavalā (for °kaṇānvitā nipatitā), D41 D43 Z1 Z4 °kaṇāmbudhāmadhavalā, Z2 °kaṇāvalī 'va patitā, N1 N21 °kaṇānvitā vilasitā; Z11 (PA only) nandadyutiḥ; Y2 Z1 Z2 Z4 Z11 (except PA which reads with the text) vaḥ

64 a DG1 DG2 DG3 D43 N21 R22 °prālambi°

b C21(t) antarnimitam; H31(t) °śakala° (for °nikala°), D64 °nikula°; C51(t) C52(t) G11 K1 P72(t) °ānukāra° (for °ānukāri°), G1 °ānukārī, M21 °ānukārā; C22(t) C51(t) C52(t) DG1 DG2 DG3 DG5 DG6 D1 D12 D14 D45 D64 E41(p) K1 M1 M6 M21 R22(t) S21(t) U1 °dyutiḥ, (for °dyuti), C22(t) E41(p) G1 dyutiḥ, G11 °dyutī

c N21 lajjādyājam; D12 U1 murāre;

d C51(t) D1 M1 U1 paśyanti; D71 G11 K1 lakṣmī°; U1 °otsavaḥ

65 a Y2 Y11 Y14 Y32 Y33 Z5 (S reads with critical text) 'dya (for 'mba); Y33 Z5 (for S reading see below) Z7 (c only) rantumanasā (for rantum adhunā), Z4 Z5 (p found only in S) rantum asakṛn, Z7 (k kh only) rantum asamā°

b all mss. except the following C51(t) C52(t) DG1 DG2 DG3 DG5 DG6 D1 D12 D21 D41 D43 D45 D71 G1 G2 M21 M24 N1 N21 P72 S21(t) Y2 Y11 Y14 Y21 Y31 Y32 Y33 YY1 Z2 Z4 Z5 Z7 Z22 Z26 tathyaṃ (for satyaṃ); Y2 Y11 kim etad āha (for ka evaṃ āha), Y21 kim eṣa prāha, Y14 mame 'tad āha (incorrect for?), G11 paśye 'ti mithyā 'nanam; N1 mityā 'ha (corrected to 'mithyā 'mba)

c Y2 Y21 Y31 Z2 Z5 (p found only in S) Z22 Z26 vikāsite (for vidārite), Y14 Y32 vikāśite, Y11 vikiśite (incorrect for?), C51(t) vivārite; D1 D12 D71 H21(t) P71 P72 T71 Y2 Y11 Y14 Z4 Z5 (p found only in S) Z7 ca vadane (for 'tha vadane), Y31 Y32 Y33 tu vadane, V1 śiśumakhe, Y21 suvadane, all mss. except preceding and DG1 DG2 DG3 DG5 DG6 D21 D41 D43 G1 G2 M6 N1 N21 S21(tp) Z2 Z22 śiśumukhe; Z2 Z26 mātā (for dṛṣṭvā), Z4 Z26 samagraṃ (for samastaṃ), M1 samas taj°

d Z2 Z26 dṛṣṭvā (for mātā); Y2 Y11 Y14 tasya; Z2 vismayavaśaṃ; D41 D43 N1 S21(t) Y2 Y14 Y21 Y31 Y32 Y33 YY1 Z2 Z4 Z5 Z7 Z22 Z26 vaḥ (for naḥ)

66 a D71 svāmī (for svātī), K1 kārakāṇāṃ

b no variants

c D41 svā° (for sā); H31(t) asūta putraṃ

d P72(te) kṛtvāspadaṃ (for kṛtāspadaṃ), U1 kṛpāspadaṃ, D1 dṛtāsyadaṃ

67 a D21 °vilocanīyaṃ (for °vilokanīyaṃ) D71 Y2 °vilokanīya-

b D1 D14 kṛṣṇa; D12 mṛgastambha°; H21(t) °stambhakṛtaṃ; C51(t) D43 U1 mṛgākṣi

c S21 vilokya; D41 D43 sākṣād api; Y12 agrair

d D45 E41 dvedhā; C22 'karot tan (for vitene), N21 tu mene, D12 vibhe te, M24 vidhene (incorrect for?); D12 khaṇḍam (for ekam), E41 golam, Y31 Y32 piṇḍam, N21 coram, Y2 Y11 Y14 ekā

68 a Y14 prabhātam (for vibhātam), C21(t) vibhāgam, D1 vibhātim

b S21 Y14 Y31 Y32 Y51 Y52 kṛṣṇa (for jīva), Y21 putra; Y1 Y2 vatsa (for kṛṣṇa), S21 Y14 Y21 Y31 Y32 Y51 Y52 jīva; M21 śataṃ sukham (for śataṃ śataṃ),

N1 śataṃ hare, N21 śataṃ vibho, Y31 śatam śivam, C21 śatam (metrically incorrect)

c U1 ruciraṃ (for surciraṃ), N1 N21 madhuraṃ. Y21 Y51 vacanaṃ, Y51 bahuśo

d D41 D43 vīkṣyamāṇa° (for dṛśyamāna°) Y21 pīyamāna°, Y31 Y32 cumbyamāna°; D45 °vadanāmbumaṃ bhaje (for °vadanaṃ bhaje mahaḥ), N1 °vadanaṃ bhajāmahaḥ (incorrect for?), N21 °vadanaṃ bhajemaḥ (metrically and otherwise incorrect for?), D1 °vadanaṃ bhajāmaho (incorrect for?), all mss. except preceding and G1 G2 Y1 Y2 Y14 Y21 Y31 Y32 Y51 Y52 bhaje mahaḥ

69 a all mss. except C21 (t) C22(t) C51 (t) C52(t) DG1 DG2 DG3 DG6 D1 D11 D12 D14 D21 D41 D43 D64 D71 G1 G2 K1 M1 M6 N1 N21 P72(t) R22(t) T21 T71 U1 Y31 Y32 jighrañ chiśur

b D21 kaṇṭhe (for kaṇṭhaṃ), DG6 N1 karṇaṃ C21 (t) C22(t [c omitted for this part]) C51 (t) C52(t) DG6 D1 D11 D12 D14 D21 D41 D43 D64 D71 G1 G2 H21 (t) H31 (t) K1 M1 M6 M24 P72(t) R22(t) T21 T71 U1 Y31 Y32 jighrann aruṇita°; Y31 Y32 āliṅgātmā

c U1 doṣā (for doṣṇā), D1 doṣāṃ, D41 D43 karṣan; D11 D41 °paṭam (for °padam), °vadam; N1 api (for abhi°); D1 D12 ekam (for aṅkam); Y31 Y32 āropito 'sau

d no variant readings

70 a D1 ye te (for ete), Z11 (PB VS) te te; C52(t) D21 lakṣaṇa (for lakṣmaṇa), D1 lakṣmaṇe U1 °virahituṃ (for °virahitaṃ), Z5 Z11 Z23 °virahiṇaṃ; D12 khedayann

b D41 D43 marmāṇy eva (for marmāṇī 'va), N21 marmāṇī 'ṣa; M24 mama (for 'va ca); N21 ni° (for ca), DG6 D11 D71 G1 G11 M1 M6 M21 N1 T21 Z11 (AKG only) Z25 vi°; Z5 (IO ZDMG Sp read with text) Z23 (S3 only khaṇḍayanty (for ghaṭṭayanty), Z11 (PA only) me tudanty, Z11 (AKG only) °ṣīdanty; D71 N1 N21 ati° (for amī)

c Z23 (P only) vyākṛta° (for vyāhṛta°), D14 vyāhṛti°; D11 °sahito (for °carito), Z5 Z11 Z23 °viraho, all mss. exept preceding and C22(t) C52(t) DG6 D1 D12 D21 D41 D43 D45 E41 G1 G2 G11 H31 (t) M6 M21 M24 N1 N21 P71 T71 U1 °caritaṃ; D41 D43 vīkṣito rādhayā; K1 dīkṣitaḥ

d D41 D43 mohāc chaṅkitayā; DG6 D71 serṣya° (for serṣyaṃ), DG1 DG2 DG3 DG5 D11 D21 H21 (t) N1 N21 S21 (t) serṣyā°, M21 U1 serṣyaḥ ,K1 śerṣyāṃ, D1 śreṣyāṃ, Z11 (PT only) serṣaṃ, D11 D71 seṣyaṃ, D1 śreṣyāṃ (incorrect for?), Z5 (p found only in S) sarvaṃ; Z11 (PB TB) sadā° (for sa naḥ), N21 nasaḥ; D12 D41 D43 D71 H21 (t) N1 Z5 Z11 (except PB TB) Z25 vaḥ (for naḥ); H21 (t) U1 sukhayataḥ (for sukhayatu), D1 sukhayataṃ, K1 sukhyat (metrically incorrect); K1 svapnāyatāt vo hariḥ

71 a DG2 vṛṣṭam (for oṣṭhaṃ); D21 D41 pūjanā

b K1 kaṇṭhākleśam; N21 imaṃ (for amuṃ); C51 C52 H21 (t) jahāhi (for jahīhi), G1 G11 jahīti; DG1 DG2 DG3 DG5 'liṅgane sā 'rjunau

c U1 dhehi; DG1 DG2 cyutaṃ (metrically incorrect for churitaṃ), DG3 churi° (also metrically incorrect); DG6 N21 °kaśipuṃ; N21 nakhair vadhyanām (incorrect for?)

d G1 rādhā° (for lakṣmyā), C22(t) D64 lakṣmyo; C21(t) D12 'pahārād (for 'pahāsād), D1 'pahāsyād

72 a Y21 drutaṃ (for huṃ tad°); D14 °abalī; G2 Y2 tat° (for tāṃ), C22(t) H21(t) H31(t) N21 P71(t) S21 T21 T71 V1 Z1 tau, C21(t) C52(t) D1 D14 D21 G11 K1 Y21 tā

b D45 G2 V1 °taṭe (for °vane), Z8 °tale; Y14 Z1 Z4 Z11 (ASA PB SSP read with text) nivasatas (for viharatas), Y21 vicaratas, N21 viviratas; C22(t) C52(t) G2 P71(t) S21(t) T21 T71 V1 Y2 Z1 tām ā (for tasyā)

c^1 Y2 Z1 Z4 Z7 have the following variant line kṛṣṇene 'ti purātanīṃ nijakathām ākarṇya mātreritāṃ. The following variants to this: Y2 kṛṣṇaś ce 'ti (for kṛṣṇene 'ti) Z11 (PA reads with other c^1 texts) kṛṣṇasye 'ti

c^2 as in text with the following variants: DG1 DG2 DG3 Z8 (g gh only) nidrārdhe (for nidrārthe), Y14 Y21 nidrālor; U1 hare 'laṃ°; Z8 (g gh only) huṃkṛṇvataḥ; D12 saṃyutā (for śṛṇvataḥ)

d Z11 dhanur dhanur iti tvarāṃ (incorrect for?); Z4 proktā (for vyāgrā) D43, vyāgre; all mss. except C21 C22 DG3 DG5 D45 D64 E41 G2 H31(t) M24 P71 P72(c) T21 V1 Y2 Y21 Z1 Z4 Z7 Z8 Z11 pātu; D1 D45 V1 Y2 Z1 Z4 Z8 Z11 vaḥ (for naḥ)

73 a C51(t) DG1 DG2 DG3 N1 N21 T71 °oddharaṇogra° (for °oddharaṇāgra°) Y14 Y21 Y31 Y32 °oddharaṇe sam°, D41 °ddharaṇāya; Y14 Y21 Y31 Y32 °artho (for °pāṇir)

b M1 viro (for nīlo 'pi), D12 vilo 'pi, D1 nilāsi; M1 M24 °tama° (for °tamaḥ°); U1 °tamaṃ, Y21 °tapaḥ

c D41 D43 G2 Y14 Y31 Y32 vīro (for dhīro), Y14 karo, D1 darau, C51(t) dhirau (incorrect for?); G1 hi (for 'pi); N21 dhārā° (for rādhā); Y14 Y21 Y31 Y32 °ānta° (for °āva°), D1 °ād a°

d H31(t) Y14 Y21 Y31 Y32 sāro (for jāro); K1 °paraḥ (for °haraḥ), C51 C52 °hataḥ, D1 °haraṃ; D41 kumas (for kutas), D1 nutas

74 a M1 vapuṣo; Y2 Y11 Y14 Y21 Y31 Y32 Y33 Y61 Y62 Y63 Y64 tanu° (for nava°)

b M21 Y11 Y14 jvālā° (for jālā°), N1 mālā, C51(t) N21 jalā°, Y2 dhyāna°, Y32 dhvanā°, Y31 Y33 Y51 Y52 dhvāna°

c Y11 omits lines c and d; Y2 Y14 Y21 Y31 Y32 Y33 YY1 bhāsvattarakṣu (for śārduladivya°), D1 °para° (for °nakha°), Y21 bhita°; Y32 °bhūṣitakaṃ (for bhūṣanabhū°), Y21 °bhūṣitabhū°; Y32 °dharāya (for °ṣitāya)

d Y32 bhavabandhabhide namo 'stu; Y2 Y21 Y31 Y33 Y61 Y62 Y63 Y64 YY1 °bhuje (for °muṣe), Y14 °bhaje, Y32 °bhujo; Y2 Y14 Y31 Y33 Y51 Y52 YY1 namo 'stu

75 a C21(c) C22(c) C51(c) C52(c) H21(c) H31(c) P71 P72(c) R22(c) savye (for pāṇau), T71 sakhye; S21 °bhakṣam; E41(p) īhitarasaṃ; D1 āhitanavaṃ; D1 R22(t) rakṣiṇe

b C21(c) C22(c) C51(c) C52(c H21(c) H31(c) P71 P72(c) R22(c) pāṇau (for savye), T21 navye, D21 sakye; C52(t) P71 vahan (for dadhat), M24 madhan (incorrect for?)

c M1 kaṇḍe; N1 kalpiti (incorrect for?) D21 S21(p) U1 aty° (for apy); C51(t) amudām a° (for apy uddāma°), S21(t) uddhāma°; DG1 DG2 DG3 DG5 H31(te) M1 M21 M24 °kāntiṃ (for °dīptiṃ), C21(e) C51(e) C52(e) D1 D12 D71 H21(te) K1 P71(t) P72(e) T71 °dīptaṃ; C22 C51 C52(c) D12 D45 D64 H21(c) H31 K1 M1 M24 P71 P72 R22(t[c omitted]) T21 dadhat

d D1 divye (for devo); D21 diśatanuḥ; K1 sāṃhkyāṃ (for saukhyaṃ); N1 N21 °sutaḥ (for °śiśuḥ)

76 a D12 has °kiṇi° times 3, DG2 D1 R22(t) times 1 (the preceding readings are metrically incorrect); Y14 Y21 Y31 Y32 °raṇitair (for °rabhasair), Y2 °kiṇitair

b DG2 DG3 DG5 G1 G2 H31(te) M1 M6 M21 M24 N21 añkaṇa° (for aṅgaṇa°), DG6 ms. destroyed here; Y14 Y31 Y32 °parirambhaṇaiḥ (for °bhuvi riñkhaṇaiḥ), Y21 °parirañgaṇaiḥ, Y2 °pariraṃṣanaiḥ (incorrect for?); C52 D12 D14 D21 D45 P71 P72 T71 V1 riñgaṇaiḥ; D41 saṭā° (for sadā) D14 ratam (metrically incorrect for 'ṭantam), K1 pantam, Y21 santam

c Y14 Y21 indicate that the half verse break precedes sadā; C22 D12 D41 D43 D45 kuṇu° (for kuñ°), C21(e) D64 omit kuñ° (metrically incorrect); C21 C51 C52(c) D21 H21(c) N21 S21 T71 °kuṇu° times 3 (metrically incorrect); Y2 Y14 Y32 kuñkumanibha° (for kuñkuṇukuṇu°), Y21 kuñkumanīta°, Y31 kuñkumunibha°

d Y2 Y14 °pariśobhitaṃ (for °karabhūṣaṇaṃ), Y31 Y32 °śobhitakaraṃ, Y21 °karaṃ (metrically incorrect;

77 (Y54 line order c d a b)

a P72 sammarde (for sambādhe)

b Y52 ms. damaged here; Y51—entire line: māyāmayaṃ tam anuyāntam (metrically incorrect); Y14 Y32 āyāmayantaṃ; M24 P72(t) Y21 anuyāntam (for anuyāntīm), D1 H21(t) R22(te) anuyānti, C51(te) D41 Y14 Y32 anuyāntī, DG2 DG5 G11 K1 M1 anuyāntim

c Y21—entire line: antaraṃ nu tānucaraṃ (metrically incorrect); K1 avalambi (for avalambe), D1 avalambī

d Y21—entire line: cintaya cintāmaṇiṃ cetaḥ; Y32—entire line: bālaṃ tu vilagnajambālam; Y61 Y62 Y63 Y64 °vilambi°

78 a D12 añkita°; V1 °pīḍaṃ (for °cūḍaṃ), D41 P72((t) °cūḍaḥ

b C21 C22(t[c omitted]) C51(g) C52(tg) DG6 D1 D11 D14 D41 D43 D64 D71 H21 H31 K1 M6 M21 P71 P72 Q71 R22 (p reads with text) S21(p) T21 T71 sañcita° (for vañcita°), M24 sañjita°, G2 ms. damaged here, D12 cañcita°

c no variant readings

d R22(t) bālakṛṣṇa° (metrically incorrect for bālaṃ gopālaṃ)

79 a D45 prahrāda°

b line as in text is metrically incorrect; DG6 entire line: mantarādheyaṃ (incorrect for?); G1 nigamagirimahā° (for nigamamahā), C51(t) D11 D14 D21 D71 H21(t) P71 nigamāntamahā°, T21 nigama° (metrically incorrect); G2 nigamamahāri° (metrically incorrect), D1 nikhilanigama° (metrically incorrect); DG5 nigamamahāgiri°, N21 nigamahā° (incorrect for?), V1 nigamamahādrer; D12 G11 °āntarābhidheyam (metrically incorrect for °āntarādheyam)

b[1] D41 D43 variant line: vidhanigamaguhāntaraguṇadheyam (metically incorrect), D43 has the following variants: vivadhana° (for vidhani°); °guṇādheyam

c no variant readings

d M24 vinata° (for vibudha°); H21(t) R22(t) mahā (for mamā), D41 E41(p) mayā, U1 mano, M24 mām a° (metrically incorrect)

80 a D1 saṃsāraiḥ

b C21 C22 C51 C52 DG6 D12 D14 D21 D45 D64 D71 E41 H21 H31 K1 M1 M6 M21 M24 P71 P72 R22 (p reads with text) S21(c) T71 °yugala° (for °kamala°), D11 omits these three syllables; DG1 DG2 DG5 D21 °vari° (for °pari°); D12 D71 °caraṇam (for °vasanam), T21 sevanam, all mss. except preceding and C21 C22 C51 C52 DG1 DG2 DG3 DG5 DG6 D21 D64 H21 H31 M1 M6 M21 M24 P71 P72 R22(p reads with the excepted mss.) S21(p reads with the excepted mss.) T71 °bhajanam

c no variant readings

d N21 entire line: harer anusmaraṇam (metrically incorrect); D12 °kāre tanu° (for °kārer anu°), D1 °kāre manu°

81 a K1 R22 kalaśe; D11 D45 M6 °caure

b C51(t) DG1 DG2 DG5 D1 °hṛtkumuda°

c no variant readings

d no variant readings

82 a N1 N21 kas tvaṃ kṛṣṇam avaihi māṃ; D1 D12 balānuja; D1 D41 aha (for iha); D11 D12 D41 P71(t) re (for te)

b D11 D12 E41 G11 H21(t) M6 N1 N21 P72(t) Q71 U1 V1 yuktaṃ tan (for brūhy etan), C21(t) D14 brūhi tvaṃ, S21(t) astv etan, Y31 buddhaṃ tan, Y32 nyāyaṃ tan, M24 brūhye te,M1 brūhi etat etan (incorrect for?); DG1 DG2 DG5 Y31 Y32 °bhāṇḍavivare (for °pātravivare), DG3 DG6 G1 N1 N21 °bhajanapuṭe; D12 haste (for hastaṃ), N1 N21 M6 nyastaḥ; N21 arthyaṃ (for arthaṃ); C21(t) G11 K1 U1 nyase (for nyaseḥ), N1 N21 M6 karaḥ

cd[1] D41 D43 N1 N21 R22(p) T5 Y31 Y32 have the following variant lines:
kartuṃ tatra pipīlikāpanayanaṃ suptāḥ kim udbodhitā
bālāvatsagatiṃ vivektum api yaj jalpan hariḥ pātu naḥ

c[1] Variants to c[1]: D41 D43 mātaḥ kaṃ cana vatsakaṃ mṛgayitum suptāḥ; R22(p) yaś ca (for tatra); N1 R22(p) Y31 Y32 suptā

d[1] N1 N21 °gatīr; D41 diśantv (for vivekt°) D43 diśatv; D41 D43 °iti vadan dāmodaraḥ pātu vaḥ; Y31 ati yaṃ (for api yaj), Y32 iti ca saṃ° (metrically incorrect), N1 N21 T5 anṛtaṃ; Y31 Y32 vaḥ (for naḥ)

c no variants

d C21(t) etad (for evaṃ), D14 °vallavīm ati°; C21(t) C22(t) C52(t) DG1 DG2 DG3 DG5 DG6 D12 D14 D45 D64 D71 G1 K1 M1 S21(t) U1 kṛṣṇaḥ sa; M1 vaḥ

83 (Y2 line order a c b d)

a B1 (quoted in c to st. 1.2) D41 D43 °āṅgana° (for °ājira°), Y31 Y32 °āṅgaṇa°, D12 K1 °ājara°, D1 °ācira°, N1 °ā?iti°; D12 R22(t) virahase, S21 viharasi, NI 21 majjase

b N1 N21 U1 V1 gokula° (for godhana°) Y31 Y33 gośata°, G11 ms. damaged here; D1 K1 N1 °kṛte; D41 D43 E41 Y31 śruti° (for stuti°); G1 °padair (for °ṣatair), Y32 °śate); Y2 maunam samālambase; D41 D43 prabho (for vidām), all mss. except preceding and B1 (quoted in c to st. 1.2) DG1 DG2 DG3 DG5 D71 N1 N21 Y31 Y32 vidām

c B1 (quoted in c to st. 1.2) D12 °sundarīṣu (for °puṃścalīṣu), Y2 °nāgarīṣu; D1 M21 T21 kurute; D41 D43 tu (for na); N21 svāmyaṃ kṛtātmātmasu; DG1 DG2 DG5 nadāt ātmasu

d Y2 tavai 'va pādayugalaṃ; D21 °yujaṃ (for °yugaṃ), DG1 DG2 DG5 N1 N21 °yuge; C21(c) C22(c) C51(c) C52(c) E41 H21(c) H31(c) P71(c) P72(c) R22 (S21 omits c) V1 premṇā 'calaṃ (for premācalaṃ), T21 premāñcalaṃ; B1 (quoted in c to st. 1.2) Y31 Y32 (corrected to premai 'va labhyaṃ param) premaikalabhyaṃ param (for premācalaṃ mañjulam), Y2 premai 'va labhyaṃ sadā; D41 D43 maṅgalam (for mañjulam)

84 a Y1 Y2 Y21 Y31 Y32 tasmai nomo yaśodāyā

b Y32 putrāya yā 'stu; Y21 Y31 vedhase (for tejase), Y32 medhase

c Y31 Y32 yo hi (for yad dhi); DG2 D41 rājā° (for rādhā°), D1 rāja°

d H21(t) mukhāmbhojaṃ (for bhojaṃ bhojaṃ; D1 D64 U1 vyavardhatām (for vyavardhata), Y23 vivardhatām, E41 Y11 Y12 Y14 vivardhate, D41 D43 G11 H21(t) vyavardhate, M24 vyavardhataḥ, D21 vyavardhana

85 a R22(t) santi anye 'py avatārāḥ; D12 D41 D43 D45 santy anye

b no variants

c D1 kṛṣṇadhanyakrodhā

d D1 D12 D64 H21(c) H31(c) K1 Q71 S21 prabhavatu (for prabhavati), H21(t) prabhavat (metrically incorrect)

86 a D11 gokulamaṇḍale; D1 pratidinaṃ (for pratidiśaṃ), DG6 G11 pratidṛśaṃ, D64 diśi diśaṃ; G11 jṛmbhā° (for hambhā°), D11 vā 'mbhā°, D1 S21 V1 cā 'mbā°, M1 P72(t) bāmbhā°, R22 cā 'mbho°, all mss. except preceding and C22 DG3 DG5 D41 D43 cā 'mbhā°; DG3 DG6 D41 D43 D45 D64 H31(t) K1 M1 M21 R22(t) S21(t) V1 °ravoj° (for °ravair), C52(t) M6 S21(c) °rave, D11 G1 P71(t) T71 °raver, C21(t) C51(t) DG5 D21 M24 P72(t) U1 °ravai (incorrect for?); C21(t) DG1 DG2 DG5 D1 G1 H21(t) M24 U1 jṛmbhate (for jṛmbhite), H31(t) K1 °jṛmbhate, D41 D43 °jṛmbhataṃ

b D1 °śyāma° (for °śyāmaṃ), D11 °śyāmā°; DG1 DG2 DG3 DG5 kvaṇan° (for raṇan°) D1 kvaṇaṃ, G1 nadan°, D11 D41 K1 raṇaṃ, U1 kaṇan

c DG1 DG2 DG5 G1 bālye (for bhāle), all mss. except preceding and C22 D11 D45 E41 phāle (variant form of bhāle), D1 bhāvye, U1 sāle, DG3 phālo; C21(t) C51(t) C52(t) D1 D11 D14 D41 D43 °taṭe° (for raṭat°), C22 D12 D71 H21(t) K1 M21 P71 P72(t) R22 T71 U1 UV °raṇat°

d C21(t) C22(t) D21 K1 °kārtsnaṃ (for kārtsnyaṃ), D14 °kārtsne, D12 °kārṣṇe,

G1 °kṛṣṇaṃ, M1 °kāntaṃ; all mss. except C22 DG1 DG2 DG5 D12 D21 D71 E41(p) G1 H21(t) M6 bhaje

87 (N1 N21 combines st. 2.87.a with st. 2. 12. b c d in the order given here)
a D12 sarvato dāra; D1 °oddhāra° (for °odāra°), Y32 °oddāra°; D71 N1 °nīlaṃ (for °līlaṃ), M1 Y2 Y21 Y32 °śīlaṃ
b D11 D21 D41 D43 °vādyaikaśīlam (for °vādyai rasālam), DG1 DG2 DG3 DG5 °vādyaikalolam, M1 M24 °veṇuvāde rasālam, V1 °veṇunādai rasālam, D14 D45 G11 Y2 Y14 Y31 Y32 °veṇuvādye rasālam
c no variant readings
d Y14 Y21 Y32 (marginal p) galalulitamālaṃ (for kalitalalitamālaṃ), Y32 taruṇatulasimālaṃ, Y2 lalitakulasimālaṃ (incorrect for?)

88 a N21 °saṃgītalālaṃ
b D14 calita° (for lalita°), DG1 DG2 DG3 DG5 lulita°; D1 ṣaurya° (for caurya°), D21 caura°; D41 D43 M1 M24 °cāturyaśīlam
c D1 K1 śatamukha°; M24 śatamakhamaṇinīlaṃ; D14 śātakaumbha°; C22 D12 D14 D41 D43 D45 D64 E41 °cailaṃ (for °celaṃ)
d M24 suraripukulakālaṃ naumi

89 a C22(te) C51(e) C52(e) snigdha° (for mugdha°), S21(t) mukta°; C22 D14 D41 D43 D45 D64 E41 °cailaṃ (for °celaṃ), T21 V1 °cūḍaṃ, P71 °vālaṃ, D11 M21 T71 °bālaṃ
b D43 dayitadanuja°; D41 D43 °danujapālaṃ; D21 M1 M24 °saujanyaśīlam
c S21(t) °pālaṃ (for °helaṃ), D64 °polaṃ; D43 padmapadmā°
d D1 °jaladala°; D12 G11 °dharalīlaṃ; T21 gopālalīlam

90 a no variant readings
b no variant readings
c D41 °sumadāyaṃ
d E41 M6 P72(t) sahṛdaya° (for suhṛdaya°), D1 svahṛdaya°, D41 D43 sukhadasu° E41 °jaya° (for °jana°); T21 °līlam (for °rāyam), P72(t) °kāyam, D11 D12 D45 M1 °bālam, N21 °geyam, M24 °rāmam, C22(te) D14 K1 °dāyam

91 a no variant readings
b N21 pūrṇendunetraṃ
c D1 kāmanīyagotraṃ kāruṇyamātram (metrically incorrect); M6 tāruṇyapātraṃ
d H21(t) vande caritaṃ

92 a D1 D14 H21(t) K1 uraṃgaṃ (metrically incorrect)
b D1 D14 yamunāvartīrya (for yamunām avatīrya; D14 D41 omit vīrya° (both variant readings in b are metrically correct)
c DG1 DG2 DG3 °tiraskṛt- (for °tiraskṛti-), DG5 ms. damaged here, DG5 M24 °tirastuti- (incorrect for?), °tiraskṛtī (metrically incorrect), D14 D41 D43 D64 °tiraskṛta-, D1 °tirasmita-, K1 °tirasmṛta-
d Z2 (c only) śayana° (for śamana°), D12 śayanaḥ (metrically incorrect), G11 śamanaṃ (metrically incorrect), D41 mana° (metrically incorrect), DG6 śama-

manasama° (metrically and otherwise incorrect); D41 D43 °varataṃsa° (for °paraḥ sa), D71 P72(t) °parasukhaṃ (metrically incorrect), G11 paraḥ susukhaṃ (metrically incorrect), K1 °paraḥ su°, H31(t) °paro vaḥ saḥ, D14 °parasya; DG1 DG2 DG3 DG5 D12 H21(t) M1 °paraḥ sat°; D12 °kriyā (for kriyāt), P72(t) kriyā; P72(t) tṛṣṇaḥ

93 a C22 D41 D64 °lallāṭa° (variant spelling of°lālāṭa°)
b D1 D64 karṇe; D12 omits karṇe; N1 tālīdanam; D41 iti (for ati°); M6 atisubhagaṃ
c D21 hāraṃ (for hāro), M1 hāre, M6 hārā; G1 °mālāmadhurasa°; C22 D1 D11 D12 D14 G1 H31(t) M21 M24 N1 N21 S21(p) °bharitaḥ (for °bharite), DG1 DG2 DG3 DG5 D41 M1 M6 T71 °bharitā, D43 °bharitāṃ, DG6 °haritaḥ; G1 N1 kaustubhaṃ co 'pa° (for kaustubhasyo 'pa°), D14 D41 D43 N21 kaustubhaś co 'pa°
d H21(t) °bhṛtaḥ (for °yutaḥ), H21(c) °vṛtaḥ, M21 °jitaḥ

94 a D1 °vihāri°
b D21 M21 mugdhāṅganānāṃ muṣ°; M21 muṣitāmbarāṇām
c DG2 varadvayaṃ; DG6 D41 kā (for vā); D12 cakasaṃhatir; G11 °saṃcayaṃ (for °saṃhatir), K1 °saṃpātir, D1 saṃvṛtir,
d D21 nimīlanaṃ

95 a C21(p) C22(p) DG1 DG2 DG3 D1 D11 D21 D41 D43 G1 H21(p) H31(tp) M6 N1 N21 R22 T21 pracura° (for lasada°), M1 M24 pracara°; M1 M24 °prāñca° (for °lola°), C21(p) C22(p) H21(p) H31(tp) °prānta°; N21 °loka°; C21(p) C22(p) H21(p) H31(tp) °nīlaḥ (for °līlā°), M24 °līlāḥ
b D1 °premagaṅga°; DG1 DG2 DG5 °pravāhaḥ (for °pravāhe), D64 R22(te) °pravāho (incorrect for?)
c DG5 pheṇāyante (for mīnāyante), DG1 pheṇāyantī; N1 N21 hi (for 'pi); D41 D43 cā 'sām atibharavi°; C21(t[p given in margin to the C21 text reads with the critical text]) D1 D12 D41 D43 D71 G1 G11 N1 Q71 R22 UV °lasac° (for °calac°), M6 °rasac°, D64 °carac°, DG2 DG3 omits °calac°; C21 C51 DG1 DG2 DG3 DG5 D1 D11 D12 D21 D41 D45 D64 G11 H21(c) H31(tg) K1 P71 R22 T71 °līlā° (for °nīlā°), D45 G1 °lolā°, C22(c omitted to this part of the text); D12 °ālakānāṃ (for °ālakāntā), G11 °ālakāntāṃ C51(t) śṛṅgāyante; M24 yam aṅghri° (for yadaṅghri°), D64 G11 yadā 'ṅghri°; C51(t) C52(t) R22(t) °ruhaḥ (for °ruhe), K1 °ruho (incorrect for?)

96 a D64 °smitasuṣira°; N21 °prabhinnās
b N21 tv eṇākṣyas; D41 D43 gopaiṇākṣyaḥ samastās truṭita°; R22 svāntareṇa truṭita°; D1 svapinasvapita° incorrect for truṭita°)
c D1 G11 hastavyastā°
d D41 kāmaṃ (for kāmā°); R22(t) kāmādeśa°; G1 °veśāḥ; D12 D45 UV V1 prakarṣa° (for °prakalpya°), C21(t) D1 D43 D71 G11 R22 °pragalbha°, D12 D41 °pragalbhaṃ, N21 °prasanna°, G1 °praklptāḥ; G1 pariṇatapulakāḥ

97 a D41 jaṭharo (for jaṭharā°), D43 jaṭhavā° (incorrect for?); D41 D43 ya uditaḥ
b D41 G11 K1 M1 M21 M24 R22 °puṇyena (for °paṇyena), H21(t) °pāṇyena

c D41 D43 °āvalimukta°; DG3 D11 D21 D41 D43 G1 °ālaṃkṛtaḥ (for °ālaṃkṛtiḥ), G11 °ālaṃkṛtiṃ, DG4 K1 M1 M24 °ālaṃkṛti

d C21(c) C22 C52 D1 D12 D14 D64 D71 G11 H21 H31 K1 M24 P71 Q71 T71 vaḥ (for naḥ); C21(t) hari° (for hṛdi); C51(c) C52(c) D1 D12 E41 H21(c) S21(c) satataṃ (metrically incorrect); D45 D64 E41 M21 M24 V1 sumadhuraḥ (for samadhuraḥ); D11 D41 H21(t) M6 °madhuro gopīndranīlo

98 a D1 D21 D43 pīṭhe pīṭhe; Y52 °niyuktabālakagaṇe

b Y31 Y33(c) śikyā° (for yantrā°), Y52 sikyā (varient form of śikyā°?), D1 D41 D43 N21 Y32 yatrā; C21(te) C22 C51(te) C52(te) D12 D14 K1 P72(e) UV apa° (or ava°), C21 C22 C51 C52 D45 H21(c) K1 P72(c) Q71 UV V1 YY1 °kṛṣyā° (for °bhidyā°), H31(c) omits c on this part of the text, D14 °kṛṣṇā°, Y52 °taryā°, M24 °bhidyāś; D12 ayabhiṣv arthaṃ ca ghaṇṭā°; Y32 ghaṇṭī° (for ghaṇṭā°), Y52 bhaṇḍā; K1 °ravaḥ

c Y32 °pātta°; E41 °dhṛtāñjaliḥ; Z9 kṛtiśiraḥ°; D21 kṛtaśiriḥ; M1 °kampaḥ; C21 D1 D12 H31 M1 M21 payo yaḥ piban (for piban yaḥ payo), D45 E41 payo yo 'pibat

d D45 E41 so 'vyād; Z9 stheyād; C51 DG1 DG2 R22 °pūt° (for °phūt°), DG3 °bhūt°

99 a N1 dhanair; C21(te) C22(te) C51(te) C52(te D1 D11 D21 D43 D64 K1 M21 V1 dadhimahe (for dadimahe), D41 ya dimahe, D12 dihimahe (incorrect for?); T21 pāleṣu

b C52(te) D43 D64 H31(t) bhojamahe (incorrect for?); D41 D43 tapaś carimahe; D41 D43 duṣkaram (D11 lines c and d not found in copy of D11 ms.)

c C21(t) sa° (for su°); D12 bhave (for bhava°)

d N1 śreyaḥkarī; D1 D14 G11 N21 °puṣī; DG6 D41 śrīyuṣi (incorrect)

100 a D45 D64 M21 mayi (for mama)

b D45 D64 mayi (for mama)

c D12 bhakte (for rakte); D45 E41(p) dayite (for ca vare), D1 T21 ca nare, N21 ca dhave, N1 ms. damaged here; D45 E41(p) 'ṅganānāṃ (for vadhūnāṃ), M1 M24 vadhūnā

d D45 E41(p) vṛthā bhavet kuṅkuma°

101 a G2 ms. damaged at °virāmasamaye, all mss. except preceding and DG1 DG2 DG3 DG6 D21 D41 D43 D45 E41 G1 G11 H31 M1 M6 M21 M24 N1 N21 R22 °vasānasamaye; all mss. except DG1 DG2 DG3 DG6 D1 D11 D14 G1 G2 G11 H31(c) M1 M21 M24 R22 T21 T71 °prabhā

b K1 T71 omit °danta°

c D11 nija° (for dadhi); D41 D43 hasta kaṅkaṇa°; D1 °kaṇat° (for °jhaṇat°), N21 °khaṇat°, G1 °raṇat°; D1 °ānukārī (for °ānurūpaṃ), D21 °ānusāraṃ, D71 °ānurāvaṃ, all mss. except preceding and DG1 DG2 DG3 D41 D43 D45 E41 G1 G11 H31(t) M6 M21 N1 N21 °ānukāraṃ; G11 japād

d D45 E41 vyāloladvasanā°; G1 vyāvalganmaṇikundalo; D21 G2 H21(t) P72(t) °āñcalo; D14 vaḥ

102 a DG3 N1 N21 °hema° (for °vāma°), DG1 °vāsa°; D41 D43 °kuntala°; YY1

°yutaṃ (for °dharaṃ), C21 C51 C52 D14 D41 D43 H21(c) K1 M21 P72(c) °bharaṃ; DG2 mado° (metrically incorrect); D43 °ollasatbhrū°

b DG2 D1 C21(t) sācī° (for sāci°), DG3 D41 sācit°; Z1 Z11 (PB only) °prasārī°

c D64 prālolā°; D41 °pallavaṃ (for °pallavair), H21(t) °pallave; R22(t) mukulikām; K1 hārayantaṃ; YY1 mudāṃ

d D41 D43 Y2 Z1 Z11 °bhaṅga°; C21 C51 C52 D12 D14 H21(c) H31(c) M1 M21 M24 P71 P72 Q71 R22 YY1 jāne (for dhyāye), K1 jñāne, N1 ms. damaged: either dhyāye or dhyāyej, all mss. except preceding and D1 D11 D45 D71 H31(t) T71 Y2 dhyāyej; Y2 jaganmohanaḥ

103 a D43 malle; Z2 (C D only) mallendraiḥ śailakalpaḥ; Z2 akhila° (for itara°); C52(t) puṇya° (for puṣpa°); D11 °bāṇo (for °cāpo), Y21 °śākhā

b M6 gopālākhyaḥ kṛtātmā; G11 bhuvi

c N21 kiṃ sena (for kaṃsena), N1 damaged here; Z2 (C and D only) kaṃsena kruddhamṛtyuḥ bhaya°; D14 P72(t) R22 (vs. 2.103 [t]) R22 (vs. in c to vs. 2.104) °dṛśo; DG1 DG2 DG3 D14 D43 dheya° (for dhyeya°), D1 deya

d T21 kṛṣṇo (for dṛṣṭo), D1 viṣṇo; G1 raṅgo (for raṅgā), D1 naṅgā°; G1 °āvatārī (for āvatāre), D45 E41 R22 (vs. 2.103 [t]) R22 (vs. in c to vs. 2.104) °āvatāro; D12 haritvam; G2 Z2 °janānanda°; D11 G1 cā 'smān (for yuṣmān), C21(c) C51 C52 M6 R22 (vs. 2.103 [c]) so 'smān, R22(2.103 [t]) R22 (vs. in c to vs. 2.104) no 'smān

104 a D12 D41 D43 karatale (for 'ṅkatalama°), DG1 prakalitā°, DG2 ms. damaged here; D12 madhyastha° (for °dhyāsīna°), D41 D43 cādhyasya; D45 °rādhāmukhe

b D12 vicarayan

c P72(t) °sthita°; M1 °cakrikā°

d G1 °parivrato; M24 °vṛte; D1 G11 C52(t) jaganmohanam

105 a D1 D64 H21(te) ākṛṣṇe (for ākṛṣṭe), N21 ākarṣan; N21 °āñcalaṃ; M1 M24 śyāmām upālaṃ kṛtā; D45 hriyā (for trapā°); D12 °ātaḥ (for °ādhaḥ°); N21 °kṛtāṃ

b DG3 vṛṣṭiḥ; DG1 DG2 G1 G2 G11 saṃcalitā (for saṃvalitā), N1 N21 saṃcitayā, D11 saṃlulitā; G2 P72(t) kucā (for rucā); D1 D11 D14 śrīmatiḥ (for śrīmati), D64 G11 R22(t) śrīmatī

c DG1 DG2 G2 N1 N21 coraḥ (for bālaḥ); C21(p) C51(p) C52(p) DG1 DG2 G2 H21(p) H31(p) N1 P71(p) P72(p) R22 coravallabha (for cūtapallava); G1 corapallava, N21 āttapalla (metrically and otherwise incorrect); V1 prāpta° (for bhrānta°), D11 bhrāntyā, D45 bhrāntya°, all mss. except preceding and DG1 DG2 D1 D21 G1 G2 R22 prānta°; P72(t) °sthitā° (for °smitā°), D14 °sthitaṃ, M24 °smitaḥ; D1 H21(t) R22(t) °sva° (for °sya°), DG1 DG2 °sā°, M24 sa°, D11 °tya°; DG1 DG2 °smitā (for °śriyaṃ), D11 °śriyā, D1 °kriyā

d G11 rukmiṇī; G2 nakhamukhīṃ; D21 °mukhiṃ (for °mukhīṃ), G11 °mukhī; D1 °mukhaṃ kṛṣṇasya; M1 M24 N1 vaḥ

106 a D12 Z31(p) ūrvyāṃ (for urvyāṃ), D21 urvyā; D12 kā (for ko); C21(p) C51(p)

C52(p) H21(p) H31(p) P72(p) dṛḍhataro; N21 bhṛto (for dhṛto), K1 dṛto, D1 dṛti

b R22(t) yena; T21 bhuvi (for divi); H21(t) vidi; C21(t) D11 D12 R22(t) 'pi (for ca); D41 D43 vidito (for satataṃ); P72(t) govardhanaṃ; M6 nīyase (for gīyase), D1 D14 M24 gīyate, D12 D41 D43 D45 V1 'ddhārakaḥ, N1 something indiscernible corrected to gīyase

c D1 D14 tvaṃ; D11 °vahaṃ (for °dharaṃ), M21 P71 (t [c to this part of the text omitted]) T71 °dhuraṃ; C21(t) R22 agreṇa; D1 raṇyate

d D12 bhāṣitena; Z31(p) gaṇyair; D43 lakṣyate

107 a D11 G11 N21 Z11 (only in ASB Comm DC DD PT VSPA) bhavato; M6 N1 N21 T21 he (for bhoḥ), Z9 omits bhoḥ; M1 snāni

b D1 D21 bhūdevāḥ; N1 N21 Z9 he (for bho)

c DG3 V1 niṣīdya (for niṣadya), C21(te) DG1 DG2 DG6 G11 N1 P72(te) niṣidya, D12 R22(te) niṣidhya, D41 niṣīddha, D43 niṣiddha, D21 niṣadhya, Z9 (vs. 28 of Kṛṣṇastutikusuma) nipatya

d D12 smārasmāram ahaṃ smarāmi; D21 maghaṃ (for aghaṃ), C51(t) D14 adyaṃ; D11 sakalaṃ (for tad alaṃ), G1 N1 N21 satataṃ; D12 anye namaḥ

108 a D12 kṛpālajanidhe; M21 siddhakanyāpate

b C21(t) °pāṭhīna (for °pārīṇa), M1 M24 °vārīṇa (incorrect), D12 °pālīna (incorrect)

c M21 °vibho (for °guro), D41 °pate

d H21(t) śrīgopījananātha; Z11 (PB only) jānāmi na tvatparam

109 (N21 omits everything after °phalake)

a D1 D11 D12 D45 Y2 Y14 Y21 Y31 °paṭale (for °phalake), H21(t) omits this word

b D11 Y1 Y31 vara° (for nava°), Y33(t [unable to determine reading in the c]) Y51 gaja°, D1 janaja° (metrically incorrect); Y51 °mauktikaṃ sakalakaṃ kaṇṭhe ca muktāvaliḥ; D11 Y31 veṇuḥ (for veṇuṃ), C51(t) D1 D12 D14 veṇu°

c Y51 °candanaṃ karatale veṇuḥ kare kaṅkaṇaṃ; D11 D14 Y2 Y31 °candana° (for °candanaṃ); Y11 Y33 sakalayan (for ca kalayan), D1 kuvalayaṃ, C21 (noted in margin of t) kuvalayan, YY2 suvilale, D11 Y31 °sulalitaṃ, Y21 sulalitaṃ, Y2 °sya tilakaṃ, Z2 suvimalaṃ, Y2 Y14 Y32 malayajaṃ, D12 ca kalayat; YY2 kaṇṭhe ca hāran dadhat; D1 D64 M1 M24 P72(t) Z2 (B reads with text) muktāvalīṃ (for muktāvaliṃ, C51(t) D21 muktāvali, D11 D12 Y2 Y14 Y21 Y31 Y32 muktāvalī

d Z2 bibhratstrī°; C51(t) °veṣṭitā (for °veṣṭito), D1 °veṣṭitaṃ; YY2 °cūlā° (variant form of °cūḍā°)

110 a[1] The following variant line found in all mss. ecxept D1 D41 D43 D45 E41(p G2 G11 M6 N1 N21 U1 UV V1 kālindībahulapravāharabhasaṃ saṃstambhayaṃs tatkṣaṇāc Variants to this line: P72(t) kālindīrabhasa°; D71 °rabhasaḥ; E41(p) taṃ (for saṃ°); C51(t) C52(t) tatraṇac (for tatkṣaṇac), C21(t) D14 tatkṣaṇam, M24 tatkṣaṇaś

a[2] Variants to the line as found in the text D1 D41 D43 D45 E41 G11 M6 T21 lokān uddharayan; D41 D43 G11 śrutiṃ (for śrutīr), D1 D21 śruti°; G11 mukulayan; D41 D43 U1 karṣayan

b M24 celān (for chailān [or śailān]), N21 śailon°; G2 prītimathan (for vidravayan)

c D12 N1 N21 R22(c) U1 pulakayan (for mukulayan), R22(t) kuvalayan, M24 mukurayan, E41(p) vikalayan; N21 °svarāṃ; D41 D43 bṛṃhayann

d G11 °ārthamadīrayan; D1 °ārtham udaṃ cayan; C51(t) D1 °ninādaṃ (for °ninādaḥ), N21 °ninādan; H21(t) haraḥ (for śiśoḥ), R22(t) śiśuḥ

Śataka III

1 a Y1 Y2 Y14 Y21 Y31 Y32 Y51 Y52 astu; U1 °padmā° (for °lakṣmī°); Y14 °stana- (for °stanaṃ), Y32 °stane

b N21 °tamohir (for °tamobhir), Y21 °tamotir

c U1 astodasta° (for hastodasta°), Y21 hasto hasta°; Y31 hastād asta°; Y52 °bhara° (for °taru°), Y32 °taruḥ; R23 °prasāra° (metrically incorrect for °prastāra°); D1 D12 °vistāritaḥ (for °vistārita-), D64 °vistāritas, N1 N21 °vistāritaṃ, Y2 °nisvādita-, Y21 °nistāḍitā, Y31 Y32 °nistāḍitaḥ, Y2 Y3 Y51 Y52 °nistādita-

d D64 trasta° (for srasta°), Y1 Y2 śrasta°; DG1 DG2 DG3 DG5 °nūna° (for °sūna°), K1 Y1 Y2 Y21 °sūnu°, Y51 Y52 °mūla°; Y3 °saṃśrava° (for °sūnasaṃ°); G2 °stuta° (for °stara°), Y3 °nava°, Y51 Y52 °bhava°; Y1 Y2 Y3 Y14 Y21 Y31 Y51 Y52 °rasa° (for °lasat°), Y32 °rasaḥ; D11 Y32 °prastāri (for °prastāvi), Y3 Y51 Y52 °prastāra°, D64 Y1 Y2 Y14 Y21 Y31 Y32 (p in margin), D44 °prastāpa° (incorrect); Y1 Y3 Y21 Y51 Y52 °dhārā° (for rādhā°), M rodhā°, N1 rārā° (incorrect), N21 dhārā° corrected to rādhā°; C51 (t) Y32 °stanam (for °stutam), Y2 °stutām, G2 °dbhūtam, Y51 Y52 °plutam

2 a D11 D45 R23 V1 lāvaṇyaratnākāraṃ; Y31 °ratnāṅkuraṃ

b DG1 DG2 °vada° (for °pada°), C51(t) Y32 °padaṃ; Y32 °sahajaṃ; N21 °smairā°;

c Y51 kila (for hari°), Y52 mahi°; Y31 Y33 Y51 Y52 °ratna° (for °garva°), D12 D64 Y1 Y2 Y3 Y21 Y32 °varga°; K1 N1 T21 °garutā° (for °gurutā°), C51(t) G11 T71 U1 °gurutāṃ, G1 °garuta° (metrically incorrect), C51(c[tp read with text]) C52 (p reads with text) D1 D11 D64 H21(t) H31(t) P71(p reads with text) °garutāṃ; Y32 °sarvasya; G1 Y1 Y2 Y3 Y14 Y21 Y31 Y51 Y52 °nirvāsanaṃ (for °nirvāpaṇaṃ), Y32 nirvāsanam

d DG1 DG2 Y14 bālā°; T21 vaiṇavikāmpi (for vaiṇavikeṣu), D11 veṇuninādа°, Y21 °veṇuvikeṣu), DG1 DG2 °vaiṇuvikeṣu, Y14 veṇuvikeṣu, Y2 veṇavikeṣu, all mss. except preceding and G1 G2 M24 N1 N21 Y3 Y31 Y32 Y51 Y52 vaiṇavikaṃ vi°; H31(t) muktamadhuraṃ; T71 muhuḥ (for mahaḥ)

3 a Y1 Y21 kariṇā 'valaṅghya° (for kariṇām alaṅghya°), Y2 Y14 kariṇā 'valambya°; N1 N21 paraṃ (for bhaje)

b DG2 kariṇā (for karuṇā°), C21(t) Y14 karaṇā°; N21 karuṇām a° (for karuṇāva°), Y11 Y12 karuṇāvi°

c D1 yamunām; Y31 Y32 yamināṃ nirantara° (for yaminām anārata°), D44 yamunārata° (metrically incorrect); D1 U1 Y1 Y2 Y11 Y12 Y13 Y14 °vihāra°; Y11 Y12 Y13 Y14 °mānasaṃ

d Y32 °taraṃga° (for °vanānta°), D44 °varṇāta° (incorrect), M24 °vanāṃda° (incorrect), D11 D71 M24 °caraṃ (for °sikaṃ); D12 bhajāmahe (for paraṃ mahaḥ), N1 bhaje mahaḥ, M24 varaṃ mahaḥ, N21 bhajemaḥ (metrically and otherwise incorrect)

4 a D71 M24 ayantrita° (for atantrita°), DG1 DG2 Y1 Y13 Y14 Y21 Y51 Y52 ayantritaṃ, C21(t) D11 D21 atandrita°, K1 niyantrika°, N1 atandritaṃ, D1 G11 N21 atantritaṃ, U1 adantriva° (incorrect); DG1 DG2 trijagati yad (for trijagad api), Y52 vrajad api ca, Y51 jayati ca yad; D1 vajrāṅganāṃ (metrically incorrect for vrajāṅganā-), Y31 prajāṅganā-, Y52 vrajāṅgane

b Y14 nirantaraṃ vipula°; DG1 DG2 virocanā°; Y51 °vilocanādinā

c C51 C52 D12 G11 M21 P71 T71 samantataḥ sarasataraṃ vijṛmbh°; D12 G11 vijṛmbhitāṃ (for vijṛmbhatāṃ), Y21 vijṛmbhato, M21 Y2 vijṛmbhatā

d C51 C52 D12 G11 M21 P71 T71 samantataḥ sarasataraṃ paraṃ; DG1 DG2 varaṃ (for paraṃ), C52 mahat

5 a Y2 °pravimalla°; Y52 °pratimendu° (for °pratimalla°), Y14 °pratimatta°, °pratimalli°

b N1 N21 bādhāraṇya° (for vṛndāraṇya°), G1 bālāraṇya°; N1 °nivāsinā° (for °vilāsinī°), N21 °vilāsinā°, M1 °vilāsini°; Y51 Y52 °vyavasitā° (for °vyasaninaṃ), N21 °vyasasinā, Y1 Y2 Y21 °vyasanitā°, D64 vyasanitaṃ, Y31 °vyasanināṃ, all mss. except the preceding and DG1 DG2 G1 N1 Y13 Y14 Y32 °vyasaninaṃ; Y31 Y32 °vaham (for °mayam), D1 °vayam

c DG1 DG2 G1 G2 kunda° (for manda°), M24 kanda°, N21 klinnaṃ, N1 klinna°; D1 Y13 Y14 Y21 Y31 Y32 madhurimā°; D64 °vyādhitṛ° (for vyāmṛṣṭa°), K1 °tyāhṛṣṭa° (incorrect), D1 °vyāmuṣṭa°; Y52 °vyāmṛṣṭanetrotsavaṃ

d Y2 °ārdrā° (metrically incorrect); Y1 Y2 Y13 Y14 Y21 Y31 Y32 Y51 Y52 °bharaṃ (for °vanaṃ), M24 omits these two syllables; DG1 D11 Y13 Y21 °kaiśorikaṃ; K1 Y13 Y14 śārṅgiṇaṃ

6 a DG2 D1 amuktamānuṣam

b D21 āgupta° (for ārūḍha°); V1 °yauvanam (for °vigraham), Y2 Y12 Y13 Y14 Y21 Y31 Y32 °vibhramam; R23(e) ārūḍha° (for arūḍha°), all mss. except preceding and DG1 DG2 G1 G2 N1 N21 R23(g) U1 Y2 Y12 Y13 Y14 Y21 Y31 Y32 agūḍha°; K1 °nīlam (for °līlam), Y12 ms. damaged here

c C21(te) C52(e) aniṣṭa° (for amṛṣṭa°), N1 ms. damaged here, H21(c) omitted, all mss. except preceding and D1 G11 M21 M24 N1 P71(t[c omitted]), Y2 Y12 Y13 Y14 Y31 Y32 anaṣṭa°; Y14 °bhāram

d Y13 kam api; D71 rocatu (for mādyati), D11 dīpyati, DG2 mādy api; all mss. except D1 D12 D21 G1 G2 M1 M24 N1 N21 R23 T21 mānasaṃ

7 a R23 ete bhāvāḥ; D12 sukala°; N1 N21 °jananī° (for °jagatī°), D12 Y14 Y32 °jagatāṃ; U1 °pradhānā

b Y21 °hṛṣṭā° (for °tṛṣṇā°), Y14 °kṛṣṇā°, D71 K1 °tṛṣṇāḥ; C21(t) C51(t) C52(t)

D12 D21 G11 hṛdi hṛdaye; M24 māman (for kāman), Y2 kāme; Y2 mādmavantu (metrically and otherwise incorrect for āvirbhavantu); D12 āvi° for āvir°); C21(t) °bhajantu (for °bhavantu), D21 °bhavanti

c C52(t) D11 D12 G11 K1 M21 M24 N1 N21 P71 Q71 U1 Y1 Y2 Y12 Y14 Y31 Y32 līlā° (for viṇā°), Y21 nānā°; DG1 °veṇī°; D12 G2 M1 M24 Y1 Y2 Y12 Y14 Y21 Y31 Y32 °lalita° (for °lasita°), C51(t) H31(t) °lasitaṃ; D1 D44 K1 °āravindaṃ

d Y2 Y2 jāne nā 'haṃ madhuram; D44 kā 'haṃ (for nā 'haṃ), DG2 nāna° (metrically incorrect); Y31 Y32 madhurimaparaṃ (for madhuram aparaam), D44 madhurimapadaṃ; Y14 manda° (for nanda°), G11 nandi°; Y1 Y2 Y12 Y14 Y31 Y32 °puṇyāvapūrāt (for °puṇyāmbupūrāt), Y21 °puṇyāvadhāran, K1 °puṇyāntapūrāt, V1 °puṇyāmburāśeḥ

8 a D1 sukṛtabhir; D1 U1 ādhṛte (for ādṛte), Y2 āvṛtte, Y13 Y14 Y21 āvṛte, Y31 ādṛter; Y31 arasa° (for sarasa°), Y13 sarasi°; G2 °reṇu° (for °veṇu°); N1 °sudhālasita- (for °ninādasudhā-), N21 °sudhāsitaj- (metrically and otherwise incorrect)

b D1 K1 lasa° (for rasa°), N1 saril° (metrically incorrect), N21 jharī° (metrically incorrect); N21 °lahari° (metrically incorrect); N1 N21 omit °vihāra°; U1 °niravigraha° (for °niravagraha°), Y13 °niravigraha° corrected to °niravagraha°; D44 °pathipūre (metrically incorrect for °putaiḥ), all mss. except preceding and Y1 Y2 Y21 Y31 Y32 °puṭe

c Y1 Y2 Y31 Y33 °jana° (for °vara°), G1 °varade (metrically incorrect), C52(t) °varṇa° (metrically incorrect), D11 D21 Y32 omit °vara°, Y14 Y21 °mada°, Y13 °manda° (metrically incorrect); Y1 Y2 Y13 Y14 Y31 °hāsakare (for °sārasike), Y21 °hāsakaraṃ, Y31 °hāsyakare, Z9 °sārasake, U1 °sāralike

d G11 sarasi (for mahasi), G2 mahati; Y31 sajjati

9 a G11 K1 N1 kṛṣṇāture (for tṛṣṇāture), N21 muṣṇātuvaś, Y12 tuṣṇāture, D11 tṛṣṇākule, D1 kṛṣṇātare, DG2 tṛṣṇāturaṃ; C52(t) D12 G2 P71(t) jṛmbhamāṇe

b D64 Y14 muhur (for muṣṇan), U1 muṣṇir, C51(t) muṣṇān, D1 mṛṣṭān; Y12 mohi°

c Y1 muṣṇātu; Y1 Y2 Y12 Y14 Y21 Y31 Y32 pūrṇadayai°; D12 °padaikasindhoḥ; Y14 °siddhāḥ (for °sindhoḥ), Y32 °sindhuḥ

d U1 kṛṣṇāsya; Y12 kāruṇyaṃ; R23 °heliḥ (for °keliḥ), M24 Y12 Y21 °keli

10 a V1 nikhilāgama° (for nikhilanigama°); Y14 °mūla° (for °mauli°), Y13 °mūla° corrected to °mauli°, M24 °vallī° (metrically incorrect), D64 omits °mauli°, K1 Y21 (vs. 152) °maulī° (metrically incorrect); Y21(vs. 299) °lālite (for °lālitaṃ), D1 U1 °lālita° (metrically incorrect), DG1 DG2 M24 °lālitaṃ yat (shift in meter by addition of one syllable), N1 damaged here but some indication that the reading was °lālitaṃ yat

b N21 °yugalaṃ (for °kamalaṃ), Y21(vs. 299) °kamale

c Y13 vrajabhuvir; C21(t) omits bahu°; Y1 Y2 mṛgyatetaraṃ (for °manmahetarāṃ), Y21(vs. 152) °manmadetarāṃ; Y13 both °te° and °he° entered for °he° and both crossed out: M24 vayaṃ (for °tarāṃ); Y13 Y14 Y32 taṃ added to end of line (shift in meter), DG1 DG2 taḥ (incorrect for?), G11 sa (ms. damaged here)

d N1 starasa° (for sarasa°), Y21(vs. 152) sahasa°; M24 °śirīṣa°; T21 °bhūṣitaṃ paraṃ mahaḥ (meter incorrect for °viśeṣabhūṣitam), DG1 °vibhūṣitaṃ maho yat (shift to aupacchandasikā meter); DG2 ms. damaged for °śeṣa°; Y13 omits °śeṣa°; DG3 P71 V1 °rūṣitam (for °bhūṣitam), Y13 Y14 °bhūṣitāṅgaṃ (shift to aupacchandasikā meter), Y21(vs. 299) °bhūṣite, D64 °bhūṣitām

11 (YY1 lines a b = lines c b of st. 3.11; Y21(vs. 301) line a = line a of st. 3.76 and lines b c d = lines b c d of st. 3.11)

a D11 N1 N21 °madhura° (for °mṛdula°), Y13 °mṛdu° (metrically incorrect) corrected to °madhura° in margin; K1 °smitaṃ; D71 omits °vyati°; D44 °ābhirāmādbhutaṃ nananda (too many syllables)

b M24 omits line b; Y51 YY1 muhuḥ (for mudā); DG1 DG2 udīrṇaye (for udīrṇayā), N21 udīrṇayan (incorrect); DG1 DG2 YY1 °manobhir ā° (for mano 'mbujā), D12 °manāmbujā°; C21(t) °āmreḍanam

c C21(t) D1 D64 G11 K1 M21 M24 N21 Y32 Y51 Y52 Z9 °locanaṃ (for °locana°), N1 ms. damaged here, YY1 °locanair; C21(c) DG1 DG2 D44 D64 G1 G2 H21(t[c damaged]) H31 °madā° (for °mukhā°), D21 °sukhā°, K1 °mṛdu°, Y1 Y2 Y13 Y14 Y21 Y32 Y51 Y52 °samā°, YY1 °janaiḥ; D44 K1 °svādituṃ (for °svāditaṃ), N1 ms. damaged, D12 °khāditaṃ, Y21 °sāditaṃ, YY1 °sādaraṃ

d Y52 tu (for nu), Y31 'pi

12 (Y1(vs. 117) lines c d = st. 3.12 lines c d; Y2(vs. 118) lines c d = st. 3.12 lines c d; Y3(vs. 127) lines c d = st. 3.12 lines c d)

a Y1 Y2 Y3 Y14 Y31 Y32 Y51 Y52 °samadana° (for °janamada°), Y12 Y13 °madanava°, Y21 °madaguru°, U1 °janamatha°, K1 °janapada°, Z9 °kulamada°; Y1 °ācheka° (for °ocheṣa°), N21 °ācheṣa°, C21(t) D1 °obhiṣṭa°, Y21 °otśeka°, Y2 °otjeka°, Y3 °ocheka° (all preceding forms incorrect), Y12 Y13 Y14 Y31 Y32 °otseka°, all mss. except preceding and DG1 DG2 G1 N1 °cchiṣṭa°

b M24 T21 iti (for api), all mss. except preceding and C52(t) G11 K1 P71 T71 Y1 Y2 Y3 Y12 Y13 Y14 Y21 Y31 Y32 Y51 Y52 ati°; DG1 DG2 M24 udābhyām (for ubhābhyām), D1 sukhābhyām, C21(t) mukhābhyām, Y52 amubhyām

c Z9 akṛd api; Y51 Y52 tad (for te); G1 pādayāmaḥ

d N1 kāmarūpaṃ (for kāntipūraṃ), Y1(vs. 100), Y2(vs. 101) sadā nu; Y12 Y14 kadā tu

13 (Y13[vs. 130] line d = st. 3.14 line c)

a Y14 gopa° (for ghoṣa°); DG2 °anubhīta°; all mss. except DG1 DG2 D44 D45 G1 G2 M21 M24 N1 N21 R23 U1 Y1 Y2 Y13 Y14 Y31 Y32 Y51 Y52 °yauvanaṃ (for °vaibhavaṃ)

b Y31 kāmalo° (for komalo°); U1 °kvaṇita° (for °svanita°), Y1 Y2 °svarita°, Y31 Y32 °ollasita°, M24 Y13 °dhvanita°, Y51 Y52 °sphurita°, all mss. except preceding and C21(e) DG1 DG2 D21 M21 N1 N21 R23 Y14 °stanita°; Y14 °svanitam eva; C51(t) D45 Y1 Y2 °niḥsvanam (for °nisvanam), Y14 niḥsvanam, U1 °kisvanam c Y1 Y2 °bhūtanidhisāra°; C21(t) abhisāra°; K1 °saṃpadaṃ (for saṃpadāṃ), °saṃpradāṃ, T21 °saṃpadā

d Y13 omits line d (see above); D12 vāmarasa°

14 a DG2 valitayā (for lalitayā), Y51 Y52 lalanayā; Y2 Y12 'vilambitaṃ; G2 ms. damaged here

b H31(t) °vega° (for °geha°), DG2 °roha°, Y1 Y2 Y12 Y14 Y21 Y31 Y32 Y51 Y52 °bhūmi°, Y13(vs. 59) omits the rest of the verse after °bhū°; G1 °ida° (incorrect for iva); M24 mukti° (for mūrti°), G1 mūrta°, Y21 Y52 pūrva°, Y31 Y32 Y51 sarva°; K1 °saṃpadam (for °sampadām), D1 °saṃpradā, Y21 saṃpadā

c N1 tāla° (for nīla°); Y12 Y14 °nīraja° (for °nīrada°), Y13(vs. 130—see critical apparatus to st. 3.13) °nīrada° corrected to nīraja°; DG1 DG2 G2 H31(t) N1 N21 R23 Y13(vs. 130), Y14 °vikāsi° (for °vikāsa°), D1 Y32 °vikāśa°, Y1 Y2 Y12 Y21 Y31 Y51 Y52 °vikāśi°; U1 Y21 °saṃbhramaṃ (for °vibhramaṃ) M24 N1 N21 °vigrahaṃ

d D1 dayam (for vayam), D44 vamam, N1 omits °va°; D1 D44 D45 D71 H31(t) K1 Y51 Y52 āśrayāmahe (for ādriyāmahe), U1 āśritāmahe, G11 ādritāmahe, M24 ādṛtāmahe

15 a D1 surāreś (for murāreś), U1 murāre; D1 D21 D64 N21 Y1 Y2 Y12 Y14 Y21 Y31 °āravindaṃ

b Y32 dvayam (for dvaṃdvaṃ), M24 dvaṃdvā°; N1 yadā (for dayā)°, N21 omits °da°; DG2 °varṣita°; T21 °vaibhavasya (for °śaiśavasya), N21 °locanasya

c D1 D44 K1 N21 Y2 vṛndāravṛndāraka°; Y1 Y2 °bāla° (for °bṛnda°), Y51 Y52 °pāla°; G11 °mauliṃ (for °mauli), D1 Y21 °maulī

d N21 vandāru° (for mandāra°); D1 D12 D71 U1 UV Y1 Y12 Y14 Y21 Y31 Y32 Y51 Y52 °makaranda° (for °vinimarda°), K1 °vinimanda°, N21 °nivimarda°; Y1 Y2 Y12 Y14 Y31 Y32 Y51 Y52 °gauram (for °bhīru), Y21 °gaurī, DG1 DG2 D1 °bhīruḥ

16 a C51(t) paśya; N1 N21 °taraiḥ (for °bharaiḥ), G2 °bhagaiḥ C21(t) °bhareḥ; Y14 krānta° (for krauñca°), DG2 krāñca°, M24 krāñja°; C52(t) D11 H21(t) °dviṣac (for °dviṣaś), Y31 °dviṣaṃś, Y14 °dvipaṃ; D11 °candrikā (for candrakī), M1 candrikī, D1 M24 candraki

b (G1 after yasya in line b ms. damaged and rest of vs. gone) D1 K1 nṛtyati (for dṛpyati), Y1 Y2 rajyati, Y21 Y31 Y32 Y52 tṛpyati, D44 N21 dṛṣyati (incorrect), Y13 dṛṣyati corrected to nṛpyati, M24 bhūpyati, G11 N1 dhṛṣyati, G2 copyist enters both tuṣyati and hṛṣyati as possible readings for the illegible ms. entry, D45 hṛṣyati; G11 °surabhir (for °surabhiṃ), K1 Y1 Y21 °surabhi° (meter wrong), Y11 Y31 Y32 Y52 °surabhīr, Y2 Y14 °surabhī°, Y13 both the i and ī strokes are entered between °surabh and r; D44 vṛṣā (for vṛṣo), D1 viṣo; G2 Y11 Y14 °jaṭiḥ (for °jaṭeḥ), M1 °jate, Y2 °jataiḥ (D64 omits lines c and d)

c Y1 nṛtyati (for sajjati), Y2 sṛpyati, Y11 Y13 Y14 Y21 Y31 Y32 rajyati Y52 °ṣataṃ (for °gatiṃ), G11 °gatir, N1 N21 Y1 Y2 Y11 Y13 Y14 Y21 °gataṃ, G1 ms. damaged here; Y11 vo 'ñchan; G2 hariḥ (for hareḥ), N21 tviśāṃ; D11 kuñjaras (for sindhuras), D1 sundaraṃ, Y2 sindhuraṃ, Y11 sindhurā d Y11 °kelya° (meter wrong for °kalpaka°), Y32 °kalpa° (meter wrong), Y13 °kalpa° corrected to °kalpaka°; Y1 Y2 °kalpapādapa; K1 °vasaṃ (for °vanaṃ), Y52 °vanā°, Y31 Y32(p) °vane; Y31 Y32(p) vande (for taṃ vā), Y52 °lambaṃ, DG2 ms. damaged here; Y31 Y32(p) mahaḥ (for bhaje), Y14 bhaja, D1 bhavet

17 a H21(t) aruṇāmṛtādhara°; D44 °viśeṣitaṃ vibhuṃ (for °viśeṣitasmitaṃ), Y3 °viśeṣinir mitaṃ

b T71 taruṇālayā°; Y1 °karma° (for °varṇa°), Y2 °karṇa°, Y12 °varṣa°, H21(t) °varṇaṃ ,T21 °varṇya°

c N1 aruṇā°; G11 °divyalocanaṃ

d C21(c) C51 C52 D21 D44 D71 H21 H31 K1 P71 R23 T71 UV Y1 Y2 Y51 Y52 karuṇāmayaṃ, M1 karuṇākaraṃ, C21(t) karuṇālayā; DG2 D1 Y11 Y51 Y52 kim api; D64 bālayā 'śraye (for bālam āśraye), Y51 dhāma cintaye, Y52 dhāma cakāstu ciram (meter wrong), Y12 bālam āśrāyā (incorrect)

18 a DG1 DG2 N1 N21 °vīthī° (for °vīcī°), Y14 °vācī; C21(t) C51(t) C52(t) D45 R23 °lalitā°; M21 °bhūṣā

b K1 bhūpā°; D12 K1 °vadā° (for °padā°), D64 °vahā°, D1 °vadhā°, Y1 °spadā‘$_{o}$ Y2 °spadāṃ; Y14 °roṣita°; Y1 Y3 °puṣpa° (for °puṇya°), N21 °barhi°; K1 Y1 °barham (for °barhām), G2 °bastām

c D21 lāvaṇya° (for kāruṇya°), K1 tāruṇya°, C51(t) kāruṇyaṃ; Y2 °dhārāli° (for °dhārāla°), D45 °dhārāccha°, Y32 °kārāla° (°dhārāla° given in margin); D1 D71 °mālaṃ

d DG1 DG2 lolāṃ (for bālāṃ), M24 balāṃ, D1 D71 M1 U1 bālaṃ, N1 Y13 omit (Y13 corrects omission to bālāṃ); D44 insetrs 2 extra syllables after bhaje (sadā); D12 pallava° (for vallava°), Y32 pallave (pallavaṃ given in margin); N1 N21 kām api gopalakṣmīm; D1 Y21 °lakṣmī

19 a D64 °rasaṃ bhavibhor vapu (incorrect for?); G11 madhur (for vapur), Y21 (vs. 340) puṭai (incorrect for?), Y51 Y52 paraṃ, K1 T21 vapurasya (metrically and otherwise incorrect); D1 D12 K1 Y14 Y32 vibho (for vibhor), C51(c) C52 D71 G11 H21(t) M21 P71 R23 T71 U1 Y21(vs. 196) vibhos tan (shift to aupacchandasikā meter)

b Y14 madhurī° (for mathurā°); D12 Y13 Y14 Y21 (vs. 340) °vīci° (for °vīthi°); D1 D21 °ciraṃ (for °caraṃ), M24 °paraṃ, Y13 °ciraṃ corrected to °caraṃ, Y14 °varaṃ; Y21(vs. 196), Y51 bhaje mahaḥ (for bhajāmahe), Y13 bhajāmahe corrected to bhaje mahaḥ, G2 ms. damaged here

c V1 nagarībala; C21 C51 C52 D1 D11 D12 D21 D44 D45 D64 D71 G2 H21 H31 K1 M1 M21 N21 P71 T21 T71 U1 °locanānāṃ (for °locanā-) (shift to aupacchandasikā meter), Y32 °locane

d Y13 °harṣa° (for °varṣa°), N21 °vatma° (for °vartma°?), N1 damaged here; Y1 Y2 Y21(vs. 196) Y31 Y32 Y51 Y52 °dharṣitam (for °varṣitam), Y21(vs. 340) °dharṣitā, Y13 °pūritam, N1 °dharṣitām, C21(t) °dharṣita

20 a Y2 Y14 nayanena (for nayanānta°), Y21 Y31 Y32 °vilokitena (for °vijṛmbhitena)

b Y2 Y32 kampreṇa (incorrect for kamreṇa), all mss. except preceding and DG1

DG2 G2 M21 N1 N21 R23 Y1 Y14 Y21 Y31 Y51 Y52 vaktreṇa; D45 V1 °dara° (for °mada°), Y31 Y32 Y51 Z9 °tara°, G11 R23(e) °manda° (meter wrong), D1 D11 D71 Y52 °mṛdu°, N1 °tama°, N21 °ma° (for °tama°?), Y2 °muda°, Y1 °mida° (for °muda°), Y21 °mukha°; N1 °vigraheṇa

c M24 mantreṇa

d Y13 Y14 nandatanayo; V1 tanaye (for tanayo, T71 tanayaṃ; C21 C51 C52 DG1 DG2 D21 D64 D71 H21 H31 M21 P71 T71 Z9 dhinoti (for dhunoti), G11 dhinotu, D1 duṇāti (incorrect), Y1 Y2 Y21 punāti, Y13 Y14 Y31 Y32 Y51 punātu, Y52 jahāra

21 a Y31 Y32 °vṛndair (for °bandīr)

b D11 °ākṣībhir alakṣyamāṇān (for °ākṣīr abhilakṣyamāṇān), Y32 °ākṣībhir avekṣyamāṇān, Y31 °ākṣībhir avekṣamāṇān; D45 abhilāṣamāṇān (for abhilakṣyamāṇān), Y1 Y2 Y14 Y21 abhilakṣamāṇān, N21 abhivīkṣamāṇān, N1 abhiniṣyamāṇān, DG1 abhirīṣyamānān, DG2 DG3 abhirīpsyamānān (the preceding three entries incorrect for?)

c T71 Y1 Y2 Y13 Y14 Y21 Y31 Y32 °smitodāra°; U1 °smitādhāramukhendubimbān; Y32 °āravindaṃ

d D64 °dhūrtadānāt

22 a DG1 DG2 G2 N1 N21 Y1 Y2 Y13 Y14 Y21 Y31 Y32 līlākopa° (for līlāṭopa°), R23 līlākṣepa°, Y51 Y52 līlālola°; DG1 °prasādā° (for °prasaṅga°), K1 °praśasta°); K1 Y1 Y2 Y21 °ādhikaṃ (for °ādhika-), D11 °ādhiṣu, D1 °ādhiraḥ

b H21(t) prītaṃ (for prīte), D71 prītī°, C21(t) prīti°; C21(te) D21 H21(t[c damaged here]) V1 gīti° (for rīti°), N1 Y31 prīti°; C52 G11 M21 P71 T71 °vibhāga° (for °vibhaṅga°), N1 N21 °vihaṃga°; Y2 Y13 Y14 Y21 Y31 Y32 °saṅkara° (for °saṅgara°), Y51 Y52 °bhaṅgivi°; Y51 Y52 °ādṛte (N21 omits lines c and d)

c Y2 rādhāyāvana°; Y52 °lāñchita° (for °locana°; D21 lasite (for lalita°), C21(t) vilāsa°, N1 lasita°; K1 °smeraṃ (for °smere), U1 °smerā; Y1 Y2 Y31 Y51 Y52 mahā (for mudā), Y14 Y21 Y32 maho

d Y13 lagnaṃ madīyaṃ mama; D1 madīyaṃ mahaḥ

23 a Y2 °pāda° (for °vajra°), M1 M24 °vaktra°

b no variant readings

c D12 hṛta° (for dhṛta°), G2 kṛta°, D1 D44 K1 dṛta°; Y1 Y2 dhṛtavigrahe sadā (for dhṛtagopavigrahe)

d N21 prabhuṃ anyan (for kiyad anyan), N1 prabhu (two syllables omitted), K1 kriyad anyaṃ, D1 kiṃ yad asyaṃ, Y1 kiyamanyan (incorrect for?), DG1 DG2 kiyad U1 anyaṃ

24 a T21 jayat (for jagat°); Y1 Y2 Y13 Y14 Y21 Y52 Z9 °trayīkānta° (for °trayaikānta°; Z9 °manoja° (for °manojña°), Y2 °mano'nya°; D45 K1 M1 V1 Y1 Y2 Y52 °bhūmi (for °bhūmiś), D1 °bhūmī

b no variant readings

c C21(t) C51 C52 D44 D64 D71 G11 H21 H31(t) K1 M21 P71 T21 Y52 rāmā° (for ramā°), M24 rāmaṃ, D1 vāma°, Y14 rādhā°, Y21 rasā°; M24 °ramā° (for

°samā°), T21 °rasā°; D1 °āsvādite; Y14 °saukumārye
d K1 rādhāsthanā°; D1 D12 M24 Y13 °stanāṃbhoga°; G11 oṣaḥ

25 (G1 lines a b—ms. damaged)
a Y32 eva (metrically incorrect for ete), D64 ete tvayi (again metrically incorrect), K1 Y1 Y2 viśvasinaḥ, Y32 viśvasitāḥ, G2 viśāsituḥ (incorrect)
b V1 Y1 Y2 °mūrti° (for kīrti°); DG1 DG2 °kiṃpaṭhantyā (for °kiṃvadantyā G2 °kiṃvadantyāt (incorrect for?), D45 °kiṃvadanty a°, Y32 °kiṃvadat te; D11 K1 M21 P71 T71 V1 'ṅge (for te), D45 °gre, C51 C52 'gre, D44 G11 H21(te) H31(te) T21 'ge, U1 'le, D71 'ste, D1 'ke, M24 Y1 Y2 Y31 M24 'nte, C21(t) G2 M1 Y32 omit this syllable
c Y1 Y2 Y14 Y31 Y31 api na (for api ca), Y13 correct api na to api ca, Y21 api bhu° (incorrect); Y1 Y2 nava° (for tava); Y1 Y2 Y13 Y14 Y32 carite (for lalite), Y31 carito
d D1 Y1 capalatarām itir iyaṃ; D12 mativīrya (meter wrong for matir iyaṃ), Y14 malinir iva (meter all right); Y1 Y2 Y13 Y14 Y21 Y31 bālā (for bālye), Y32 cāpalā (meter wrong), D12 bāle

26 a C21 C51 C52 D1 D12 D21 G11 H21 H31 UV VI vatsabāla° (for vatsavāṭa°), G2 H21(p) M21 N1 N21 R23 U1 vatsavāṭī°, C21(p) vatsavāti°, C51(p) C52(p) as in text, H31(p) ms. damaged here, G1 vatsavana°, M1 vatsamāla°, Y14 vatsavāpi°, M24 vatsavrāta°
b M1 vatsaṃ
c DG1 DG2 G1 G2 K1 N1 N21 T71 U1 utsukāya (for utsavāya), M1 upabhavāya (meter wrong)
d H21(t) utsuko (for utsuke), G11 utsome, D1 D12 D64 utsake, Y1 Y2 Y13 utsavo, Y14 Y21 utsave

27 a DG1 DG2 madhurasa° (for madhurima°), M1 madhurīṃ (meter wrong); Y21 °dharite mano'bhirāmo
b Y1 mṛdutarala° (for mṛdulatara°), D64 mṛdutara° (meter wrong), DG1 DG2 mṛdulatarā°, Y13 mṛdulatarā° corrected to mṛdulatara°; U1 Y14 °ānanendo (for °ānanendau), M1 °ānanendoḥ, Y21 °ānanandaiḥ
c K1 °nayanaikya°, Y32 °lokanīye
d Y2 Y21 °lālasā sma

28 a D45 niṣpanda° (for niṣyanda°), D1 D12 D44 Y14 Y21 nisyanda° (variant form of niṣyanda°), Y2 nispanda°, Y31 nisyandi°, Y32 niḥspanda°
b Y21 °musalī°
c D11 Y13 Y14 vrajāṅganāyāṃ gata° (for vrajāṅganāpāṅgata°), M6 vrajāṅganānāṃ śata°; D1 D12 D21 Y14 Y31 K1 M24 T71 °bhaṅga- (for °bhṛṅga-), D64 °bhṛṅgaṃ
d D44 sagrāma°; Y2 saṃgrāmamaule; D11 Y2 Y13 Y14 Y21 Y31 Y32 bata (for tava); Y14 lālasāḥ syuḥ (for lālasāḥ smaḥ), M24 Y13 Y31 lālasā sma

29 a DG2 ātātmā° (for ātāmra°), Y2 Y14 ātāmrayita; Y1 Y2 Y12 Y13 Y14 Y21 °locanāmbu° (for °locanāṃśu°), Y51 °locanāśru°; Y14 °laharīṃ; C51(t) °lālā°

(for °līlā°), Y51 °nānā°, Y51 °madhu° (for °sudhā°); M1 M24 °vyāyataiḥ (for °pyāyitaiḥ), C21(t) DG1 DG2 D1 G1 H21(t) U1 °pyāyataiḥ (incorrect for?), K1 °pyādṛter (incorrect), Y1 Y2 Y21 Y32 Y51 °vyāpitaiḥ, Y12 Y33(te[g reads with text]), N21 °pyāyite

b Y21 gantā° (for gītā°); G2 °haritaiḥ (for °bharitaiḥ), H21(t) Y21 Y51 °racitaiḥ, Y1 Y2 Y13 Y14 Y31 Y32 °caritaiḥ, N21 °bharite; G2 pītaṃ; U1 °śrījanaiḥ (for °strījanaiḥ), D1 °śrījaraiḥ, DG1 DG2 °strīśataiḥ

(N21 omits lines c and d)

c Y13 Y14 svedāntaḥ°; all mss. except DG1 DG2 D44 G1 G2 R23 T21 U1 Y2 Y12 Y13 Y14 Y21 Y31 Y32 Y51 °bhūṣitena; D71 kam api (for kim api), N1 kim iva; D1 smareṇa; DG1 DG2 vaktre manā;

d Y1 Y2 Y12 Y14 °mahah° (for °mṛdu°), Y51 °mahaṃ, Y13 °mayas°; Y12 °pravāra° (for °pracāra°), Y13 °payoda°; C21 C51 C52 D1 D11 D12 D45 D64 G11 H21(t[c is damaged here]) K1 M24 P71 T21 °sulabhaṃ; Y51 paśyāmy adṛśyaṃ; G2 vaśyaṃ (for dṛśyaṃ), N1 hṛdyaṃ, Y13 hṛśyaṃ (incorrect for?); K1 manaḥ (for mahaḥ)

30 a D1 K1 Y1 Y2 veṇuḥ); U1 °kusumārā° (for °sukumārā°), M1 sukumāre; Y1 Y2 °sukṛtau yā parā bālyalakṣmīh; N1 omits prakṛti—... kṛtau but a space is left in the ms. for this omission; G2 °āhitau (for °ākṛtau), M1 °ātena, (meter wrong); D44 pālya° (for bālya°), Y14 bāla°, N1 omits first letter of (?) uṇya°

b U1 pārśvau; D1 D64 D71 M1 U1 Y1 Y2 Y11 Y12 Y14 Y21 Y31 Y51 Y52 bālā ;Y1 Y2 Y31 Y32 Y51 Y52 °kupitā° (for °sarasā°), G11(st. 3.30) °sarasāṃ; DG1 DG2 G1 G2 N1 R23 Y1 Y2 Y11 Y12 Y14 Y21 Y31 Y32 Y51 Y52 °lokite (for °lokitā°), H31(t) °likine, D1 °lokitāṃ; G1 G2 N1 'pāñgalīlā (for °pāñga-līlāḥ), Y1 Y2 Y11 Y12 Y14 Y21 Y31 Y32 Y52 kā 'pi līlā, Y51 kā 'pi bālā, U1 °pāñgalīlā

c G2 barhiṃ (incorrect); K1 madana° (for vadana°); Y11 Y12 °vadanambhau° (incorrect); K1 °ruho; D12 D64 maugdha° (for maugdhya°); Y1 Y2 Y11 Y12 Y14 Y31 Y32 Y51 Y52 maunamudrā (for maugdhyamudre)

d C21(t) tv ārdrākāraṃ (for 'ty ārdrākāraṃ), G11(2.74) 'ty āgrākāraṃ, Y1 Y2 Y11 Y12 hṛdy oṃkāraṃ, Y14 Y21 Y31 Y32 Y51 Y52 hṛdy ākāraṃ; D1 G1 N1 kam api (for kim api), DG1 bahala°, DG2 omits; G11(2.74) M25 kitava° (for kitavaṃ); N1 jñātam (for jyotir); G2 anveṣayāmi (for anveṣayāmaḥ), Y51 ālokaye nu, Y52 ālokayemaḥ

31 (C21 D1 D11 D12 D45 D71 G11 M21 P71 T71 have the line order a b d c)

a Y11 Y14 Y21(vs. 341) ālīḍhaveṇu°; DG1 DG2 D11 G2 H21(e) N21 R23 Y12 Y14 Y21 (vs. 341) °veṇur aruṇā° (for °veṇutaruṇā°), K1 N1 U1 °veṇuṃ aruṇā°, M21 °veṇukaruṇā°, Y1 Y2 Y21(vs. 166) Y31 Y32 Y51 °veṇumadhurā°, Y13 °veṇuramaṇā°; Y51 °pallavena (for °vibhramena), Y13 °pallavena given as a p in the margin, Y1 Y2 Y12 Y14 Y21 °vidrumena

b C21(t) mādhuryasāda°; D12 udvamantī (for udvahantī), K1 M1 U1 Y21 (vs. 166) udvahanti

c Y1 Y2 Y13 ālokitāḥ (for ālokyatāṃ), D64 ālokitāṃ, Y12 Y14 Y21(vs. 341) Y31 Y32 Y51 ālokitā, Y21(vs. 166) ālokitām Y2 Y13 (character much remade)

Y31 Y32 kim anaghā (for kim anayā), Y1 Y14 kim anathā, Y21(vs. 166) api nadha (incorrect), Y21(vs. 341) kim anadha (incorrect), Y51 kim adhunā Y51 bhava devatā ca (for vanadevatā naḥ), D21 G1 N1 N21 vanadevatāyāḥ, DG1 DG2 G2 R23 Y31 Y32 vanadevatā naḥ, K1 vanadevatāpaḥ

d Y13 Y14 kaiśorike; M1 T21 omits vayasi; DG1 DG2 G1 M21 N1 N21 P71 R23 U1 V1 kā 'pi ca (for kā cana), D12 D64 T21 Y1 Y2 Y12 Y13 Y14 Y21 Y32 Y51 kāṃ cana; Y1 Y2 Y12 Y13 Y14 Y21(vs. 166) Y51 kānta° (for kānti°), Y21(vs. 341) kāṃ ca; Y13 Y14 Y21 (vs. 166) Y31 °dṛṣṭiḥ (for °yaṣṭiḥ), Y12 °draṣṭiṃ (incorrect), G2 ms. damaged here

32 a Y12 °kānikāntam; D11 °kānta- (for °kāntam), D1 K1 °kāntā-, G11 °mātra te (one extra syllable)

b D44 akrānta°; Z9 °ghoṣa° (meter wrong for °gopī°); D1 Y1 Y2 Y51 Y52 °vadanā° (for °nayanā°)

c DG1 DG2 G11 U1 punaḥ purāṇasya

d D12 D71 H31 M1 M24 Y11 Y12 Y14 Y21 Y31 Y32 Y51 pūrṇena puṇyena (for puṇyena pūrṇena), Y52 puṇyena pūrvena

33 (C51 C52 line order b a c d)

a K1 Y1 Y2 aṣṭāṅga°; K1 °pādam (for °pātam), M1 °vādam, N21 °bhāvam, Z9 °pītam; G2 M21 abhivādya (for abhivandya), V1 abhinandya, N1 ms. damaged here; M1 °bhāve

b N1 ms. damaged for sarvān sur°; N1 °deva° (for °endra°); G1 N21 °nivahān (for °nikarān), N1 ms. damaged here

c DG2 mandāsmita°; M1 M24 °smitārdra° (incorrect); N1 N21 °vadanāmbuja° (for °madhurānana°), N21 °sūrya° (for °candra°), M1 °bimbo

d D1 G1 puṇyanilaye

34 a M21 bhavapravhedeṣu (for eṣu pravāheṣu), D1 eṣu prabhāveṣu; T21 na (for sa); D1 saheṣu (for sa eva); Y51 nirarṇaveṣu (for sa eva manye); M1 madhye (for manye), D11 D71 U1 nā 'nyo, D1 manya (incorrect)

b C51(t) C52(t) Y14 kṣaṇe 'pi (for kṣaṇo 'pi), K1 kṣaṇeṣu, H21(t) kṣaṇopa°, M24 kṣaṇo 'ṣṭa°, DG1 DG2 N1 kṣaṇo 'bhi°, N21 kṣaṇābhi°; G1 G2 Y2 Y11 Y12 Y14 Y21 gamyaḥ (for gaṇyaḥ), N1 N21 °gamyaḥ, K1 gaṇyāḥ, M1 gaṇyaṃ, D1 raṇyāḥ, D1 puruṣāyateṣu

c Y1 Y2 Y11 Y12 Y14 Y21 Y51 Y52 āsādyate; D1 M21 Y1 Y2 kathā (for kayā); M1 'livṛtyā (for 'pi vṛttyā), U1 pravṛtyā, M21 pravṛttyā, D64 'bhiratmā (incorrect); C51(te) DG1 DG2 D1 D12 D71 G1 G2 K1 M24 N1 N21 R23(e) T21 vṛtyā (for vṛttyā), V1 bhaktyā, Y21 vṛddhyā

d Y32 nandasya (for nīlasya); D44 vicitram (for caritam)

35 a D11 °sarasānanaṃ; U1 °kṛpā° (for °dayā°), N21 °yadā° (incorrect), DG2 °daryā°; M1 M24 Y32 °ādra° (incorrect); Y1 Y2 Y31 Y32 Y51 Y52 °ramye° (for °divye°), Y14 °ranve° (incorrect)

b G1 G2 M21 U1 Y1 Y2 Y14 Y21 Y31 Y32 Y51 Y52 °vadanāmbujaṃ (for °mukhapaṅkajaṃ), N1 N21 °hṛdayāmbujaṃ, DG1 DG2 °vacanābujaṃ; Y32 Y33 madhuram ārdra° (for madhurasārdra°), N1 madhurimārdra°, N21 madhurimadārdra° (one extra syllable), DG1 DG2 D12 G2 M1 T21 U1 UV °sāndra° (for °sārdra°), Y51 °bhāva°; Y51 °śānta° (for °manda°), K1 °smitaḥ

c Y14 rasasya (for rasajña°); Y52 valita° (for ramita°), H21(t) ramata°, D12 °rocanaṃ

d no variants

36 a Y1 Y2 Y11 Y12 Y14 Y21 Y31 Y32 Y51 gopaḥ (for bālaḥ); DG1 DG2 D1 °ruhākṣī

b U1 °dhūliṃ

c U1 mahaṃs (for muhus), Y51 mahas, Y31 mahus (incorrect); Y13 evaṃ (for etad); Y21 Y51 vimalam (for yugalaṃ), Y11 yugulaṃ (incorrect)

d D11 M1 me muhyamāne (for monmuhyamāne), Y51 mumukṣumāne, Y12 momudyamāne, M21 momuhyamāno, DG2 momuhyamānā; M1 tu (for 'pi), Y1 namasy (for manasy), Y2 manas v; D1 G2 N1 Y14 udeti (for udetu), Y12 udetuḥ (incorrect), Y21 udenuḥ (incorrect)

37 a U1 praṇāmābhimukhe (for prayāṇābhimukhe), DG1 DG2 prayāṇe 'bhimukhe; Y1 Y2 Y11 Y12 Y14 Y21 Y31 Y32 'pi (for ca), N1 N21 tu

b K1 sthana° (for stana°), Y1 Y2 Y11 Y12 Y14 Y31 Y32 kuca°, Y21 kruddha°; U1 °dvayā°; N1 N21 °saṃmuditaḥ (for °durlalitaḥ), G1 sallalitaḥ; C21(t) DG1 D1 °durlalitasya; U1 ca (for sa), C51(t) C52(t) D21 svabhāvaḥ (one syllable short for sa bālakaḥ); C21 C51(c) C52(c) D11 D12 D71 G1 H21 H31(c) P71 R23 T71 U1 bālaḥ (one syllable short for bālakaḥ), G1 lālakaḥ, K1 bālaḥ sta (incorrect)

c Y11 Y12 śravati (meter wrong for śrāvita°); D45 U1 °niḥsvano (for °nisvano), Y11 Y12 °niḥsvanaḥ, Y1 Y2 Y14 Y21 Y31 Y32 °nisvanaḥ

d Y1 Y2 Y11 Y12 Y14 Y21 Y31 Y32 kiśoraveśeṇa; C51(t) C52(t) D1 D21 G2 G11 N1 T21 punaḥ; Y2 Y11 Y12 Y14 Y21 Y31 Y32 pratiṣṭhatām (for pratīyatām), T21 pragīyatām, D1 G2 pradīyatām

38 a N1 atibhūtim abhūtim; M1 matibhūmim; G2 abhūdi (incorrect for?); H21(t) Y1 ve (for me)

b N21 madhuraṃ (for vacasām); Y14 vacasā (for vacasām), Y11 Y12 vacasa (meter wrong); Y14 °svanam (for °stanam), Y11 °staranam (one extra syllable—shift to aupacchandasikā meter), D1 °stananām (incorrect for?); C21(t) C51(t) C52(t) D11 D12 D21 D44 H21(t) K1 Y32 vā added to end of line (one extra syllable—shift to aupacchandasikā meter)

c Y31 Y32 apadaṃ; D44 vā added to the end of line (one extra syllabel—shift to aupacchandasikā meter)

d Y11 Y12 Y14 muhur advaitam (for madhurādvaitam), DG1 DG2 U1 madhurasmera°, N1 madhurāsyaṃ sam°, N21 madhurāsyaṃ kim

39 a Y2 janatāntare (for jananāntare), Y31 janmāntare (one syllable short); Y21 °maṇḍale (for °maṇḍane)

b Y51 Y52 ramaṇīya° (for kamanīya°); Y1 Y2 Y14 Y21 Y31 Y32 kamalāruṇekṣaṇe (for kamalāyatekṣaṇe), G2 kamalākarekṣaṇe, Z9 kamalojjvalekṣaṇe

c Y2 °āvṛte (for °āmṛte)

d K1 taralāni santu capālendriyāni; K1 omits me (meter wrong)

40 a U1 °vandye; Y1 Y2 Y13 Y14 Y31 Y51 Y52 °calad° (for °lasad°), Y21 Y32° valad°
b C21(tg) C51(g) C52 D45 D64 H21(g) H31(g) M21 P71 R23 U1 V1 Y2 Y32 stanaśroṇī°; Y51 °viśvaksthagita° (for °bimbastimita°) Y52 °viśvaksnapita°, K1 U1 °bimbe stimita°, N1 N21 °saṃgastimita° (for °saṅgastimita°?), N1 N21 °nayanābhoja°; G11 M24 Y21 °yugalam (for °subhagam)
c G2 upaślāghā°; D1 D21 D71 Y21 Y31 Y32 °ślāghyā° (for °ślāghā°), D64 °ślāghyāṃ; D1 D21 M24 °bhūmīṃ (for °bhūmiṃ); Y1 Y2 Y13 Y51 Y52 °tanuṃ (for °hṛdāṃ), G2 °hṛdā, D64 °garāṃ, K1 °gavāṃ, Y32 °bharaṃ, M1 M24 °giraṃ, Y14 °tanur, all mss. except preceding and C51 C52 DG1 D12 D71 G1 N1 N21 R23 °girāṃ
d C51(t) D21 ghanaḥ; U1 Y13 Y21 Y51 kam api; G1 G2 H21(t) H31(t) P71(t) T71 Y13 Y14 mahanīyākṛti; Y51 °ākṛtim iha

41 a N1 N21 aticumbatām, (for anucumbatām), C21(t) C51(t) D1 D11 G11 M21 U1 anucumbitām. Y14 anubimbitām; D45 V1 Y12 Y13 Y14 Y21 Y31 Y32 avicalena (api calena), D21 abhinavena, D71 K1 aticalena, D64 api balena, Y1 Y2 iva calena, D44 api ca tena; M21 N1 N21 tejasā (for cetasā), Y21(vs, 537) cetaso
b R23 Y12 Y13(p in margin) Y31 Y32 madhurākṛter (for manujākṛter), Y13 madhurīkṛter, Y14 madhurākṛte; T71 madhurimāśrayaṃ (for madhurimaśriyaṃ), Y1 Y2 madhuritaśriyaṃ Y32 madhurimāśriyaṃ; Y14 vibho
c DG1 DG2 G2 N1 N21 Y13 api (for ayi); Y31 kṛṣṇa deva (for deva kṛṣṇa); M24 dadhiya (for dayite); C51(t) M1 nijalpatām; C21(t) D64 N21 Y12 Y21 (vs. 310) Y32 jalpitām
d Y32 ayi (for api); M21 M24 vā sarāḥ (for tādṛśāḥ), D71 vā saraḥ, Y31 vā daśāḥ, C51(t) D21 D45 P71(t) Y1 Y2 tādṛśaḥ, K1 tādṛśam, D1 omits N1 N21 tādṛśām

42 a N21 Y31 kṛśodarīṇāṃ (one syllable short)
b Y1 Y2 Y11 Y12 Y14 Y21 Y31 Y32 viśeṣamṛgyeṇa
c Y21 lamba° (for labdha°), Y11 Y12 laṣca° (incorrect); N21 labdhamahṛdayāmbudhiṃ (incorrect for?); D71 G2 K1 °yaśodayāmbudhiṃ; DG1 DG2 G2 °āmbudaṃ (for °āmbudher), C51(t) D21 D44 D45 M1 N1 Y1 Y2 Y11 Y12 Y14 Y21 Y31 Y32 °āmbudhiṃ
d M1 Y1 Y2 niśām ahe (for niśāmaye); N1 N21 nīladivākaraṃ; G2 Y11 Y12 Y14 Y31 Y32 sadā (for kadā), Y1 Y2 Y21 mahaḥ

43 a N1 N21 pratiravatu (one syllable short for prakṛtir avatu), Y2 Y21 prakṛtiḥ khalu (also one syllable short); G1 N1 N21 Y3 Y11 Y12 Y14 Y21 Y31 Y32 vo (for no); C51(t) DG1 DG2 D12 D21 M24 viśāla° (for vilāsa°), G1 G11 T71 °lakṣmyā (for °lakṣmyāḥ), D64 °lakṣmāḥ, K1 °lakṣyāḥ Y12 °lakṣmīḥ
b M1 °jayaṃ (for °jaḍaṃ), K1 Y31 °jaḍa°; M24 prakṛtā° (for praṇatā°), C21(t) praṇitā°; D64 °pratāpa° (for °parādha°), Y21 °yaśaga°, Y31 °parāga°, Y32 °parādhaṃ, N1 N21 °parādhya°; G2 U1 °vidyām (for °vīthyām), N1 N21

°vītām, Y31 °vikṣaṇeṣu (two syllables extra), Y11 Y12 Y14 Y21 °vīkṣyam, Y32 °vīkṣya, K1 °vidyā

c N1 N21 Y1 Y2 Y11 Y14 Y31 sukṛta° (for sukṛti°), Y21 prakṛti°; M1 °kṛti° (for °kṛta°), DG2 N1 N21 Y11 Y12 omit °kṛta°; N1 omits kiśorabhāve; C21(t) D11 °bhāvaiḥ (for °bhāve), Y1 Y2 Y3 Y11 Y12 Y14 Y21 Y31 Y32 °bhāvaṃ

d Y1 Y2 Y14 sukṛta° (for sukṛti°) C51(c[p reads with text]), C52(c[p reads with text]), D12 D71 G11 P71 T71 °kṛta° (for °manaḥ°), U1 °kṛtaḥ, N1 Y1 Y2 °mataḥ; D12 °pratidhāna° (for °praṇidhāna°), N1 °praṇatidhāna° (one extra syllable), Y3 °prādhaṇidhāna° (one extra syllable); M21 °mātram (for °pātram), Y1 Y2 Y3 °labhyam; Y31 oghaḥ (for ojas), Y11 oja; N1 adds to the end of the line: paraṃ satatam

44 a Y12 Y14 Y32 upahasita° (for apahasita°) Y13 upahasudhāva° (metrically and otherwise incorrect); Y1 Y2 Y13 Y14 Y31 Y32 °mudhā° (for °mada°), Y12 Y21 °sudhā°, D12 N1 N21 omits °mada°, G1 G2 °mudā°, Z9 °vibhā°; G2 °āraveṣair (for °āvalepair), Y13 °āvahalair, Y12 °ātaleyair (incorrect for?)

b Z9 atirucirānanam (for atisumanoharam), C21 (c omits e and g for °su° syllable) C51 C52 D12 D21 D71 G2 G11 H31 N1 N21 U1 ati hi manoharam, Y2 ati hi manohara°, D11 H21 P71 R21 T71 adhikamanoharam, Y12 Y13 Y14 api hi manoharam, Y31 Y32 amaramanohara°, DG1 avīsumanohara° (metrically incorrect), DG2 atisumanohara°, Y1 ms. damaged here, D64 atimanoharam (one syllable short); Y1 Y2 Y31 °sārdra° (for °m ārdra°), DG1 DG2 °māndra°; Z9 °hāsaḥ

c Y12 Y13 Y14 surayuvati°; U1 °āpalehyaṃ (for °āvalehyaṃ), M21 °āvaleśaṃ, K1 °āvalepyāṃ, M24 °āvalehaṃ

d Y12 Y13 Y14 ramayati; DG1 rāmavarodhanaṃ paraṃ saḥ (for dhāma ramāvarodhanaṃ naḥ), DG2 rāmavarodhanaṃ saḥ (omits 2 syllables), Y13 dhāma ramāya rocanaṃ vaham, Y21 dhāma samāvarodham antaḥ; M1 °āparodhanaṃ; N21 °rodhajaṃ naḥ (for °rodhanaṃ naḥ), N21 °rodhaṃ janaḥ (metrically incorrect); Y1 Y2 Y12 Y31 Y32 vaḥ (for naḥ), G2 ms. damaged here

45 a N1 N21 ākuñcita° (for aṅkūrita°), G1 alaṃkṛta°, D12 ākārita°, M1 akrūrata° (incorrect for?); K1 Y14 °dṛśāṃ (for °daśā°), Y12 °dṛśā, T21 °dayā°; Y1 Y2 Y13 °āvaśeṣam (for °āviśeṣair), Y12 Y31 Y32 °āviśeṣam, Y14 viśeṣa-

b Y14 viśrānta° (for aśrānta°), M24 āśrānta°, M21 ākrānta°, D64 aspanda°, D21 aśnānta°, Z9 asānta°; H21(t) H31(t) K1 °harṣam (for °varṣam), D44 °vamam; Y32 °varṣaṇakṣamam (for °varṣam akṣṇām), Y13 °varṣam akṣaṇam (both preceding have one extra syllable), M1 °varṣamṛkṣṇam (incorrect for?), Y12 °varṣī marṣa, DG1 DG2 °varṣam akṣmām (incorrect for?), N1 N21 °varṣalakṣaṇam (one extra syllable)

c D64 H31(t) saṃkrīḍitāṃ

d D64 Y14 dhana° (for dhanya°); D44 D45 UV V1 Y1 Y2 Y12 Y13 Y31 Y32 ghana°

46 (D1 omits line a and line b before °gairika°)

a N1 °rasa° inserted after °paṅka° (metrically incorrect); Y13 °śaṃkara° (for

°saṃkara°), K1 °saṃkaca°; G1 N1 °maho (for °mahā-)

b Y1 Y2 omit °taṭagaṇḍagairika°; G2 Y12 Y13 Y14 Y21 Y31 Y32 °gandha° (for °gaṇḍa°), N1 ms. damaged here; D21 D64 Y21 °dhana° (for °ghana°), Y12 Y13 Y14 °vana°; T21 °vrata° (for °drava°), M24 °druva°, Y12 Y13 Y14 Y21 °druma°; T21 °vibhramitam (for °vidrumitam), U1 °vidṛtam (meter incorrect), M21 °vidramitam (incorrect for?), D71 °vidravitam, Y2 °vikramitam, N1 °citram idam

c G2 ajitaṃ (metrically incorrect for ajita°), D1 omits; N1 °bhuvanā° (metrically incorrect for °bhujā°), D1 °bhajā°; M1 °bhūjāntarantaraṃ (one syllable short for °bhūjāntaraṃ bhajata); DG1 DG2 bhajita (for bhajata), C21(t) bhajati, G11 he vraja°; Y21 bhaja maho (for bhajata hā), D71 bhajimahe; D1 H31 (t[c omitted for bata]) M1 R23 T21 V1 he bata gopavadhū- (for hā bata gopavadhū-), D11 D12 D71 H21 U1 he vrajagopavadhū-, C21(t) C51(t) hā vrajagopavadhū- (C21c and C51c omitted for bata; both give he for hā); C52(t[c gives he gopavadhū-, c for bata omitted]) P71 T71 UV gopavadhūpṛthula-, M21 he gopavadhū- (two syllables short), G11 ms. damaged here, Y12 Y13 (bho corrected to hā) Y14 bho bata ghoṣavadhū-, Y31 bho ghanadhoṣavadhū-, Y32 hāvayutaghoṣastana- (one syllable extra), Y2 gopavadhū- (three syllables short), D44 hā 'rpi bhajata gopavadhū (two extra syllables), K1 hā pitagopavadhū- (incorrect for?)

d K1 °sthaleṣu sṛṇa° (for °sthalīghusṛṇa°), Y13 °sthalīṣu sṛṇa°, G2 °sthalīsusṛṇa° (the three preceding incorrect for?); Y32 omits °mardana°; N1 omits °marda°; D1 G1 M1 °kardam idam

47 a Y14 °nīlam (for °līlam), Y51 °jīvam; G2 agāñgajātair (for apāñgajālair, M1 anañgajālair; Y1 Y2 Y11 Y12 Y14 Y21 Y31 Y32 Y51 Y52 °varṣair (for °jālair)

b G2 N1 R23 U1 āpiñchatī (for āsiñcatī), M24 āsiñjatā°, Y1 Y2 āśiñcatī (incorrect for?); C21(t) DG1 DG2 N1 āvṛta° (for ādṛta°), D1 ādhṛta°; Y2 ādṛgatopaveṣā (incorrect for?); D64 °veṣāṃ (for °veṣā), DG2 °veṇa (incorrect for?)

c D12 M1 M24 R23 V1 Y1 Y2 Y11 Y12 Y14 Y21 Y31 Y32 Y51 Y52 bālā° (for bālyā°), N1 bālyā° corrected to bāla° (metrically incorrect); G11 °kṛtaṃ (for °kṛtir); D1 D21 D64 H21 H31 M1 M24 Y1 Y2 Y11 Y12 Y14 Y21 Y31 Y51 Y52 madhura° (for mṛdula°); M21 Y1 Y2 Y51 Y52 °bimba- (for °bimbā), D1 K1 °bimbaṃ, Y32 °vidyā

d D71 H31(t) M1 M24 T21 °sindhur (for °siddhir; Y1 Y2 Y11 Y12 Y14 vaḥ (for naḥ)

48 a D12 vicaran° (for viraṇan°), M1 virājan°, D1 viralan°; DG1 DG2 K1 N1 UV Y1 bhaje (for vraje); D45 vrajac (for vraje), D1 vrajaś, Y14 vraja-

b Y1 °āmbhojanapāsya° (incorrect for °āmbhojam upāssva); C21(t) D12 G2 M24 upāsma (for upāssva), G1 upāsmi, D64 upāśya, C51(t) D44 M1 T21 U1 Y2 Y11 Y12 Y13 Y14 Y31 upāsya; Y11 śārñgiṇīḥ

c DG1 DG2 surase (for sarase), D1 D44 K1 sarasī, D71 sarasaṃ, Y14 sarasi (metrically incorrect); Y1 Y2 Y13 sarasaḥ (for sarasi), D44 K1 sarasa, D64 sarasī, Y31 na hi kiṃ; D1 D71 H21(t) N1 T71 'śriyaṃ (for 'śritaṃ) Y31 'vṛtaṃ (metrically incorrect) d G2 kalpisa° (metrically and otherwise incorrect for kalahaṃsa°); G1 Y13 sanādinam

49 a Y51 duḥkhadāridryabhājāṃ (for śāradāmbhojanetraṃ); DG1 DG2 G1 G2 N1 N21 R23 °āmbhoruhākṣaṃ (for °āmbhojanetraṃ), Y1 Y2 Y11 Y12 Y14 Y31 Y32 °āmbhoruhābhaṃ, Y52 °āmbhoruhāṇāṃ; N1 N21 nīlarūpena dṛśyam

b no variant readings

c N1 °hara° (for °śara°), N21 °vaśa°; Y21 °tara° (for °para°), D64 °pada°; Y11 omits everything after °para°; D1 G11 U1 °tantraṃ (for °tantra°), C51(t) °tantraḥ, C21(t) °tantrā°; K1 M24 N1 N21 U1 Y31 Y32 °vaktra° (for °netra°)

d Y1 °yuvatir abhidyād; Y14 saṃviṣṭitaṃ (for saṃveṣṭitam); Y1 Y2 Y14 Y31 Y32 vaḥ (for naḥ), Y12 vā

50 a D71 suvyakti°; D44 °kāntibhir asaurabha°; D1 °madhu° (for °bhara°); G2 °saubhara° (for °saurabha°), Y32 °saubhaga°, D44 °saurama°, D21 °saurabhe° (metrically incorrect); D1 N1 Y2 Y14 °gātraṃ (for °gātram), Y21 °mātram

b N1 Y1 Y2 Y14 suvyakta° (for avyakta°), D1 gavyakta° (incorrect for?); Y14 °kiśoraparītabhāvam; N1 N21 °rūpam (for °bhāvam), C21(t) D11 °veṣam, D1 °bhāvaḥ

c D12 gadyānulāpanavidhāv; Y1 Y2 Y14 Y21 Y31 Y32 °ābhipālana° (for °ānu pālana°), N21 °ānudbhāvana°, C21(p) C51(p) C52(p) H21(p) H31(p) P71(p) °ānupāraṇa°; Y1 Y2 Y14 Y21 Y31 Y32 °vidhau viniviṣṭam avyād; C21(t) °vidhān anu°

d D64 ravyāja°; H31(t) °mugdham (for °ramyam); Y21 °vaibhavantaḥ; Y1 Y2 Y31 Y32 vaḥ (for naḥ), Y14 ca

51 a D12 avagatam (for anugatam), G2 anugamam; Y2 Y12 Y13 Y14 Y21(vs. 303), Y32 (marginal p) ramaṇīnām (for amarīṇām); Y31 antarā° (for ambarā°), Y2 Y52 añcalā° Y13 aṅgasaṃ°; D12 D71 M24 °lambanīnāṃ

b Y2 Y12 Y13 Y14 Y21 Y31 Y52 °madhukara°; D12 Y2 Y21(vs. 303) °śrīr (for °śrī); C21(t) D11 Y2 Y12 Y13 Y31 Y32 °nirvāṇa° (for °nirmāṇa°), Y21 (vs. 303) °nivāsi° (metrically incorrect(; G1 °sīma (for °sīmnām), DG1 DG2 D11 M21 N1 N21 Y2 Y31 Y32 °sīmnā, Y1 Y21(vs. 303) °nimnā (incorrect for?)

c D71 U1 °vilāsā° (for °vilāsa°), M21 °vilāse; C21(t) D1 D12 D44 D64 K1 M1 N1 U1 Y13 Y14 Y21(vs. 331) °vyāvṛta° (for °vyāpṛta°), M24 °vyāhata°, Y21 (vs. 303) °vyāhṛta°, Y32 °vyākṛta°; H21(te) H31(e) M1 T21 °āpāṅgalīlām

d Y12 °kusumāraṃ; M24 divya° (for deva°), C21(t) DG1 DG2 D1 D12 D71 H31(t) K1 M1 T21 T71 U1 Y2 Y12 Y13 Y21(vs. 331) Y32 daiva°; Y21(vs. 303) °kiśorikaṃ namaḥ (one extra syllable); Y2 Y12 Y13 Y14 Y21 (vs. 331) Y52 vaḥ (for naḥ); K1 saḥ

52 a U1 āpādamūlāvayava°

b DG1 āpīyamāno (for āpīyamānā), G1 āpīyamānaṃ, D12 āpīyamānāṃ; D21 yamanāṃ (for yamināṃ), Y2 yam imāṃ Y14 sunobhiḥ

c DG2 Y2 Y12 Y21 Y31 Y32 Y51 Y52 gopīstana° (for gopījana°), Y14 gopīrasa°; Y14 Y21 °jñāta°; DG1 DG2 'vataṃso (for 'vatān no), Y2 'vṛtād vā, K1 'vatāṅgo, Y21 'vatāho (incorrect for?), C21 C51 C52 D11 D12 D44 D64 G11

H21 H31 M1 M24 P71 Q71 R23 T21 T71 UV Y12 Y31 Y32 Y52 vo (for no), D1 yo, Y14 vā

d K1 gogopagopālakumāra°; Y2 Y12 Y14 Y21 Y31 Y32 Y51 Y52 °kiśoramūrtiḥ

53 a DG1 D1 N1 N21 Y1 Y2 Y13 dṛṣṭyā (for diṣṭyā), DG2 Y21 dṛṣṭvā, Y14 vṛṣṭyā, Y31 Y32 iṣṭaṃ; Y1 Y2 vṛndāvane tu pramada° (three extra syllables for vṛndāvana°); D64 °mṛgadaśāṃ; Y1 Y2 Y21 °prayogāṅganānāṃ (for °prayogākulānāṃ), Y12 °prayogāt kulānāṃ, M24 °prayogākalānāṃ

b Y1 Y2 Y12 Y14 Y21 pratyāpannaṃ (for pratyāsannaṃ), Y13 pratyānannaṃ corrected to pratyāsannaṃ; Y14 °taraṃgaḥ

c G1 G2 N1 U1 °śyāmakaṃ (for °śyāmalaṃ), M1 °śyāmagaṃ; T21 kāmadhāmā (for dhāmakāmān), D71 Y21 kāmadhāmān, D1 dhāmakarmā

d N21 puṣṇāyāṃ (for puṣṇīyān), U1 puṣṇeyān (both preceding are incorrect forms); C21 C51 C52 D11 D44 D64 D71 G11 H21 H31 M1 M24 Q71 R23 T21 T71 Y1 Y2 Y12 Y14 vaḥ (for naḥ), Y13 vaḥ corrected to naḥ, D1 D12 yaḥ; D1 Y1 °viśeṣām (for °viśeṣam), T21 Y12 Y21 °viśeṣaḥ

54 a N1 N21 śubha° (for guha°), D44 giri°, Y13 guru°; D44 °śikhendra°

b Y1 Y2 Y12 Y13 Y14 Y21 Y31 Y32 Y51 Y52 maṇi° (for sura°), Y2 °kandara° (for °gairika°)

c Y1 Y2 Y31 Y32 Y51 Y52 vraja° (for sura°), Y13 sura° corrected to vraja°; K1 Y2 °sūnu° (for °sūna°), D12 Y14 °stana°, N1 N21 °puṣpa°; Y51 °prasūna- (one syllable short for °sūnavarṣa-)

d G1 °kuṇḍalaḥ (for °kuntalaḥ), G2 kundalaḥ (incorrect for?), Y12 Y14 Y21 °kuntala° (for °kuntalaḥ), Y13 °kuntala° corrected to °kuntalaḥ, K1 °kuntalaṃ

55 a G1 °mṛdu° (for °śuci°), DG1 DG2 Y12 Y14 °mita°, G2 N1 N21 Y1 Y2 Y51 Y52 °mada°, Y31 °sita°; Y21 °smitamita° (for °śucismita°); N21 °smitamaṇḍanaṃ

b Y21 añjana° (for aṅgaja°); DG1 DG2 D1 D64 G1 G2 H31(t) N1 N21 R23 T21 Y1 Y2 Y12 Y14 Y21 Y31 Y32 Y51 Y52 °valgitam (for °vellitam)

c Y2 vijayatād; U1 °mugdha° (for °bāla°), Y32 °pāla°; C21(c) D1 D21 D64 H21(c) H31(c) Q71 °stana- (for °jana-), C21(t) °dvaya-, D44 N1 omit these two syllables, N21 °dṛḍhaṃ

d C21(c) D1 D21 D64 H21(c) H31(c) Q71 dvaya° (for stana°), K1 sthana°, D12 stanas; DG1 DG2 G1 N1 N21 °taṭe° (for °taṭī°, D1 °taṭaṃ; M1 °vipurannayanaṃ (for °viluṭhannayanaṃ), DG1 °viluvannayanaṃ (incorrect for?); G2 Y14 vibho

56 a DG2 N1 N21 °vilasaṃ; D1 manda° (for mugdha°), M24 dugdha°, T21 omits two syllables; N21 °smera° (for °snigdha°), D45 °snigdhaṃ, C51(t) C52(t) K1 omits these two syllables; D1 U1 Y32 °smitavraja°; Y51 °sundarīgaṇa- (two extra syllables for °sundarī-), M1 omits °sundarī-

b Y51 prabalamadanasnigdhaṃ ramyaṃ valad vadanāmbujam (entire line); M24 vadana° (for madana°), Y13 illegible, M1 omits; DG1 DG2 kadane; K1 °klinnaṃ (for °svinnaṃ), D12 Y2 Y13 (entered in margin as correction or p)

°snigdhaṃ; Y31 °khinnaṃ; Y2 dhanvaṃ; DG1 DG2 D12 M21 R23 Y2 Y11 Y14 Y31 vahad (for mahad), N1 N21 Y13 Y32 vahan

c M24 karuṇataruṇa° (for taruṇam aruṇa°), Y11 Y14 taruṇa° (three syllables short), Y13 taruṇa° corrected to taruṇam aruṇa°; DG1 DG2 D44 G1 G2 N1 R23 U1 Y2 Y13 Y14 Y32 °kṛtsna° (for °kārtsnya°), D12 H31(t) °kārtsnyaṃ, Y52 °pūra°, N21 °kāla°, Y21 Y31 °kṛṣṇa°, Y11 °kṛśna° (incorrect for?) DG1 DG2 M21 N1 N21 Y2 Y11 Y13 Y14 Y21 Y31 Y32 Y51 °prati° (for °smita°)

d M21 R23 vijayi (for vijaya°), Y11 Y14 viyati, Y21 jayatī°, Y31 vijayati (one extra syllable), Y32 vijati°, Y2 vijayate (one extra syllable); Y51 vijayaśrīr eṣā preyasaḥ samadaṃ mahaḥ; M21 °śreṇīhariṇī° (for °śreṇīm eṇī°), Y14 Y21 Y31 Y32 °śreṇīr eṇī°, Y2 °śreṇīṃ raṇī°, Y11 °śreṇī raṇī°, Y13 °striṣtrereṇī° (incorrect for?); eṇīdṛśā M1 M24 madanaṃ (for madayan), T21 omits

57 a N21 rādhālola°; U1 °lakṣitamahā°; Y13 °vṛkṣa° (for °vakṣaḥ°), Y2 °kalpa°; K1 M24 °maṇḍalā (for °maṇḍanā), M1 °maṇḍalāṃ, Y32 °maṇḍanaṃ, DG1 Y31 °maṇḍanāj

b Y2 āñkuśās (for °āñkurās), Y21 °āñkuśaḥ Y32 °āñkuras, N21 °āñkura°, N1 °āñkurā°, DG2 °āñkurāṃ; M1 tribhavana°; D11 °bhuvanāsvādīyasas

c Y31 vakṣo 'ntaḥ° (for krīḍānta°), Y32 vakṣojaṃ, U1 krīḍāntaḥ°, N21 omits °prati° D12 °pratisupra°; DG1 DG2 N21 Y2 Y14 °mugdha° (for °dugdha°); DG1 DG2 K1 °nayanā° (for tanayā°), N21 °taralā°; Y14 °āvarodha° (for °āvabodha°), Y21 °āvabodhaḥ; C21(t) D21 D64 H31(t) K1 °kṣaṇā- (for °kṣaṇa-), D11 °kṣaṇās, D12 Y21 kṣaṇas, Y13 Y14 Y32 °kṣaṇaṃ

d C21(t) tāsāṃ (for trāsā°); D12 Y13 Y14 Y32 °dṛśo° (for °dṛḍho°) V1 °gūhanamahā° (for °gūḍhagahanāḥ), G2 °gūhagahanā°, H21(t) H31(t) P71 R23 °gūhagahanāḥ, G51(t) D12 G11 M21 M24 °gūḍhagahanā, C21 C51(c) C52 D11 D44 D45 D64 H21(c) H31(c) P71(p) T21 T71 °gūḍhagahanāḥ (as in text), U1 gūhanaghanā°, C21(p) DG1 DG2 D71 G1 H21(p) °gūhanaghanāḥ, D21 °gūḍhagamanā°, K1 °gūḍhajaghanā°, Y2 °gūḍhanatanuḥ, M1 N21 °gūḍhanayanāḥ, N1 °gūhanayanāḥ, Y13 Y14 Y21 Y31 Y32 °gūhanapunaḥ; C51(t) °striyaḥ

58 a N1 N21 snuta° (for smita°), DG1 DG2 smitaṃ; M1 °stabakitā° (for °snutasudhā°), Y2 Y21 Y32 Y51 °srutarasā°, Y31 °snutarasā°, Y33 °stutarasā°, D11 Y13 Y14 °srutasudhā°, D12 G1 °stutarasā°, DG1 nutā°, sudhā°, DG2 na tu sudhā°, N1 N21 °smita°; Y13 Y14 °karā° (for °dharā°)

b N21 viśā° (one syllable short for viśāla°); N1 °vadanāmbuja° (for °nayanāmbujā), C21(t) N21 Y21 Y32 °nayanāmbuja°, D64 °nayanāmbujai (incorrect for?), G11 ms. damaged here; D11 °vilāsisaṃvāsitāḥ (for °vilāsinīvāsitāḥ), C21(t) °vilāsibhir vāsitā; Y2 Y14 Y21 Y32 Y51 °vāsitā

c Y21 Y31 Y32 vibudha° (for manojña°), Y2 Y14 vidagdha°, Y51 prabuddha°; Y2 Y21 Y31 Y32 Y51 śiśiraveṇunādāmṛtā (for madhuraveṇunādadravā), Y14 madhuraveṇunādāmṛtā

d Y2 Y14 Y21 nayanti (for jayanti), G1 N21 jayantu, Y31 Y32 nayāti, Y51 nayeta; M24 cetasāṃ (for cetasaś), Y51 cetasaḥ, D64 K1 N21 cetasā, DG1 DG2 cetanaś, M1 cetasiś (incorrect for?); Y51 sthiram (for ciram); Y51 upāsitasyā 'kṛtiḥ; C21(t) DG1 DG2 D11 U1 Y2 Y21 upāsanā (for upāsitā), M24 upāsinā; M21 vāsitāḥ (for vāsanāḥ), G2 U1 Y2 Y14 Y21 Y31 Y32 vāsanā

59 a Y2 °śikhaṇḍi°; U1 °āvataṃsaḥ (for °āvataṃsā), D12 Y14 °āvataṃsa, Y11 °āvataṃsaṃ

b D64 Y2 sāsiddhikī; Y11 °samṛddhim

c C21(t) °keśa° (for °leśa°), D64 °kalikā°; D21 D45 D64 H21(t) K1 U1 V1 °parimāṇa°; V1 °bhāgyaḥ (for °bhāgyāt), D45 T21 °bhāgya-, N1 N21 °bhāgyān, DG1 DG2 M25 °bhāgyā, M24 °bhaṅgyā

d D21 °somaparam; U1 pañcabālaḥ

60 a D44 ārāmeṇa (for āyāmena), D71 āyāsena, G1 āyasena (metrically incorrect), C21(t) D11 āmīnāṅga° (incorrect for?); C21(t) Y14 dṛśo; D71 Y2 vilāsatarayor (for viśālatarayor), U1 viśālatanayor; D71 akṣīṇam; M21 U1 ārdasmita- (for ārdrasmita-), Y11 ārdristhitaḥ, Y14 ārdhasthita-, N1 N21 Y32 ārdrasmitaṃ, M24 ārdrasmitaḥ, Y13 ārdrasmite, D64 ārdrasmitā

b D71 G1 N1 T21 Y13 °varṣita° (for °dharṣita°), Y11 °varṣati, Y14 °varṣata°, U1 °darpita°, DG1 DG2 °vardhita°, R23 °ghūrṇita°, N21 °carcita°, M1 omits; DG1 DG2 D71 Y2 Y11 Y13 Y14 Y21 Y31 Y32 cāpalyamātraṃ; Y2 Y11 Y13 Y31 Y32 dṛśām (for śiśoḥ), H31(t) dṛśoḥ, Y21 dṛśaṃ

c Y11 omits all of verse after āyāsā°; Y32 āyāsena pareṇa vividharasikair (one extra syllable); D44 āyāsānuparān (for āyāsān aparān), M1 āśāsān v aparān, D11 āvāsān aparān, DG1 DG2 āsāyān aparān, K1 N1 āyāsān na parān; N21 vilāsa° (for vidhūya); C21(t) āsādyamānaṃ (for āsvādyamānaṃ), Y13 Y21 āvādyamānaṃ, Y2 āvāsyamānaṃ

d N21 unnata° (for unmada°), Y13 mantharaṃ (metrically incorrect); C21(t) N21 °pallavī° (for °vallavī°) Y21 Y31 Y32 °taṭī° (for °bharā°), Y2 Y13 Y14 °bhara°, N1 °mugā° (incorrect for?); C21(t) D11 °bhāraṃ (for °dhāraṃ), K1 °dāraṃ, M1 °dhārāṃ, Y2 Y13 Y14 Y21 Y31 Y32 °ślāghyaṃ; Y2 Y21 Y31 Y32 manojñaṃ (for kiśoraṃ)

61 (D64 omits line a)

a G1 °dhāna° (for °vāra°), N1 °dhāra°; C21(t) C51(t) C52(t) D21 D44 D45 °sadaḥ (for padaṃ), C51(p) C52(p) H31(p) P71(p) V1 °sado, D11 °sadā; D11 G1 K1 R23 T21 vrajāḥ (for vrajaḥ), C21(t) C51(t) C52(t) DG1 DG2 D21 D44 D45 G2 M1 N1 N21 prajāḥ, M1 prajaṃ; D71 K1 sahāyodayāḥ (for sahāyādayaḥ), M1 suyogadayaḥ, N21 sahasrādayaḥ, M24 sahāyāmaya

b DG1 D12 skandālambini; N1 N21 skandhālambitavatsadāmanidhanāgopāṅganā°; C21(t) DG2 G1 G2 K1 M1 Y14 Y21 °dhāmni; M1 gaṇikā (for dhanadā), G2 dhanadhā, Y14 Y21 Y32 dhanadhī, Y31 dhanadhīr, Y2 dhanuṣī, D71 M24 dhanatā; D12 D64 D71 G11 H21(t) H31(t) K1 M1 M21 M24 U1 Y2 Y14 Y21 Y32 gopāṅganā° (for gopāṅganāḥ); M1 °pāṅganā (for svāṅganāḥ), M24 °svāṅganā, Y14 °svāṅgatāḥ, H31(t) °svāṅganām

c M24 N21 U1 śṛṅgāraṃ (for śṛṅgārā), C21(t) D71 Y2 Y14 Y31 Y32 śṛṅgāro, Y21 śṛṅgāre; K1 T21 °gairikāḥ, M1 kairikā (incorrect for?); N21 śirasi vai (for śiva śiva); U1 Y32 śrīmanta°; D45 D71 V1 ca (for vā)

d M24 °grāhatayā (for °grāhikayā), M1 T21 °grāhitayā; N21 kathā (for tathā);

N1 N21 hi (for 'pi); C21(t) C51(e) D11 D21 D64 G11 H21(te) H31(te) P71(te) T71 U1 V1 tad (for tam); C21 C51(c) C52(c) D11 D21 H21 H31(c) M1 N1 N21 P71 T71 idaṃ; T21 imāḥ; D64 G1 G2 M1 M24 N1 N21 R23(p) Y2 Y21 Y31 Y32 trilokīśvaram

62 (Y2 has a line order a c d plus a line at the end no found elsewhere in the Bilvamaṇgala anthologies. Line b is omitted. The evidence of Y1 is lost. Y3 reads with the critical text.)

a T71 °barha°; K1 M1 N1 U1 Y2 Y32 °śikhaṇḍi°; N1 U1 °khaṇḍana° (for °maṇḍana°), Y32 °maṇḍala°; M1 °yuje (for °juṣe), D64 °juṣa°; N21 rāma° (for śyāma°); D1 Y2 Y21 Y31 °ābhirāmānviṣe (for °ābhirāmatviṣe), D12 D64 °ābhirāmātviṣe), G1 °ābhirāmatyuṣe

b Y3 Y21 Y31 Y32 °āvasakta°; G1 °lasat° (for °saraḥ°), C51(t) Y14 °sara°, N1 N21 °dhara°, C52(t) °rasaḥ, Y12 °rasaṃ, Y3 Y21 Y31 Y32 Y51 °rasa°

c C21(te) D1 D11 D21 K1 R23 (p reads with text) U1 Y2 Y14 °kṛṣṇa° (for °kṛṣṭa°); Y2 Y12 Y21 Y31 Y32 °varga° (for °dharma°), Y14 °garva°, Y32 °varṇa°, Y51 °rañga°, Y2 °varya°; G2 °vapuṣe (for °manase), D12 °mahase, C21(t) °vaṃsaine (incorrect for?; Y31 Y32 krīḍāmṛta'; D1 D12 Y11 Y14 Y31 °śrotase (for °srotase), Y21 °śrotasi, Y2 °srotasi

d Y2 Y3 no (for na); Y2 Y3 Y12 Y14 Y21 gandha° (for hanta), Y31 Y32 gopa°, Y51 sarva°, D44 hanti; Y51 °rahase (for mahase), Y21 mahati (metrically incorrect), N1 manasā, D1 G1 K1 M1 T21 manase; Y3 Y12 Y14 Y21 Y31 Y32 Y51 gopīstana°; D11 Y12 °śreyase (for °preyase), Y21 °preyasi, G1 ms. damaged here (Y2 line d: śrīrāme hṛdi vā bibharti vadane gopālanāmāśrite)

63 a D64 āpāṭalāṃ; Y2 āpāṭalāya dharadhīra°; D1 adhīram udīkṣamāṇam; M1 Y31 Y32 °viśālanetram

b G1 ālola° (for āmoda°), Y14 ānanda°

c G2 āviśramā° (for āviḥsmitā°), C21(t) DG1 DG2 D64 H21(t) K1 M1 M24 N2 Y21 āvismṛta°, M21 Y14 āviḥsmṛta°, all mss. except preceding and C21(c) C51(c) C52(c) D45 G1 H21(c) H31(c) P71 Q71 R23 āvismita°; Y31 °āmṛta-manaḥ° (for °āmṛtam anu°), M1 omits °m anu°; T71 anusmita°

d Y2 Y11 Y14 Y21 Y31 Y32 āmugdham ānanam; K1 ahā; U1 madhurāṃ; DG2 D12 D21 K1 M1 U1 Y11 Y14 murāre

64 a Z9 kṛṣṇe prajāgṛhi cetaś

b P71 T71 na cirāya kṛtārthatā bhavataḥ; C21(c) C51(c) C52(c) H21(c) H31(c) cirāya kṛtārthatā bhavataḥ (metrically incorrect); G2 citāya; N21 calitārthatā; Y2 Y14 Y21 °ārthatāṃ dṛśau vahatām (for °ārthatā bhavataḥ), Y32 °ārthitaṃ dṛśau vahatām, Y31 °ārthatāṃ yaśo vahatām (preceding three metrically correct)

c M21 anubhūyad idam amitaṃ; Z9 anubhūyatāṃ tvaye 'daṃ; Y2 anubhūya vā; N21 imam idaṃ

d N1 N21 Y32 pūrvanirvāṇam (for pūrṇanirvāṇam), D71 puṇyanirvāṇam

65 a U1 karuṇodaye (for karuṇārdrayoḥ), Z9 kamalābhayoḥ

b N1 N21 tava hare (for kacabhare), G2 Y2 kucabhare; C51(t) C52(t) D12 D44

G2 R23 T21 Y2 vipulaṃ bahulaṃ (for bahulaṃ vipulaṃ), M1 bahalaṃ vipulaṃ bahalaṃ (three extra syllables), M1 M24 bahalaṃ vipulaṃ; D1 kabalaṃ vipulaṃ (incorrect for?), Y2 vimalaṃ bahulaṃ, Y51 bahulaṃ vimalaṃ, Z9 vipulaṃ bahalaṃ

c N21 vañjulam añjuna° (for mañjulam añjana°), DG2 mañjalam añjuna°, D1 mañjulam añjuna° (the three preceding incorrect for?); N21 °mecakaṃ (for °mecake), Y51 °mecaka

d D21 vapuṣi; D44 bālyam; N21 ahaṃ (for aho), M1 M24 abhūn

66 a D21 bālā° (for mālā°), M24 sālā°; Y2 °kuntalatarāṃ sunau bhūṣitāṃ; Y12 Y13 Y14 Y21 °oṣitāṃ (for °okṣitāṃ), N21 °ojjvalāṃ, N1 °otthitāṃ

b Y12 śaileyāṃ gurukḷpta° (for śaileyadravakḷpta°), Y21 śaileyāgarutkḷpta°, Y14 śaileyāgarullipta°, U1 śaileyādivakḷpta°; Y31 Y32 °pratilabdha° (for °dravakḷpta°), Y2 °pratibaddha°, N1 N21 °dravatapta°; C21(t) N1 °citralatikāṃ; N1 N21 śyāmaṃ (for śaśvan°); C21(t) D64 °hārinī

c Y31 °varā° (for °ravā°), C51(t) N1 °rasā°; D21 T21 °mayī (for °mayīṃ), D12 M1 °mayaṃ

d D64 bālaṃ (for bālāṃ); DG1 DG2 D21 G1 Y2 °vapuṣiṃ (for °vapuṣaṃ), C21(t) K1 M1 Y32 °vapuṣāṃ

67 (M21 omits line b)

a Y2 Y11 gurum ṛju° (for guru mṛdu°), Y13 gurum ṛju° corrected to guru mṛdu°; N21 rūpaṃ (for gūḍhaṃ), K1 gūḍhe

b DG1 DG2 Y32 valitam (for nalinam), Y11 Y14 Y31 valinam, Y21 balinam; DG1 DG2 G1 M1 bāhau dīrghaṃ (for vīraṃ bāhvor), M24 bāhau dīrgham, V1 dīghaṃ bāhvor, H21(t[c omitted]) vīryaṃ bāhvor, K1 T21 bāhvo dīrghaṃ, R23 bāhau vīraṃ, G2 Y2 Y11 Y14 Y32 vīraṃ bāhau, N1 N21 vīryaṃ bāhau; M1 vidāram (for viśālam), M24 udāram; M1 N21 udara° (metrically incorrect for uraḥ°); DG1 DG2 G1 G2 M1 M24 Y11 Y14 °taṭe (for °sthale)

c U1 madhuramadhuraṃ (for madhuram adhare), D1 D44 K1 Y11 Y14 Y21 madhuramadhure; G11 vaktre mugdhaṃ; Y11 Y14 Y21 ramyaṃ (for mugdhaṃ); D12 cakre (for vaktre); G2 viśāli (for vilāsi), H31(t) vilāsa°, R23(p) visāri, D12 D64 viśālaṃ (metrically incorrect), N1 vilola°, all mss. except preceding and C21(t) V1 Y2 Y11 Y14 Y21 Y31 Y32 viśāla°

d K1 Y21 bahu is omitted; M24 kuca° (for kaca°); C51(t) D21 °bharaṃ; G2 M24 T21 dhanyaṃ (for vanyaṃ), G11 veṣaṃ (for veṣe), Y11 veṣa (metrically incorrect); M24 manojñam aho), M1 manojñamahaṃ; U1 ahā (for aho), Y2 ado

68 a DG2 dihānaṃ dihānaṃ; D12 M1 M24 N1 N21 T21 T71 U1 Y2 Y14 Y21 na (for nu), C21(t) V1 su°, Y32 Y33 ca, Y31 ga° (incorrect for?), K1 ni°, D1 ta (incorrect for?); D71 R23 maugdhyaṃ na jāne; D21 jñanena (for jānena), Y31 Y32 Y33 gānena, N21 vaktreṇa, H31(t) hānena, DG1 DG2 jāne sa; D12 H31(t) mugdhaṃ

b H21(t) mihānaṃ mihānaṃ; Y2 sudānaṃ (for the first duhānaṃ); G1 sudhāmardanaṃ (for duhānaṃ sudhāṃ), DG1 DG2 sudhāṃ durdinaṃ, G1 Y2 Y14 Y21 Y31 Y32 sudhādurdinaṃ, M1 sudhā durdiśaṃ

c G1 M1 dihānaṃ vihānaṃ (for lihānaṃ lihānaṃ), DG1 DG2 R23 dihānaṃ

dihānaṃ, U1 vihānaṃ vihānaṃ, Y21 Y31 Y32 dihānaṃ lihānaṃ, Y13 lihānaṃ corrected to dihānaṃ lihānaṃ; C21(t) D64 R23 V1 Y13 Y14 Y21 su° (for nu), G1 G2 N1 N21 na, DG1 DG2 M1 ca, D12 Y2 Y31 Y32 tu; D45 divyair (for dīrghair)

d DG1 DG2 G2 maho (for mahā°); N21 °sarvārthadaṃ manmahe manmaho naḥ (three extra syllables and otherwise incorrect); N1 °sarvārtham (for °sarvasvam), T21 °parasvam (metrically incorrect) M1 °sarvasvamate mate me (metrically incorrect); DG1 DG2 D45 G1 G2 H31(t) K1 V1 Y2 Y14 Y31 Y32 etan; U1 namas te (for namet tam), K1 M21 name tat, D45 H31(t) T71 name tam, V1 namastāt (incorrect for?), DG1 DG2 Y2 Y14 Y21 Y32 mame 'ti, N1 mamete (incorrect for?), D44 namet (one syllable short), G2 mamai 'tat, T21 tvam eti

69 (C51[t] line order: c b c d)

a Y14 lasadbarhaiḥ; D64 °pīḍālalita°; N1 vihita° (for the first lalita°), T21 rasita°; U1 °phalita° (for the second °lalita°), DG1 DG2 °madhura°, K1 T21 °mṛdula°, D1 °vadanaṃ, D64 °lalitā°, D45 °sadṛśaṃ, Y11 °vacanā°, N1 N21 °lulita°, Y2 Y21 Y31 Y32 °viśada°, Y14 omits these three syllables; D1 °madhuraṃ (for °vadanaṃ)

b DG2 Y2 Y11 Y21 Y31 Y32 °āpāṅgapraṇata°; D64 praṇati°; D1 U1 °janitā° (for °janatā°), K1 °jagatā°, D12 °jagatāṃ; Y11 °nirmiti° (for °nirvṛti°), G2 K1 °nirvṛta°

c C21(t first occurrence of line c) °madhurimāsmeravadanaṃ; D45 V1 °āmoda° (for °ābhoga°), U1 °caritaṃ (for °bharitaṃ), Y11 °duritaṃ, Y14 Y21 °haritaṃ, Y2 °rahitaṃ

d D21 K1 padaṃ; C21(t) DG1 DG2 D12 D71 M21 N1 N21 daivaṃ; D64 G1 K1 N1 N21 Y2 Y11 Y14 Y31 parimalita°; DG1 DG2 °kaiśorika°; Y11 Y32 °kaiśorasarasam; Y14 °kaiśorasadṛśam

70 (Y11 omits everything after ivā 'nane°)

a G2 harasya (for sārasya°), D1 sarasya; N21 °sāmastyam (for °sāmagryam), N1 omits, U1 °sāmagram, D12 °sāmagrim; U1 ivā 'sanena

b no variant readings

c Y2 tāruṇyatāruṇyam (for kāruṇyatāruṇyam), all mss. except preceding and DG1 DG2 D71 G1 G2 H31(t) M1 M24 N1 N21 R23 V1 Y31 Y32 tāruṇyakāruṇyam; V1 'kṣitena (for 'kṣaṇena), C21(t) 'kṣitena corrected to 'kṣaṇena

d M1 imaṃ (for idaṃ), C51(t) C52(t) iva (metrically incorrect)

71 a Y21 yaṃ ya (for yatra); Y2 Y21 vādapravāde ca (for vā tatra vā deva), N1 N21 kutrā 'pi nā 'vāso, G1 tatra vayaṃ deva

b Y21 yatra (for yadi); C21(t) DG1 DG2 M1 Y2 Y32 viśvasitas

c U1 nirvābhināni kiṃ punaḥ (incorrect for?); G11 H31(t) avi° (for api); D71 T71 kurvāṇa- (for kiṃ punaḥ), N1 kurvāṇo, N21 kurvāṇe; DG1 DG2 durvāra-

d N1 N21 garhitaiḥ kiṃ phalais tu naḥ; DG1 murvācānānīkaṃ (incorrect for?); DG2 murkhācānāni kiṃ (incorrect for?)

72 (C 21[t] line order: a d b c)

a Y31 kṣmāgāndha° (for rāgāndha°), G11 rāgāndhi; N1 °paṇḍitābhyāṃ (for °vanditābhyāṃ), N21 °maṇḍitābhyāṃ), Y2 Y12 Y14 Y21 Y31 Y32 Y33 °cumbitābhyāṃ

b C51(t) D12 D21 Y2 Y12 yogendra° (for yogīndra°), G1 gobhīndra° (incorrect for?); U1 °bhṛṅgair anuseditābhyām (incorrect for?); D71 T21 Y14 Y31 Y32 Y33 °bhogīndra° (for °bhṛṅgendra°), D64 Y11 °bhogendra°, K1 °bhṛṅgīndra°, D1 °mṛgīndra°, Y2 °mṛgendra°, R23 °vṛndena, D11 °vṛndaika°

c Y2 Y12 Y14 Y21 °komalābhyāṃ

d Y2 Y12 Y14 Y21 Y32 Y33 ābhyāṃ (for svāmin); M1 M24 sadābhyām (for padābhyām), D1 kayābhyām; D1 U1 mayam (for ayam); Y14 Y21 me (for te), Y2 sma

73 a C21(g) C51(g) C52(g) D21 G1 G11 H21(t[c damaged here]) H31 P71 T71 U1 ardhā° (for arthā°); T21 Y1 Y2 Y14 Y21 Y31 Y32 ārdrā°; G1 °ānurohaṃ (for °ānulāpān), C52(te) D1 Y21 °ānupālān, U1 °ānulāpā°; DG1 DG2 °ānuloman, T71 °ānukūlān, D64 omits, Y1 °ānulepān, Y31 °ānvilāsān, Y14 °ānulepān, Y2 °ānulepā°, Y21 °ānuvādān

b no variant readings

c DG1 DG2 ārdrāñcalena (for ārdrāśayena), D44 Y14 ārdrāśrayena

d N1 N21 saṃbodhayantaṃ (for saṃbhāvayantaṃ), D1 saṃbhāṣayantaṃ, Y14 saṃbhāvayantī, M21 saṃbhāvitaṃ taṃ; D44 taruṇīṃ; G1 bhajemaḥ (for gṛṇīmaḥ), N1 N21 T21 Y14 gṛhīmaḥ M24 gṛṇīma

74 a YY10 vacasi (for manasi), U1 manase DG2 manasaṃ nidhattāṃ

b Y1 Y2 Y12 Y14 Y31 Y32 YY10 °smitabharita° (for °mukhā), Y21 °smita° (metrically incorrect), H31(t) °mukhān, N21 °mukha°, D1 °mukhāṃ; D1 D12 manmathā° (for mantharā°), M24 mandhurā°; N1 manthana°, D64 matara° (metrically incorrect), G2 manthā° (metrically incorrect), T21 manmathara° (metrically incorrect), H21(t) ms. damaged here; C51(t) C52(t) D1 D21 G2 H31(t) M1 M21 N1 N21 P71 U1 Y1 Y2 Y12 Y14 Y31 Y32 YY10 °āpāṅgāḥ (for °āpāṅgā), G1 K1 °āpāṅgī, DG1 DG2 °āpāṅgi, D71 G11 T71 °āpāṅgām, T21 °āsāṅgī, D44 °āgī (metrically incorrect); H21(t) ms. damaged N21 °talaka° (metrically incorrect for °kalitala°)

c G1 °līna° (for °lalita°), Y1 Y2 °lalana°; G2 °lalitam avyāt; Y21 °śyāmi (for °vaṃśā), C21(t) °vaṃśa, Y32 °vaṃśī

d U1 ko 'pi; Y1 Y2 Y12 Y14 kṛśodarīkṛpā° (for kiśorā kṛpā°), M21 kiśorākṛtir, M24 kiśorākṛtil (incorrect for?), V1 kiśorākṛtā C21(t) D45 D64 U1 kiśorākṛtiḥ kṛpā°, G11 kiśorakatibā° (metrically incorrect), C52(t) D11 P71 Y31 Y32 YY10 kiśorī kṛpā°, C51(t) kiśorāṃ kṛpā°, D71 K1 Y21 kiśorakṛpā° (metrically incorrect), D1 kiśorakṛtiḥ (metrically incorrect), DG1 kiśorikṛpā° (metrically incorrect), DG2 kiśorakṛpā° (metrically incorrect), H21(t) ms. damaged here; D71 °mūrtiḥ (for °laharī)

75 a M1 M24 rakṣas tu naḥ; Y1 Y14 Y32 vaḥ (for naḥ), Y31 omits; Y14 śikṣatu (for śikṣita°), Y1 Y2 śikṣi tu); H31(t) °pāśa° (for °pāśu°), Y14 pāśa°; H31(t) °bālyaṃ (for °pālyā), K1 °bālyāḥ, M1 °bālyā

b D11 D71 R23 V1 Y2 Y14 Y21 Y31 Y32 Y52 bālyā° (for bālā°); DG1 DG2 M1

Y2 °ādhṛtā° (for °āvṛtā°), M24 °ābhṛtā°, G1 N1 R23 Y31 °ādṛtā°, D71 °āmṛtā°, K1 °āvatā°, D1 °ākṛtā°, Y1 °ādvanā°, Y21 °ādbhutā°, Y14 °ādhutā°, Y32 °ātkṛtā°, Y52 °ārdratā°; C21(t) D1 G11 K1 Y1 Y2 Y14 barha°; C51(t) H31(t) M1 Y1 Y2 Y14 °āvataṃsā (for °āvataṃsāḥ), G11 °āvataṃsām, D12 K1 °āvataṃsaḥ, Y21 °āvasānam

c D1 Y21 prāṇā° (for prāṇa°), D12 prāyā°, Y1 prāṇaḥ, Y2 Y14 Y31 Y32 Y52 prāṇāḥ; V1 °priyāḥ (for priya°), Y1 °priyaḥ Y14 Y21 Y31 Y52 °śriyaḥ, Y32 °śriye, H31(t) ms. damaged here M1 omits; Y31 prasruta°; C21(p) C51(p) C52(p) H21(p) H31(p) P71(p) °gītaśītāḥ (for °veṇugītāḥ)

d N21 °nādā (for gītāḥ), C51(t) D1 D12 G11 H31(t) Y1 Y2 Y14 Y21 °gītā, M24 °hītāḥ (metrically incorrect), M1 °gīta; U1 sītā° (for śītā°), Y52 nītā°, N21 etā°, D44 śitā°, G2 sphītā°, M1 hitā°, M24 omits; D21 R23 °dṛśaḥ (for °dṛśoḥ), Y52 °ntarā, N1 N21 °dṛśāḥ; DG1 DG2 G1 Y1 Y2 Y14 Y31 Y32 śilita° (for śītala°), D71 śevita° (incorrect for?), Y51 sundara°; D12 K1 M1 Y1 Y2 Y21 °gopakanyā (for °gopakanyāḥ), Y14 °gopakaṃ yāḥ

76 a U1 smitaṃ cakitā° (for smitastabakitā°) D64 smitaṃ stabakitā°, N1 smitasastabakitā° (metrically incorrect); D21 °āghaṭaṃ (for °ādharaṃ), Y21(vs 301) °ānanaṃ; N21 madhura° (for śiśira°), Y21 śikhara°; D1 °veṇunādadravaṃ

b Y21 mahat (for muhus), D12 mukus; G1 tarali° (for tarala°), Y32 taruṇa°; Y1 Y14 Y31 Y32 Y51 °locanā° (for °locanaṃ); Y14 °muda° (for mada°), Y32 °manda°, T21 mayi; N21 madakatakamālāṅkuram (metrically incorrect); D45 U1 °vṛtam (for °kulam), N1 ms. damaged here, Y14 °kulām

c DG1 DG2 D12 D71 G1 G2 G11 H31(t) M24 N1 N21 P71(t) R23 T21 Y1 Y2 Y14 urastaṭa°; U1 °vinīlayā (for °vilīnayā), N21 Y1 Y2 Y14 Y21 Y31 Y32 Y52 °nilīnayā, C21(t) °vihīnayā, H31(t) °phalī nayā (incorrect for?)

d DG1 DG2 D44 G2 M1 M24 N21 T21 bhuvastaṭam (for bhuvastalam), G11 H21(t) H31 M21 P71 T71 U1 bhuvaḥsthalam, C21(t) D11 D12 K1 Y21 bhuvasthalam, C52(t) Y32 bhuvaḥstalam (incorrect for?); K1 upāsmahe (for upāgataṃ); D1 D71 °devataṃ; Y1 Y14 Y21 Y31 Y32 Y52 vaḥ (for naḥ)

77 Y14 Y21 line order: a d b c)

a G2 caraṇāmbujaṃ (for nayanāmbuje), Y21 nayanāntake; G1 M1 bhajita° (for bhajata), Y21 bhajana°, Y31 bhajatu; G1 sāmasakhaṃ (for kāmadughaṃ), T71 kāmaṃ dughaṃ, K1 kāmarūpyaṃ, D12 kāmadugdhaṃ Y2 Y14 Y21 kāmaduhaṃ

b D12 °āmbujaiḥ; C21(t) D44 M21 N1 N21 T71 kam api; DG2 kāruṇam (metrically incorrect)

c G2 vadanāmbuje (for caraṇāmbuje), DG1 DG2 nayanāmbuje; Y51 inserts kim api after °āmbuje (metrically incorrect); G1 U1 kuladhanaṃ munīnāṃ (for munikulaikadhanaṃ), C21(c) DG1 DG2 D12 G2 M1 M24 N1 N21 T21 Y1 Y2 Y14 Y21 Y31 Y32 Y51 Y52 kuladhanaṃ yamināṃ, T71 kuladharaṃ yamināṃ, K1 kuladhanaikarasaṃ, H21(c) damaged here, D44 munikulaiḥ kadanaṃ

d G2 nayanāmbuje; G1 °vibhramam (metrically incorrect for °vibhavam)

78 a R23 nirvāpaṇaṃ (for nirvāsanaṃ), Y1 nirvāsaṃ (one syllable short), DG2 nirvāsa° (one syllable short); D1 sarva° (for hanta)

b M21 °sāmrājyam atīvaramyam; N1 N21 'vakīrṇam
c no variant readings
d C21 C51(c) C52(c) DG1 DG2 D1 D11 D64 G1 G2 H21 prajānām (for vrajānām); M1 N1 dvijānām; M21 api (for adhi°); Y3 Y14 vaḥ (for naḥ)

79 a D71 gopīnām atiramaṇīyagīta°; D1 °mada° (for °mata°), D12 D21 °matta° (metrically incorrect); DG1 DG2 N1 N21 T21 U1 °gopa° (for °gīta°), Y3 Y52 °m aṅga°, Y51 °saṅga°, D44 Y14 Y21 Y34 omit; H31(t) °veṇu° (for °veṣa°), M21 M24 °jāta°; Y3 Y51 °gīta°, Y52 °śīta°, Y31 Y32 °harṣa°, Y1 Y2 Y11 Y12 Y14 Y21 °varṣa°; ;Y3 Y31 Y32 Y52 °varṣād (for °harṣād), G1 ms. damaged here
b H31(t) āpīta°; Y1 Y2 Y3 Y51 Y52 °nirbharena gūḍham
c Y51 atula° (for avatu), Y1 Y2 janair (for rasair), N21 rathair; Y11 Y12 upāsyamāna-
d Y11 Y12 Y21 °varaṃ (for °caraṃ); G11 rasaṃ (for paraṃ), C21(t) D11 D71 N1 N21 U1 ciraṃ, Y51 omits; Y1 Y3 vaḥ (for naḥ), M1 omits

80 (D12 D71 G11 H21 H31 P71 T71 line order: a b d c)
a M1 °ātmanā- (for °āṅganā-), D64 °āṅganāṃ (one extra syllable)
b N1 °nija° (for °mṛdu°); DG1 DG2 K1 Y3 Y11 Y12 Y14 Y21 Y31 Y32 °nisvanam (for nisvanaiḥ), Y1 Y2 °niḥsvanam, D45 G1 G11 H21 H31 M21 P71 U1 U1 °niḥsvanaiḥ
c M21 aparaṃ (for api naḥ); Y1 Y2 Y3 vaḥ (for naḥ); C21 C51 C52 D1 D11 D12 D21 D64 D71 G11 H21 H31 P71 T21 T71 U1 kṛpāspadaṃ
d Y11 Y12 Y14 Y21 Y31 Y32 °kalabhodvahaṃ (for °kalahodvahaṃ), K1 °kalapodvahaṃ, M24 °kalagodvahaṃ, Y2 Y3 °kalahodvayaṃ; K1 mahataḥ (one extra syllable for mahaḥ)

81 a Y11 Y14 pāṇī° (for eṇī°); Y51 eṇaśyāma° (for eṇīśāba°); T21 °śābaralocanā°; M24 °locanārasalasa°; Y3 asasa° (for alasa°); DG1 D11 G1 G2 T71 Y2 °śreṇībhara° (for °śroṇībhara°), DG2 omits, U1 °śroṇībharā° Y12 Y14 °śreṇībhir ā°, Y21 °śroṇībhir ā°, Y51 °śroṇībhir a°
b DG2 omits entire line; Y51 premabaddha° (for veṇībhūta°), D12 vāṇībhūta°; N21 °manaḥ° (for °rasa°), N1 °manu° corrected to °mana°; Y14 °kṣamā° (for °kramā°), Y32 °ktamā°; G1 ajitaḥ (for abhitaḥ), V1 Y21 amitaḥ, N21 ahita°, N1 ahi° corrected to abhi° (one syllable short), T21 ms. damaged here; Y1 Y2 Y21 śroṇī° (for śreṇī°); Y21 °bhūtānirvṛtaḥ; C52(t) D12 D21 G1 H21(t) H31(t) P71(t) vṛtāḥ (for vṛtaḥ), DG2 U1 vṛtam, DG1 vṛtām, Y32 dhṛtaḥ, N1 damaged (T21 c d: ms. damaged)
c M1 M24 vāṇīnām api (for pāṇī nāma vi°), C21(t) N21 Y2 pāṇīnām api, K1 N1 vāṇīnām avi°; V1 pāṇī dvau ca (for pāṇī nāma), Y51 gopīprema°, R23 veṇīdāma°, D1 D44 H21(t) pāṇī veṇu°; Y51 vivardhayan (for vinodayan); D44 N21 °śaraiḥ (for °śayaiḥ)
d Y51 tarṇālīm api lālayan (for vāṇīnām apadaṃ paraṃ); G11 N21 veṇīnām; M21 apadaḥ param (for apadaṃ paraṃ), DG1 DG2 D44 G2 N21 R23 Y14 apadaṃ padaṃ, K1 T71 Y12 Y32 aparaṃ padaṃ, M24 padasaṃpadaṃ; DG1 DG2 G2 M24 vrajasatī° (for vrajajana°), T71 U1 vrajajanaḥ, N1 N21 R23

vrajapati°, Y1 Y2 Y3 Y12 Y14 Y31 Y32 vrajapadaṃ, Y51 vrajapada°; Y3 kṣoṇīpati; Y1 Y2 Y3 Y12 Y14 Y21 Y31 Y32 vaḥ (for naḥ)

82 a D1 yan nāma smaraṇaṃ (for kalindīpuline); G11 °pulinaika° (for puline ta°), K1 °puline 'ti; DG2 omits °māla°; N1 °nicaya° (for °nibiḍa°); M21 T21 punaḥ (for puraḥ°); DG1 DG2 M1 °saṃcaraṃs (for °saṃcarat-), C51(t) D1 D21 °saṃcaras, D11 D12 G11 N1 °saṃcaran (incorrect for?)

b no variant readings

c D1 pādā° (for vāme); U1 veṇur; H21(t) niṣāṇaṃ (for viṣāṇaṃ), D64 viṣālaṃ; D64 N1 N21 kaṭī- (for kaṭi-), D1 G11 kaṭiṃ

d M24 sāci (for gāś ca); C21(t) DG1 DG2 G2 H31(t) N1 N21 R23(g) °yann anukalaṃ (for °yan pratikalaṃ), D11 G1 M21 R23(e) °yann anukulam, K1 M24 T21 °yann anudinam, U1 °yaṃ ratikalaṃ, D71 °yan pratipadaṃ, D1 °yan pratikulaṃ, M1 °yann anuntaṃ (metrically and otherwise incorrect); M21 kṛṣṇaḥ sa puṣṇātu naḥ (for bālam ālokaye); N21 ālaye (one syllable short for ālokaye)

83 a M21 T71 °nayane° (for vadane°), N21 °vane° (one syllable short); N1 N21 Y31 °vadaneṣu; Y2 Y14 Y21 Y32 Y51 Y52 °bhittiṣu gataṃ (for °maṇḍanam abhūt), Y31 bhittiṣu gataṃ; C21 C51(p) C52(p) D44 G2 H21(c) H31(c) °maṇḍalam; M21 °vidhau (for °m abhūt), D71 °juṣe; Y14 Y21 Y31 Y32 kastūrivibhramaṃ (one syllable short), Y2 Y51 Y52 kastūrikāvibhramaṃ, K1 G11 M1 kastūrikāpatrikaṃ

b D44 Z9 °koca° (for °kuca°), G2 °kula°; D71 N1 °kumbhaśāta° (for °śātakumbha°); C52(t) DG1 DG2 D1 D71 G1 H21(t) H31(t) M1 M21 P71(t) Y21 Y31 Y51 Y52 °kalaśe (for °kalaśa°), N1 °kalasī°; G1 M1 Y21 Y31 vyākośam (for vyākocam), T21 V1 Y2 Y14 Y32 °vyākośam, Y51 Y52 vyākoṣam; N21 °vyākocakendī°

c T21 nirmāṇa°; DG1 DG2 K1 N1 M1 N21 T21 U1 Y2 Y14 Y52 Z9 °vidhāna° (for °nidhāna°), D21 °nidhāya°; G2 snigdhāñjanaṃ; D71 °āñjane (for °āñjanaṃ), M1 °āñjanā°

d G2 M1 Z9 tadvac chyāma°; N1 saydyaḥ (for tan naḥ), C21(t) D1 Y14 tan na, Y2 Y21 Y31 Y32 Y51 Y52 tad vaḥ; C51(te) C52(te) śāmalam; D44 kṛṣṭā°; Y2 Y14 Y21 Y31 Y32 Y51 Y52 °dheyaṃ (for °dhānaṃ)

84 a C21 C51 C52 H21 H31(c) M21 P71 R23 °kāntam indu° (for °kāntim indu°), Z11 (PB only), °indukānti°; U1 barhāvataṃsaṃ priyaṃ

b DG1 DG2 pītāmbarālaṃkṛtam

c M1 gopāpa° (for gogopa°); DG2 °saṃhāvṛtaṃ; M1 °saṃghārcitaṃ

d C21(t) D12 Z11 Z13 °veṇuvāda°; C21(t) D1 D11 D12 H31(t) R23 UV °rasikaṃ (for °niratam), U1 °navaraṃ, D44 °m aparaṃ, DG1 DG2 D71 G1 G2 G11 K1 M1 M21 M24 T21 Z11 Z13 °naparaṃ

85 a G2 °puṭī; K1 vidhar

b M21 T21 kamalānivāsa° (for kamalāvilāsa°), G11 kamalādhivāsa°; G2 °nayanaṃ (for °sadanaṃ); D12 N1 bhāskarau (for c 'endvinau), G1 dvendvinau

c D71 tatpāda°; C21 C51(t) C52(t) D21 D44 D64 H21(t) H31(e) M24 N21 T71

°nisṛtā (metrically incorrect for °niḥsṛtā), K1 °nistutā, D1 °niśrutā, N1 °nusruta
d D44 K1 N1 vaḥ (for naḥ)

86 a YY1 °jalajanmāñjaliḥ (for °jalajair añjaliḥ), G2 °jalajanyarpitāḥ; DG1 DG2 mūrtiḥ (for °mūle)
b DG1 DG2 U1 nābhīḥ (for nābhī°), D12 nābhiṃ; G11 K1 sarasahṛdaye; U1 pūrabāṇā; M1 murāre
c D12 M1 hārā (for hārāḥ), H31(t) hāraṃ, G11 hārāṃ; M1 kande (for kaṇṭhe), T21 °maṇimaye; U1 °padma° (for °padme); D12 M1 M24 dvirephā (for dvirephāḥ), G11 dvirephāṃ, K1 T71 dvirephaḥ
d DG1 DG2 pañcacūḍāś; C21(t) D11 R23(p reads with critical text) °cūḍaṃ (for °cūḍāś), D64 °cūḍaś, M1 M24 °cūḍa; K1 M1 M24 T21 gopa° (for ghoṣa°); DG2 D12 °ākṣaḥ

87 a H31(t) matha° (for dadhi°); D64 D71 K1 M21 T71 U1 °nidra° (for °nidraḥ), M1 °nidrā
b T21 vivṛtapadam; DG1 DG2 G1 M24 T21 agārān (for agāraṃ), M1 akārā°; U1 praviṣṭāḥ
c K1 U1 °samīpair; M24 nirvyāpa° (for nirvāpya), DG2 nirvāpa°, D12 nirvāṇa°
d M21 navanītaṃ; N1 N21 Z11 māṃ bālakṛṣṇaḥ (for gopālabālaḥ), M21 T21 gopālakṛṣṇaḥ, M24 gopālako naḥ

88 a U1 rathi° (for dadhi°); D12 V1 °vinīta° for °vidhūta°); G11 K1 °nidrāṃ
b no variant readings
c Y21 Y31 Y32 navanītacauram (for nayanābhirāmam), Y14 navanītacīram
d Y14 Y21 Y31 Y32 nayanābhirāmam (for navanītacoram); D11 Y2 Y51 °cauram (for °coram), T21 °cāram

89 a N1 °hemaka° (for °hallaka°), M1 °kalpa° (one syllable short), T21 °halla-kalpakā° (two extra syllables); H21(t) H31(c) P71 UV °ojjvalad- (for °ollasad-)
b G2 gaṇḍam (for gallam), M1 mallim, N21 bhallam, D12 hallam; N1 gallagarbham adhunagaveṣitam (entire line); T71 gallamānamuralīviśeṣitam (entire line); G1 °gavīraveṣṭitam (for °gavīgaveṣitam), M1 °gavīṇaveṣitam (incorrect for?), U1 °gavinaveṣitam
c N21 °kucavarāsitā° (for °cikuravāsitā°); H31(t) °yāsitā° (for °vāsitā°), U1 °vācitā°; N1 °āñguliṃ
d D44 pallavī (for pallavaṃ); D64 K1 U1 kim api; U1 pallavaṃ (for vallavaṃ), D21 G1 G11 M21 M24 Q71 vallabhaṃ

90 a Y21 harir (for harer), M24 hare, G1 haraty; G1 api ca (for harati), N21 hati (one syllable short); K1 °coraṃ
b M1 jāras tvam asya gurumatya°
c Y21 °mṛtī (for °hatir), K1 °pūrtir (metrically incorrect), M1 N21 °harir, M24 °hatiṃ; C21(c omitted) C51 C52 D11 D71 G1 G11 H31 M1 M21 P71 T71 °goṣṭhīṃ (for °doṣaṃ), D12 °goṣṭhiṃ, M1 °goṣṭhaṃ, H21(t reads with critical text; c is omitted)
d G2 tat° (for yat°), D12 yaḥ, M1 yaṃ; K1 °sthana° (for °stana°); D64 kṛṣṭāḥ (for kṛṣṇaḥ)

91 a all mss. except DG1 DG2 G1 G11 H21(t) H31(c damaged) M1 M21 M24 N1 N21 P71 T21 T71 Y1 Y2 Y21 mā 'vasa

b no variant readings

c UV V1 śrīramāpatir ihā 'gamed asau (entire line); Y1 hā (for he); Y1 vāryatām ayaṃ (for vāryatām asau), Y2 vāryatā vayaṃ

d Y1 Y2 Y21 °luṇṭhanam (for °laṅghanam), N1 N21 °maṅgalam, M1 °lambanam

92 a D1 N21 ākuñcataṃ (for ākuñcitaṃ), M24 ākuñci taj; T71 padaṃ (for karaṃ), D12 N1 N21 caraṃ; N21 bālaṃ (for vāmaṃ)

b D1 G1 H31(t) M1 M24 N1 nyastaṃ kṣitau (for nyasya kṣitau), P71 nyasyā 'vanau, DG1 DG2 nyasya sthitau, C21(t) nanv asthito, N21 stanya sma kṣitau (one extra syllable); M24 N21 T21 U1 °padmam (for °padme), M21 °pakṣe, N1 °padam (metrically incorrect)

c K1 °bhāṇḍaṃ (for °khaṇḍaṃ), D44 °coraṃ

d N21 ihā 'sitāṅgam (for upānatāṅgam), D11 N1 upāsitāṅgam, K1 upālatāṅgam, D1 G11 upānatāṅgaḥ

93 a no variant readings

b no variant readings

c no variant readings

d C51(t) C52(t) °varṇacandram

94 a C21(t) D11 D12 D21 api (for abhi°)

b V1 pāṇi° (for bāhu°), N21 jānu°, C21(c) C51 C52 D1 D12 D21 D64 D71 G11 H21 H31 P71 R23 T71 api (for ati°), U1 abhi°

c C21(t) D11 kuṇḍalālaṃkṛtaṃ bālaṃ (entire line); C21(c) C51 C52 D1 G11 H21 H31 N1 P71 R23 T71 U1 sa° (for su°); N1 °kuntalālakaṃ; H31(t) vande (for bālaṃ)

d D21 gopāle; N21 mahaḥ (for uṣaḥ)

95 a D71 apāsya (for vihāya); M1 °śaraṃ (for °śarān), C21(c) D11 D12 D64 G11 H21 H31 M21 P71 T71 U1 V1 °śarau; D1 D64 N21 T21 muhūrte (for muhūrtaṃ), N1 muhus te

b D71 pānau kuru tvaṃ maṇi°; DG2 °cāra°;

c DG1 DG2 'āṅgaṃ

d N21 śriṣapatiṃ tvāṃ (incorrect for?); DG1 DG2 tvaṃ (for tvāṃ); C21(c) C51(c) C52(c) D11 D12 D64 G2 H21 H31(p reads with critical text) P71(p reads with critical text) R23(p reads with text) T71 rāghavarāmacandra (for tvāṃ praṇamāmi paścāt), U1 rāghavarāmacandram, D1 rāghavarāmacandraḥ, D21 tvāṃ praṇato 'smi nityam, N21 tvāṃ śaraṇaṃ prapadye

96 a Y31 Y32 dugdhā° (for kṣīrā°), N21 gavā° (metrically incorrect); V1 °āmbhodaḥ (for °āmbhodeḥ), C51(t) M1 °āmbhodhaiḥ, D12 D21 Y14 °āmbhodhe, D1 °āmbādhe; N21 Y21(vs. 362) pālaya (for pālaka), T21 pālana

b DG1 DG2 G11 M1 M21 N21 śruto (for śrito); N21 'bhābhiḥ (for 'smābhiḥ); D12 tṛṣṇataralitadhiyā; Y31 Y32 dugdhopanayana°; Y32 nanda° (for gopa°); M1 °tanaya (for °tanayaḥ), N1 °tanayāḥ (for °tanayā) c U1 na tena (for anena); T21 vyacarata tadā (for vyaraci satataṃ), M1 M24 vyacarata tathā, Y21(vs. 362) vyacarata yathā, Y21 (vs. 276) vyaracata yathā, H31(t) vyaruci satataṃ, DG1 DG2 vyaraci dhṛtamā (incorrect for?), Y14 vyaracatu (incorrect for?), Y32 vyaraci ca tathā, N1 N21 vyaraci śatadhā, Z9 vyaraci sumahāṃs, G1 vyaraci nu tathā, G2 vyaraci sa tathā; Z9 tena (for yena), N1 rajanī

d D1 sarādhyasy (for stanād apy); Z9 amāska (incorrect for asmākaṃ); Y14 Y21 punar (for sakṛd), D12 R23(p with critical text) UV nijam

97 a M21 hastam āpyāyato yāti; U1 Y21 Y31 Y32 Y51 Y52 utkṣipya

b Y21 Z2 balād iti; D12 G11 H31(t) kṛṣṇe 'dam (C51[t] D1 omit lines c and d)

c G11 H31(t) api (for yadi)

d no variant readings

98 a D11 mañjulaṃ (for majjatām); Z11 aplavānāṃ (for amburāśau)

b C51(t) tṛpitānāṃ; Z11(PA only) barhiṇāṃ varṣameghaḥ (for svāduvarṣī 'va meghaḥ), D12 svāduveṣai 'va meghaḥ

c C21(t) D11 D12 D64 D71 G11 H21(t) H31(t) M21 P71(t) T71 U1 Z11 nidhanānāṃ (for vidhanānāṃ), P71(c) R23 nirdhanānāṃ, D44 nidadhānāṃ; Z11 tīvraduḥkhāmayānāṃ

d D64 dhātum; D71 H21(t) P71 T71 U1 Z11 (DD reads with critical text) āyāti

99 a C21(c) D21 H21 K1 N1 N21 madhuraṃ (for masṛnaṃ); K1 gandha°; N1 N21 °āṅkuśān

b D21 D44 D64 K1 N1 N21 U1 haimaṃ (for haimīṃ); D21 veṇulatākaraṃ ca (for veṇulatāṃ karaiś ca), K1 N1 N21 veṇulatāṅkuraṃ ca, D44 veṇulatāṅkuraiś ca, D21 D64 °pūjā° (for °puñjā°)

c YY2 karpūrā° (for kandarpā°); N1 N21 kandarpāyuta°

d N1 N21 gopālaṃ madhurākṛtiṃ manumahe trailokya°; K1 U1 °ābhidhaṃ (for °ādhipaṃ) ,D11 T71 °ādhikaṃ; D71 °ābhipālam (for °ādhipaṃ taṃ); YY2 hṛdi bhaje (for tam abhajaṃ), K1 tam udaye, U1 tam abhaje (incorrect for?), YY2 trailokyasaṃmohanam

100 a N1 N21 °śayane (for °samaye)

b C51(t) °ākarṣaṇānaṃ; D71 suragaṇa° (for suranara°), K1 suravara°; N21 °mohanānaṅga°; H21(t) °līlam (for °mūrtim), D71 °lolam

c U1 °sahasraṃ

d G11 govindaṃ (for vande 'haṃ), D71 vede 'haṃ; D12 N1 N21 rāsakeliṃ; N1 N21 ratipati° (for °ratam ati°); C21(te) C51(t) C52(t) D11 D21 D64 H21(t) °ratim (for °ratam), C52(e) °taram; M21 atimuditaṃ (for atisubhagaṃ), G11 atisulabhaḥ, N1 atisulabhaṃ, K1 atisukhadaṃ; D12 D64 G11 H21(e) H31(te) K1 N1 N21 paśya° (for vaśya°), U1 vanya°, C21(t) D21 D71 vaṃśa°

101 a no variant readings

b C51 C52 D64 M21 °niṣevitam (for °niveśitam), C21(t) D11 D12 D21 G11 H31(t) K1 U1 °niveśanam, N1 N21 T71 °niveśinam

c M21 V1 padmāsanasthitaṃ; C21 C51(c) C52(c) H21(g) U1 devaṃ (for vande)

d no variant readings

102 a D1 omits bālaṃ... °jāla°; D1 D11 G11 K1 °baddhaṃ
b C21(t) G11 H31(t) K1 śreṇī; D21 °rasadhana° (for °rurunakha°), K1 °m urutarā°; G11 H31(t) °karṇa° (for °kaṇṭha°)
c C21(te) phallā°; D1 D21 D44 M21 °jāta°; M21 °netraṃ (for °vaktraṃ); V1 °marut° (for °patat°; K1 prapātaṃ (for prasannam)
d D12 °endrāghamara°; D1 °maramaram aji; D21 pūjayad

103 a C21(t) mukundair; D12 indīvarābhaṃ
b D12 K1 V1 gogopī° (for gopīgo°), C21(t) gopī° (one syllable short); D44 °pītaṃ (for °vītaṃ), K1 °sītaṃ; M21 °hāraṃ (for °hāsaṃ
c M21 °ābha° (for °āgrya°), D1 °āgri°; D45 G11 H31 T71 V1 °piñchagrathana° (for °piñchākalana°), M21 °piñchagrathita°; C51(t) C52(t) D11 D44 G11 °kuṇḍalaṃ (for °kuntalaṃ), C21(t) °kaṇḍalaṃ
d D12 madhyāhne vai ramāyai yaja yaja dinaśaḥ sādhu pītāmbarāḍhyaṃ (entire line); C21(t) C51(t) C52(t) D1 D11 D21 D44 K1 vande (for devaṃ); D44 yamijana° (for yaja yaja), C51 C52 D11 D21 K1 T71 jaya jaya; D44 °sudṛśo (for dinaśo), D1 vinaśo; G11 H31(t) M21 P71(t) T71 dinaśas taṃ ramāyai mukundam; V1 ramāya (for ramāyai

104 a D1 D12 G11 H31(t) K1 °vairī; D1 D12 K1 ayāstā° (for apāsta°), H31(t) apāsyā°; K1 °bhāvam
b D1 D21 G11 āpītaṃ (for āvītaṃ); T71 āvirbhūtaṃ surādyair; D44 tatra (for tattva°); K1 °hetum (for °hetoḥ), D12 °hetau
c D12 viśvosyo 'tpattihetuṃ sthitaharaṇapadaṃ cintayen nīlabhāsaṃ (entire line—partially incorrect); G11 H21(t[c omitted here]) H31 M21 P71 T71 mantrī taṃ (for sāyāhne); C21 C51 C52(c) D1 D44 D45 °upamam aciraṃ;
d D12 sāyaṃkāle yuvānaṃ nirupamam ajaraṃ muktidaṃ vāsudevam (entire line); G11 H21 H31 M21 P71 T71 sāyaṃ (for mantrī); D44 vidyodaya°

105 a D71 N1 N21 YY2 anekaśaraṃ (for akhaṇḍam iṣuṃ); C51(t) D21 D44 D45 pauṣyaṃ
b M21 cakrāṅkuśābjasṛṇi°
c M21 aṣṭabhujam iṣṭadam agragaṇyaṃ; N1 N21 YY2 °mita° (for °vidha°)
d no variants

106 a D1 vidurārpitair (for vidurārpite), M6 vidurārpito; G11 T71 °ripoḥ; D12 M21 kuntyā 'rpite
b C21(t) yo govardhana°
c Z11(PA only) omits line c; C21(t) phale (for 'dhare); N1 N21 kucelārpite (for 'dhare yoṣitāṃ
d C51(t) C52(t) D21 D45 G2 hy (for py); Z11 yā vā te bhāvinīvinihite 'nne 'trā 'pi tām arpaya (entire line). Variants to this line: Z11(AKG PA only) bhāminī° (for bhāvinī°); Z11(PB only) netre 'pi (for 'nne 'trā 'pi)

Additional Verses

āttaṃ padavyāṃ

(T21 ms. damaged; no evidence after āttaṃ padavyāṃ viga°)

a M1 padavyā

b G1 eka° (for eva)

c DG2 kulo (for °karo); M24 kraya° (for phala°); M1 °vikrayiṇyāṃ

d no variant readings

karayoḥ kaṅkaṇa°

a DG2 °rāyaṃ (for °rāvaṃ)

b no variant readings

c N1 omits entire line. N1 scribe indicates with a + sign after the midverse stop (/) that part of the verse is missing.

d N21 āmaraṇā

karṇāmṛtaṃ bhagavataś

(MGOL ms. no. 15809 [G62] first line only collated; evidence for lines b c d not available)

a M1 rasajñāḥ (for rasajñaḥ), M24 rasajñā

b no variant readings

c no variant readings

d no variant readings

Sources outside the KK from which the verse was collated: This verse is quoted by Ullur Paramesvara S. Aiyar in an article on Bilvamaṅgala. (Ullur S. Paramesvara Aiyar, "Saint Vilvamaṅgala," *Proceedings of the All India Oriental Conference*, 1937 [Poona, 1938], p. 475.)

kalāttamāyālava°

a M6 kalārtamāyā° (for kalāttamāya°), Z41 (TPC) kalāktamāyā°, D21 kalottamāya°, N21 kālāttamāyā°, G2 kālāktamālaya° (one extra syllable), N1 karā° (ms damaged after first two syllables); N1 °vala° (for °lava°), D21 °dava°; Z41 (B) Z41 (Ch) Z41 (BORI) Z41 (TPC) °lavakāttamūrtiḥ (for °lavakāntamūrtiḥ), G2 °lavakrāntamūrtiḥ

b Z41 (B) Z41 (S) kvaṇat° (for kala°)

c D21 N1 N21 Z41 (Ch commentary) sthito (for śrito), M6 śrite, Z41 (TPC) ms. damaged here; M6 trilokī

d Z41 (BORI) unable to determine reading for naḥ, all mss. except preceding and D21 M6 N1 N21 read vaḥ

Sources outside the KK from which the verse was collated: YY1 2.26 (line d only) and 3 printed editions of the Kramadīpikā [Z41 (B) Z41 (Ch) Z41 (S)] and 3 mss. [Z41 (N) Z41 (TPC) Z41 (BORI)]

govālamūle

a D1 G11 gopālamūle

b D1 pūrite (for pūryase), N21 pūryate; N1 °payādhikārtham (for °payodharārtham), N21 °payaḥsravārtham

c D21 N21 payovihīnau ca kucau madīyau (entire line), N1 payovihīnau tu kucau madīyau
d D21 tāṃ tāṃ (for etāṃ)

ghaṭodakeṣu pratimā°
a no variant readings
b Y31 Y52 nirīkṣya (for vilokya)
c Y31 ādātukāmas tad alābhakhedād; Y52 ādātukāmas tadanāptiduḥkhād
d Y31 Y61 vilokya dhātrīvadanaṃ ruroda; Y52 vilokya dhātrīmukham āruroda; Y62 Y63 Y64 vilokya mātur vadanaṃ ruroda; G1 tadaprāpta°; M24 °samākulena
Sources outside the KK from which the verse was collated: Y31 Y52 Y61 Y62 Y63 Y64

jayatu jayatu devo
a M21 kṛṣṇo (for devo)
b no variant readings
c D21 N22 meghaḥ śyāmalḥ
d D45 Y21 °bhārahāro
Sources outside the KK from which the verse was collated: Y21

dadhimathananinādair dīrghikā°
a K1 dīrghikāvaṃśanādaiḥ
b no variant readings
c K1 ātmavibhramanādair
d no variant readings

nigamataroḥ
no variant readings

pādadvaṃdve vinimaya°
a DG vinimayavati (metrically incorrect); G1 °yugme (for padme)
b DG2 T21 pādo (for pātho°), DG6 pā° (metrically incorrect); G1 °cchavir (for °dyutir)
c T21 kiṃ cid
d DG vaṃśanī (incorrect for?); G1 vāsarā

prātar namāmi manasā
a N21 bhajāmi (for namāmi); N22 vacasā (for manasā); M21 śirasā (for vacasā), N21 vapuṣā, N22 manasā; M21 vācā (for mūrdhnā)
b no variant readings
c no variant readings
d M21 N22 °pravara° (for pravaṇa°)
Sources from outside the KK from which the verse was collated: Z42

prātar bhajāmi bhajatām
a Z42 prātaḥ smarāmi; N1 ms. damaged (for °m abha°)

b Z42 prāgjanmakoṭiduritaughabhayāpahatyai
c no variant readings
d N21 N22 °oddhṛta° (for °odyata°), N1 °oddhata°; M21 N1 N21 N22 °śaṅkha-cakraḥ (for °cakrapāṇiḥ)
Sources from outside the KK from which the verse was collated: Z42

prātaḥ smarāmi bhava°
a M21 prātar namāmi bhavabhīti°
b no variant readings
c M21 °mada° (for °vara°)
d M21 karuṇa° (for tarala°)
Sources from outside the KK from which the verse was collated: Z42

barhāpīḍaṃ
a C21 (t) nara° (for naṭa°); DG G1 G2 M6 N1 R21 T21 °nara° (for °vara°)
b no variant readings
c no variant readings
d D14 nṛpati° (for svapada°), C21(t) N1 svapati°; G11 bhīta° (for gīta°); C21(t) C14 gopamūrtiḥ (for gītamūrtiḥ)
Sources outside the KK from which the verse was collated: Y11 Y12 Y21 Z43(M) Z43(G)

bahuśāstrakathā°
a no variant readings
b DG1 mṛdhena (for vṛddhena)
c DG5 anveṣṭavyā (for anveṣṭavyaṃ)
d DG5 DG6 jñātir (for jyotir°); DG5 āntarī (for °ānataram)

maṇiviḍambitatasya
a no variant readings
b DG1 DG2 DG5 DG6 (All manuscripts, in which this verse appears, read °manā for °mano°. The emendation was suggested by the copyist, N Ranganathasastri.) DG1 DG2 DG5 DG6 (All manuscripts, in which this verse appears, read °maṇḍale for °maṇḍalāḥ. The emendation was suggested by the copyist, N. Ranganathasastri.)
c no variant readings
d DG2 (ms. damaged for vratam amuñcata)

mugdhe dhyāyasi
a G2 ms. damaged for dhyāyasi kiṃ gṛhāṇa
b no variant readings
c G2 sakhī; N21 śrutigiro
d N1 ms. damaged for ujjhita°; G2 entire last line much damaged

lakṣmīsuvarṇatilakā°
a N1 °latikā° (for °tilakā°)
b no variant readings
c N21 °yamunāraṅgaṃ (metrically incorrect—one syllable short)
d N1 °pātra° (for °patra°)

vanamālini yāti

a N1 ms. damaged (for vanamālini yāti)

b N1 ms. damaged (for pari°)

c no variant readings

d N1 eva vāsaḥ (for pītavāsāḥ); N21 ms. damaged (for final ā of °vāsāḥ)

SYNOPTIC CHARTS OF VERSE SEQUENCES

GUIDE TO READING "CHART OF STANDARD VERSE SEQUENCES"

The 70 to 80 mss., from which the KK has been collated, are entered horizontally across the tops of the following pages. Six of these units comprehend the entire standard sequence of the 330 standard verses of the KK.

If the column, or any part of the column, beneath a ms. entry which has no preceding bracket is empty, this indicates that the verse numbering of the ms. is identical with that of the standard version. For example, on the first page of the "Chart of Standard Verse Sequences" only B2 B3 C51 C52 have the verse numbering identical with that of the standard version.

If the column, or any part of the column, beneath a ms. entry has numbers, these numbers will usually differ from the standard numbers given to the standard verses. This difference is just the difference between the numbering of the standard version and the numbering of the particular ms. For example, on the first page of the "Chart of Standard Verse Sequences" see DG1: Standard verse 1.2 (st. 1.2) is DG1 verse 1.1 (DG1 1.1).

The numbering and the actual sequence of the verses are identical unless a note, indicated by an asterisk(*), calls attention to significant misnumbering. A chart of actual sequence and actual numbering would be twice as long as this already lengthy chart.

It is to be noted that the Y mss. are not here considered as KK mss. but anthologies of Bilvamañgala verses which include many KK verses. The "Chart of Standard Verse Sequences" must be read somewhat differently for Y mss.: If the column or any part of the column beneath a ms. entry is empty, this indicates that the standard verse or verses included in that column or part of column are not found in the Y ms. entry at the head of the column.

If the column, or any part of the column, beneath a ms. entry has signs other than numbers, they are to be interpreted as follows:

x indicates loss or destruction of ms. where the expected vs. or vss. would be entered.

o indicates that vs. is omitted.

[preceding a ms. entry at the top of the page indicates that all the st. vss. listed on that page are not found in the ms. To determine whether these vss. have been lost or omitted, see description of the ms. in the "Manuscripts Used" section. For example, on the first page of the "Chart of Standard Verse Sequences" C22, which is prefixed with a bracket ([C22), is a ms. which is represented only by *śataka* 2. Therefore, the C22 ms. does not include the *śataka* 1 verses listed on the first page of the "Chart of Standard Verse Sequences." It is necessary to see the "Manuscripts Used" section to determine whether the C22 colophon indicates that *śatakas* 1 and 3 have been lost or are not considered to be part of the KK.

– Underlining of numbers is to facilitate detection of sequences which differ from the standard sequence.

+ indicates that a verse (or verses), not found in the standard version of the KK, is entered in the ms. before or after the standard verse so affixed with a plus. This additional verse is entered in the "Chart of Additional Verse Sequences." For example, see the column under C21 on the first page of the "Chart of Standard Verse Sequences." After the blank space, which indicates that C21 has the standard numbering for the standard vs. 1.20, there is a plus. Refer now to the "Chart of Additional Verse Sequences" under st. 1.20. There also locate the listing of the ms., C21. We find here that in ms. C21 after st. 1.20 the additional verse calaccikuramaṇḍalaṃ (add. calaccikuramaṇḍalaṃ) is entered, but it is unnumbered (unn.) and does not change the numbering of the C21 ms. from that of the standard version. S indicates that, of the mss. collated, C21 is the only one which includes this verse. If, however, we look in the section entitled "Additional Verses", we will find that this verse also occurs in the KK ms., IO ms. No. 3900/1605c (D13), whose verses have not been collated for this edition.

* indicates a note which is entered in the "Notes to Chart of Standard Verse Sequences." Pertinent information, which could not be accomodated in a chart, is given in the notes.

/// indicates that the verse, thus marked, is the last verse in the *śataka*.

t This sign is used only for mss. which include both text and commentary. It indicates that the ms. has only the text for the verse specified.

c This sign is used only for mss. which include both text and commentary. It indicates that the ms. has only the commentary for the verse specified.

Chart of Standard Verse Sequences

A1	B1 (GA only)	B1	B2	B3	C21	[C22	C51	C52	DG1	I
x	x								o	1
x	x								1	2
x	x								2	3
x	x								3	4
x	x								4+	5
x	x								o	6
x	x								+6	7
x	x								7	8
x	x								o	9
x	x								8	10
x	x								9	11
x	x								10	12
x	x								11	13
x	x								12	14
x	x								13	15
x	x								14	16
x	x								15	17
x	x								16	18
x	x								17	19
x	x					+			18	20
x	x				+				19	21
x	x								20	22
x	x								21	23
x	x								22	24
x									23	25
x									24	26
x									25	27
x									o	28

A1	B1 (GA only)	B1	B2	B3	C21	[C22	C51	C52	DG1	I
x									26	29
x									27	30
x									28	31
x									29	32
x									30	33
x									31	34
									o	35
									o	36
									32	37
									o	38
x	x								33	39
x	x								34	40
x	x								35	41
									36	42
									37	43
									38	44
									39	45
									40	46
	48	48							41	47
	47	47							42	48
									43	49
									44	50
									45	51
									46	52
									47	53
									48	54
									49	55
									50	56

DG2	[DG3	DG4	[DG5	[DG6	D1	D11	D12	[D14	D21	I
o		o								1
1		1								2
2		2								3
3		3								4
4+		4+								5
o		o								6
+6		+6								7
7		7								8
o		o								9
8		8								10
9		9								11
10		10								12
11		11								13
12		12								14
13		13								15
14		14								16
15		15								17
16		16								18
17		17								19
18		18								20
19		19								21
20		20								22
21		21								23
22		22								24
23		23								25
24		24								26
25		25								27
o		o								28

DG2	[DG3	DG4	[DG5	[DG6	D1	D11	D12	[D14	D21	I
26		26								29
27		27								30
28		28								31
29		29								32
30		30								33
31		31								34
o		o								35
o		o								36
32		32								37
o		o								38
33		33								39
34		34								40
35		35								41
36		36								42
37		37								43
38		38								44
39		39								45
40		40								46
41		41								47
42		42								48
43		43								49
44		44								50
45		45								51
46		46								52
47		47								53
48		48								54
49		49								55
50		50								56

[D41	[D43	D44	D45	D64	D71	[E41	[E42	[E43	F41	I
									2/1*	1
										2
										3
										4
										5
										6
										7
										8
										9
										10
										11
										12
										13
										14
										15
										16
										17
			19						19	18
			20						20	19
			$\overline{18}$						$\overline{18}$	20
										21
										22
									3/1*	23
				26					2	24
				$\overline{25}$					3	25
									4	26
									5	27
									6	28

[D41	[D43	D44	D45	D64	D71	[E41	[E42	[E43	F41	I
									7	29
									8	30
									9	31
									10	32
									11	33
									12	34
									13	35
									14	36
									15	37
									16	38
									17	39
									18	40
									19	41
									20	42
									21	43
									22	44
									23	45
									24	46
									25	47
									26	48
									27	49
									28	50
									29	51
									30	52
									31	53
									4/1*	54
									2	55
									3	56

G1	G2	G11	H21	H31	K1	M1	[M6	M21	M24	I
o						+2			x	1
1						3			x	2
2						4			x	3
3						5			x	4
4						6			x	5
5						7			x	6
6						8			x	7
7						9			x	8
8						10			x	9
9						11			x	10
10						12			x	11
11						13			x	12
12						14			x	13
13						15			x	14
14						16			x	15
15						17				16
16						18				17
17						19				18
18						20				19
19						21				20
20						22				21
21						23				22
22						24				23
23						25				24
24		*				26				25
25		25				27				26
26		26				28				27
o		27				29				28

G1	G2	G11	H21	H31	K1	M1	[M6	M21	M24	I
27		28				30				29
28		29				31				30
29		30				32				31
30		31				33				32
31		32				34				33
32		33				35				34
o		34				36				35
33		35				37				36
34		36				38				37
35		37				39				38
36		38				40				39
37		39				41				40
38		40				42				41
39		41	c			43				42
40		42	c			44				43
41		43				45				44
42		44				46				45
43		45		t		47				46
44		46				48				47
45		47				49				48
46		48				50				49
47		49				51				50
48		50				52				51
49		51				53			53*	52
50		52				54			o	53
51		53				55				54
52		54				56				55
53		55	c			57				56

N1	N21	N22	P71	P72	Q71	R21	[R22	[R23	S21	I
1										1
1*										2
2										3
3										4
4										5
5										6
5*	6*									7
6										8
7										9
8										10
9										11
10										12
11										13
12										14
13										15
14		o								16
15		o								17
16		16								18
17		17								19
18		18								20
19		19								21
20	21*	20								22
21	22	21								23
22	23	22								24
23	24	23								25
24	*	24								26
25		25								27
26		26								28

N1	N21	N22	P71	P72	Q71	R21	[R22	[R23	S21	I
27		27								29
28		28								30
29		29								31
30		30								32
31		31							x	33
32		32							x	34
33		33							x	35
34		34								36
35		35							38	37
36		36							$\overline{37}$	38
37		37								39
38		38								40
39		39								41
40		40								42
41		41								43
42		42								44
43		43								45
44		44								46
45		45								47
56		46								48
47		47								49
48		48								50
49		49								51
50		50								52
51		51								53
52		52								54
53		53								55
54		54								56

T5	T21	T71	U1	V1	V2	V22	V25	W1	I
									1
									2
									3
									4
									5
									6
									7
									8
									9
									10
									11
									12
	x								13
	x								14
	x								15
	x								16
	x							t	17
	x								18
	x								19
	x								20
									21
									22
									23
									24
									25
									26
									27
									28

T5	T21	T71	U1	V1	V2	V22	V25	W1	I
									29
									30
x									31
x									32
x									33
x									34
x									35
x									36
x									37
x									38
x									39
x									40
									41
									42
									43
									44
									45
									46
									47
									48
									49
									50
			53						51
			$\overline{51}$						52
			52						53
									54
									55
									56

Y1	Y2	Y3	Y11	Y12	Y13	Y14	Y21	[Y54	I
x	197	193	x	x	235	235	183		1
x	49	46	x	x	199	204	112		2
									3
									4
									5
x	45	42	x	x	197	202	108		6
									7
									8
x	237	44	x	x	198	203	110		9
									10
									11
									12
									13
									14
									15
									16
x	46	43	199	x	196	201	109		17
x	85	90	x	x	226	226	143		18
x	81	78	99	x	98	106	92		19
									20
									21
x	238*	76*	x	x	241*	241*	188*		22
									23
									24
x	212	79	x	x	95	103	93		25
									26
									27
									28

Y1	Y2	Y3	Y11	Y12	Y13	Y14	Y21	[Y54	I
x	77	72	222	x	223	223	138		29
									30
									31
									32
									33
									34
									35
									36
									37
									38
									39
									40
									41
									42
									43
									44
									45
									46
									47
									48
									49
									50
									51
									52
									53
									54
									55
									56

A1	B1 (GA only)	B1	B2	B3	C21	[C22	C51	C52	DG1	I
					t		o	o	51	57
					57		57	57	52	58
					58		58	58	53	59
					59		59	59	54	60
					60		60	60	55	61
					61		61	61	56	62
					62		62	62	57	63
					63		63	63	o	64
					64		64	64	58	65
					65		65	65	59	66
					$\overline{67}$		66	66	60	67
					$\overline{66}$		67	67	61	68
					$\overline{68}$		68	68	62	69
					69		69	69	63	70
					70		70	70	64	71
					71		71	71	65	72
					72		72	72	66	73
					73		73	73	67	74
					74		74	74	68	75
					75		75	75	69	76
					76		76	76	70	77
					77		77	77	71	78
					78		78	78	72	79
					79		79	79	73	80
					80		80	80	74	81
					81		81	81	75	82
					82		82	82	76	83
					83		83	83	77	84

A1	B1 (GA only)	B1	B2	B3	C21	[C22	C51	C52	DG1	I
					84		84	84	78	85
					85		85	85	79	86
					86		86	86	80	87
					87		87	87	81	88
					88		88	88	82	89
					89		89	89	83	90
					90		90	90	84	91
					91		91	91	85	92
					92		92	92	86	93
					93		93	93	87	94
					94		94	94	88	95
					95		95	95	89	96
					96		96	96	90	97
					97		97	97	91	98
					98		98	98	92	99
					99		99	99	93	100
					100		100	100	94	101
					101		101	101	95	102
					102		102	102	96	103
					103		103	103	97	104
					104		104	104	98	105
					105		105	105	99	106
					106		106	106	100	107
					107		107	107	101	108
					108		108	108	102	109
					109		109	109	103	110
					110		110	110	104	111
					111		*111*	*111*	*105*	*112*

DG2	DG3	DG4	[DG5	[DG6	D1	D11	D12	[D14	D21	I
51	x	51								57
52	x	52								58
53	x	53				59/60*				59
54	x	54				61				60
55	x	55				62				61
56	x	56				63				62
57	x	57				64				63
o	x	o				65				64
58	x	58				66				65
59	x	59				67				66
60	x	60				68			68	67
61	x	61				69			67	68
62	x	62				70				69
63	x	63				71				70
64	x	64				72				71
65	65	65				73				72
66	66	66				74				73
67	67	67				75				74
68	68	68				76				75
69	69	69				77				76
70	70	70				78				77
71	71	71				79				78
72	72	72			*	80				79
73	73	73			o	81				80
74	74	74			o	82				81
75	75	75			o	83				82
76	76	76			o	84				83
77	77	77			o	o				84

DG2	DG3	DG4	[DG5	[DG6	D1	D11	D12	[D14	D21	I
78	78	78			o					85
79	79	79			79*					86
80	80	80			80					87
81	81	81			81					88
82	82	82			82					89
83	83	83			83					90
84	84	84			84					91
85	85	85			85					92
86	86	86			86					93
87	87	87			87					94
88	88	88			88					95
89	89	89			89					96
90	90	90			90					97
91	91	91			91					98
92	92	92			92					99
93	93	93			93	+				100
94	94	94			94	+102				101
95	95	95			95	103				102
96	96	96			96	104				103
97	97	97			97	105				104
98	98	98			98	106				105
99	99	99			99	107				106
100	100	100			100	108				107
101	101	101			101	o				108
102	102	102			102					109
103	103	103			103					110
104	104	104			104					111
105	x	*105*			*105*	*105*	*105*		*105*	*112*

[D41	[D43	D44	D45	D64	D71	[E41	[E42	[E43	F41	I
		o	o	o	o				o	57
		57	57	57	57				4	58
		58	58	58	58				5	59
		59	59	59	59				6	60
		60	60	60	60				7	61
		61	61	61	61				8	62
		62	62	62	62				9	63
		63	63	63	63				10	64
		64	64	64	64				11	65
		65	65	65	65				12	66
		66	66	$\overline{67}$	$\overline{67}$				13	67
		67	67	$\overline{66}$	$\overline{66}$				14	68
		68	68	$\overline{68}$	$\overline{68}$				51	69
		69	69	69	69				16	70
		70	70	70	70				17	71
		71	71	71	71				18	72
		72	72	72	72				19	73
		73	73	73	73				20	74
		74	74	74	74				21	75
		75	75	75	75				22	76
		76	76	76	76				23	77
		77	77	77	77				24	78
		78	78	78	78				25	79
		79	79	79	79				26	80
		80	80	80	80				27	81
		81	81	81	81				28	82
		82	82	82	82				29	83
		83	83	83	83				30	84

[D41	[D43	D44	D45	D64	D71	[E41	[E42	[E43	F41	I
		84	84	84	84				31	85
		85	85	85	85				32	86
		86	86	86	86				33	87
		87	87	87	87				34	88
		88	88	88	88				35	89
		89	89	89	89				36	90
		90	90	90	90				37	91
		91	91	91	91				38	92
		92	92	92	92				5/1*	93
		93	93	93	93				2	94
		94	94	94	94				3	95
		95	95	95	95				4	96
		96	96	96	96				5	97
		97	97	97	97				6	98
		98	98	98	98				7	99
		99	99	99	99				8	100
		100	100	100	o				9	101
		101	101	101	100				10	102
		102	102	102	101				11	103
		103	103	103	102				12	104
		104	104	104	103				13	105
		105	105	105	104				14	106
		106	106	106	105				15	107
		107	107	107	106				16	108
		108	108	108	108				17	109
		109	109	109	108				18	110
		110	110	110	109				19	111
		111	*111*	*111*	*110*				*20*	*112*

G1	G2	G11	H21	H31	K1	M1	[M6	M21	M24	I
54		56	58	t		58				57
55		57	$\overline{59}$*			59				58
56		58	$\overline{57}$			60				59
57		59	$\overline{59}$		61	61				60
58		60	60		60	62				61
59		61	61		63	63				62
o		62	62		64	64				63
o		$\overline{64}$	63		$\overline{60}$	65				64
60		$\overline{63}$	$\overline{65}$c	o		66		66		65
o		$\overline{65}$	$\overline{64}$	65		67		$\overline{65}$	+	66
61		66	$\overline{67}$	$\overline{67}$		68		$\overline{68}$	69	67
62		67	$\overline{66}$	$\overline{66}$		69		$\overline{67}$	+$\overline{68}$	68
63		68	$\overline{68}$	$\overline{68}$		70			70	69
64	+	69	69	69		71			71	70
65	+73	70	70	70		72			72	71
66	74	71	71	71		73			73	72
67	75	72	72	72		74			74	73
68	76	73	73	73		75			75	74
69	77	74	74	74		76			76	75
70	78	75	*	75		77			77	76
71	79	76		76		78			78	77
72	80	77		77		79			79	78
o	81	78		78		80			80	79
73	82	79		79		81			81	80
74	83	80		80		82			82	81
75	84	81		81		83			83	82
76	85	82		82		84			84	83
77	o	83		83		85			85	84

G1	G2	G11	H21	H31	K1	M1	[M6	M21	M24	I
o	86	84		84		86			86	85
78	87	85		85		o			87	86
79	88	86		86					88	87
80	89	87		87					89	88
81	90	88		88					90	89
82	91	89		89					91	90
83	92	90		90				o	92	91
84	93	91		91				91	93	92
85	94	92		92				92	95	93
86	95	93		93				93	94	94
87	96	94		94				94	96	95
88	97	95		95				95	97	96
89	98	96		96				96	98	97
90	89	97		o				97	99	98
91	90	98		97				98	100	99
92	91	99		98				99	101	100
93	x	100		99				100	102	101
94	x	101		100				101	103	102
95	109	102		101				102	104	103
96	110	103		102				103	105	104
97	111	104		103				104	106	105
98	112	105		104				105	107	106
99	113	106		105				106	108	107
100	114	x		106				107	109	108
101	115	x		107				108	110	109
102	116	109		108				109	111	110
103	117	110		109				110	112	111
o	118+*	111	///	110	///			///*	///*	112

N1	N21	N22	P71	P72	Q71	R21	[R22	[R23	S21	I
55		55	o	o	o				58	57
56		56	57	57	57				$\overline{57}$	58
57		57	58	58	58					59
58		58	59	59	59					60
59		59	60	60	60					61
o		60	61	61	61					62
60	64	61	62	62	62					63
o	$\overline{63}$	62	63	63	63					64
61		63	64	64	64					65
62		64	65	65	65					66
63	68	$\overline{66}$	$\overline{67}$	$\overline{67}$	$\overline{67}$	68			x	67
64	$\overline{67}$	$\overline{65}$	$\overline{66}$	$\overline{66}$	$\overline{66}$	$\overline{67}$			x	68
65		$\overline{67}$	$\overline{68}$	$\overline{68}$	$\overline{68}$				x	69
66		68	69	69	69				69	70
67		69	70	70	70				70	71
68		70	71	71	71				71	72
69		71	72	72	72				72	73
70		72	73	x	73				73	74
71		73	74	x	74				74	75
72		74	75	75	75				75	76
73		75	76	x	76				77*	77
74		76	77	77	77				76	78
75		77	78	78	78				77	79
x		78	79	79	79				78	80
x		79	80	80	80				79	81
x		80	81	81	81				80	82
x		81	82	82	82				81	83
x		82	83	83	83				82	84

N1	N21	N22	P71	P72	Q71	R21	[R22	[R23	S21	I
x		83	84	84	84				83	85
x		84	85	85	85				84	86
x		85	86	86	86				85	87
x		86	87	87	87				86	88
84		87	88	88	88				87	89
85		88	89	89	89				88	90
86		89	o	90	o				89	91
o	o	90	90	91	90				90	92
87	92	91	91	92	91				92*	93
88	93	92	92	93	92				93	94
89	94	93	93	94	93				94	95
o	95	94	94	95	94				95	96
91	96	95	95	96	95				96	97
92	97	96	o	97	96				97	98
90	98	97	96	98	97				98	99
93	99	98	97	99	98				99	100
94	100	99	98	100	99				100	101
o	101	100	o	101	100				101	102
95	102	101	o	102	101				102	103
o	o	102	99	103	102				103	104
96	103	103	100	104	103				104	105
97	104	o	101	105	104				105	106
98	105+	o	102	106	105				*	107
99	+109	103	103	107	106					108
100	110	104	104	108	107				+	109
///*	112	105	105	109	108				111	110
o	113	105	106	110	109				112	111
o	111	o	107	111	110	//1			113	112

T5	T71	T21	U1	V1	V2	V22	V25	W1	I
	o								57
	57								58
	58								59
	59								60
	60								61
	61								62
	62								63
	63								64
	64								65
	65								66
	$\overline{67}$	68				68	68		67
	$\overline{66}$	$\overline{67}$				$\overline{67}$	$\overline{67}$		68
	$\overline{68}$								69
	69								70
	70								71
	71			o	o	o	o		72
x	72			72	72	72	72		73
x	73			73	73	73	73		74
x	74			74	74	74	74		75
x	75			75	75	75	75		76
x	76			76	76	76	76		77
x	77			77	77	77	77		78
x	78			78	78	78	78	t	79
x	79			79	79	79	79	c	80
	80			80	80	80	80		81
	81			81	81	81	81		82
	82			82	82	82	82		83
	83			83	83	83	83		84

T5	T71	T21	U1	V1	V2	V22	V25	W1	I
	84			84	84	84	84		85
	85			85	85	85	85		86
	86			86	86	86	86		87
	87			87	87	87	87		88
	88			88	88	88	88		89
	89			89	89	89	89		90
	90			90	90	90	90		91
	91			91	91	91	91		92
	92			92	92	92	92		93
	93			93	93	93	93		94
	94			94	94	94	94		95
	95			95	95	95	95		96
	96			96	96	96	96		97
	97	o		97	97	97	97		98
	98	98		98	98	98	98		99
	99	99	+	99+	99+	99+	99+		100
	100	100	+102	+	+	+	+		101
	101	101	103						102
	102	o	$\overline{105}$						103
	103	o	$\overline{104}$						104
	104	o	$\overline{106}$						105
	105	o	107						106
	106	102	108						107
	107	103	109						108
	108	o	110						109
	109	104	///*	///	///	///	///		109
112	110	105	o	o	o	o	o		111
$\overline{111}$	111	106	o	o	o	o	o	///	112

Y1	Y2	Y3	Y11	Y12	Y13	Y14	Y21	Y54	I
									57
									58
									59
									60
									61
x	240	o	243	243	244	244	202		62
									63
									64
									65
									66
									67
									68
									69
									70
									71
									72
									73
								109	74
									75
									76
									77
									78
									79
									80
									81
									82
									83
									84

Y1	Y2	Y3	Y11	Y12	Y13	Y14	Y21	Y54	I
									85
									86
									87
									88
									89
									90
									91
x	84	89	x	x	o	341	142		92
									93
									94
									95
									96
									97
									98
									99
									100
									101
									102
									103
									104
									105
									106
									107
									108
									109
									110
									111
									112

[A1	[B1 (GA only)	[B1	[B2	[B3	C21	C22	C51	C52	DG1	II
										1
										2
										3
										4
										5
										6
										7
										8
										9
										10
										11
										12
										13
										14
										15
										16
										17
										18
										19
										20
										21
										22
									24	23
									23	24
										25
										26
										27
										28

[A1	[B1 (GA only)	[B1	[B2	[B3	C21	C22	C51	C52	DG1	II
										29
										30
										31
										32
										33
									+	34
									+36	35
									o	36
									o	37
						39			o	38
						40			o	39
						$\overline{38}$	o	o	o	40
							40	40	o	41
							41	41	o	42
							42	42	37+	43
							43	43	o	44
							44	44	+39	45
							45	45	40	46
							46	46	41	47
							47	47	42	48
							48	48	43	49
							49	49	44	50
							50	50	45	51
							51	51	46	52
							52	52	$\overline{48}$	53
							53	53	$\overline{47}$	54
							54	54	$\overline{49}$	55

DG2	DG3	[DG4	DG5	DG6	D1	D11	D12	D14	D21	II
						+			+2	1
						+3			3	2
						4+			*	3
						+6				4
						7				5
						8				6
						9				7
						10				8
						11				9
						12				10
						13				11
						14				12
						15		14		13
						16		13		14
						17				15
						18				16
						19				17
						20				18
						21				19
						22				20
						23				21
						24				22
24	24		24			25				23
23	23		23			26				24
						27				25
						28				26
						29				27
						30				28

DG2	DG3	[DG4	DG5	DG6	D1	D11	D12	D14	D21	Ii
						31				29
						32				30
						33				31
						34				32
						35				33
+	+		+			36				34
+36	+36		+36		36	37			36	35
o	*		o		37	38			37	36
o	*		o	o	38	39			38	37
o	*		o	o	39	41			41	38
o	*		o	o	40	40			39	39
o	*		o	o	41	42			40	40
o	*		o	o	42	43			42	41
o	*		o	o	43	44			43	42
37+	37+		37+	37	44	45			44	43
o	o		o	38	45	46			44*	44
+39	+39		+39	39	46	47	46		45*	45
40	40		40	40	47	48	45		47	46
41	41		41	41	48	49			48	47
42	42		42	42	49	50			49	48
43	43		43	43	50	51			50	49
44	44		44	44	51	52			51	50
45	45		45	45	52	53			52	51
46	46		46	46	o	54			53+	52
48	48		48	48	o	55			57	53
47	47		47	47	o	56			+56	54
49	49		49	49	o	57+			58	55

D41	D43	[D44	D45	D64	D71	E41	E42	E43	[F41	II
										1
										2
			4							3
			3							4
										5
			7							6
			6							7
										8
										9
										10
										11
										12
										13
										14
										15
										16
										17
										18
										19
										20
										21
										22
										23
										24
										25
										26
										27
										28

D41	D43	[D44	D45	D64	D71	E41	E42	E43	[F41	II
										29
										30
										31
										32
										33
										34
										35
										36
o	o					o	o	o		37
o	o					37	37	37		38
o	o					38	38	38		39
o	o					39	39	39		40
o	o					40	40	40		41
o	o					o	o	o*		42
36	36					41	41	42		43
37	37					43*	42	43		44
38	38					44	43	44		45
39	39					45	44	45		46
40	40					46	45	46		47
41	41					47	46	47		48
42	42					48	47	48		49
43	43					49	48	49		50
44	44					50	49	50		51
45	45					51	50	51		52
46	46					52	51	52		53
47	47					53	52	53		54
48+	48+					54	53	54		55

G1	G2	G11	H21	H31	K1	M1	M6	M21	M24	II
	x									1
										2
										3
										4
										5
										6
										7
										8
										9
										10
										11
							13			12
							14			13
							$\overline{12}$			14
										15
		18								16
	x	$\overline{16}$								17
		17								18
		$\overline{19}$								19
										20
										21
										22
										23
										24
										25
										26
										27
										28

G1	G2	G11	H21	H31	K1	M1	M6	M21	M24	II
										29
										30
										31
										32
										33
+	+									34
+36	+36									35
o	o									36
o	o									37
o	o						39			38
o	o						$\overline{38}$			39
o	o			t						40
o	o	42								41
o	o	$\overline{41}$								42
37+	37+									43
o	o						*110*			44
+38	+39						44			45
39	40						45			46
40	41						46			47
41	42						47			48
42	43						48			49
43	44						49+			50
44	45						+51		+	51
45	46						52		+53	52
$\overline{47}$	$\overline{48}$						$\overline{54}$+		54	53
$\overline{46}$	$\overline{47}$						53		55	54
$\overline{48}$	$\overline{48}$						$\overline{87}$		56+	55

N1	N21	N22	P71	P72	Q71	[R21	R22	[R23	S21	II
										1
										2
										3
										4
										5
										6
										7
										8
										9
										10
										11
+15	+15									12
16	16						22*			13
12	12						23			14
17	17						21			15
18	18						20			16
19	19						19			17
20	20						18			18
21	21						16		x	19
22	22						17		x	20
23	23						15		x	21
24	24						14		x	22
25	25						13		x	23
26	26								x	24
27	27								x	25
28	28								x	26
29	29								x	27
41	41								x	28

N1	N21	N22	P71	P72	Q71	[R21	R22	[R23	S21	II
30	30								x	29
31	31									30
32	32									31
42	42									32
43	43									33
33	33									34
44	44									35
45	45									36
46	46									37
49	49								40	38
48	48								38	39
47	47								39	40
50	50									41
51	51									42
34	34									43
o	o									44
52+	52+									45
35	35									46
36	36									47
37	37								o	48
38	38								48	49
39	39								49	50
+54	+54								50	51
40	40								51	52
56	56	54							53	53
55	55	53							52	54
58	58								54	55

T5	T21	T71	U1	V1	V2	V22	V25	[W1	II
									1
									2
									3
			7						4
			$\overline{4}$						5
			5						6
			6						7
									8
									9
		11							10
		$\overline{10}$							11
									12
									13
									14
									15
									16
o									17
17									18
18									19
19									20
20									21
21									22
22			24*						23
23			25						24
24			26						25
25			27						26
26			28						27
27			29						28

T5	T21	T71	U1	V1	V2	V22	V25	[W1	II
28			30						29
29			31						30
30			32						31
31			33						32
32			34						33
33			35						34
34	36		37						35
o	37		38						36
o	38	o	40						37
o	39	37	41						38
o	40	38	39						39
o	41	39	43						40
o	42	40	42						41
o	43	41	44						42
35+	44	42	45						43
o	45	43	46						44
+37	46	44	47						45
38	47	45	48						46
39	48	46	49						47
40	49	47	50						48
41	50	48	51						49
42	51	49	52	o		o	o		50
43	52	50	53	50		50	50		51
44	o	51	54	53	54	53	53		52
45	54	52	55	51	52	51	51		53
46	53	53	56	52	53	52	52		54
47	56+*	54	58*	54	55	54	54		55

Y1	Y2	Y3	Y11	Y12	Y13	Y14	Y21	Y31	Y32	II
										1
										2
										3
							480	2	2	4
										5
o	225	o	x	162	162	170	104	171	172	6
			x	259	o	262	210	249	250	7
										8
			x	299	o	301	269	248	248	9
o	245	o	x	245	247	247	206	87	88	10
x	60	56	209	x	206	211	121	191	192	11
										12
94	95	102	55	55	55	61	51	66	67	13
			o	298	o	300	368	92	93	14
							375	25	25	15
										16
										17
x	20	17	x	x	x	20	19	162	163	18
										19
										20
x	4	2	x	x	6	6	2	72	73	21
x	23	20	26	x	x	23	22	91	92	22
x	252	o	253	253	254	255	205	34	34	23
x	34	31	x	35	x	35	33*	149	150	24
o	272	o	x	x	o	298	243	188	189	25
x	37	35	x	44	x	49	40	112	113	26
										27
x	27	24	x	x	x	28	27	36	36	28

Y1	Y2	Y3	Y11	Y12	Y13	Y14	Y21	Y31	Y32	II
x	276	o	x	x	o	348	432	303	o	29
x	93	100	x	x	51	58	48	246	246	30
								125	126	31
205	204	202	x	x	94	102	91	93	94	32
										33
o	251	o	x	x	253	254	213	280	280	34
x	38	36	x	42	x	39	232	200	201	35
o	o/234*	o	x	x	184/7*	41/6*	234/7*	203/6*	204/7*	36
o	230	o	x	x	185	42	235	202	203	37
o	234/2*	o	x	x	o	46/7*	239/4*	206/7*	207/8*	38
o	231	o	x	x	186	43	236	204	205	39
o	233	o	x	x	187	45	238	205	206	40
o	229	o	x	x	183	40	233	201	202	41
o	232/0*	o	x	x	0/184*	47/1*	237/9*	207/3*	208/4*	42
								220	220	43
										44
x	186*	182	x	184	182	192	175	81	82	45
x	73	68	217	x	213	218	133	294	294	46
										47
										48
x	170	166	x	x	172	181	169	146	147	49
										50
x	24	21	x	x	x	24	23	179	180	51
										52
										53
							285*	13*	13*	54
x	33	30	x	34	x	34	33*	5	5	55

Y33	Y51	Y52	Y54	Y61	Y62	Y63	Y64	YY1	II
								1. 58	1
									2
									3
2		109		2	2	2	2		4
									5
172								1.108	6
249	107	107	119	133	133	133	131	1.157	7
									8
248									9
87								1. 10	10
192								1.138	11
									12
66	23	23	24	53	53	53	53		13
92								2. 14	14
25	98	89	130	130	130	130	127		15
									16
									17
163	6	6	6	37	37	37	37		18
								1. 79	19
72									20
									21
91									22
34									23
150									24
189									25
112	33	33	34	62	62	62	62		26
									27
36	12	12	12	43	43	43	43	1. 50	28

Y33	Y51	Y52	Y54	Y61	Y62	Y63	Y64	YY1	II
303									29
246									30
125	35	35	37	64	64	64	64		31
93									32
288									33
280									34
201	95	102	100	127	127	127	124	1. 87	35
204/7*									36
203									37
207/8*									38
205									39
206									40
202									41
208/4*									42
220	96	o	101	128	128	128	125	1. 13	43
									44
81									45
294	32	32	33	61	61	61	61	1. 11	46
									47
									48
147									49
									50
180	69	70	74	101	101	101	100		51
									52
									53
13*		87*		10*	10*	10*	10*		54
5	5	5	5	36	36	36	36	1.160	55

[A1	[B1 (GA only)	[B1	[B2	[B3	C21	C22	C51	C52	DG1	II
							55	55	50	56
							56	56	51	57
							57	57	52	58
							58	58	53	59
							59	59	54	60
							60	60	55	61
							61	61	56	62
							62	32	57	63
							63	63	58	64
							64	64	59	65
							65	65	60	66
							66	66	61	67
							67	67	62	68
							68	68	63	69
							69	69	64	70
							70	70	65	71
							71	71	66	72
							72	72	67	73
							73	73	68	74
							74	74	69	75
							75	75	70	76
							76	76	71	77
							77	77	72	78
						o	78	78	73	79
						79	79	79	74	80
						80	80	80	75	81
						81	81	81	76+	82
						82	82	82	+78	83

[A1	[B1 (GA only)	[B1	[B2	[B3	C21	C22	C51	C52	DG1	II
						83	83	83	79	84
						84	84	84	80	85
						85	85	85	81	86
						86	86	86	82	87
						87	87	87	83	88
						88	88	88	o	89
						89	89	89	84	90
						90	90	90	85	91
						91	91	91	86	92
						92	92	92	87	93
						93	93	93	88	94
						94	94	94	89	95
						95	95	95	o	96
						96	96	96	90	97
						97	97	97	91	98
						98	98	98	92	99
						99	99	99	93	100
						o	o	o	94	101
						o	101	101	95	102
					+	o	102	102	96+	103
				+		o	103	103	+99	104
						o	104	104	100	105
						o	105	105	101	106
						o	106	106	102+	107
						o	107	107	o	108
						o	108	108	o	109
						o	109	109	o	110

DG2	DG3	DG4	DG5	DG6	D1	D11	D12	D14	D21	II
50	50	x	50	50	o	+59+			59	56
51	51	x	51	51	o	+76			60	57
52	52	x	52	52	53	+68+			61	58
53	53	x	53	53	54	77			62	59
54	54	x	54	54	$\overline{56}$	78			63	60
55	55	x	55	55	57	79			64	61
56	56	x	56	56	$\overline{55}$	80			65	62
57	57	x	57	57	$\overline{58}$	81			66	63
58	58	x	58	58	59	82			67	64
59	59	x	59	59	60	83			68	65
60	60	x	60	60	61	84			69	66
61	61	x	61	61	62	85			70	67
62	62	x	62	62	63	86			71	68
63	63	63	63	63	64	87			72	69
64	64	64	64	64	65	88			73	70
65	65	65	65	65	66	89			74	71
66	66	66	66	66	67	90			75	72
67	67	67	67	67	68	91			76	73
68	68	68	68	68	69	92			77	74
69	69	69	69	69	70	93			78	75
70	70	70	70	70	71	94			79	76
71	71	71	71	71	72	95			80	77
72	72	72	72	72	73	$\overline{97}$			81	78
73	73	73	73	73	74	$\overline{96}$			82	79
74	74	74	74	74	75	$\overline{98}$			83	80
75	75	75	75	75	76	99			84	81
76+	76+	76+	76+	76	77	100			85	82
+78	+78	+78	+78	77	78	101			86	83

DG2	DG3	DG4	DG5	DG6	D1	D11	D12	D14	D21	II
79	79	79	79	78	79	102			87	84
80	80	80	80	79	80	103			88	85
81	81	81	81	80	81	104			89	86
82	82	82	82	81	82	105			90	87
83	83	83	83	82	83	106			91	88
o	o	84	84	83	84	$\overline{108}$			92	89
84	84	85	85	84	85	$\overline{107}$			93	90
85	85	86	86	85	86	$\overline{109}$			94	91
86	86	87	87	86	87	110			95	92
87	87	88	88	87	88	111			96	93
88	88	89	89	88	89	112			97	94
89	89	90	90	89	90	113			98	95
o	o	91	91	90	91	114			99	96
90	90	92	92	91	92	115			100	97
91	x	93	93	92	93	116			101	98
92	x	94	94	93	94	117			102	99
93	x	95	95	94	95	118			103	100
94	x	96	96	95	96	119			104	101
95	x	97	97	96	97	120			105	102
96+	x	98+	98+	97	98+	121		+	106+	103
+99	x	+101	+101	98	+100	122		+105	+109	104
100	x	102	102	99	101	123		106	110	105
101	x	103	103	100	102	124		107	111	106
102+	x	104	104	101	103	125		108	112	107
o	x	o	o	102	104	126		109	$\overline{114}$+	108
o	x	o	o	103	105	127+		110	$\overline{113}$	109
o	x	105+	105+	104+	35	+129	///	111	$\overline{35}$	110

D41	D43	[D44	D45	D64	D71	E41	E42	E43	[F41	II
+50	+50					55	54	55		56
51	51					56	55	56		57
52	52					57	56	57		58
o*	53					58	58*	58		59
54	54					59	59	x		60
55	55					60	60	x		61
56	56		63			61	61	x		62
57	57		62			62	62	62		63
58	58					63	63	63		64
59	59					64	64	64		65
60	60					65	65	65		66
61	61					66	66	66		67
62	62					67	67	x		68
63	63					68	68	x		69
64	64					69	69	x		70
65	65					70	70	x		71
66	66					71	71	x		72
67+	67+					72	72	x		73
+69	+69					73	73	x		74
70	70					74	74	x		75
71	71					75	75	x		76
72	72					76	76	x		77
73	73					77	77	x		78
74	74					78	78	78		79
75	75					79	79	79		80
76	76					80	80	80		81
77	77					81	81	81		82
78	78					82	82	82		83

D41	D43	[D44	D45	D64	D71	E41	E42	E43	[F41	II
79	79					83	83	83		84
80	80				87	84	84	x		85
81	81				85	85	85	x		86
82	82					86	86	86		87
83	83					87	87	87		88
84	84					88	88	88		89
85	85					89	89	89		90
86	86					90	90	90		91
87	87					91	91	91		92
88	88					92	92	92		93
89	89					93	93	93		94
90	90		97			o	o	x		95
91	91		98			o	o	x		96
92	92		96			95	95	x		97
93	93		99			96	96	x		98
94	94		101			98	98	98		99
95	95		100			97	97	97		100
96	96		102			99	99	99		101
97	97		103			100	100	100		102
98	98		104			101	101	101		103
99	99		105			x	102	102		104
o	o		106			x	103	103		105
100	100		107			x	104	104		106
102	102		108			x	105	105		107
101	101		109			x	106	106		108
o	o		110+			x	107+	107+		109
35	35		95	///	///	94	94	x		110

G1	G2	G11	H21	H31	K1	M1	M6	M21	M24	II
49	50						o		+59	56
50	51						+56		60	57
51	52						57		61	58
52	53+						58		62	59
53	+55						59		63	60
54	56						60		64	61
55	57						61		65	62
56	58	114+					62		66	63
57	59	$\overline{63}$					63		67	64
58	60	64					64		68	65
59	61	65					65		69	66
60	62	66					66		70	67
61	63	67					67		71	68
62	64	68					68		72	69
63	65	69					69		73	70
64	66	70					70		74	71
65	67	71					71		75	72
66	68	72					72		76	73
67	69	73+					73		77	74
68	70	+					74		78	75
69	71						75		79	76
70	72						76		80	77
71	73						77		81	78
72	74						78		82	79
o	75						o		83	80
73	x						79		84	81
74	x						$\overline{81}$		85	82
75	x						$\overline{84}$		86	83

G1	G2	G11	H21	H31	K1	M1	M6	M21	M24	II
76	x						85		87	84
77	x						86		88	85
78	x						88		89	86
79	x						o		90	87
80	x						82		91	88
o	x						o		92	89
81	x						83		93	90
o*	x						80		94	91
83	x						o		95	92
84	x						89		96	93
85	x						90		97	94
86	x						91		98	95
87	x						92		99	96
88	x						93		100	97
89	91						94		101	98
90	92						95		102	99
91	93						96		103	100
92	94						97		104	101
93	95						98		105	102
94+	96+						99+		106	103
+97	+99						+102		107	104
98		+					o		108	105
99		+107					103		109	106
100	102	108	c				104		110	107
o	103+	109					105		111	108
o	o	110				///	106+		112	109
o	54	111+	///	///	///	o	+109		113+	110

N1	N21	N22	P71	P72	Q71	[R21	R22	[R23	S21	II
o	60								55	56
57	57								56	57
o	$\overline{59}$								57	58
59	$\overline{61}$								58	59
$\overline{62}$	$\overline{64}$								59	60
$\overline{60}$	$\overline{62}$								60	61
61	63								61	62
$\overline{63}$	$\overline{65}$								62	63
o	$\overline{67}$								63	64
64	68								64	65
65	69								65	66
66	69								66	67
67	70								67	68
68	71								68	69
69	72								69	70
$\overline{71}$	73								70	71
o	74								71	72
70	75								72	73
$\overline{72}$	76								73	74
73	77								74	75
o	+91								75	76
o	92								76	77
+86	93								77	78
87	94								78	79
o	+$\overline{97}$								79	80
88+	$\overline{95}$+								80	81
+90	98								81	82
91	99								82	83

N1	N21	N22	P71	P72	Q71	[R21	R22	[R23	S21	II
o	o								83	84
o	o	o							84	85
o	o	o							85	86
o	o	85							86	87
74	78	86							87	88
o	o	87							88	89
75	79	88							89	90
76	80	89							90	91
o	o	90							91	92
77	81	91		x					92	93
13+	13+	92		x					93	94
83	87	93		x					x	95
o	88	94		x					x	96
78	82	95		x					x	97
79	83	96							x	98
80	97	97							x	99
81	85	98							x	100
82	86	99							x	101
84+	89+	100							x	102
92+	100+	101					+		x	103
+94	o	102					+105		x	104
95	o	104					106		x	105
o	o	103					107		x	106
96	o	105					105		x	107
97+	o	106					109		x	108
o	o	107					110		x	109
o	o	o					111+		x	110

T5	T21	T71	U1	V1	V2	V22	V25	[W1	II
48	+64	55	60	55		55	55		56
49	65	56	59	56		56	56		57
50	66+	57	61	57		57	57		58
51	+74	58	62	58		58	58		59
52	x	59	63	59		59	59		60
53	x	61	64	60		60	60		61
54	x	60	65	61		61	61		62
55	x	62	66	62		62	62		63
56	x	63	67	63		63	63		64
57	80	64	68	64		64	64		65
58	81	65	69	65		65	65		66
59	82	66	70	66		66	66		67
60	83	67	71	67		67	67		68
61	84	68	72	68		68	68		69
62	85	69	73	69		70*	69		70
63	86	70	74	70			70		71
64	87	71	75	71			71		72
65	88	72	76	72			72		73
66	89	73	77	73			73		74
67	90	74	78	74			74		75
68	91	75	79	75			75		76
69	92	76	80	76			76		77
70	93	77	o	77			77		78
71	94	78	81	78			78		79
72	95	79	82	79			79		80
73	96	80	83	80			80		81
74	97	81	84	81			81		82
x	105	82	85	82			82		83

T5	T21	T71	U1	V1	V2	V22	V25	[W1	II
x	98	83	86	83			83		84
x	99	84	87	84			84		85
x	100	85	88	85			85		86
x	101	86	x	86			86		87
x	102	87	x	87			87		88
x	103	88	x	88			88		89
x	104	89	x	89			89		90
x	105	90	x	90			90		91
x	106	91	x	91			91		92
x	108*	92	x	92			92		93
x	109	93	x	93			93		94
x	110	94	x	94			94		95
x	111	95	x	95			95		96
x	112	96	x	96			96		97
x	113	97	x	97			97		98
x	114	98	x	98			98		99
x	115	99	x	99			99		100
x	116	100	x	100			100		101
x	117	101	x	101			101		102
x	118	102	x	102			102		103
x	119+	103	x	103			103		104
x	+121	104	x	104			104		105
x	122	105	x	105			105		106
x	123	106	x	106			106		107
x	124	107	x	107			107		108
x	o	108	x	108			108		109
x	35	x	36t	109+	+	///	109		110

Y1	Y2	Y3	Y11	Y12	Y13	Y14	Y21	Y31	Y32	II
			x	x	o	295	244	354	345	56
x	19	16	22	x	x	19	18	214	214	57
x	18	o					252			58
										59
										60
o	271	o	x	x	o	294	287	45	45	61
										62
x	42	o								63
										64
x	264	o	275	x	o	278	224	27	27	65
										66
x	90	33	40	40	x	37	36	38	38	67
114	115	124	x	x	x	71	59	28	28	68
								21	21	69
										70
										71
o	274	o	x	x	o	318	227			72
x	192	187	x	x	o	323	178	185	186	73
x	78	73	223	x	224	224	139	41	41	74
										75
x	44	41	x	x	194	199	107	17	17	76
						306	270*	43	43	77
										78
										79
										80
										81
								24	24	82
x	52	o						268	268	83

Y1	Y2	Y3	Y11	Y12	Y13	Y14	Y21	Y31	Y32	II
106	107	115	x	144	144	150	156*	181	182	84
										85
										86
x	5	3	x	x	7	6	3	102	103	87
										88
										89
										90
										91
										92
										93
										94
										95
										96
										97
								23	23	98
										99
										100
										101
x	12	o								102
							352	273	273	103
										104
										105
										106
										107
										108
201	201	198	171	x	170*	179	186	131	133	109
										110

Y33	Y51	Y52	Y54	Y61	Y62	Y63	Y64	YY1	II
356								1.132	56
215	9	9	9	40	40	40	40	1. 26	57
									58
									59
45									60
									61
									62
								1.161	63
									64
27								1. 55	65
									66
38				29	29	29	29		67
28	24	24	25	54	54	54	54		68
21				17	17	17	17		69
									70
									71
									72
186									73
41	31	31	32	31	31	31	31	1.109	74
								1. 32	75
17									76
43	36	36	37	65	65	65	65		77
									78
									79
									80
									81
24				20	20	20	20		82
268									83

Y33	Y51	Y52	Y54	Y61	Y62	Y63	Y64	YY1	II
182									84
									85
102									86
									87
									88
									89
									90
									91
									92
									93
									94
									95
									96
									97
23		100	107	19	19	19	19		98
								2. 12	99
									100
									101
								1. 2	102
273									103
									104
									105
									106
									107
									108
132	100								109
								1. 6	110

A1	B1 (GA only)	B1	B2	B3	C21	[C22	C51	C52	DG1	III
										1
										2
										3
										4
										5
										6
										7
										8
										9
										10
										11
										12
										13
										14
										15
										16
										17
									22	18
									18	19
									19	20
									20	21
									21	22
									23	23
									25	24
									24	25
									26	26
									28	27

A1	B1 (GA only)	B1	B2	B3	C21	[C22	C51	C52	DG1	III
									27	28
										29
										30
										31
										32
										33
										34
										35
										36
										37
										38
										39
										40
										41
										42
										43
										44
										45
										46
										47
										48
										49
										50
										51
										52
										53

DG2	DG3	DG4	DG5	[DG6	D1	D11	D12	[D14	D21	III
		+3	+3							1
		4	4							2
		5	5							3
		6	6				5			4
		7	7				4			5
		8	8							6
		9	9							7
		10	10							8
		11	11							9
		12	12							10
		13	13							11
		14	14							12
		15	15							13
		16	16							14
		17	17							15
		18	18							16
		19	19			18				17
22	22	24	24			17				18
18	18	20	20							19
19	19	21	21							20
20	20	22	22							21
21	21	23	23							22
23	23	25	25							23
25	25	27	27							24
24	24	26	26							25
26	26	28	28							26
28	28	30	30							27

DG2	DG3	DG4	DG5	[DG6	D1	D11	D12	[D14	D21	III
27	27	29	29							28
		$\overline{31}$	$\overline{31}$							29
		32	32							30
		33	33							31
		34	34							32
		35	35							33
		36	36							34
		37	37							35
		38	38							36
		39	39							37
		40	40							38
		41	41							39
		42	42							40
		43	43		*					41
		44	44		o					42
		45	45		o					43
		46	46		o					44
		47	47		o					45
		48	48		41*					46
		49	49		42/43*					47
		50	50		42					48
		51	51		43					49
		52	52		44					50
		53	53		45					51
		54	54		46					52
		55	55		47					53

[D41	[D43	D44	D45	D64	D71	[E41	[E42	[E43	[F41	III
					+2					1
					3					2
					4					3
					5					4
					10					5
										6
										7
										8
										9
					11					10
					12					11
					13					12
					14					13
					15					14
					16					15
					17					16
					18					17
					19					18
					20					19
					21					20
					22					21
					23					22
					24					23
					25					24
					26					25
					27					26
					28					27

[D41	[D43	D44	D45	D64	D71	[E41	[E42	[E43	[F41	III
					30					28
					$\overline{29}$					29
					$\overline{31}$					30
					32					31
					33					32
					34					33
					35					34
					36					35
					37					36
			38		38					37
			$\overline{37}$		39					38
					40					39
					41					40
					42					41
					43					42
					44					43
					45					44
					46					45
					47					46
					48					47
					49					48
					50					49
					51					50
					52					51
					53					52
					54					53

G1	G2	G11	H21	H31	K1	M1	[M6	M21	M24	III
										1
								5	+4+	2
								$\overline{2}$+	2+	3
								+4	+6	4
								$\overline{6}$	7	5
								7	8	6
								8	9	7
								9	10	8
								10	11	9
								11	12	10
						12		12	13	11
						13		13	14	12
						$\overline{11}$		14	15	13
		15						15	16	14
		$\overline{14}$						16	17	15
								17	18	16
o								18	19	17
o								19	20	18
o								20	21	19
o								21	22	20
o								22	23	21
o								23	24	22
o								24	25	23
o								25	26	24
o								26	27	25
17								27	28	26
18								28	29	27

G1	G2	G11	H21	H31	K1	M1	[M6	M21	M24	III
19+								29	30	28
+21								30	31	29
22								31	32	30
23								32	33	31
24								33	34	32
25								34	35	33
26								35	36	34
27								36	37	35
28								37	38	36
29								38	39	37
30								39	40	38
31								40	41	39
32								41	42	40
33								42	43	41
34								43	44	42
35								44	45	43
36								45	46	44
37								46	47	45
38								47	48	46
39								48	49	47
40						+		49	50	48
41						+51		50	51	49
42						52		51	52	50
43						53		52	53	51
44						54		53	54	52
45						55		54	55	53

N1	N21	N22	P71	[P72	Q71	[R21	[R22	R23	[S21	III
	+11									1
	12									2
	13									3
+84	+90									4
85	91									5
4	14									6
5	15									7
86	92									8
7	17									9
6	16									10
8	18									11
87	93									12
9	19									13
10	20									14
11	21									15
89	94									16
12	22									17
13	23									18
14	24									19
15	25									20
90	95									21
91	96*									22
16	26							24		23
o	o							25		24
o	o							26		25
88	27		o					27		26
17	28		26					28		27

N1	N21	N22	P71	[P72	Q71	[R21	[R22	R23	[S21	III
o	o		27					29		28
92	96*		28					30		29
93	o		29					31		30
94+	97		30					32		31
18	29		31					33		32
19	30		32					34		33
+96	98		33					35		34
20	31		34					36		35
21	32		35					37		36
22	33		36					23		37
23	99		37							38
24	34		38							39
25	35		39							40
97	100		40							41
26	36		41							42
98	101		42							43
99	o		43							44
27	37		44							45
100	o		45							46
28	o		46							47
29	o		47					o		48
30	38		48					48		49
31	39		49					49		50
33	o		50					50		51
o	o		51					51		52
34	o	52	52					52		53

[T5	T21	T71	U1	V1	V2	V22	V25	[W1	III
		x							1
									2
									3
									4
									5
									6
									7
									8
									9
									10
									11
									12
									13
									14
					15/16*				15
					17				16
					18				17
					19				18
					20				19
					21				20
					22				21
					23				22
					24				23
					25				24
					26				25
		27*			27				26
		28			28				27

[T5	T21	T71	U1	V1	V2	V22	V25	[W1	III
		29	35		29				28
		30	28		30				29
		31	29		31				30
		32	30		32				31
		33	31		33				32
		34	32		34				33
		35	33		35				34
		36	34		36				35
		37			37				36
		38			38				37
		39			39				38
		40			40				39
		41			41				40
		42			42/43*				41
		43			44				42
		44			45				43
		45			45*				44
		46			46				45
		47			47				46
		48			48				47
		49			49				48
		50			50				49
		51			51				50
		52			52				51
		53			53				52
		54			54				53

Y1	Y2	Y3	Y11	Y12	Y13	Y14	Y21	Y31	Y32	III
139	141	98	x	x	x	56	46	110	111	1
140	142	99	x	x	x	57	47	101	102	2
207	206	204	54	54	54	60	50	150	151	3
x	94	101	x	x	52	59	49	144	145	4
95	96	103	x	x	134	140	149	236	236	5
x	15	12	x	17	18	14	13	235	235	6
96	97	104	x	122	122	128	150	231	231	7
97	98	105	x	x	126	132	151	82	83	8
98	99	106	x	56	56	62	52	109	110	9
99	100	107	x	x	127	133	152*	67	68	10
141	143	o	x	x	129	135	194*	211	211	11
100*	101*	108*	x	57	58	63	53	228	228	12
142	144	o	x	x	130	136	195	127	129	13
101	102	109	x	58	59	64	54	75	76	14
102	103	110	x	59	x	65	55	63	64	15
143	145	111	139	x	139	142	153	151	152	16
103	104	112	x	60	x	66	56	57	57	17
104	105	113	x	x	131	137	154	79	80	18
144	146	o	x	x	132	138	196*	272	273	19
105	106	114	x	x	133	139	156*	121	122	20
107	108	116	x	x	135	141	157	166	167	21
109	110	118	x	x	136	143	158	183	184	22
145	147	119	x	x	x	68	58	107	108	23
110	111	120	x	x	137	144	159	184	185	24
111	112	121	x	x	138	145	160	270	270	25
113	114	123	x	x	141	147	162	59	59	26
115	116	125	x	x	142	148	163	122	123	27

Y1	Y2	Y3	Y11	Y12	Y13	Y14	Y21	Y31	Y32	III
x	55	51	x	x	143	149	117	135	136	28
118	119	128	x	146	146	152	165	198	199	29
119	120	129	65	65	65	72	61	167	168	30
119*	121	130	x	147	147	153	166*	193	194	31
120	122	131	66	66	66	73	62	137	138	32
121	123	132	91	x	91	98	89	230	230	33
122	124	133	67	67	67	74	63	69	70	34
123	125	134	x	x	231	231	342	134	135	35
126	128	137	68	68	68	75	64	233	233	36
127	129	138	73	73	73	76	65	159	160	37
128	130	139	69	69	69	77	66	172	173	38
124	126	135	x	x	93	101	90	232	232	39
125	127	136	x	x	153	161	328	170	171	40
130	131	140	x	148	148	154	310*	247	247	41
131	132	141	70	70	70	78	67	157	158	42
154	156	151	72	72	72	80	69	155	156	43
155	157	152	x	159	159	167	282	136	137	44
146	148	o	x	160	160	168	197	175	176	45
147	149	153	x	161	161	169	293	209	209	46
157	158	154	74	74	74	82	70	99	100	47
148	150	o	x	163	163	171	o	o	o	48
158	159	155	75	75	75	81	71	194	195	49
206	205	203	x	x	92*	100	88	234	234	50
x	163	159	x	164	164	172	303*	158	159	51
x	164	160	x	76	76	83	72	160	161	52
159	160	156	x	165	165	173	313	192	193	53

Y33	Y51	Y52	Y54	Y61	Y62	Y63	Y64	YY1	III
110	56	57	59	88	88	88	87*		1
101	43	44	o	74	73	74	73		2
									3
145	79	80	o	110	110	100	o		4
236	27	26	27	56	56	56	56		5
									6
									7
									8
									9
									10
212	42	43	46	73	72	73	72	152*	11
228	80	81	84	111	111	111	o		12
128	41	42	43	72	71	72	71		13
75	81	82	85	112	112	112	o		14
63	82	83	86	113	113	133	o		15
152	o	58	60	89	89	89	82*		16
57	26	27	28	57	57	57	57		17
79									18
272	57	59	61	90	90	90	89*		19
121	38	38	39	68	67	68	67		20
167									21
184	39	39	40	69	68	69	68		22
107									23
185	o	40	41	70	69	70	69		24
270									25
59									26
122									27

Y33	Y51	Y52	Y54	Y61	Y92	Y63	Y64	YY1	III
136									28
199	83	o	87	114	114	114	o		29
168	30	30	31	60	60	60	60		30
194	85	o	89	116	116	116	o		31
138	84	84	88	115	115	115	o		32
230	94	98	99	126	126	126	123		33
69	29	29	30	59	59	59	59		34
135	86	85	90	117	117	117	o		35
233	89	o	93	120	120	120	o		36
160									37
173									38
232	87	97	91	118	118	118	o		39
171	88	93	92	119	119	119	o		40
247									41
158									42
156									43
137									44
176									45
210									46
99	62	63	66	94	94	94	93*		47
									48
195	63	64	67	95	95	95	94*		49
234									50
159	o	67	70	97	97	97	96		51
161	66	68	71	98	98	98	97		52
193									53

[A1	[B1 (GA only)	[B1	[B2	[B3	C21	[C22	C51	C52	DG1	III
										54
										55
										56
										57
										58
										59
										60
										61
										62
										63
										64
										65
										66
										67
										68
										69
										70
							72	72		71
							71	71		72
										73
										74
										75
										76
										77
										78
							80	80		79
							79	79		80

[A1	[B1 (GA only)	[B1	[B2	[B3	C21	[C22	C51	C52	DG1	III
									+	81
									+84	82
									85	83
									86	84
									87	85
									88	86
									89	87
									90	88
									91	89
									92	90
									93	91
									94	92
									95	93
									o	94
									96	95
									97+	96
					98				o	97
					$\overline{97}$				o	98
									o	99
									o	100
									o	101
									o	102
									o	103
									o	104
									o	105
					///		///	///	o	106

DG2	DG3	DG4	DG5	[DG6	D1	D11	D12	[D14	D21	III
		56	56		50					54
		57	57		51					55
		58	58		52					56
		59	59		*					57
		60	60		o					58
		61	61		o					59
		62	62		o					60
		63	63		o					61
		64	64		53*					62
		65	65		54					63
		66	66		55					64
		67	67		56					65
		68	68		57					66
		69	69		58					67
		70	70		59					68
		71	71		60					69
		72	72		61					70
		73	73		62					71
		74	74		63					72
		75	75		64					73
		76	76		65					74
		77	77		66					75
		o	78		67					76
		o	x		68					77
		78/88*	x		69					78
		79/89	x		70	80	80			79
		80/90	x		71	$\overline{79}$	$\overline{79}$			80

DG2	DG3	DG4	DG5	[DG6	D1	D11	D12	[D14	D21	III
+		+	x		72					81
+84	x	+84	x		$\overline{75}$					82
85	x	85	x		76					83
86	x	86	x		$\overline{73}$					84
87	x	87*	x		74					85
88	x	o	x		o					86
89	x	o	x		o					87
90	x	o	x		o					88
91	x	91	x		o					89
92	x	92	x		o					90
93	x	93	x		77					91
94	x	94	x		78					92
95	x	95	x		79					93
o	x	o	x		80					94
96	x	96	x		81					95
97+	x	97+	x		82					96
o	x	o	x		*					97
o	x	o	x		o					98
o	x	o	x		o					99
o	x	o	x		o					100
o	x	o	x		o					101
o	x	o	x		83*					102
o	x	o	x		84					103
o	x	o	x		85					104
o	x	o	x		86					105
o	x	o	x		87+	+	+			+106

[D41	[D43	D44	D45	D64	D71	[E41	[E42	[E43	[F41	III
					55					54
					56					55
					57					56
					58					57
					59					58
					60					59
					61					60
					62					61
					63					62
					64					63
					65					64
					66					65
					67					66
			o		68					67
			67		69					68
			68		70					69
			69		71					70
			70		72					71
			71		73					72
			72		74					73
			73		75					74
			74		76					75
			75		77					76
					o					77
					78					78
					$\overline{80}$					79
					$\overline{79}$					80

[D41	[D43	D44	D45	D64	D71	[E41	[E42	[E43	[F41	III
			82							81
			$\overline{81}$							82
										83
										84
										85
										86
			76		88					87
			$\overline{87}$		$\overline{\text{o}}$					88
			88		87					89
			89		$\overline{89}$					90
			90		90					91
			91		o					92
			92		91					93
			93		92					94
			94		93+					95
			95		o					96
			96		+95					97
					96					98
					97					99
		o		///	98+					100
		o		o	o					101
		100		o	o					102
		101		o	o					103
		102	+	o	o					104
		103	+107+	o	+100+					105
		104+	97	o	+102					106

G1	G2	G11	H21	H31	K1	M1	[M6	M21	M24	III
46						56		55	56	54
47						57		56	57	55
48						58		57	58	56
49						59		58	59	57
50						60		59	60	58
51						61		60	61	59
52						62		61	62	60
53						63		62	63	61
54						64		63	64	62
55						65		64	65	63
56						66		65	66	64
57						67		66	67	65
58						68		67	68	66
59						69		68	69	67
60						70		69	$\overline{71}$	68
61						o		70	$\overline{70}$	69
62						71		$\overline{72}$	$\overline{72}$	70
$\overline{64}$						72		$\overline{71}$	73	71
$\overline{63}$				t		73		$\overline{73}$	74	72
$\overline{65}$				t	o	o		74	75	73
66				t	73			75	76	74
67					74			76	77	75
68					75			77	78	76
69					76			78	79	77
70					77			79	80	78
71		80		80	78			80	81	79
72		$\overline{79}$		$\overline{79}$	79			81	82	80

G1	G2	G11	H21	H31	K1	M1	[M6	M21	M24	III
73+					80			82+	83+	81
+76					81			+85	+85	82
77					82			86	86	83
78					83			87	87	84
79					84			88	88	85
80		87	x		85+	+		89	89+	86
81		$\overline{86}$	x			+88		90	+91	87
82						89		91+	92	88
83						90		+95	93	89
84						91		96	94	90
85						92		97	95	91
86						93		98	96	92
87		o				94		99	97	93
o	o	93			95	o		o	o	94
88	94	94			$\overline{94}$	95		100	98	95
89+	95	95			$\overline{96}$	96+		101	99+	96
o	o	96			o	o		102	o	97
o	o	97			o	o		103+	o	98
o	o	98			97	o		106	o	99
o	o	99			98	o		+$\overline{105}$	o	100
o	o	100			99	o		107	o	101
o	o	101			100	o		108	o	102
o	o	102			101	o		109	o	103
o	o	103			102	o		110	o	104
o	o	104			103+	o		111	o	105
o	o	105	///	///	o	o		112	o	106

N1	N21	N22	P71	[P72	Q71	[R21	[R22	R23	[S21	III
32	40	53	53					53		54
35	41	54	54					54		55
36	42	55	55					55		56
37	43	56	56					56		57
38	44	57	57					o		58
39	45	58	58					57		59
40	46	59	59					58		60
41	47	60	60					60*		61
42	48	61	61					61		62
43	49	62	62					62		63
44	50	63	63					o		64
45	51	64	64					63		65
46	52	65	65					64		66
47	53	66	66					65		67
48	54	67	67					66		68
49	55	68	68					67		69
50	56	69	69					68		70
51	57	70	o					69		71
52	58	71	70					70		72
53	59	72	71					71		73
54	60	73	72					o*		74
55	61	74	73					73		75
57	63	75	74					74		76
56	62	76	75					o		77
58	64	77	76					75		78
59	64*	78	78		80			76		79
61	66	79	77		79			77		80

N1	N21	N22	P71	[P72	Q71	[R21	[R22	R23	[S21	III
62	67	80	79					78		81
60	65	o	80					79		82
65	71	82	81					80		83
o	o	81	82					82		84
66	72	o	o					81		85
o	o	o	83					83		86
67	73	o	84					85		87
71+	77+	95+	85					86		88
63	69*	83	86					84		89
64	70	84	87					87		90
+76	+82	85	88					88		91
+74+	+80+	86	89					89		92
69	75	87	90					90+		93
68	74	88	91					+92		94
70	76	89	92					93		95
o	83	90	93					94		96
77	84	91	94					95+		97
o	o	93	95					108		98
78	o	o	96					o		99
81+	87+	o	97					o		100
80	86	+98+	o					o		101
o	o	o	98					o		102
o	o	o	99					o		103
o	o	o	100					o		104
79	85	94	101					o		105
o	o	92	102		///			+107		106

[T5	T21	T71	U1	V1	V2	V22	V25	[W1	III
		55			55				54
		56			56				55
		57			57				56
		58			58				57
		59			59				58
		60			60				59
		61			61				60
		62			62				61
		63			63				62
		64			64				63
		65			65				64
		66			66				65
		67			67				66
		68			68				67
		69			69				68
		70			70				69
		71			71				70
		72			72				71
		73			73				72
	74	74			74				73
	73	75			75				74
		76			76				75
		77			77				76
		78			78				77
		79			79				78
		81			80				79
		80			t				80

[T5	T21	T71	U1	V1	V2	V22	V25	[W1	III
		82			82				81
	+	83			83				82
	+84	84			84				83
	85	85			85				84
	86	86			86				85
	87+	87			87				86
	+89	88			88				87
	90	89			89				88
	91	90			90				89
	92	91			91				90
	93	92			92				91
	94	93			93				92
	95+	94	94*	o	o	o	o		93
	o	95	$\overline{93}$	93	94	93	93		94
	+97	96	94	94	95	94	94		95
	98+	97	$\overline{95}$	95	96	95	95		96
	o	98	96	96	101*	96	96		97
	o	99	97	97	102	97	97		98
	o	100	98	98	103	98	98		99
	o	101	99	99	104	99	99		100
	o	102	100	100	105	100	100		101
	o	103	x	101	106	101	101		102
	o	104	x	102	107	102	102		103
	o	105	x	103	108	103	103		104
	o	106	x	104+	109+	105*	104		105
	o	107	x	+107+	+112+	*	105		106

Y1	Y2	Y3	Y11	Y12	Y13	Y14	Y21	Y31	Y32	III
160	161	157	x	166	166	174	304	1	1	54
161	162	158	x	77	77	84	73	169	170	55
x	165	161	168	x	168	176	317	237	237	56
x	166	162	169	x	169	177	314	182	183	57
x	167	163	x	x	170	178	167	143	144	58
x	169	165	79	x	79	86	74	116	117	59
x	168	164	172	x	171	180	168	174	175	60
x	172	168	x	x	174	183	171	242	242	61
x	173	169	x	177	176	185	172	177	178	62
x	174	170	92	x	92*	99	87	119	120	63
x	14	11	x	x	15	12	11	256	257	64
152	154	10	x	x	14	11	10	8	8	65
x	177	173	x	90	90	97	86	65	66	66
x	178	174	80	x	80	87	76	117	118	67
x	180	176	x	x	82	89	78	98	99	68
x	181	177	x	182	180	189	174	153	154	69
x	179	175	81	x	81	88	77	118	119	70
x	188	184	x	x	191	195	177	260	261	71
x	191	188	x	89	88	96	85	257	258	72
132	133	142	x	x	150	158	279*	238	238	73
133	134	143	x	149	149	157	300	156	157	74
134*	135	144	x	x	151	159	279*	104	105	75
134*	137	145	x	x	152/3*	160	454*	168	169	76
135*	138	146	x	x	154	162	292	142	143	77
136	o	147	x	x	155	163	311	o	128	78
135*	136	148	137*	157	157	165	283	199	200	79
137	139	149	71	71	71	79	68	128	130	80

Y1	Y2	Y3	Y11	Y12	Y13	Y14	Y21	Y31	Y32	III
138	140	150	x	158	158	166	312	195	196	81
										82
x	25	22	x	x	x	26	25	145	146	83
										84
										85
										86
										87
x	89	95	x	x	x	51	42	29	29	88
										89
							487			90
212	211						344			91
										92
										93
										94
								353	344	95
						353	276*	108	109	96
							476	271	271	97
										98
										99
										100
										101
										102
										103
										104
										105
										106

Y33	Y51	Y52	Y54	Y61	Y62	Y63	Y64	YY1	III
o	64	65	68	1	1	1	1		54
170	65	66	69	96	96	96	95*		55
237	90	o	94	121	121	121	o		56
183									57
144	91	o	95	122	122	o	125		58
116									59
175	o	o	96	123	123	123	120		60
242									61
178	93	o	98	125	125	125	122		62
119									63
255									64
8	61	62	65	7	7	7	7		65
65									66
117									67
98									68
154									69
118									70
260									71
257									72
238									73
157	50	51	52	81	81	81	80		74
104	o	53	54	83	83	83	82		75
169	52	54	55	84	84	84	83		76
143	53	55	56	85	85	85	84		77
127									78
200									79
129	54	56	57	86	86	86	85*		80

Y33	Y51	Y52	Y54	Y61	Y62	Y63	Y64	YY1	III
196	55	o	58	87	87	87	86*		81
									82
146	7	7	7	38	38		38		83
									84
									85
								1.83	86
									87
29	22	22	23	52	52	52	52		88
									89
								1.91	90
									91
									92
									93
									94
355			106						95
108			108						96
271	99	108	104	131	131	128	134		97
									98
									99
									100
									101
									102
									103
									104
									105
									106

Notes to Chart of Standard Verse Sequences

st. 1.1(F1) The verses of century one are further divided into four parts which are numbered 2, 3, 4, 5. (Part 1 is an introduction written in Marathi.)
st. 1.2(N1) Note the misnumbering. Verse sequence is as in standard version.
st. 1.7(N1 and N21) Note misnumbering. Verse sequence is as in standard version.
st. 1.22(N21) Note misnumbering. Verse sequence is as in standard version.
st. 1.22(Y) Line d of this verse is the same as line d of Y2 86 (Y3 92, Y13 228, Y14 228, Y21 144, Y31 178, Y32 179, Y33 179, Y51 74, Y52 75, Y61 105, Y62 105, Y63 104, Y64 108)
st. 1.23(F1) See footnote to st. 1.1.
st. 1.25(G11) Verse, unnumbered, is entered in the margin.
st. 1.26(N21) The number 25 is omitted. No verse is numbered 25.
st. 1.52(M24) Number 52 is omitted. No verse is numbered 52.
st. 1.54(F1) See footnote to st. 1.1.
st. 1.58(H21) The number 59 occurs twice. The sequence of H21: st. 2.56, 59, 57, 58, 60.
st. 1.59(D11) This verse occurs twice, as 59 and 60.
st. 1.76(H21) The number 75 is omitted.
st. 1.77(S21) Note misnumbering. The verse sequence is as in the standard version. Also the commentary to st. 1.76 skips by haplology to the commentary to st. 1.77. There is no text for st. 1.77.
st. 1.79(D1) The first three words of the first line of st. 1.79 (so 'yaṃ vilāsa°) are combined with the last word of line c of st. 1.86 and the whole of line d (°śriyau vilokaya vilocanā°).
st. 1.86(D1) See above.
st. 1.93(F1) See footnote to st. 1.1.
st. 1.93(S21) The number 91 is omitted. No verse is numbered 91.
st. 1.107(S21) The number 106 is omitted. No verse is numbered 106.
st. 1.110(N1 and U1) The verse is entered here, but it is unnumbered.
st. 1.112(G2) Verses are entered after st. 1.112 at the end of the manuscript. The manuscript is so damaged it is impossible to read the verses.
st. 1.112(M21 and M24) The verse is entered here but it is unnumbered.
st. 2.3(D21) Note the misnumbering.
st. 2.13(R22) The manuscript is much disordered here, and the commentary does not match the text.
st. 2.23(U1) The number 23 is omitted. No verse is numbered 23.
st. 2.24(Y21) Number 33 occurs twice, the second 33 immediately next the first 33. The first 33 is st. 2.55 and the second is st. 2.24.
st. 2.36(DG3) st. 2.36–42 are entered between DG3 2.36 and 37 (st. 2.35 and 43). They are numbered 36–42 as in the standard version.
st. 2.36(Y) To be read as in following example: Y2 reads 0/234 for st. 2.36, 234/232 for st. 2.38, 232/0 for st. 2.42. This indicates that lines a and b of st. 2.38 are combined with lines c and d of st. 2.36 to form a verse numbered 234. st. 2.42 a-b is combined with st. 2.38 c-d to form a verse numbered 232.
st. 2.38(Y) See above.

st. 2.42(E43) st. 2.42 and the number 41 are omitted.
st. 2.42(Y) See footnote to st. 2.36.
st. 2.44(D21) Note the misnumbering.
st. 2.44(E41) The number 42 is omitted. No verse is numbered 42.
st. 2.45(D21) Note misnumbering.
st. 2.45(Y2) This verse occurs a second time as number 228.
st. 2.54(Y21, Y31, Y32, Y33, Y52, Y61, Y62, Y63, Y64) See notes on add. ghaṭodakeṣu.
st. 2.55(T21) Number 55 is omitted. No verse is numbered 55.
st. 2.55(U1) Number 57 is omitted. No verse is numbered 57.
st. 2.55(Y21) See st. 2.24.
st. 2.59(D41) st. 2.59 and the number 53 are omitted.
st. 2.59(E42) The number 57 is omitted. No verse is numbered 57.
st. 2.70(V22) Number 69 is omitted. No verse is numbered 69.
st. 2.77(Y21) Y21 270 is formed from st. 2.77 a-b plus Y21 130 c-d (Y2 70 c-d, Y3 65 c-d etc.)
st. 2.84(Y21) Number 156 occurs twice. The second number 156 occurs immediately next the first 156. st. 3.20 is the first 156 and st. 2.24 is the second.
st. 2.91(G1) st. 2.91 and the number 82 are omitted.
st. 2.93(T21) Number 107 is omitted. There is no number 107.
st. 2.109(Y13) Number 170 occurs twice. The second number 170 occurs immediately next the first number 170. st. 2.109 is the second 170 and st. 3.58, the first.
st. 3.1(Y64) st. 3.1 occurs a second time as 111.
st. 3.10(Y21) st. 3.10 occurs a second time as 299.
st. 3.11(Y21) Y21 301 has st. 3.11bcd as lines bcd and st. 3.76a as line a. Y21 194 is st. 3.11 and Y21 454 is st. 3.76.
st. 3.11(YY1) st. 3.11cb is YY1 152ab.
st. 3.12(Y1, Y2, and Y3) Y1 117cd(Y2 118cd, Y3 127cd) is st. 3.12cd.
st. 3.15(V2) The text is numbered 15 and the commentary is numbered 16.
st. 3.16(Y64) st. 3.16 occurs a second time as 112.
st. 3.19(Y21) st. 3.19 occurs a second time as 340.
st. 3.19(Y64) st. 3.19 occurs a second time as 113.
st. 3.20(Y21) See st. 2.84.
st. 3.22(N21) N21 2.96 is st. 3.22ab plus st. 3.29cd.
st. 3.26(T71) Number 26 seems to be omitted so that st. 3.26 is numbered 27, but the manuscript is much damaged here so that it is possible that a verse was entered between st. 3.25 and 26.
st. 3.29(N21) See st. 3.22(N21).
st. 3.31(Y1) Number 119 occurs twice. Sequence of st. 3.30 and 31 in Y1 is as in standard version.
st. 3.31(Y21) This verse occurs a second time as 341.
st. 3.41(D1) D1 combines st. 3.41 and 64 thus: °dayite 'ti of st. 3.41c precedes °gairika° of st. 3.46b. paraṃ is interposed between these. The whole combination is numbered 41.
st. 3.41(V2) The text is numbered 42 and the commentary 43.
st. 3.41(Y21) This verse occurs a second time as ~~537~~.

st. 3.44(V2) Note misnumbering.
st. 3.46(D1) See footnote to st. 3.41.
st. 3.47(D1) Lines ab are number 42 and lines cd, 43.
st. 3.47(Y64) The verse occurs a second time as 117.
st. 3.49(Y64) The verse occurs a second time as 118.
st. 3.50(Y13) Number 92 occurs twice immediately next each other. The first 92 is st. 3.63 and the second is st. 3.50.
st. 3.51(Y21) This verse occurs a second time as 111.
st. 3.55(Y64) This verse occurs a second time as 119.
st. 3.57(D1) D1 combines st. 3.57 and 62 thus: °svādīya° of st. 3.57b precedes st. 3.62 which is given in full. The combination is numbered 53.
st. 3.61(R23) Note the misnumbering.
st. 3.62(D1) See st. 3.57.
st. 3.63(Y13) See st. 3.50.
st. 3.73(Y21) Number 279 occurs twice immediately next each other. The first is st. 3.73 and the second, st. 3.75.
st. 3.74(R23) st. 3.74 and number 72 are omitted.
st. 3.75(Y21) See above.
st. 3.75(Y1) st. 3.75, 79, 76, 77 occur with the sequence as given and are numbered respectively 134, 135, 134, 135.
st. 3.76(Y13) Lines ab are numbered 152 and lines cd, 153.
st. 3.76(Y21) See footnote to st. 3.11.
st. 3.78(DG4) The combination of st. 3.85ab and 78cd is numbered 88. There is no number 87; st. 3.85cd is omitted.
st. 3.79(N21) Number 64 is repeated twice. Sequence is as in N1.
st. 3.79(Y11) This verse is incorrectly numbered 137. The correct number would be 157.
st. 3.80(Y64) This verse occurs a second time as 109.
st. 3.81(Y64) This verse occurs a second time as 110.
st. 3.85(DG4) See footnote to st. 3.78.
st. 3.89(N21) The number 68 is omitted. Sequence is as in N1.
st. 3.93(U1) Note the misnumbering. Verse sequence is st. 3.92, 94, 95, 93, 96, 97.
st. 3.96(Y21) This verse occurs a second time as 362.
st. 3.97(D1) D1 combines st. 3.97 and 102 thus: kam adbhu° of st. 3.97b precedes °bandham of st. 3.102a. This combination is numbered 83.
st. 3.97(V2) Note the misnumbering. Verse sequence is st. 3.96, 97.
st. 3.102(D1) See footnote to st. 3.97.
st. 3.105(V22) Note the misnumbering. Number 104 is omitted.
st. 3.106(V22) Verse is entered here but is unnumbered.

Guide to Reading "Chart of Additional Verse Sequences"

Sixty-six verses, not entered in the standard version of the KK, are entered in one or more of the 59 KK mss. collated for this edition. These verses are called additional (add.) verses. Standard verses have also been treated here as additional verses if they occur in a century other than the century in which their position is standard.

In the "Chart of Standard Verse Sequences" the occurrence of additional verses is noted with a plus (+). No other information about an additional verse is given in this chart. Further information about an additional verse is given in the "Chart of Additional Verse Sequences" according to the standard verse to which the plus has been suffixed in the "Chart of Standard Verse Sequences." (Additional verses are arranged in the "Chart of Additional Verse Sequences" according to the standard verse or verses they follow.

An additional verse is not entered in the "Chart of Additional Verse Sequences" according to the verse it precedes unless that verse is the first verse. If the first verse in the "Chart of Standard Verse Sequences" is prefixed with a plus, this plus, unlike other prefixed pluses, indicates the place where the additional verse has been entered in the "Chart of Additional Verse Sequences."

For an alphabetical listing of all additional verses, except those verses which are also standard verses, see the section entitled "Additional Verses." Here their positions after standard verses are given.

The column headings in the "Chart of Additional Verse Sequences" are abbreviated. The full description is as follows:

Standard Verse	Standard verse after which additional verse is entered.
Manuscript	Manuscript in which additional verse is found.
Verse Number	Number of additional verse in the manuscript in which it is found.
Occurrence	Number of occurrence of additional verse after standard verse.
Total Occurrences	Total number of occurrences of additional verse after standard verse.
Identification	Identification of additional verse as standard verse or echo of standard verse (+indicates that verse is entered twice in the manuscript: as a standard verse and as an additional verse.)

The use of the terms, "Occurrence" and "Total Occurrences", in the column heads should be further clarified by an example. See 'dadhimathananinādair' listed in the "Chart of Additional Verse Sequences" under st. 1.5. Note that this is its occurrence after a st. vs. This is indicated by the number 1 entered in the "Occurrence" column. This verse occurs after one other st. vs. This is indicated by the number 2 entered in the "Total Occurrences" column. To find the other verse, check add. dadhimathana-ninādair where it is listed in the "Additional Verses" section. In this section it is noted that add. dadhimathananinādair is entered under st. 1.5 and st. 3.86. If the "Chart of Additional Verse Sequences" is checked after st. 3.86, add. dadhimathananinādair will be found there.

The signs in the "Chart of Additional Verse Sequences" are to be read as follows:

ā indicates that the additional verse precedes rather than follows the standard verse. This sign is used only with the first st. verse in each of the three centuries.

unn. indicates that the additional verse is unnumbered.

S indicates that, of the KK mss. collated for this edition, this verse is found only in the ms. here entered.

SS indicates that, of all the KK mss. examined including perhaps 100 which are not collated for this edition, this verse is found only in the ms. here entered.

\+ after the notation of an add. vs. as a st. vs. indicates that this vs. is entered twice in the ms., as a st. vs. and as an add. vs.

Chart of Additional Verse Sequences

Additional Verse	Standard Verse	Manu-script	Verse Number	Occurrence	Total Occurrences	Identification
	st.1					
ramāpatipadāmbhoja-	ā1	M1	1	S		
dadhimathananinādair	5	DG1	5	1	2	echos st.3.87
dadhimathananinādair	5	DG2	5	1	2	echos st.3.87
dadhimathananinādair	5	DG4	5	1	2	echos st.3.87
calaccikuramaṇḍalaṃ	20	C21	unn.	S		
keśava tava kala°	66	M24	67	SS		
uttuṅgastanamaṇḍalo	70	G2	71	S		st.2.64+
kṛṣṇenā 'mba gatena	70	G2	72	S		st.2.65+
mandāramūle madanā°	100	D11	101	1	1	st.3.93+
mandāramūle madanā°	100	U1	101	1	1	st.3.93+
mandāramūle madanā°	100	V1	100	1	1	st.3.93
mandāramūle madanā°	100	V2	100	1	1	st.3.93
mandāramūle madanā°	100	V22	100	1	1	st.3.93
mandāramūle madanā°	100	V25	100	1	1	st.3.93
apahasitasudhā°	107	N21	106	S		st.3.44
anugatam amarīṇām	107	N21	107	S		st.3.51
diṣṭyā vṛndāvana°	107	N21	108	S		st.3.53
udayagiri taṭānte	107	S21	110	S		
	st.2					
gogopagopījana°	ā1	D21	1	SS		
dhanyānāṃ sarasā°	1	D11	2	1	2	st.1.111+
anugrahadviguṇa°	3	D11	5	S		st.1.112+
pallavāruṇapāṇi°	34	DG1	35	1	1	st.1.9
pallavāruṇapāṇi°	34	DG2	35	1	1	st.1.9
pallavāruṇapāṇi°	34	DG3	35	1	1	st.1.9

pallavāruṇapāṇi°	34	DG5	35	1	1	st.1.9
pallavāruṇapāṇi°	34	G1	35	1	1	st.1.9+
pallavāruṇapāṇi°	34	G2	35	1	1	st.1.9+
mukulāyamāna°	43	DG1	38	1	1	st.1.6
mukulāyamāna°	43	DG2	38	1	1	st.1.6
mukulāyamāna°	43	DG3	38	1	1	st.1.6
mukulāyamāna°	43	DG5	38	1	1	st.1.6
mukulāyamāna°	43	G1	38	1	1	st.1.6+
mukulāyamāna°	43	G2	38	1	1	st.1.6+
mukulāyamāna°	43	T5	36	1	1	st.1.6+
mukhāravinde	45	N1	53	1	3	st.3.26
mukhāravinde	45	N21	53	1	3	st.3.26
mukhāravinde	50	M6	50	2	3	st.3.26
mukhāravinde	51	M24	52	3	3	st.3.26+
nidrāvatīṃ rahasi	52	D21	54	S		
govālamūle vadanā°	52	D21	55	1	4	
he kṛṣṇa viṣṇo	53	M6	55	1	2	echos st.2.56
dṛṣṭvā hariṃ	55	D41	49	1	1	
dṛṣṭvā hariṃ	55	D43	49	1	1	
he kṛṣṇa viṣṇo	55	D11	58	2	2	echos st.2.56
he kṛṣṇa viṣṇo	55	M24	57	2	2	echos st.2.56
he kṛṣṇa viṣṇo	55	T21	57	2	2	echos st.2.56
prabhātasaṃcāragatā	55	T21	58	2	2	echos st.2.56
pravālaśobhā iva	55	T21	59	2	2	echos st.2.56
ulūkhale saṃbhṛta°	55	T21	60	2	2	echos st.2.56
bhajasva mantraṃ	55	T21	61	2	2	echos st.2.56
agre kurūṇām api	55	T21	62	2	2	echos st.2.56
gṛhe gṛhe gopavadhū°	55	T21	63	SS		echos st.2.56
kvacit prabhāte	56	D11	60	SS		echos st.2.56

Additional Verse	Standard Verse	Manu-script	Verse Number	Occurrence	Total Occurrences	Identification
	st.2					
agre kurūṇām api	56	D11	61	2	2	echos st.2.56
ulūkhale saṃbhṛta°	56	D11	62	2	2	echos st.2.56
vṛndāvanasthaṃ harim	56	D11	63	SS		echos st.2.56
pravālaśobhā iva	56	D11	64	2	2	echos st.2.56
prabhātasaṃcāragatā	56	D11	65	2	2	echos st.2.56
bhajasva mantraṃ	56	D11	66	2	2	echos st.2.56
tāsāṃ prasanno	56	D11	67	SS		echos st.2.56
ālokya mātur mukham	58	D11	69	1	1	echos st.2.58
ālokya mātur mukham	58	T21	69	1	1	echos st.2.58
yamasva sānta°	58	D11	70	1	1	echos st.2.58
yamasva sānta°	58	T21	72	1	1	echos st.2.58
śikye nidhāyā	58	D11	71	1	1	echos st.2.58
śikye nidhāyā	58	T21	69	1	1	echos st.2.58
lambālakaṃ lambita°	58	D11	72	1	1	echos st.2.58
lambālakaṃ lambita°	58	T21	70	1	1	echos st.2.58
ulūkhale baddham	58	D11	73	1	1	echos st.2.58
ulūkhale baddham	58	T21	71	1	1	echos st.2.58
saṃhṛtya lokān vaṭa°	58	D11	74	1	1	echos st.2.58
saṃhṛtya lokān vaṭa°	58	T21	68	1	1	echos st.2.58
indīvaraśyāmalam	58	D11	75	SS		
avyaktacūḍaṃ sura°	58	T21	173	SS		
jaro 'si coro 'si	73	D41	68	1	1	
jaro 'si coro 'si	73	D43	66	1	1	
pāṇau veṇuprakṛti°	74	G11	74	S		st.3.30+
karayoḥ kaṅkaṇarāvaṃ	82	DG1	77	1	1	
karayoḥ kaṅkaṇarāvaṃ	82	DG2	77	1	1	
karayoḥ kaṅkaṇarāvaṃ	82	DG3	77	1	1	

karayoḥ kañkaṇarāvaṃ	82	DG4	77	1	1	
karayoḥ kañkaṇarāvaṃ	82	DG5	77	1	1	
karayoḥ kañkaṇarāvaṃ	81	N1	89	1	1	
karayoḥ kañkaṇarāvaṃ	81	N21	96	1	1	
vanamālini yāti	94	N1	14	1	1	
vanamālini yāti	94	N21	14	1	1	
barhāpīḍaṃ naṭa°	102	N1	85	1	1	
barhāpīḍaṃ naṭa°	102	N21	90	1	1	
barhāpīḍaṃ naṭa°	103	C21	unn.	2	5	
barhāpīḍaṃ naṭa°	103	DG1	97	2	5	
barhāpīḍaṃ naṭa°	103	DG2	97	2	5	
barhāpīḍaṃ naṭa°	103	DG4	99	2	5	
barhāpīḍaṃ naṭa°	103	DG5	99	2	5	
barhāpīḍaṃ naṭa°	103	D1	99	2	5	
barhāpīḍaṃ naṭa°	103	D14	104	2	5	
barhāpīḍaṃ naṭa°	103	D21	107	2	5	
barhāpīḍaṃ naṭa°	103	G1	95	2	5	
barhāpīḍaṃ naṭa°	103	G2	97	2	5	
barhāpīḍaṃ naṭa°	103	M6	100	2	5	
barhāpīḍaṃ naṭa°	103	R22	104	2	5	
yā prītir vidurā°	103	DG1	98	1	1	st.3.106
ya prītir vidurā°	103	DG2	98	1	1	st.3.106
yā prītir vidurā°	103	DG4	100	1	1	st.3.106
yā prītir vidurā°	103	DG5	100	1	1	st.3.106
yā prītir vidurā°	103	D21	108	1	1	st.3.106+
yā prītir vidurā°	103	G1	96	1	1	st.3.106
yā prītir vidurā°	103	G2	98	1	1	st.3.106
yā prītir vidurā°	103	M6	101	1	1	st.3.106
yā prītir vidurā°	103	N1	93	1	1	st.3.106

Additional Verse	Standard Verse	Manu-script	Verse Number	Occurrence	Total Occurrences	Identification
	st.2					
yā prītir vidurā°	103	N21	*101*	1	1	st.3.106
barhāpīḍaṃ naṭa°	104	T21	120	3	5	
barhāpīḍaṃ naṭa°	105	G11	106	4	5	
nigamataroḥ prati°	107	DG1	103	1	2	
nigamataroḥ prati°	107	DG2	103	1	2	
maṇiviḍambita°	107	DG1	104	1	2	
maṇiviḍambita°	107	DG2	104	1	2	
bahuśāstrakathā°	107	DG1	*105*	1	2	
bahuśāstrakathā°	107	DG2	*105*	1	2	
kalāttamāyā°	108	D21	*115*	1	3	
kalāttamāyā°	108	G2	104	1	3	
kalāttamāyā°	108	N1	98	1	3	
lakṣmīsuvarṇatilakā°	108	N1	99	1	2	
mugdhe dhyāyasi	108	G2	*105*	1	3	
mugdhe dhyāyasi	108	N1	*105*	1	3	
barhāpīdaṃ naṭa°	109	D11	128	5	5	
yasya 'tmabhūtasya	109	D45	*111*	1	2	
yasya 'tmabhūtasya	109	E42	*108*	1	2	
yasya 'tmabhūtasya	109	E43	*108*	1	2	
kalāttamāyā°	109	M6	107	2	3	
mugdhe dhyāyasi	109	M6	108	2	3	
īśānadevacaraṇā°	110	DG6	*105*	S		st.1.110
nigamataroḥ prati°	110	DG4	106	2	2	
nigamataroḥ prati°	110	DG5	106	2	2	
maṇiviḍambita°	110	DG4	107	2	2	
maṇiviḍambita°	110	DG5	107	2	2	
bahuśāstrakathā°	110	DG4	*108*	2	2	

bahuśāstrakathā°	110	DG5	*108*	2	2	
dhanyānāṃ sarasā°	110	G11	112	2	2	st.1.112+
navanavanīta°	110	G11	113	SS		
aṅgulyā kaḥ kavāṭaṃ	110	G11	115	1	3	
govālamūle vadanā°	110	G11	116	2	4	
kṛṣṇasya duṣṭa°	110	G11	*117*	S		
mugdhe dhyāyasi	110	M24	*114*	2	3	
karacaraṇakṛtaṃ	110	R22	*112*	S		
yasya 'tmabhūtasya	110	V1	*110*	2	2	
yasya 'tmabhūtasya	110	V2	*112*	2	2	
	st.3					
he gopālaka he	āl	DG4	1	1	2	
he gopālaka he	1	DG5	1	1	2	
he gopālaka he	1	N21	5	5	2	
kastūritilakaṃ	āl	DG4	2	1	2	st.2.109
kastūritilakaṃ	1	DG5	2	1	2	st.2.109
kastūritilakaṃ	1	N21	6	1	2	st.2.109
urvyāṃ ko 'pi	1	N21	1	1	3	st.2.106
saṃviṣṭo maṇi°	1	N21	2	1	2	st.2.104
ākṛṣṭe vasanā°	1	N21	3	S		st.2.105
sandhyāvandana	1	N21	4	S		st.2.107
kalāttamāyā°	1	N21	7	3	3	
lakṣmīsuvarṇatilakā°	1	N21	8	2	2	
mugdhe dhyāyasi	1	N21	9	3	3	
cintāmaṇir jayati	1	N21	10	1	2	st.1.1+
vyākhyā mudrālasat°	1	D71	1	S		
uddaṇḍavāma°	2	M24	5	SS		
ābhīramugdhākṣi	3	M21	3	1	1	

Additional Verse	Standard Verse	Manu-script	Verse Number	Occurrence	Total Occurrences	Identification
	st.3					
ābhīramugdhākṣi	3	M24	3	1	1	
ātāmrapāṇikamala°	28	G1	20	S		st.2.46+
urvyāṃ ko 'pi	31	N1	95	2	2	st.2.106
kṛṣṇo rakṣatu māṃ	48	M1	49	SS		
he jihve rasasārajñe	48	M1	50	SS		
madhuram adharam	81	DG1	82	1	2	st.1.64
madhuram adharam	81	DG2	82	1	2	st.1.64
madhuram adharam	81	DG4	82	1	2	st.1.64
madhuram adharam	81	G1	74	1	2	st.1.64
madhuram adharam	81	M21	83	1	2	st.1.64+
madhuram adharam	81	M24	84	1	2	st.1.64+
bālena mugdhe°	81	DG1	83	1	2	st.1.35
bālena mugdhe°	81	DG2	83	1	2	st.1.35
bālena mugdhe°	81	DG4	83	1	2	st.1.35
bālena mugdhe°	81	G1	75	1	2	st.1.35
bālena mugdhe°	81	M21	84	1	2	st.1.35+
madhuram adharam	82	T21	83	2	2	st.1.64+
dadhimathananinādair	86	K1	86	1	2	echos st.3.87
dadhimathananinādair	86	M1	87	2	2	echos st.3.87
dadhimathananinādair	86	M24	90	2	2	echos st.3.87
dadhimathananinādair	86	T21	88	2	2	echos st.3.87
prātar smarāmi bhava°	88	M21	92	S	1	
prātar namāmi manasā	88	M21	93	1	1	echos st.3.58
pratar namāmi manasā	88	N1	72	1	1	echos st.3.58
prātar namāmi manasā	88	N21	78	1	1	echos st.3.58
pratar namāmi manasā	88	N22	96	1	1	echos st.3.58
prātar bhajāmi	88	M21	94	1	1	echos st.3.58

prātar bhajāmi	88	N1	73	1	1	echos st.3.58
prātar bhajāmi	88	N21	79	1	1	echos st.3.58
prātar bhajāmi	88	N22	97	1	1	echos st.3.58
govālamūle vadanā°	92	N1	75	3	4	
govālamūle vadanā°	92	N21	81	3	4	
gopījanodvīkṣaṇam	92	R23	91	S		echos st.3.59
kastūritilakaṃ	93	T21	96	2	2	st.2.109
gopāla iti kṛṣṇa tvāṃ	95	D61	94	SS		
cintāmaṇir jayati	96	DG1	98	SS	u	st.1.1
cintāmaṇir jayati	96	DG2	98	SS	u	st.1.1
cintāmaṇir jayati	96	DG4	98	SS	u	st.1.1
cintāmaṇir jayati	96	G1	90	SS	u	st.1.1
pādadvaṃdve vinimaya°	96	DG1	99	1	1	
pādadvaṃdve vinimaya°	96	DG2	99	1	1	
pādadvaṃdve vinimaya°	96	DG4	99	1	1	
pādadvaṃdve vinimaya°	96	G1	91	1	1	
pādadvaṃdve vinimaya°	96	M1	97	1	1	
pādadvaṃdve vinimaya°	96	M24	100	1	1	
pādadvaṃdve vinimaya°	96	T21	99	1	1	
ghaṭodakeṣu pratimā°	96	DG1	100	1	2	echos st.2.54
ghaṭodakeṣu pratimā°	96	DG2	100	1	2	echos st.2.54
ghaṭodakeṣu pratimā°	96	DG4	100	1	2	echos st.2.54
ghaṭodakeṣu pratimā°	96	G1	92	1	2	echos st.2.54
ghaṭodakeṣu pratima°	96	M1	98	1	2	echos st.2.54
ghaṭodakeṣu pratimā°	96	M24	101	1	2	echos st.2.54
ghaṭodakeṣu pratimā°	96	T21	100	1	2	echos st.2.54
āttaṃ padavyāṃ	96	DG1	101	1	2	
āttaṃ padavyāṃ	96	DG2	101	1	2	
āttaṃ padavyāṃ	96	DG4	101	1	2	

Additional Verse	Standard Verse	Manu-script	Verse Number	Occurrence	Total Occurrences	Identification
	st.3					
āttaṃ padavyāṃ	96	G1	93	1	2	
āttaṃ padavyāṃ	96	M1	99	1	2	
āttaṃ padavyāṃ	96	M24	102	1	2	
karṇāmṛtaṃ bhagavataś	96	M1	100	1	2	
karṇāmṛtaṃ bhagavataś	96	M24	109	1	2	
kṛṣṇa tvadīyapada°	96	M24	103	SS		
vaṃśivibhūṣitakarāt	96	M24	104	SS		
urasijamukham ekam	96	M24	105	SS		
ālolatulasīmālam	96	M24	106	SS		
vyatyastapādam	96	M24	107	S		st.2.22+
ārūḍho garuḍaṃ	96	M24	108	SS		
he gopālaka he	96	M24	101	2	2	st.2.108+
kisalayamṛdupādaṃ	97	R23	96	1	2	
indīvarābham aravinda°	97	R23	97	1	2	
ānīlagātram alakā°	97	R23	98	1	2	
maulau māyūrabarhaṃ	97	R23	99	1	2	echos st.2.93
mūle kalpataro smaro	97	R23	100	S		
mandāradrumamūlam	97	R23	101	S		
āyur dīrgham ārogatāṃ	97	R23	102	S		
saṃviṣṭo maṇiviṣṭare	97	R23	103	2	2	st.2.104+
urvyāṃ ko 'pi	97	R23	104	2	3	st.2.106+
rājan nūpurakiñkiṇi	97	R23	105	S		
saṃviṣṭan kamalāsane	97	R23	106	S		
jayatu jayatu	98	M21	104	1	1	
dehimat kantukaṃ	100	D71	99	SS		
maulau māyūrabarhaṃ	100	N1	82	2	2	echos st.2.93
maulau māyūrabarhaṃ	100	N21	88	2	2	

lokān unmadayan	100	N1	83	1	1	st.2.110
lokan unmadayan	100	N21	*99*	1	1	st.2.110
jayatu jayatu	101	N22	99	2	4	
añgulyā kaḥ kavāṭaṃ	104	D45	105	2	3	
rādhāmohana mandirād	104	D45	106	1	2	
jayatu jayatu	105	D45	108	3	4	
kṛṣṇāusmaraṇād	105	D45	*109*	1	2	
kiyān ahaṃ kṛṣṇa	105	D71	101	SS		
añgulyā kaḥ kavāṭaṃ	105	V1	105	3	3	
añgulyā kaḥ kavāṭaṃ	105	V2	110	3	3	
rādhāmohanamandirād	105	V1	106	2	2	
rādhāmohanamandirād	105	V2	111	2	2	
ghaṭodakeṣu pratimā°	105	K1	*104*	2	2	echos st.2.54
jayatu jayatu	106	D1	88	4	4	
jayatu jayatu	106	D11	*107*	4	4	
jayatu jayatu	106	D21	107	4	4	
jayatu jayatu	106	D44	*106*	4	4	
govālamūle vadanā°	106	D1	*89*	4	4	
gopījanāliñgita°	106	D12	107	S		
kisalayamṛdupādaṃ	106	D12	108	2	2	
indīvarābham aravinda°	106	D12	109	2	2	
ānīlagātram alakā°	106	D12	*110*	2	2	
gopīkucasthahāreṣu	106	D21	108	SS		
nārāyaṇa puṇḍarīka°	106	D21	*109*	SS		
alikulanibhanīlaṃ	106	D44	105	S		
kṛṣṇānusmaraṇād	106	V1	*108*	2	2	
kṛṣṇānusmaraṇād	106	V2	*113*	2	2	

NOTES ON THE ADDITIONAL VERSES

Sixty-six verses, not found in the standard version of the KK, are entered in one or more of the KK mss. collated for this edition. A first line index of these additional verses is given on the following pages. Notes are also given which identify sources of the add. vss. outside the KK and which describe the occurrence of the verse within the KK mss. and its relationship to other KK vss. The affiliation of these with the KK tradition is further defined in the Introduction and in the section "Manuscripts Used."

Nineteen verses, indicated by an asterisk (*) prefixed to the first lines, have been edited and translated. Eighteen of these 19 verses are found in the crucial G, N, and DG mss. which are intermediate between the standard KK tradition and the tradition of the Northern anthologies (the Y mss.). The 19th vs., add. karṇāmṛtaṃ bhagavataś is an interesting verse colophon.

Unlike the standard verses which are noted by their number, e.g. st. 1.67, additional verses are noted by their *pratīkas*, e.g. add. agre kurūṇāṃ.

Abbreviations Used in "First Line Index of 66 Additional Verses with Notes"

ASP	Āndhra Sāhitya Pariṣad, Kakinada.
BORI	Bhandarkar Oriental Research Institute.
Flo	Biblioteca Nazionale Centrale, Florence.
IO	India Office Library, London.
Ker	University of Kerala Manuscripts Library, Trivandrum.
Mar	Staatsbibliothek, Marburg.
MGOL	Madras Government Oriental Library, Madras.
Mys	University of Mysore Oriental Research Institute, Mysore City.
Osm	Osmania University Library, Hyderabad—Dn.
TP	H.H. The Maharajah's Palace Library, Trivandrum. (The mss. are now deposited in the University of Kerela Manuscripts Library.).
Tri	Government Sanskrit College, Tripunithura.

There are KK mss., mentioned in the following pages, which have not been used to edit the text presented in this edition. These mss. have not been described in the "Description of Mss." section; after their mention in the following pages, they are very briefly described in parenthesis according the system outlined in the "Manuscripts Used" section.

First Line Index of Sixty-Six Additional Verses With Notes

agre kurūṇām api pāṇḍavānāṃ
Upajāti meter.
Preceded by st. 2.55 and st. 2.56.
See entry under add. he kṛṣṇa viṣṇo.

aṅgulyā kaḥ kavāṭaṃ praharati kutile mādhavaḥ kiṃ vasanto
Sragdharā meter.
Preceded by st. 2.110, st. 3.104, st. 3.105.
This verse occurs in three anthologies (Z1 Z5 Z11) where it is listed as anonymous. It also occurs as vs. 3 of MGOL ms. D9905 called Kṛṣṇastotra. This ms., written in the Grantha script, contains 7 vss. 4 of these verses are KK st. vss. (st. 2.98 is vs. 1, st. 2.5 is vs. 2, st. 2.7 is vs. 4, st. 2.72 is vs. 5). Vs 7 has the same line d as st. 2.98; the verse is also found as vs. 3.102 in Mys. ms. no. 2321 (G12).

alikulanibhanīlaṃ barhibarhāvataṃsaṃ
Mālinī meter.
Preceded by st. 3.106.
The only other occurrence of this verse in KK mss. is in BORI ms. no. 627/1883-84 (D62). No occurrence of this verse was found outside the KK.

avyaktacūḍaṃ surakāryaniṣṭha-
Upajāti meter.
Preceded by st. 2.58.
See entry under add. ālokya maturmukham

*āttaṃ padavyāṃ vigalayya dhanyaṃ
Upajāti meter.
Preceded by st. 3.96.
No occurrence of this verse was found outside the KK.

ānīlagātram alakāvṛtavaktrabimbaṃ

Vasantatilaka meter.

Preceded by st. 3.97 and st. 3.106.

This verse occurs as vs. 503 in Y21.

ābhīramugdhākṣi bhajasva dhairyaṃ

Upajāti meter.

Preceded by st. 3.3.

This verse is found only in the Malayalam mss. of the KK. No occurrence of this verse was found outside the KK.

āyur dīrgham arogatāṃ priyavadhūṃ

Śārdūlavikrīḍita meter (?).

Preceded by st. 3.97.

The only other occurrence of this verse in KK mss. is in ASP ms. no. 1813 (T22). Only the *pratīka* is available, because R23 includes the commentary only, and a *pratīka* rather than a complete copy of T22 was made. Most probably this would be a Śārdūlavikrīḍita verse. No occurrence of this verse was found outside the KK.

ārūḍho garuḍaṃ bhujāntataralaśrīvanyamālāvalīṃ

Śārdūlavikrīḍita meter.

Preceded by st. 3.108.

No occurrence of this verse was found outside the KK.

ālokya mātur mukham ādareṇa

Upajāti meter.

Preceded by st. 2.58.

This verse, plus the seven verses listed after it in the sequence chart for additional verses, have the same line d as st. 2.58. An *aṣṭaka* chosen from these nine verses is entered in D11 and T21 mss. No other KK mss. have this *aṣṭaka*. This *aṣṭaka* exists as an independent stotra in 8 mss. deposited in the MGOL (Mss. No. D18368 and D18206 [Kannarese script], D10207, D10208, and R3174 [Telugu script], D10209, D10210, and D10211 [Grantha script]). These *aṣṭakas* have varying verse sequences and vary as to the verse omitted (R3174 includes all 9 verses). None omit st. 2.58, add. ālokya, add. yamasva, add. ulūkhale, and add. saṃhṛtya. None of these verses occur in Y mss., but it is to be noted that Y21 has 13 verses with the same line d as st. 2.58. None of the 13 verses of Y21 are the same as the above

8 verses. Y21 vs. 253 is st. 2.58 and the 13 echo verses are entered after Y21 vs. 253 as numbers 254–266.

ālolatulasīmālam
Anuṣṭubh meter.
Preceded by st. 3.96.
No occurrence of this verse was found outside the KK.

indīvaraśyāmalam āyatākṣam
Upajāti meter.
Preceded by st. 2.58.
See under add. ālokya matur mukham.

indīvarābham aravindadalāyatākṣaṃ
Vasantatilaka meter.
Preceded by st. 3.97 and st. 3.106.
No occurrence of this verse was found outside the KK.

udayagiritaṭānte rukmiṇīsatyabhāmā-
Mālinī meter.
Preceded by st. 1.107.
This verse is also found in YY1 vs. 1.172. In the KK this verse is found only in three Telugu mss. (S21, ASP No. 1813 [T22], and MGOL No. D13408 [T26]).

uddaṇḍavāmadordaṇḍa-
Anuṣṭubh meter.
Preceded by st. 3.2
No occurrence of this verse was found outside the KK.

urasijamukham ekaṃ śrīmukhenā 'dadānaḥ
Mālinī meter.
Preceded by st. 3.96.
No occurrence of this verse was found outside the KK.

ulūkhale baddham udāraśauryam
Upajāti meter.
Preceded by st. 2.58.
See entry under add. ālokya matur mukham

ulūkhale saṃbhṛtataṇḍulāṃś ca
Upajāti meter.

Preceded by st. 2.55 and st. 2.56.
See entry under add. he kṛṣṇa viṣṇo.

*karṇāmṛtaṃ bhagavataś caritaṃ rasajñaḥ
Vasantatilaka meter.
Preceded by st. 3.96.
The only other occurrence of this verse in KK mss. is in MGOL ms. No. D15809 (G62). In the MGOL ms. the verse is numbered 3.100 and is entered after st. 3.96. As one would expect, no occurrence of this verse was found outside the KK.

karacaraṇakṛtaṃ vā karmavākkāyajaṃ vā
Mālinī meter.
Preced by st. 2.110.
No occurrence of this verse was found outside the KK.

*karayoḥ kaṅkaṇarāvaṃ
Anuṣṭubh meter.
Preceded by st. 2.82.
No occurrence of this verse was found outside the KK.

*kalāttamāyālavakāntamūrtiḥ
Upajāti meter.
Preceded by st. 2.108 and st. 2.109. Precedes st. 3.1.
This verse occurs in the *Kramadīpikā* (Z41) as vs. 1.1. Line d is the same as line d of YY1 vs. 2.26.

kvacit prabhāte dadhipūrṇapātre
Upajāti meter.
Preceded by st. 2.56.
See entry under add. he kṛṣṇa viṣṇo.

kiyān ahaṃ kṛṣṇadivyān
Anuṣṭubh meter.
Preceded by st. 3.105.
No occurrence of this verse was found outside the KK.

kisalayamṛdupādaṃ kiṅkiṇīnādaramyaṃ
Mālinī meter.
Preceded by st. 3.97 and st. 3.106.
No occurrence of this verse was found outside the KK.

kṛṣṇa tvadīyapadapaṅkajapañjarānta-
Vasantatilaka meter.
Preceded by st. 3.96.
No occurrence of this verse was found outside the KK.

kṛṣṇasya duṣṭacaritaṃ sakhi kiṃ bravīmi
Vasantatilaka meter.
Preceded by st. 2.110.
This verse is found only in the Grantha manuscripts of the KK. No occurrence of this verse was found outside the KK.

kṛṣṇo rakṣatu māṃ carācaraguruḥ kṛṣṇaṃ namasye sadā
Śārdūlavikrīḍita meter.
Preceded by st. 3.48.
No occurrence of this verse was found outside the KK.

kṛṣṇānusmaraṇād eva
Anuṣṭubh meter.
Preceded by st. 3.105 and st. 3.106.
This verse is found only in the following KK mss.: D45 V1 V2 and IO Book San. C. 211 (V26). It also occurs in Madhvācārya's *Kṛṣṇāmṛtamahārṇava* as vs. 46. (*Śrīmat Sarvamūlam; The Collected Works of Madhvācārya*, Vol. 2, ed. R. Kṛṣṇācārya and Rāmācārya [Bombay: Nirnaya Sagar Press, 1892], folios 737.)

keśava tava kalamuralī-
Āryā meter
Preceded by st. 1.66.
No occurrence of this verse was found outside the KK.

gṛhe gṛhe gopavadhūkadambāḥ
Upajāti meter.
Preceded by st. 2.55.
See entry under add. kṛṣṇa viṣṇo.

gogopagopījanavallabhāya
Upajāti meter.
Precedes st. 2.1.
No occurrence of this verse was found outside the KK.

gopāla iti kṛṣṇa tvāṃ

Anuṣṭubh meter.

Preceded by st. 3.95.

No occurrence of this verse was found outside the KK.

gopīkucasthahāreṣu

Anuṣṭubh meter.

Preceded by st. 3.106.

No occurrence of this verse was found outside the KK.

gopījanāliṅgitamadhyabhāgaṃ

Upajāti meter.

Preceded by st. 3.106.

This verse occurs in Z11 (vs. 292) where it is ascribed to Puruṣottamadeva

gopījanodvīkṣaṇam aprameyaṃ

Upajāti meter.

Preceded by st. 3.93.

Line d of this verse is the same as line d of st. 3.93.

*govālamūle vadanānilena

Upajāti meter.

Preceded by st. 2.52, st. 2.110, st. 3.92, st. 3.106.

This verse is often quoted in Madras State today as from the KK.

*ghaṭodakeṣu pratimāśaśāṅkaṃ

Upajāti meter.

Preceded by st. 3.96.

The variant lines c and d, which are found only in the Y mss., are same as lines c and d of st. 2.54. This verse occurs in the following Y mss.: Y13 vs. 14, Y33 vs. 14, Y52 vs. 88, Y61 vs. 11, Y62 vs. 11, Y63 vs. 11, Y64 vs. 11. In these Y mss. note that st. 2.54 immediately precedes add. ghaṭodakeṣu.

calaccikuramaṇḍalaṃ jagadavāryalīlākulaṃ

Mālinī meter.

Preceded by st. 1.20.

The only other occurrence of this verse in KK mss. is in IO ms. 3900/1605c (D13). No occurrence of this verse was found outside the KK.

*jayatu jayatu kṛṣṇo devakīnandano 'yam

Mālinī meter.

Preceded by st. 3.98, st. 3.101, st. 3.105, st. 3.106.

This verse is found in Y21 as vs. 482. It also occurs as vs. 3 in the Nirṇaya Sāgara Press edition of the Mukundamālā in the *Bṛhatstotraratnākara* [Z42(N)], but it is not found in the Annamalai University Sanskrit Series edition edited by K. Rama Pisharoti [Z42(A)].

jāro 'si coro 'si jagannivāsa

Upajāti meter.

Preceded by st. 2.73.

This verse is found only in D41 and D43. No occurrence of this verse was found outside the KK.

tāsāṃ prasanno harir āvirāsa

Upajāti meter.

Preceded by st. 2.56.

See entry under add. he kṛṣṇa viṣṇo.

*dadhimathananinādair dīrghikāvaṃśanādaiḥ

Mālinī meter.

Preceded by st. 1.5 and st. 3.86.

The first half of line a is the same as the first half of st. 3.87 line a. They are echo or parallel verses. No occurrence of this verse was found outside the KK.

dṛṣṭvā hariṃ paravadhūgalitāṅgarāgaṃ

Vasantatilaka meter.

Preceded by st. 2.55.

This verse is found in Y31(vs. 233), Y32(vs. 223), Y33(vs. 223).

dehimat kantukaṃ rādhe

Anuṣṭubk meter

Preceded by st. 3.100.

No occurrence of this verse was found outside the KK.

navanavanītaṃ nītaṃ

Āryā meter.

Preceded by st. 2.110.

No occurrence of this verse was found outside the KK.

nārāyaṇa puṇḍarīkanayana śrīrāma sītāpate

Śārdūlavikrīḍita meter.

Preceded by st. 3.106.

Note that the meter fails. A long syllable needs to be inserted after the second syllable.

No occurrence of this verse was found outside the KK.

*nigamataroḥ pratiśākhaṃ

Āryā meter.

Preceded by st. 2.107 and st. 2.110.

No occurrence of this verse was found outside the KK.

nidrāvatīṃ rahasi gopavadhūṃ vilokya

Vasantatilaka meter.

Preceded by st. 2.52.

No occurrence of this verse was found outside the KK.

*pādadvaṃdve vinimayavatī pāṭalāpāṇipadme

Mandākrāntā meter.

Preceded by st. 3.96.

No occurrence of this verse was found outside the KK.

prabhātasaṃcāragatā nu gāvas

Upajāti meter.

Preceded by st. 2.55 and st. 2.56.

See entry under add. he kṛṣṇa viṣṇo

pravālaśobhā iva dīrghakeśā

Upajāti meter.

Preceded by st. 2.55 and st. 2.56.

See entry under add. he kṛṣṇa viṣṇo

*prātar namāmi bhavabhītimahārtiśāntyai

Vasantatilaka meter.

Preceded by st. 3.88.

The first word of line a is the same as the first word of line a in st. 3.88, prātar namāmi manasā, add. prātar bhajāmi bhajatām. These four verses are echo verses; all are in the Vasantatilaka meter. add. prātar namāmi bhava° occurs as vs. 27 of the Annamalai edition of the *Mukundamālā*, Z42(A). add. prātar bhajāmi bhajatām occurs as vs. 28, and add. prātar namāmi manasā occurs as vs. 29. •

These three verses do not occur in the Nirnaya Sagara Press edition of the Mukundamālā in the *Bṛhatstotra ratnākara* [Z42(N)]. st. 388 does not occur in the *Mukundamālā.*

*prātar namāmi manasā vacasā ca mūrdhnā
Vasantatilaka meter.
Preceded by st. 3.68.
See entry under add. prātar namāmi bhava°

*prātar bhajāmi bhajatām abhayaṃkaraṃ taṃ
Vasantatilaka meter.
Preceded by st. 3.88.
See entry under add. prātar namāmi bhava°

*barhāpīḍaṃ naṭavaravapuḥ karṇayoḥ karṇikāraṃ
Mandākrāntā meter.
Preceded by st. 2.102, st. 2.103, st. 2.104, st. 2.105, st. 2.109.
This verse is found in Y11(vs. 180), Y12(vs. 180), and Y21(vs. 231). It is to be noted that Y13 and Y14, which share the manuscript tradition of Y11 and Y12, omit this verse. Otherwise this verse occurs in the *Bhāgavata Purāṇa* [Z43] as vs. 10.21.3.

*bahuśāstrakathākanthā
Anuṣṭubh meter.
Preceded by st. 2.107 and st. 2.110.
No occurrence of this verse was found outside the KK.

bhajasva mantraṃ bhavabandhamuktyai
Upajāti meter.
Preceded by st. 2.55 and st. 2.56.
See entry under add. he kṛṣṇa viṣṇo

*maṇiviḍambitatasya manohare
Drutavilambita meter.
Preceded by st. 2.107 and st. 2.110.
No occurrence of this verse was found outside the KK.

*mugdhe dhyāyasi kiṃ guhāṇapurataḥ kundaṃ vikāsonmukhaṃ
Śārdūlavikrīḍita meter.
Preceded by st. 2.108 and st. 2.109. Precedes st. 3.1.
No occurrence of this verse was found outside the KK.

mandāradrumamūlam alpitam ahā

Śārdūlavikrīḍita meter(?).

Preceded by st. 3.97.

The only other occurrence of this verse in KK mss. is in ASP ms. no. 1813 (T22). Only the *pratīka* is available, because R23 includes the commentary only, and a *pratīka* rather than a complete copy of T22 was made. Most probably this would be a Śārdūlavikrīḍita verse. No occurrence of this verse was found outside the KK.

mūle kalpataro smaro ruhagataṃ

Śārdūlavikrīḍita meter(?).

Preceded by st. 3.97.

Same remarks as for add. āyur dīrgham and add. mandāradrumamūlam.

maulau māyūrabarhaṃ marakatamakarīkuṇḍale gaṇḍamūle

Sragdharā meter.

Preceded by st. 3.97 and st. 3.100.

The first part of line a is the same as the first part of st. 2.93; both are in the Sragdharā meter. They are echo verses. No occurrence of this verse was found elsewhere.

yamasva sāntasthitakāliyasya

Upajāti meter.

Preceded by st. 2.58.

See entry under add. ālokya mātur mukham

yasyā 'tmabhūtasya guroḥ prasādād

Upajāti meter.

Preceded by st. 2.109 and st. 2.110.

This verse is entered in V2, as noted in the sequence chart, but no Telugu verse translation is given.

No occurrence of this verse was found outside the KK.

ramāpatipadāmbhoja-

Anuṣṭubh meter.

Precedes st. 1.1.

This verse also precedes st. 1.1 in Ker. ms. no. 20156/TP no. 1148 (M71) and the introduction to the Pāpayallaya Sūri commentary in Tri ms. no. 36/36 (M31). No occurrence of this verse was found outside the KK.

rājan nūpurakiñkiṇīmaṇiraṇat
Śārdūlavikrīḍita meter (?).
Preceded by st. 3.97.
Same remarks as for add. āyur dīrgham, add. mandāradrumamūlam, add. mūle kalpataro.

rādhāmohanamandirād upagataś candrāvalīm ālapat
Śārdūlavikrīḍita meter.
Preceded by st. 3.104 and st. 3.105.
This verse is found in Y31(vs. 189), Y32(vs. 190), and Y33(vs. 190).

*lakṣmīsuvarṇatilakākhacitendranīlaṃ
Vasantatilaka meter.
Proceded by st. 2.108. Precedes st. 3.1.
This verse is found only in N1 and N21. No occurrence of this verse was found outside the KK.

lambālakaṃ lambitahārayaṣṭiṃ
Upajāti meter
Preceded by st. 2.58.
See entry under add. ālokya mātur mukham

vaṃśivibhūṣitakarāt
Anuṣṭubh meter.
Preceded by st. 3.96.
No occurrence of this verse was found outside the KK.

*vanamālini yāti vastracore
Upajāti meter.
Preceded by st. 2.94.
This verse is found only in N1 and N21. No occurrence of this verse was found outside the KK.

vyākyāmudrālasatpāṇi-
Anuṣṭubh meter.
Precedes st. 3.1.
This verse regularly precedes the introduction to the Pāpayallaya Sūri commentary to century 3. No occurrence of this verse was found outside the KK.

vṛndāvanasthaṃ hariṃ āśu buddhvā
Upajāti meter.

Preceded by st. 2.56.
See entry under add. he kṛṣṇa viṣṇo

śikye nidhāyā 'mbupayodadhīni
Upajāti meter.
Preceded by st. 2.58.
See entry under add. ālokya mātur mukham

saṃviṣṭan kamalāsane maṇimaye
Śārdūlavikrīḍita meter (?).
Preceded by st. 3.97.
Same remarks as for add. āyur dīrgham, add. mandāradrumamūlam, add. mūle kalpataro, add. rājan nūpura°

saṃhṛtya lokān vaṭapatramadhye
Upajāti meter.
Preceded by st. 2.58.
See entry under add. ālokya mātur mukham

he kṛṣṇa viṣṇo madhukaiṭabhāre
Upajāti meter.
Preceded by st. 2.53 and st. 2.55.
This verse plus the nine verses listed after it in the sequence chart for additional verses (only where it is entered after st. 2.55) have the same line d as st. 2.56. D11 enters 10 of the 11 verses (See "Chart of Additional Verse Sequences") and T21 enters an *aṣṭaka* (See same chart.) No other KK mss. include these additional verses except M6 which substitutes add. he kṛṣṇa viṣṇo for st. 2.56 and M24 which includes both st. 2.56 and add. he kṛṣṇa viṣṇo.
These eleven verses exist as independent *daśakas* in three MGOL mss.: ms. no. D9967 (Nandināgarī script) includes nine of the eleven verses add. tāsāṃ prasanno and add. bhajasva mantraṃ are left out. ms. no. D18014 (Kannarese script) includes 10 of the eleven verses. add. tāsāṃ prasanno is left out, but another vs. not found in D11 or T21 is included to make a total of 11 vss. in this stotra. ms. D9968 (Telugu script) includes eight of the eleven verses. add. tāsāṃ prasanno, add. bhajasva mantraṃ, add. kvacit prabhāte are left out, and another verse not found in D11 or T21 is included to make a total of nine vss. in this stotra.
Three of the eleven verses are found in Y21: st. 2.56 as vs. 244, add.

he kṛṣṇa viṣṇo as vs. 462, and add. bhajasva mantraṃ as vs. 465. vss. 458 through 465 of Y21 are an *aṣṭaka* with the same line d as st. 2.56, but only vss. 462 and 465 are verses found in D11 and T21. Four of the eleven verses are found in Y31, Y32, and Y33: st. 2.56 as respectively vs. 354, 345, and 356; add. ulūkhale saṃbhṛta° as respectively vs. 355, 346, and 357; add. agre kurūṇām as respectively vs. 361, 352, 363; and add. he kṛṣṇa viṣṇo as respectively vs. 363, 354, and 365. vss. 354 through 369 of Y31 (vss. 345 through 359 of Y32 and vss. 356 through 371 of Y33) have the same line d as st. 2.56 (which is, of course, Y31 354). Y31 vss. 356, 357, 360, 366, 367, 368, 369 (Y32 vss. 347 etc. and Y33 vss. 358 etc) are found in Y21 but not D11 and T21.

All 16 of the st. 2.56 echo verses, found in Y31, Y32, and Y33, however, are included in another group of manuscripts.

21 to 71 verses including st. 2.56 and a remainder of 20 to 70 verses which share the same line d all exist as independent stotras. All the manuscripts are in the Devanāgarī script and are titled according to the recurring line d (govinda dāmodara mādhave 'ti) as Govindastotra, Govindadāmodarastotra, etc. All of these manuscripts which have 55 or more verses include all the verses found in D11, T21, Y21, Y31, Y32, Y33, the three MGOL mss., except for the fact that 12 out of the total of 17 mss. (D11, T21, Y21, Y31, Y32, Y33, the three MGOL mss., plus the 7 to be described below), which include 8 or more st. 2.56 echo verses, have one verse which is peculiar to them alone. The seven mss. in the Devanāgarī script are: Flo ms. Indiani no. 84 (57 vss.), Osm. ms. no. B25/2 (56 vss.), BORI ms. no. 274/1895–98 (69 vss.), BORI ms. no. 396/1887–91 (21 vss.), BORI ms. no. 491/1891–95 (55 vss.), Mar. ms. or. oct. 781 (57 vss.). The seventh is not a manuscript but is printed as the "Govindadāmodarastotra" (71 vss.) in the *Stotraratnavalī* [ed. anon., (Gorakhpur: Gītā Press, 1935), pp. 210–227.].

he jihve rasasārajñe

Anuṣṭubh meter.

Preceded by st. 3.48.

No occurrence of this verse was found outside the KK.

LIST OF WORKS CITED

See also: 1) "Description of the Manuscripts". This section includes a description of the manuscripts and printed editions used to prepare the KK text in this dissertation. 2) "Identity of the Author. Works." This section includes description of the manuscripts and printed editions of works attributed to Bilvamaṅgala and not elsewhere mentioned in the dissertation.

Aiyar, Ullur S. Paramesvara. "Saint Vilvamaṅgala," *Proceedings and Transactions of the Ninth All-India Oriental Conference: Trivandrum, 1937*. Poona, 1938. Pp. 471–91.

Aufrecht, Theodor. *Catalogus Catalogorum*. 3 parts. 1962 edition. Wiesbaden: Franz Steiner Verlag GMBH, 1962.

Barua, Birinchi Kumar. *History of Assamese Literature*. New Dehli: Sahitya Akademi, 1964.

Bhandarkar, R. G. *Collected Works of Sir R. G. Bhandarkar*. 4 vols. Edited by Narayan Bapuji Utgikar. Government Oriental Series, Class B. Nos. I–IV. Poona: BORI, 1927–33.

——. *Report on the Search for Sanskrit Manuscripts in the Bombay Presidency during the year 1883–84*. Bombay: Government Central Press, 1887.

——. *Report on the Search for Sanskrit Manuscripts in the Bombay Presidency during the years 1887–88, 1888-89, 1889-90* and *1890-91*. Bombay: Government Central Press, 1897.

Brown, W. Norman. "Early Vaishnava Miniature Paintings from Western India," *Eastern Art* II (1930), pp. 167–206.

——. ed. *The Saundaryalaharī...* The Harvard Oriental Series, Vol. 43. Cambridge: Harvard University Press, 1958.

Burrow, T., and M. B. Emeneau. *A Dravidian Etymological Dictionary*. Oxford: Clarendon Press, 1961.

Chandrasekharan, T., ed. *Stotrārṇavaḥ*. Government Oriental Manuscripts Series, No. 70. Madras, 1961.

Choudhury, P. C. *A Catalogue of Sanskrit Manuscripts at the D.H.A.S.* Gauhati: Dept. of Historical and Antiquarian Studies in Assam, 1961.

Dasgupta, S. N. *A History of Indian Philosophy*. 4 vols. Cambridge: Cambridge University Press, 1923–49.

De, S. K. "Kāvya," *A History of Sanskrit Literature*. Vol. I. Edited by S. N. Dasgupta. Calcutta: University of Calcutta, 1962.

——. *Aspects of Sanskrit Literature*. Calcutta: Firma K. L. Mukhopadhyay, 1959.

——, ed. *The Kṛṣṇakarṇāmṛta*... University of Dacca Oriental Publication Series, No. 5. Dacca, 1938.

——. "Miscellany: The Viṣṇu-stuti and Kṛṣṇakarṇāmṛta," *The Indian Historical Quarterly*, XX, no. 2 (June, 1944), pp. 179–181.

——. "A Note on the Text of the Kṛṣṇa-karṇāmṛta," *Annals of he Bhandarkar Oriental Research Institute*, XVI, pts. 3–4 (April–July, 1935), pp. 173–188.

Farquhar, J. N. *An Outline of the Religious Literature of India*. Oxford: Oxford University Press, 1920.

Gode, P. K. "Kavīndra Paramānanda and Keḷadi Bhasavabhūpāla," *Bhāratīya Vidyā*, III, pt. 1 (November, 1941), pp. 40–46.

Guttal, P. Hayagrīvācārya. "śrīmadānandatīrthabhagavatpādācāryāṇāṃ sarvamūlagranthāntyavākyam idam. bilvamaṅgalaḥ sādhuḥ iti," *Saṃskṛti* (Poona, 1960?). (The text available was from an offprint which provided little bibliographical information.)

Katre, S. L. "Kṛṣṇa, Gopas, Gopīs, and Rādhā," *P. K. Gode Commemoration Volume*. (The text available was from an offprint which provided little bibliographical information.)

Kavi, M. Ramakrishna, ed. "Bṛndāvanastutiḥ," *Tirumalai Sri Venkatesvara*, I, No. 3 (1932), pp. 225–30.

——. "Kālavadham." *Tirumalai Sri Venkatesvara*. Serial publication of *sargas* 1–3 in Vol. I, no. 4 and 5 (1932), pp. 307–312 and 393–398.

——. "Literary Gleanings: No. 9 Bilvamaṅgalasvāmin," *The Quarterly Journal of the Andhra Historical Research Society*, III, pt. 1 (July, 1928), pp. 66–77.

Keith, A. Berriedale. *A History of Sanskrit Literature*. Oxford: Oxford University Press, 1956.

Kosambi, D. D., ed *The Epigrams Attributed to Bhartṛhari*. Singhi Jain Series, No. 23. Bombay: Bharatiya Vidya Bhavan, 1948.

——, and V. V. Gokhale, edd. *The Subhāṣitaratnakoṣa*... The Harvard Oriental Series, Vol. 42. Cambridge: Harvard University Press, 1957.

Krishnamachariar, M. *History of Classical Sanskrit Literature.* Madras: Tirumalai-Tirupati Devasthanams Press, 1937.

Līlāśukaviracitaśrīkṛṣṇakarṇāmṛtamu Āndhrapadyaṭīkātātparyasahitamu. Madras: V. Rāmasvāmi Śāstrulu and Sons, 1918 A.D. (IO San. C. 211)

Madhvācārya. *The Collected Works of Madhvācārya.* 3 vols. Edited by R. Kṛṣṇācārya and Rāmācārya. Bombay: Nirnaya Sagar Press, 1892

Mitra, Rājendralāla. *Notices of Sanskrit Mss.* Series I, Vol. IX. Calcutta, 1888.

Monier-Williams, Monier. *A Sanskrit-English Dictionary.* Oxford, 1899.

Nābhādāsajīviracitā Śrībhaktamālā. Bombay, Vaibhav Press, 1924.

Narahari, H. G. (under the supervision of C. Kunhan Raja). *Descriptive Catalogue of Sanskrit Manuscripts in the Adyar Library.* Vol. 5. Madras: The Adyar Library, 1951.

——. "Manuscript Notes: An Early Manuscript of the Kṛṣṇakarṇāmṛta of Bilvamaṅgala," *The Adyar Library Bulletin,* VIII, pt. 1 (February, 1944), pp. 37–46.

Neog, Maheswar, ed. *Bilvamaṅgala's Kṛṣṇa-Stotra.* Gauhati: Lawyer's Book Stall, 1962.

Nirṇayasāgarapres-prakāśita Saṃskṛta, Hindī, Gujarātī Pustakoṃkā Sūcīpatra. Bombay: Nirṇaya Sāgara Press, 1964.

Pillai, K. Raghavan, ed. *Kālavadhakāvyam...* University of Kerala Sanskrit Series, No. 199 Trivandrum, 1962.

——. "On the Līlātilaka." This was an unpublished typescript copy of the author's English translation of an article written in Malayalam and published in the *Matṛbhūmi* (June 10 and 17, 1962).

——, ed. "Śrīcihnakāvyam." *Journal of the Kerala University Oriental Manuscripts Library.* Serial publication of *sargas* 1–7 in Vol. XII, no. 4 through Vol. XV, no. 4 (1963–66).

——. *Stotrasamāhāra.* Part I. University of Kerala Sanskrit Series, No. 211. Trivandrum, 1964.

Pisharoti, K. Rama. *Bulletin of the Rama Varma Research Institute,* VI, pt. 2 (July, 1938), pp. 69–86.

Raghavan, V. *Prayers, Praises and Psalms.* Madras: G. A. Natesan and Co., n.d.

Raja, K. Kunjunni. *The Contribution of Kerala to Sanskrit Literature.* Madras: University of Madras, 1958.

——. "The Text-Problem of the Kṛṣṇakarṇāmṛta," *The Indian Historical Quarterly,* XXII, no. 1 (March, 1946), pp. 66–71.

Ranganathasvami, S. P. V. "On the Seshas of Benares," *The Indian Antiquary*, XLI (November, 1912), pp. 245–253.

Raya, Amar Nath. "Reviews: The Kṛṣṇakarṇāmṛtam." *The Indian Historical Quarterly*, XV, no. 1 (March, 1939), pp. 147–153.

Sarkar, Jadunath. *Caitanya's Pilgrimages and Teachings.* London: Luzac and Co., 1913.

Sastri, G. Harihara, and V. Srinivasa Sastri. *Madhura Vijaya*... Trivandrum, 1924.

Śastrī, K. Sāmbaśiva. *A Descriptive Catalogue of Sanskrit Manuscripts in the Curator's Office Library: Trivandrum.* Vol. III. Trivandrum, 1938.

——. *A Descriptive Catalogue of Sanskrit Manuscripts in H. H. The Maharājah's Palace Library: Trivandrum.* Vol. V. Trivandrum, 1938.

Sastri, M. Seshagiri. *Report on a Search for Sanskrit and Tamil Manu scripts for the Year 1893–94.* No. 2. Madras: 1899.

Sastri, P. P. S. *A Descriptive Catalogue of the Sanskrit Manuscripts in the Tanjore Mahārāja Serfoji's Sarasvatī Mahāl Library: Tanjore.* Vol. XIX. Srirangam: Sri Vani Vilas Press, 1934.

Śāstrī, Rāmadāsa, Hindī comm. *Kṛṣṇakarṇāmṛta.* Vṛndāvana: Cār Samprādaya Āśrama, n.d.

Sastri, S. Subrahmanya, ed. "Śaṅkarahṛdayaṅgamā," *Annals of Oriental Research.* Madras University, 1952.

Sastri, T. Ganapati, ed. *Abhinavakaustubhamala and Dakshinamurtistava* ... Trivandrum Sanskrit Series, No. 2. Trivandrum, 1905.

——, ed. *The Daiva of Deva with the Puruṣakāra Commentary of Kṛṣṇalīlāśuka.* Trivandrum Sanskrit Series, No. 2. Trivandrum, 1904 (?).

Sharma, B. N. K. *A History of the Dvaita School of Vedānta and Its Literature.* 2 vols. Bombay: Booksellers' Publishing Co., 1962.

Stotraratnāvalī: Anon. ed. Gorakhpur: Gītā Press, 1934.

Upadhye, A. N. "Siriciṃdhakavvaṃ...," *Bhāratīya Vidyā*, III, pt. 1 (November, 1941), pp. 60-76.

Vivekananda, Swami. *The Complete Works of Swami Vivekananda.* Vol. I. Calcutta, 1957.

Wariyar, A. Govinda. "Vilvamaṅgalam Svāmiyārs," *The Indian Historical Quarterly*, VII, no. 2 (June, 1931), pp. 334–358.

(The following are manuscripts not listed in the "Description of the Manuscripts" section or in the "Identity of the Author. Works." section. For explanation of abbreviations used below, see "Abbreviations Used

in 'First Line Index of Sixty-Six Additional Verses with Notes'".)
KK manuscripts.
ASP ms. no. 1813 (T22)
BORI ms. no. 627/1883-84 (D62)
IO ms. no. 3900/1605c (D13)
Ker ms. no. 20156/TP 1148 (M71)
MGOL ms. no. 13408 (T26)
MGOL ms. no. 15809 (G62)
Mys ms. no. 2321 (G12)
Tri ms. no. 36/36 (M31)
Y manuscripts (The following manuscript does not belong to any of the Y versions described in the "Description of the Manuscripts" section.)
Vīrapustakālaya (Kathmandu) ms. no. 79 (Devanāgarī scripts, 296 vss., 1739 A.D. Colophon: iti śrībilvamaṅgalaparamahaṃsasanyāsinā viracitaṃ gopālasvarūpāṅkakāvyaṃ samāptaṃ...)
Kṛṣṇastotra. Exists in one ms. only.
MGOL ms. no. D. 9905 (Grantha script, 7 vss., anon., no date)
Mukundāṣṭaka. (Line d in all of the verses of this *aṣṭaka* the same as line d in st. 2.58)
MGOL ms. no. D. 10207 (Telugu script)
MGOL ms. no. D. 10208 (Telugu script)
MGOL ms. no. R. 3174 (Telugu script)
MGOL ms. no. D 10209 (Grantha script)
MGOL ms. no. D. 10210 (Grantha script)
MGOL ms. no. D. 10211 (Grantha script)
MGOL ms. no. D. 18206 (Kannarese script)
MGOL ms. no. D. 18368 (Kannarese script)
Gopāladaśaka. (Line d in the verses of this *daśaka* the same line d in st. 2.56.)
MGOL ms. no. D. 9967 (Nandīnāgarī script)
MGOL ms. no. D. 18014 (Kannarese script)
MGOL ms. no. D. 9968 (Telugu script)
(The seven following mss. have many more than 10 vss.
All are written in the Devanāgarī script.)
Flo Indiani ms. no. 84 (Govindadāmodara stotra, 57 vss., 1689 A.D.)
Osm. ms. no. B25/2 (Govindadāmodara stotra, 56 vss.)
BORI ms. no. 274/1895–98 (Govindadāmodara stotra, 69 vss., 1849 A.D.)

BORI ms. no. 396/1887-91 (Govindaikaviṃśatika stotra, 21 vss., n.d.)
BORI ms. no. 491/1891-95 (Govindadāmodaramādhaveti stotra, 55 vss., n.d.)
Mar. ms. no. or. oct. 781 (Govindadāmodaramādhaveti storta, 57 vss., n.d.)

INDEX OF METERS

The meters of standard verses are given below. The meters of additional verses are given in the "First Line Index of Sixty-Six Additional Verses with Notes" section.

Anuṣṭubh
st.1 16 76 83 93 103 105
st.2 84
st.3 26 71 94 97 101

Āryā
st.1 43 65 90
st.2 76 77 78 79 80 81 85 92
st.3 25 64 74

Indravajrā
st.1 23 45 69 84 89
st.2 73 91
st.3 9 15 18 21 70 72 78 92 93

Upajāti
st.1 22 29 30 36 41 63 78 85
st.2 34 51 53 54 56 57 58 66 67 100
st.3 24 28 32 34 36 45 73 95

Upendravajrā
st.1 10 99
st.2 55 94
st.3 52

Aupacchandasika
st.1 7 11 102
st.2 14 15 16 17
st.3 none

Kokilaka
st.1 5

st.2 none
st.3 8 46

Caccarī
st.1 9
st.2 none
st.3 none

Toṭaka
st.1 61 92
st.2 none
st.3 none

Drutavilambita
st.1 8
st.2 13
st.3 55 65

Puṣpitāgrā
st.1 73 108
st.2 28
st.3 27 43 44 54

Pṛthvī
st.1 20 86 88
st.2 none
st.3 11 34 58 76

Pramitākṣarā
st.1 none
st.2 none
st.3 77

Praharṣiṇī
st.1 28 44 56
st.2 none
st.3 79

Bhujāṃgaprayāta
st.1 none
st.2 none
st.3 68

Mañjubhāṣiṇī
st.1 6 17 71
st.2 none
st.3 3 17 39 41

Mandākrāntā
st.1 75
st.2 3 4 5 6 7 8 50 69
st.3 7 30 53 86

Mālinī
st.1 12 13 46 64 72 81
st.2 1 9 10 11 12 47 48 87 88 89 90
st.3 12 49 51 87 98

Rathoddhattā
st.1 77
st.2 30 31 32 33 68
st.3 13 14 80 89 91

Rucirā
st.1 112
st.2 none
st.3 4

Lalitagati
st.1 18
st.2 none
st.3 none

Vasantatilaka
st.1 1 14 15 19 25 31 32 33 35 37 38 39 40 49 50 60 66 67 68 70 74 79 80 82 91 94 97 98 107 110
st.2 18 19 20 21 22 23 24 25 26 27 44 46 74
st.3 6 20 31 33 47 50 59 63 88 90 105

Vaṃśasthavila
st.1 27 34
st.2 none
st.3 10 37 42

Vaitālīya
st.1 24 62 96
st.2 none
st.3 19 23 38 48

Śaśiśobhā (?)
st.1 51 52 53
st.2 none
st.3 none

Śārdūlavikrīḍita
st.1 2 3 4 21 54 57 58 59 87 100 106 109 111
st.2 2 43 52 59 60 61 62 63 64 65 70 71 72 75 82 83 86 97 98 99 101 102 104 105 106 107 108 109 110
st.3 1 2 5 16 22 29 57 60 61 62 66 81 82 83 84 85 99 106

Śālinī
st.1 55 95
st.2 none
st.3 none

Śikhariṇī
st.1 26 48 101
st.2 45 49
st.3 40 69 96

Sragdharā
st.1 none
st.2 93 95 96 103
st.3 100 102 103 104

Sragvīṇī
st.1 none
st.2 35 36 37 39 40 41 42
st.3 none

Svāgatā
st.1 none
st.2 29
st.3 none

Hariṇī
st.1 42 47
st.2 none
st.3 56 57

Undescribed
st.1 104
st.2 none
st.3 none

INDEX OF STANDARD VERSES

There is no index of additional verses; these verses have been alphabetically arranged in the "Additional Verses" section.

Pratīka	*KK st.*
aṃsālambitavāma°	2.102
akhaṇḍanirvāṇa°	1. 99
akhilabhuvanaika°	1. 90
agre dīrghataro	2. 43
agre samagrayati	1. 60
aṅkūritasmera°	3. 45
aṅganām aṅganām	2. 35
aṅgulyagrair	2. 5
añcitapicchā°	2. 78
atantritatrijagad	3. 4
atibhūmin abhūmin	3. 38
atyantabālam	2. 19
adharabimba°	2. 13
adhare viniveśya	2. 14
adhīrabimbādhara°	1. 36
adhīram ālokitam	1. 27
ananyasādhāraṇa°	3. 32
anugatam amarīṇām	3. 51
anugrahadviguṇa°	1.112
anucumbatām api	3. 41
antargṛhe kṛṣṇam	2. 35
apahasitasudhā°	3. 44
apāṅgarekhābhir	1. 10
api januṣi	2. 9
abhinavanavanīta°	2. 1
amunā kila	2. 16
amūny adhanyāni	1. 41
ayaṃ kṣīrāmbhodheḥ	3. 96
ayi paricinu	2. 10
ayi murali mukunda°	2. 11
araṇyānīm ārdra°	2. 49
aruṇādharāmṛta°	3. 17
arthānulāpān	3. 73
alasavilasan	3. 56
avatārāḥ santv	2. 85
avyājamañjula°	1. 15
aśrāntasmitam	1. 44
asti svastaruṇī°	1. 2
asti svastyayanaṃ	3. 1
astokasmitabharam	1. 28
ahimakarakara°	1. 51
ākuñcitaṃ jānu	3. 92
ākṛṣṭe vasanāñcale	2.105
ācinvānam ahany	1. 87
ātāmrapāṇikamala°	2. 46
ātāmrāyatalocanā°	3. 29
ānandena yaśodayā	2. 52
ānamrām asita°	1. 54
āndolitāgrabhujam	1. 70
āpāṭalādharam	3. 63
āpādam ācūḍam	3. 52
ābhyāṃ vilocanā°	1. 43
āmuktamānuṣam	3. 6
āmugdham ardha°	1. 19
āmūlapallavita°	3. 47
āyāmena dṛśor	3. 60

Pratīka	*KK st.*
ārūḍhaveṇutaruṇā°	3. 3
ārdrāvalokita°	1. 67
ālolalocana°	1. 39
īśānadevacaraṇa°	1.110
uttuṅgastana°	2. 64
udāramṛdulasmita°	3. 11
upāsatām ātmavidaḥ	2. 55
urvyāṃ ko 'pi	2.106
ulūkhakaṃ vā	2. 57
eṇīśābavilocanā°	3. 81
ete lakṣmaṇa	2. 70
eṣu pravāheṣu sa	3. 34
oṣṭhaṃ gṛhṇañ	2. 69
oṣṭhaṃ muñca hare	2. 71
kadambamūle	3.101
kadā nu kasyāṃ nu	1. 63
kadā vā kālindī°	1. 26
kandarpakaṇḍūla°	3. 21
kandarpapratimalla°	3. 5
kamanīyakiśora°	1. 7
karakamaladala°	1. 52
karāravindena	2. 58
kariṇām alaṅghya°	3. 3
karau śaradijāmbu°	1. 86
karṇalambita°	2. 31
kalakvaṇitakaṅkaṇaṃ	1. 20
kalaśanavanīta°	2. 81
kastūrītilakaṃ	2.109
kas tvaṃ bāla	2. 82
kāntākacagrahaṇa°	1. 91
kāmaṃ santu	1.100
kāruṇyakarbura°	1. 25
kālindīpuline tamālanibiḍa°	3. 82
kālindīpulinodareṣu	2. 61
kiṅkiṇikiṇi°	2. 76
kiṃcitkuñcita°	2. 63
kim idam adhara°	1. 72
kim iha kṛṇumaḥ	1. 42
kiśoraveṣena	3. 42
kusumaśaraśara°	1. 53
kṛṣṇenā 'mba	2. 65
kṛṣṇe hṛtvā	2. 8
kekikekādṛāneka°	2. 36
ke 'yaṃ kāntiḥ	1. 95
kailāso navanītati	2. 62
kodaṇḍaṃ masṛṇaṃ	3. 99
kodaṇḍam aikṣavam	3.105
kvā 'pi vīṇābhir	2. 37
khelatāṃ manasi	3. 80
galadvrīḍā lolā	1.101
gāyanti kṣaṇadā°	2.101
guru mṛdupade	3. 67
godhūlidhūsarita-komalakuntalāgraṃ	2. 26
godhūlidhūsarita-komalagopaveṣaṃ	2. 44
gopālājirakardame	2. 83
ghoṣapraghoṣa°	2. 23
gopīnām abhimata°	3. 79
ghoṣayoṣidanugīta°	3. 13
cakrāntadhvasta°	3.104
caraṇayor aruṇaṃ	3. 65
cāturyaikanidāna°	1. 3
cāpalyasīma capalā°	1. 74
cārucandrāvalī°	2. 38
cārucāmīkarābhāsa°	2. 40
cikuraṃ bahulaṃ	1. 61
citraṃ tad etac	1. 89
cintāmaṇir jayati	1. 1
jagattraikānta°	3. 24
jagadādaraṇīya°	2. 17

Pratīka	*KK st.*
jananāntare 'pi	3. 39
janubhyām abhi°	3. 94
jaya jaya jaya	1.108
jayati guhaśikhī°	3. 54
jāgṛhi jāgṛhi	3. 64
jihānaṃ jihānaṃ	3. 68
jīyād asau śikhi°	3. 59
tat kaiśoraṃ tac	1. 55
tat tvanmukhaṃ	1. 97
tad idam upanataṃ	1. 73
tad ucchvasita°	1. 88
tad etad ātāmra°	1. 85
tamasir avir ivo	3. 98
taruṇāruṇakaruṇā°	1. 18
tubhyaṃ nirbhara°	1.109
tṛṣṇāture cetasi	3. 9
tjase 'stu	1. 76
te te bhāvāḥ	3. 7
tribhuvanasarasā°	1. 81
tvacchaiśavaṃ	1. 32
tvayi prasanne	2.100
dadhimathananinādais tyakta°	3. 87
diṣṭyā vṛndāvana°	3. 53
dūrād vilokayati	1. 80
devaḥ pāyāt payasi	2. 3
devakītanayapūjana°	2. 29
devakyā jaṭharākare	2. 97
devas trilokī°	1.103
dhanyānāṃ sarasā°	1.111
dhenupāladayitā°	1. 77
nakhaniyamita°	2. 47
namas tasmai	2. 84
nayanāmbuje	3. 77
nā 'dyā 'pi	1. 94
nikhilanigama°	3.100
nikhilabhuvana°	1. 12
nidhiṃ lāvaṇyānāṃ	2. 45
nibaddhamugdhā°	1. 30
nirvāsanaṃ hanta	3. 78
nisargasarasā°	3. 35
nṛtyantam atyanta°	2. 67
param imam upa°	2. 28
parāmṛśyaṃ dūre	1. 48
paripālaya naḥ	1. 62
paryākulena nayanā°	3. 20
pary ācitāmṛta°	1. 33
pallavāruṇapāṇi°	1. 9
paśupālabāla°	1. 71
pāṇau pāyasa°	2. 75
pāṇau veṇuḥ	3. 30
pādau pādavinir°	1. 58
pārijātaṃ samud°	2. 42
picchāvataṃsa°	1. 31
pīṭhe pīṭha	2. 98
punaḥ prasannena	1. 34
puṣṇānam etat°	1. 84
prakṛtir avatu	3. 43
praṇayapariṇatā°	1. 13
prahlādabhāga°	2. 79
prātaḥ smarāmi dadhighoṣa°	3. 88
premadam ca me	1.104
phullahallaka°	3. 89
phullendīvara°	3. 84
barhaṃ nāma	1. 59
barhottaṃsavilāsa°	1. 4
bahulacikura°	1. 46
bahulajalada°	1. 47
bālaṃ nīlāmbudā°	3.102
bālāya nīlavapuṣe	2. 74
bālikātālikātāla°	2. 41

Pratīka	*KK st.*	*Pratīka*	*KK st.*
bālena mugdha°	1. 35	mugdhaṃ snigdhaṃ	2. 50
bālo 'pi śailo°	2. 73	muniśreṇīvandyaṃ	3. 40
bālo 'yam ālola°	1. 69	muralininadalolaṃ	2. 89
bhaktis tvayi	1.107	murāriṇa vāri°	2. 94
bhavanaṃ bhuvanaṃ	1.102	mṛgamadapañka°	3. 46
bhāsatāṃ bhava°	2. 30	mṛdukvaṇannūpura°	1. 78
maṇinūpuravācālaṃ	1. 16	maulimālamilan°	2. 39
madamayam adamayad	2. 92	mauliś candraka°	1. 57
madaśikhaṇḍi°	1. 8	maulau māyūrabarhaṃ	2. 93
madhuraṃ madhuraṃ	1. 92	yajñair ījimahe	2. 99
madhuratarasmitā°	1. 5	yatra vā tatra vā	3. 71
madhuram adhara°	1. 64	yad gopīvadanendu°	3. 83
madhuramanda°	3. 55	yadromarandhrapari°	2. 27
madhurimabharite	3. 27	yadveṇuśreṇirūpa°	2. 96
madhuraikarasaṃ	3. 19	yannābhīsarasī°	3. 85
madhye gokula°	2. 86	yasmin nṛtyati	3. 16
manasi mama	3. 74	yāni tvaccaritā°	1.106
mandaṃ mandaṃ	2. 6	yāṃ dṛṣṭvā yamunāṃ	2. 2
mandāramūle	3. 93	yā prītir vidurā°	3.106
mama cetasi	1. 17	yāvan na me nara°	1. 38
mayi prayāṇā°	3. 37	yāvan na me nikhila°	1. 37
mayi prasādaṃ	1. 29	yāsāṃ gopāñganānāṃ	2. 95
mallaiḥ śailendra°	2.103	rakṣantu tvām	3. 86
mātar nā 'taḥ	2. 4	rakṣantu naḥ	3. 75
mātaḥ kiṃ yadunātha	2. 60	ratnasthale jānu°	2. 54
mādhuryavāridhi°	1. 14	rāgāndhagopījana°	3. 72
mādhuryād api	1. 65	rādhākelikaṭākṣa°	3. 57
mādhuryeṇa dviguṇa°	1. 75	rādhā punātu jagad	2. 25
mādhuryeṇa vivardhantāṃ	1.105	rādhārādhita°	3. 2
mā yāta pānthāḥ	2. 34	rāmo nāma babhūva	2. 72
mārah svayaṃ	1. 68	lakṣmīkalatraṃ	2. 91
māra mā 'rama	3. 91	lagnaṃ muhur manasi	1. 50
mālābarhamano°	3. 66	lasadbarhapīḍaṃ	3. 69
mukulāyamāna°	1. 6	lāvaṇyavīci°	3. 18
mukhāravinde	3. 28	līlayā lalitayā	3. 14

Pratīka	*KK st.*
līlāṭopakaṭākṣa°	3. 22
līlānanāmbujam	1. 49
līlāyatābhyāṃ	1. 45
lokān unmadayan	2.110
vakṣaḥsthale ca	1. 66
vatsa jāgṛhi	2. 68
vatsavāṭacaraḥ	3. 26
vadane navanīta°	2. 15
vadanenduvinir°	1. 96
vande murāreś	3. 15
vandyaṃ devair	3.103
vayam ete	3. 25
vikretukāmā kila	2. 56
vicitrapatrāñkura°	1. 22
vidagdhagopāla°	2. 51
viraṇanmaṇi°	3. 48
viśvopaplava°	1. 56
vihāya kodaṇḍa°	3. 95
vṛndāvanadruma°	2. 21
veṇīmūle viracita°	2. 7
vyatyastapādam	2. 22
vrajajanamada°	3. 12
vrajayuvatisahāye	2. 48
śambho svāgatam	2. 59
śaraṇam aśaraṇā°	3. 49
śaraṇāgatavraja°	3. 23
śiśirīkurute	1. 24
śuśrūṣase śṛṇu	1. 98
śṛñgārarasa°	1. 93
śaiva vayaṃ na	2. 24
śrīmadbarhiśikhaṇḍa°	3. 62
saṃbādhe surabhī°	2. 77
saṃviṣṭo maṇi°	2.104

Pratīka	*KK st.*
saṃsāre kiṃ sāraṃ	2. 80
sa ko 'pi bālaḥ	3. 36
sajalajaladanīlaṃ darśitodāra°	2. 87
sajalajaladanīlaṃ vallavīkelī°	2. 12
sandhyāvandana	2.107
sarasaguṇanikāyaṃ	2. 90
sarvajñatve ca	1. 83
sā kā 'pi sarva°	2. 18
sācisaṃcalita°	2. 32
sāyaṃkāle vanānte	3.100
sārasyasāmagryam	3. 70
sārdhaṃ samṛddhair	1. 23
sāṣṭāñgapātam	3. 33
sukṛtibhir ādṛte	3. 8
suvyaktakānti°	3. 50
so 'yaṃ munīndra°	1. 82
so 'yaṃ vilāsa°	1. 79
skandhāvārapadaṃ	3. 61
steyaṃ harer	3. 90
stokastokanirudhya°	1. 21
smitalalitakapolaṃ	2. 88
smitastabakitā°	3. 76
smitasnutasudhā°	3. 58
syandane garuḍa°	2. 33
svātī sapatnī kila	2. 66
hastam ākṣipya	3. 97
hastāñghrinikvaṇita°	2. 20
hṛdaye mama hṛdya°	1. 11
he gopālaka he	2.108
he deva he dayita	1. 40